EFFICIENTLY INEFFICIENT

EFFICIENTLY INEFFICIENT

How Smart Money Invests and
Market Prices Are Determined

LASSE HEJE PEDERSEN

PRINCETON UNIVERSITY PRESS
PRINCETON AND OXFORD

Copyright © 2015 by Princeton University Press

Published by Princeton University Press, 41 William Street, Princeton, New Jersey 08540
In the United Kingdom: Princeton University Press, 6 Oxford Street, Woodstock, Oxfordshire
OX20 1TW

press.princeton.edu

Jacket art © akindo/Getty Images

Library of Congress Cataloging-in-Publication Data

Pedersen, Lasse Heje.
Efficiently inefficient : how smart money invests and market prices are determined / Lasse Heje
Pedersen.
       pages cm
Includes bibliographical references and index.
ISBN 978-0-691-16619-3 (hardcover : alk. paper) 1. Investment analysis. 2. Investments.
3. Portfolio management. 4. Capital market. 5. Securities—Prices. 6. Liquidity (Economics) I.
Title.
HG4529.P425 2015
332.6—dc23
       2014037791

British Library Cataloging-in-Publication Data is available

This book has been composed in Sabon Next LT Pro and DINPro

Printed on acid-free paper. ∞

Printed in the United States of America

10 9 8 7 6 5

Contents

The Main Themes in Three Simple Tables

OVERVIEW TABLE I. EFFICIENTLY INEFFICIENT MARKETS

Market Efficiency	Investment Implications
Efficient Market Hypothesis: The idea that all prices reflect all relevant information at all times.	**Passive investing:** If prices reflect all information, efforts to beat the market are in vain. Investors paying fees for active management can expect to underperform by the amount of the fee. *However, if no one tried to beat the market, who would make the market efficient?*
Inefficient Market: The idea that market prices are significantly influenced by investor irrationality and behavioral biases.	**Active investing:** If prices bounce around with little relation to fundamentals due to investors being naïve, beating the market would be easy. *However, markets are very competitive, and most investment professionals do not beat the market.*
Efficiently Inefficient Markets: The idea that markets are inefficient but to an efficient extent. Competition among professional investors makes markets almost efficient, but the market remains so inefficient that they are compensated for their costs and risks.	**Active investment by those with a comparative advantage:** A limited amount of capital can be invested with active managers who can beat the market using a few economically motivated investment styles. *This idea underlying the book provides a framework for understanding why certain strategies work and how securities are priced.*

OVERVIEW TABLE II. HEDGE FUND STRATEGIES AND GURUS

Classic Hedge Fund Strategies The profit sources for active investment	Gurus Interviewed in This Book Who personify the classic strategies
Discretionary Equity Investing: Stock picking through fundamental analysis of each company's business.	**Lee Ainslie III:** Star "Tiger Cub" and stock selector.
Dedicated Short Bias: Uncovering companies with over-stated earnings or flawed business plans.	**James Chanos:** Legendary financial detective who shorted Enron before its collapse.
Quantitative Equity: Using scientific methods and computer models to buy and sell thousands of securities.	**Cliff Asness:** Quant luminary and a pioneer in the discovery of momentum investing.
Global Macro Investing: Betting on the macro developments in global bond, currency, credit, and equity markets.	**George Soros:** The macro philosopher who "broke the Bank of England."
Managed Futures Strategies: Trend-following trades across global futures and forwards.	**David Harding:** Devised a systematic trend-detection system.
Fixed-Income Arbitrage: Relative value trades across similar securities such as bonds, bond futures, and swaps.	**Myron Scholes:** Traded on his seminal academic ideas that won the Nobel Prize.
Convertible Bond Arbitrage: Buying cheap illiquid convertible bonds and hedging with stocks.	**Ken Griffin:** Boy king who started trading from his Harvard dorm room and built a big business.
Event-Driven Arbitrage: Trading on specific events such as mergers, spin-offs, or financial distress.	**John A. Paulson:** Event master with the subprime "greatest trade ever."

OVERVIEW TABLE III. INVESTMENT STYLES AND THEIR RETURN DRIVERS

Investment Styles	Return Drivers
Ubiquitous methods used across trading strategies	Why these methods work in efficiently inefficient markets
Value Investing: Buying cheap securities with a low ratio of price to fundamental value—e.g., stocks with a low price to book or price-earnings ratio—while possibly shorting expensive ones.	**Risk premiums and overreaction:** A security that has a high risk premium or is out of favor becomes cheap, especially when investors overreact to several years of bad news.
Trend-Following Investing: Buying securities that have been rising while shorting those that are falling, i.e., momentum and time series momentum.	**Initial underreaction and delayed overreaction:** Behavioral biases, herding, and capital flows can lead to trends as prices initially underreact to news, catch up over time, and eventually overshoot.
Liquidity Provision: Buying securities with high liquidity risk or securities being sold by other investors who demand liquidity.	**Liquidity risk premium:** Investors naturally prefer to own securities with lower transaction costs and liquidity risk, so illiquid securities must offer a return premium.
Carry Trading: Buying securities with high "carry," i.e., securities that will have a high return if market conditions stay the same (i.e., if prices do not change).	**Risk premiums and frictions:** Carry is a timely and observable measure of expected returns as risk premiums are likely to be reflected in the carry.
Low-Risk Investing: Buying safe securities with leverage while shorting risky ones, also called betting against beta.	**Leverage constraints:** Low-risk investing profits from a leverage risk premium as other investors demand high-risk "lottery" assets to avoid using leverage.
Quality Investing: Buying high-quality securities—profitable, stable, growing, and well-managed companies—while shorting low-quality securities.	**Slow adjustment:** Securities with strong quality characteristics should have high prices, but if markets adjust slowly, then these securities will have high returns.

Preface

My first experience as a hedge fund manager was seeing hundreds of millions of dollars being lost. The losses came with remarkable consistency. Looking at the blinking screen with live P&L (profits and losses), I saw new million-dollar losses every 10 minutes for a couple of days—a clear pattern that defied the random walk theory of efficient markets and, ironically, showed remarkable likeness to my own theories.

Let me explain, but let's start from the beginning. My career as a finance guy started in 2001 when I graduated with a Ph.D. from Stanford Graduate School of Business and joined the finance faculty at the New York University Stern School of Business. My dissertation research studied how prices are determined in markets plagued by liquidity risk, and I hoped that being at a great university in the midst of things in New York City would help me find out what was going on both inside and outside the Ivory Tower.

I continued my research on how investors demand a higher return for securities with more liquidity risk, that is, securities that suffer in liquidity crises. Digging a layer deeper, my research showed how liquidity spirals can arise when leveraged investors run into funding problems and everyone runs for the exit, leading to a self-reinforcing drop and rebound in prices.

I tried my best to do relevant research and, whenever I had the chance, I talked to investment bankers and hedge fund traders about the institutional details of the real markets. I also presented my research at central banks and tried to understand their perspective. However, when I really wanted to understand the details of how trade execution or margin requirements actually work, I often hit a roadblock. As an academic outside the trading floors, it was very difficult to get to the bottom of how markets actually work. At the same time, traders who knew the details of the market did not have the time and perspective to do research on how it all fits together. I wanted to combine real-world insight with rigorous academic modeling.

In 2006, I was contacted by AQR, a global asset manager operating hedge funds and long-only investments using scientific methods. I was excited and started consulting shortly after. Working with AQR opened a new world to me. I became an insider in the asset management world and finally had access to people who knew how securities are traded, how leverage is financed, and how trading strategies are executed, both my colleagues at AQR and, through them, the rest of Wall Street. Most excitingly, my own research was being put into practice.

After a year, AQR convinced me to take a leave of absence from NYU to join them full time starting on July 1, 2007. Moving from Greenwich Village to Greenwich, CT, the first big shock was how dark and quiet it was at night compared to the constant buzz of Manhattan, but a bigger shock was around the corner.

My job was to develop new systematic trading strategies as a member of the Global Asset Allocation team, focusing on global equity indices, bonds, commodities, and currencies, and I also had opportunities to contribute to the research going on in the Global Stock Selection and arbitrage teams. However, my start as a full-time practitioner happened to coincide with the beginning of the subprime credit crisis.

As I began working in July 2007, AQR was actually profiting from some bets against the subprime market but was starting to experience a puzzling behavior of the equity markets. As a ripple effect of the subprime crisis, other quantitative equity investors had started liquidating some of their long and short equity positions, which affected equity prices in a subtle way. It made cheap stocks cheaper, expensive stocks more expensive, while leaving overall equity prices relatively unchanged. The effect was invisible to an observer of the overall market or someone studying just a few stocks, but became more and more clearly visible through the lens of diversified long–short quant portfolios.

In early August, a number of quant equity investors started running for the exit and things escalated in the week of Monday, August 6. All my long-term research was put aside as I was staring at the P&L screen, wondering what to do about it. The P&L updated every few seconds, and I saw the losses constantly mounting. Here was a real-life liquidity spiral, all too similar to that in my theoretical model. It is difficult to explain the emotional reaction to seeing many millions being lost, but it hurts. It hurt even though the strategies that I had worked on were actually unaffected and even though I had a tenured lifetime appointment at NYU to return to. It has been said that you cannot explain what it is like to be in a war unless you experience bullets flying over your head, and I think something similar holds for being in the midst of a trading crisis. I understand why most of the successful managers whom I interviewed for this book emphasize the importance of self-discipline.

The question that kept going through my head was "what should we do?" Should we start selling part of the portfolio to reduce risk but then contribute to the sell-off and reduce the potential gains from prices turning around? Or should we stay the course? Or add to our positions to increase the profit from a future snapback of prices? Or rotate the portfolio to our more secret and idiosyncratic factors that were not affected by the event? Although I was engaged in these important deliberations as an academic with models of exactly this type of liquidity spirals, let me be clear that I wasn't exactly running the operation. I suspect that there was a sense that I was still too much an academic and not enough a practitioner, akin to Robert Duvall's character in *The Godfather*, Tom Hagen, who was too much lawyer and not enough Sicilian to be "wartime consigliere."

To answer these questions, we first needed to know whether we were facing a liquidity spiral or an unlucky step in the random walk of an efficient market. The efficient market theory says that, going forward, prices should fluctuate randomly, whereas the liquidity spiral theory says that when prices are depressed by forced selling, prices will likely bounce back later. These theories clearly had different implications for how to position our portfolio. On Monday, we became completely convinced that we were facing a liquidity event. All market dynamics pointed clearly in the direction of liquidity and defied the random walk theory (which implies that losing every 10 minutes for several days in a row is next to impossible).

Knowing that you are facing a liquidity event and that prices will eventually snap back is one thing; knowing when this will happen and what to do about it is another. The answer is complex and, though this book will go into the details of the quant event and the general principles of risk management in an efficiently inefficient market, let me briefly tell you how it ended. In the funds with limited leverage, we managed to stay the course and made back most of the losses when the snapback finally started on Friday morning. In the more highly leveraged hedge funds, we reduced positions to limit the risk of a forced sale, but we started putting back the positions close to the bottom just before the market turned around. When the profits started, they arrived at an even wilder pace than the losses had.

I returned to my "peacetime" efforts of developing new trading strategies and other long-term research. I set out to understand each of the different types of trading strategies and their return drivers through careful research. I had the fortune of working with lots of great people across investment teams and helped develop new funds with elements of all the eight strategies discussed in this book, long–short equities, short-selling, quantitative equities, global macro, managed futures, fixed-income arbitrage, convertible bond arbitrage, and event-driven investment.

As I love the combination of theory and practice, I decided to straddle both worlds between AQR and academia, first at NYU and now also at Copenhagen Business School as I moved back to my home country, Denmark, after 14 years in the United States. I have been teaching a new course on hedge fund strategies that I developed based on my research and experience and the insights of my colleagues, interviewees, and guest-lecturing hedge fund managers. The lecture notes for this course slowly developed into this book.

WHO SHOULD READ THE BOOK?

Anyone interested in financial markets can read it. The book can be read at different levels, both by those who want to delve into the details and those who prefer to skip the equations and focus on the intuitive explanations and interviews. It is meant both as a resource for finance practitioners and as a textbook for students. First, I hope that the book is useful for finance practitioners working in hedge funds, pension funds, endowments, mutual funds, insurance companies, banks, central banks, or really anyone interested in how smart money invests and how market prices are determined.

Second, the book can be used as a textbook. I have used the material to teach courses on investments and hedge fund strategies to MBA students at New York University and master's students at Copenhagen Business School. The book can be used for a broad set of courses, either as the main textbook (as in my course) or as supplementary reading. The book can be read by students ranging from advanced undergraduates to Ph.D. students, several of whom have gotten research ideas from thinking about efficiently inefficient markets. My website contains problem sets for each chapter and other teaching resources: www.lhpedersen.com.

Acknowledgments

I am deeply grateful for countless ideas for this book from my colleagues at AQR Capital Management, New York University, Copenhagen Business School, and beyond. At AQR, I would in particular like to thank John Liew for teaching me a lot about asset management when I knew next to nothing about real-world trading; Cliff Asness for always sharing his brilliant insights (often masked as jokes) when I bust into his office; David Kabiller for his thoughtful visions about how to build a business (and for trying to make me a businessman); Andrea Frazzini, the fastest quant backtester around, for his great collaboration; Toby Moskowitz for sharing both the experience of going from academia to AQR and, initially, an office—you're a great office mate; Yao Hua Ooi for tremendous teamwork on many projects; and all the others at AQR who provided helpful comments on early drafts of the book, including Aaron Brown, Brian Hurst, Ari Levine, Mike Mendelson, Scott Metchick, Mark Mitchell, Lars Nielsen, Todd Pulvino, Scott Richardson, Mark Stein, Rodney Sullivan, and, especially, Antti Ilmanen and Ronen Israel who provided many insights for the book.

I am also extremely grateful to my colleagues and students at New York University Stern School of Business and at Copenhagen Business School. This book has really benefited from my inspiring discussions with colleagues at NYU, such as Viral Acharya, Yakov Amihud, Xavier Gabaix, Thomas Philippon, Matt Richardson, William Silber, Marti Subrahmanyam, Stijn Van Nieuwerburgh, Jeff Wurgler, and my colleagues at Copenhagen Business School, including David Lando (who first got me interested in finance when I was an undergrad), Søren Hvidkjær, Niklas Kohl, Jesper Lund, and Kristian Miltersen. A huge thanks to all my co-authors, not least the ones already mentioned, as well as Nicolae Gârleanu at Berkeley, Markus Brunnermeier at Princeton, and my Ph.D. advisors Darrell Duffie and Ken Singleton at Stanford, all of whom have meant a lot to me.

Last, but not least, I thank my wife and kids for letting me pursue multiple careers and for reminding me of what really matters in my efficiently inefficient life.

About the Author

Lasse Heje Pedersen is both a distinguished academic and an asset manager. A finance professor at Copenhagen Business School and NYU Stern School of Business, he has published a number of influential academic papers on liquidity risk, asset prices, and trading strategies. His research has been cited by Ben Bernanke and other central bank governors around the world, by leading asset managers, and in thousands of academic and industry papers. He has won a number of awards, most notably the Bernácer Prize for the best E.U. economist under 40 years of age, the Banque de France-TSE Prize, the Fama-DFA Prize, and the Michael Brennan Award.

Lasse has applied his research as a principal at AQR Capital Management, a global asset manager with more than $100 billion of assets across its hedge funds and long-only investments. He has helped start several funds, has developed trading strategies across equity markets, macro markets, and arbitrage strategies, and has performed applied research on portfolio optimization, trade execution, and risk modeling.[1]

In addition to his experience at AQR and academia, Lasse has served in the Liquidity Working Group meeting at the Federal Reserve Bank of New York to address liquidity issues during the global financial crisis, the New York Fed's Monetary Policy Panel, the Economic Advisory Boards of NASDAQ and FTSE, as a Director of the American Finance Association, and on the editorial boards of several journals such as the *Journal of Finance* and the *Quarterly Journal of Economics*. Lasse received his B.S. and M.S. from the University of Copenhagen and his Ph.D. from Stanford University Graduate School of Business.

---

[1] The views expressed herein are those of the author and do not necessarily reflect the views of AQR Capital Management, LLC, its affiliates, or its employees.

EFFICIENTLY INEFFICIENT

Introduction

This book is about the trading strategies used by sophisticated investors such as hedge funds. It shows how to implement the key trading strategies and explains why they work and why they sometimes don't.[1] The book also includes interviews with some of the best hedge fund managers, who successfully developed and traded these strategies. Finally, looking through the lens of these trading strategies, the book shows how financial markets operate and how securities are priced in an efficiently inefficient way, as seen in Overview Table I.

Hedge funds have always been highly secretive, often so secretive that their own investors have only a vague idea about what strategies the funds pursue. The secret nature of the strategies has justified high fees and reduced entry into the industry. This book puts the main hedge fund strategies out in the open. It demystifies the trading universe by describing the most important strategies, how to evaluate trading strategies, how to trade them, how to manage their risk, and how to come up with new ones.

To really understand each hedge fund strategy and bring it to life, I include interviews with one of the world's pioneers and leading hedge fund managers in each style, as seen in Overview Table II. We learn how star "Tiger Cub" Lee S. Ainslie picks stocks based on the methods he started honing working for the legendary Julian Robertson at Tiger Management. The famous short seller Jim Chanos explains how he bets against companies with flawed business plans and fraudulent managers and how he uncovered Enron before its collapse. Quant pioneer Cliff Asness discusses how his computer models buy and sell thousands of securities and how he turned his academic finding of the momentum effect into a real-world investment strategy as a complement to value and other factors. George Soros, who "broke the Bank of England," talks about his big macro bets and his ideas about the evolution of markets. David Harding discusses how he developed a systematic trend-detection

---

[1] This book provides an academic treatment of investments, not investment advice. When I say that a trading strategy "works," I use the word like finance academics and asset managers, namely to mean that they have historically produced positive average returns and may have a chance of outperforming on average in the future, but not always, not without risk, and the world can change. As Cliff Asness has said, "If your mechanic used the word 'work' to mean that your car might work 6–7 years out of 10, then you would fire your mechanic, but this is how asset management tends to 'work.'"

system and how trends defy traditional notions of market efficiency. Myron Scholes explains how he traded on his Nobel Prize–winning insights in the fixed-income markets. We hear how Ken Griffin started trading convertible bonds out of his Harvard dorm room and how he grew from "boy king" to running a large firm. Finally, John Paulson describes his methods for merger arbitrage and event-driven investment, including his famous subprime "greatest trade ever."

The managers I interviewed shine with true brilliance, and the hedge fund world has often been known as a mysterious realm in which genius managers deliver outsized returns by sheer magic. However, rather than being based on magic, I argue that much of the world of hedge fund returns can be explained by a number of classic trading strategies that work for good reasons. There exist many more hedge funds than unique hedge fund strategies in the world. If hedge fund returns are not just about magic, then the main hedge fund strategies can be learned and understood. This book teaches the general principles. To be successful in the long term, a hedge fund needs a repeatable process that makes money more often than not. This book explains many of these processes based on the lessons of top managers. Of course, putting this knowledge into action requires a lot of work, even more discipline, capital, brainpower, and trading infrastructure. Only those who master all the required skills can reap the benefits in an efficiently inefficient market.

Although the different trading strategies and the different hedge fund gurus invest in very different markets and asset classes using different methods, there are nevertheless some common overarching principles that I call "investment styles." I discuss the key investment styles and show how many investment strategies and hedge fund gurus rely on value investing, trend-following investing, liquidity provision, and a few other key styles described in Overview Table III. These styles are general enough to work across asset classes and markets, even though their specific implementations (and the words used to describe them) differ across markets and investors.

The book also shows how securities are priced and how markets operate, but not as in traditional academic finance books. Whereas traditional finance books typically write some equation for the value of a bond or a stock and claim that this is how the security is priced because this is what the theory says, this book seriously analyzes the possibility that the market price can differ from the theoretical value and what to do about it. A discrepancy between the market price and the theoretical value has two possible interpretations: (1) It presents a trading opportunity, where you buy if the market price is below the theoretical value and sell otherwise; if such opportunities arise repeatedly, which can happen for reasons we discuss in detail, they give rise to a trading strategy; (2) The discrepancy can reflect that your theoretical value is wrong. How do you know if the truth is one or the other? You implement the trading strategy—in live trading or in a simulated backtest—and, if you make money, it's (1) and, if you lose, it's (2).

In other words, the book's premise is that trading strategies present natural tests of asset pricing theories and, vice versa, asset pricing theories naturally give rise to trading strategies. The book shows how finance theory can be translated into trading ideas and how trading results can be translated into finance theory.

I. EFFICIENTLY INEFFICIENT MARKETS

To search for trading strategies that consistently make money over time, we need to understand the markets where securities are traded. The fundamental question concerning financial markets is whether they are *efficient*, a question that remains hotly debated. For instance, the Nobel Prize in economics in 2013 was awarded jointly to Eugene Fama, the father and defender of efficient markets, Robert Shiller, the father of behavioral economics, and Lars Hansen, who developed tests of market efficiency.[2] As seen in Overview Table I, an efficient market, as defined by Fama, is one where market prices reflect all relevant information. In other words, the market price always equals the fundamental value and, as soon as news comes out, prices immediately react to fully reflect the new information. If markets are fully efficient, there is no point in active investing because the prices already reflect as much information as you could hope to collect. But without active investors, who would make the market efficient in the first place? Further, given that investors are paying billions of dollars in fees to active managers, either the securities markets are inefficient (so active managers can outperform) or the market for asset management is inefficient (because investors would pay fees for nothing)—it is logically impossible that all these markets are fully efficient.[3]

Shiller, on the other hand, believes that security market prices deviate from fundamentals because people make mistakes and are subject to common biases that do not cancel out in aggregate. Humans make errors: they panic, herd, and get exuberant. But, if most investors were completely naïve and market prices had little relation to fundamentals, then shouldn't beating the market be easy?

---

[2] Testing whether the market is efficient is difficult since most tests must rely on a specific asset pricing model. Hence, observing anomalous returns is a rejection of the "joint hypothesis," meaning that either the market is not efficient or the asset pricing model is wrong, but not necessarily both. However, observing two securities with equal cash flows trading at different prices (i.e., an arbitrage) is a rejection of frictionless efficient markets.

[3] Grossman and Stiglitz (1980) showed that the theory of efficient markets entails a paradox since investors must have an incentive to collect information. They concluded that securities markets must entail an "equilibrium level of disequilibrium." Their point is strengthened by the fact that investors pay large fees for active management. Berk and Green (2004) propose that the market for money management is efficient while security markets are not. I argue instead that both security markets and the market for money management are efficiently inefficient.

In reality, beating the market is far from easy. Most investment professionals, e.g., most mutual funds, hardly beat the market. There are lots of sophisticated money managers with large amounts of capital who compete vigorously to achieve the best investment performance, and they make markets more efficient when they buy low and sell high.

I believe that the truth lies somewhere in between these extremes, but not just in some arbitrary middle ground. The truth is equally well-defined: the truth is that markets are *efficiently inefficient*.

Prices are pushed away from their fundamental values because of a variety of demand pressures and institutional frictions, and, although prices are kept in check by intense competition among money managers, this process leads the market to become *inefficient* to an *efficient* extent: just *inefficient* enough that money managers can be compensated for their costs and risks through superior performance and just *efficient* enough that the rewards to money management after all costs do not encourage entry of new managers or additional capital.

In an efficiently inefficient market, money managers are compensated for providing a service to the market, namely providing liquidity—just like burger bars are compensated for the service of combining meat, salad, and buns and delivering a burger in a convenient location. Burger bars' profits reflect their efficiently inefficient competition in light of their costs, just like the money managers' outperformance reflects the efficiently inefficient price of liquidity in light of their costs and risks. The outperformance that money managers deliver to their investors after fees reflects the efficiently inefficient market for money management.

Liquidity is the ability to transact, so when money managers "provide liquidity," it means that they help other investors transact by taking the other side of their trades. Money managers profit because demanders of liquidity value the opportunity to transact at prices that are not exactly equal to fundamental values (just like you are willing to buy a burger for more than the value of the ingredients). For example, some investors trade when they need to reduce risk (e.g., hedging by commodity producers such as farmers or commodity consumers such as airlines); others need to raise money or invest it (e.g., you sell bonds to raise cash for a wedding and later invest money you received as a wedding gift, or a mutual fund needs to rebalance its portfolio because of inflows or outflows of capital); many investors desire to sell stocks going through mergers to avoid event risk; pension funds may trade to comply with regulation; banks may prefer certain securities over other similar ones because of differential capital requirements; many investors prefer not to hold illiquid securities that are difficult to trade; and some investors prefer more speculative securities that have a chance of a large return. Money managers are compensated for taking the other side of these trades and, although their fierce competition can drive the compensation close to zero, competition doesn't drive the price of liquidity all the way to zero since doing these trades involves liquidity risk. Liquidity risk is an important concept that means the risk of being forced to sell at the worst time and incurring large transaction costs.

The transaction costs incurred by money managers lower the returns received by their investors. In addition, money managers charge fees for their efforts, skills, and internal operating costs (e.g., salaries to traders, computers, rent, legal fees, and auditors). Investors are willing to bear these costs and fees when they are outweighed by the profits that the manager is expected to extract from the efficiently inefficient market.

How close are prices and returns to their fully efficient values in an efficiently inefficient market? Well, because of competition, securities' returns net of all the relevant market frictions—transaction costs, liquidity risk, and funding costs—are very close to their fully efficient levels in the sense that consistently beating the market is extremely difficult. However, despite *returns* being nearly efficient, *prices* can deviate substantially from the present value of future cash flows. To understand this apparent paradox, note that the return to buying a cheap stock, say, depends both on the price today and the price tomorrow. If the price tomorrow can be even further from its efficient level and if liquidity costs are large, then the expected return may not be very attractive even if the price deviates significantly from its efficient level.

Markets constantly evolve and gravitate toward an efficient level of inefficiency, just as nature evolves according to Darwin's principle of survival of the fittest. The traditional economic notion of perfect market efficiency corresponds to a view that nature reaches an equilibrium of "perfectly fit" species that cease to evolve. However, in nature there is not a single life form that is *the* fittest, nor is every life form that has survived to date "perfectly fit." Similarly in financial markets, there are several types of investors and strategies that survive and, while market forces tend to push prices toward their efficient levels, market conditions continually evolve as news arrives and supply-and-demand shocks continue to affect prices.

As in nature, many social dynamics inside and outside financial markets entail an efficient level of inefficiency. For instance, the political process can be inefficient, yet politicians have an incentive to appear efficient relative to their competition. However, the competitive forces in the political system do not make the process fully efficient because of the friction caused by voters' ability to monitor their representatives (corresponding to the frictions in financial markets). Similarly, traffic dynamics can be efficiently inefficient. For example, consider what happens when you drive on a busy highway. Each lane moves approximately equally fast because lane-switchers ensure a relatively even number of cars in each lane. However, the lanes don't move exactly equally fast because of the "cost" of switching lanes and the evolving traffic situation. Lane speeds probably tend to reach an efficiently inefficient level where switching lanes hardly helps, but doing so still makes sense for those with comparative advantages in lane switching—although frequent lane switching and high speed increase the risk of driving, just as frequent trading and high leverage increase the risk in financial markets.

The economic mechanisms of an efficiently inefficient market are fundamentally different from those of neoclassical economics, as seen in table I.1. The neoclassical principles continue to be taught ubiquitously at global universities as they constitute the fundamental pillars for our understanding of economics. While economic thinking is almost always seen in reference to these neoclassical benchmarks, the belief that these pillars constitute an accurate description of the real world has been shaken by the global financial crisis that started in 2007, by earlier liquidity crises, and by decades of research. In contrast to the Modigliani–Miller Theorem, corporations trade off the benefits of debt against the costs of financial distress, and, during liquidity crises, corporations strapped for cash must change their investment policy. While the Two-Fund Separation Theorem stipulates that all investors should hold the market portfolio in combination with cash or leverage, most real-world investors hold different portfolios, where some avoid leverage and instead concentrate in risky securities, whereas others (such as Warren Buffett) leverage safer securities. Asset returns are not just influenced by their market risk (as in the CAPM); they are also influenced by market and funding liquidity risk since investors want to be compensated for holding securities that are difficult to finance or entail the risk of high transaction costs. The Law of One Price breaks down when arbitrage opportunities arise in currency markets (defying the covered interest rate parity), credit markets (the CDS-bond basis), convertible bond markets, equity markets (Siamese twin stock spreads), and option markets. Investors exercise call options and convert convertible bonds before maturity and dividend payments when they need to free up cash or face large short sale costs (defying Merton's Rule). The financial market frictions influence the real economy, and unconventional monetary policy, such as central banks' lending facility, can be important in addressing liquidity draughts.[4]

---

[4] Modigliani–Miller breaks down due to financial distress costs, taxes, and behavioral effects, see Baker and Wurgler (2012) and references therein. Calvet, Campbell, and Sodini (2007) and Frazzini and Pedersen (2014) document systematic deviations from Two-Fund Separation, where constrained individuals and mutual funds hold riskier stocks, and leveraged buyout (LBO) firms and Warren Buffett apply leverage to safer stocks. Theory and evidence suggest that required returns are influenced by transaction costs (Amihud and Mendelson 1986), market liquidity risk (Acharya and Pedersen 2005), and funding liquidity constraints (Gârleanu and Pedersen 2011). Arbitrage opportunities arise due to the limits of arbitrage (Shleifer and Vishny 1997), and specific examples are referenced throughout the book. Deviations from Merton's Rule are documented by Jensen and Pedersen (2012). Credit cycles (Kiyotaki and Moore 1997, Geanakoplos 2010) and liquidity spirals (Brunnermeier and Pedersen 2009) arise due to leverage and funding frictions. For the theoretical and empirical case for two monetary tools, see Ashcraft, Gârleanu, and Pedersen (2010) and references therein.

TABLE I.1. PRINCIPLES OF NEOCLASSICAL FINANCE AND ECONOMICS VS. THOSE IN AN EFFICIENTLY INEFFICIENT MARKET

Neoclassical Finance and Economics	Efficiently Inefficient Markets
Modigliani–Miller Irrelevance of capital structure	**Capital structure matters** because of funding frictions
Two-Fund Separation Everyone buys portfolios of market and cash	**Investors choose different portfolios** depending on their individual funding constraints
Capital Asset Pricing Model Expected return proportional to market risk	**Liquidity risk and funding constraints** influence expected returns
Law of One Price and Black–Scholes No arbitrage, implied derivative prices	**Arbitrage opportunities** arise as demand pressure affects derivative prices
Merton's Rule Never exercise a call option and never convert a convertible, except at maturity/dividends	**Optimal early exercise and conversion** free up cash, save on short sale costs, and limit transaction costs
Real Business Cycles and Ricardian Equivalence Macroeconomic irrelevance of policy and finance	**Credit cycles and liquidity spirals** driven by the interaction of macro, asset prices, and funding constraints
Taylor Rule Monetary focus on interest rate policy	**Two monetary tools** are interest rate (the cost of loans) and collateral policy (the size of loans)

II. GLOBAL TRADING STRATEGIES: OVERVIEW OF THE BOOK

Exploiting inefficiencies is challenging in an efficiently inefficient market. It requires hard work, thorough analysis, costs in setting up trading infrastructure, and opportunity costs of highly skilled people. Hence, to be a successful active investor requires specialization and often scale, so money management is usually done by managers who run pools of money such as mutual funds, hedge funds, pension funds, proprietary traders, and insurance companies. The first part of the book explains the main tools for active investment. As seen in figure I.1, we learn how to evaluate, find, optimize, and execute trading strategies.

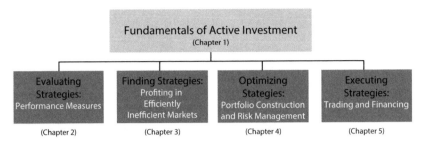

Figure I.1. Fundamental tools for active investments described in this book.

The most unrestricted and sophisticated investors tend to be the hedge funds, so I focus on hedge fund strategies. While I focus on hedge funds, the strategies in the book are also the core strategies for most other active investors. One difference is that whereas hedge funds can both invest long (i.e., bet that a security increases in value) and sell short (i.e., bet that a security decreases in value), most other investors only invest long. However, the difference is smaller than you may think. A hedge fund strategy that invests in IBM and short-sells CISCO corresponds to a mutual fund that overweights its allocation to IBM (relative to the benchmark) and underweights CISCO.

At a high level, I distinguish between *equity strategies*, *macro strategies*, and *arbitrage strategies*. Equity hedge funds invest primarily in stocks, macro hedge funds invest primarily in overall markets (e.g., currencies, bonds, equity indices, and commodities), and arbitrage funds primarily make relative-value bets across pairs of related securities. I subdivide these three broad types of trading strategies, as seen in figure I.2, which also shows the structure of the

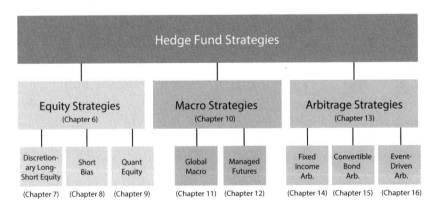

Figure I.2. Classic hedge fund strategies analyzed in this book.

rest of the book.[5] Each chapter is self-contained and can be read independently. For instance, readers most interested in event-driven investment can jump directly to chapter 16 (and use the fundamental chapters 1–5 as a reference).

Equity Strategies

I subdivide equity strategies into *discretionary long–short equity, dedicated short bias*, and *quant equity*. Discretionary long–short equity managers typically go long or short stocks based on a fundamental analysis of the value of each company, comparing its profitability to its valuation and studying its growth prospects. These fund managers also analyze the quality of the company's management, traveling to meet managers and see businesses. Furthermore, they study the accounting numbers, trying to assess their reliability and to estimate future cash flows. Equity long–short managers mostly bet on specific companies, but they can also take views on whole industries.

Some equity managers, called value investors, focus on buying undervalued companies and holding these stocks for the long term. Warren Buffett is a good example of a value investor. Implementing this trading strategy often requires being contrarian, since companies only become cheap when other investors abandon them. Hence, cheap stocks are often out of favor or bought during times when others panic. Going against the norm is harder than it sounds, as traders say:

It's easy to be a contrarian, except when it's profitable.

Another approach is to try to exploit shorter term opportunities, for example, to try to predict a company's next earnings announcement better than the rest of the market. If you think the earnings will come out higher than others expect, you buy before the announcement and sell after the announcement. More generally, such opportunistic traders try to put on a position before something is broadly known and unwind the position when the information gets incorporated into the price based on the motto:

Buy on rumors, sell on news.

If you know a rumor to be true, then you could be engaging in illegal insider trading (as Gordon Gekko, played by Michael Douglas, in the movie *Wall Street*). Whereas equity long–short managers often have more long positions than short, the reverse is true for dedicated short-bias managers. They use similar

---

[5] There are many ways to classify hedge funds, varying across hedge fund indices and databases. My classification of substrategies is similar to that of the Credit Suisse Hedge Fund Indexes, and it also shares similarities with most other classifications.

techniques as equity long–short managers, but they focus on finding companies to sell short. Short-selling means taking a bet that the share price will go down. Just like buying a stock means that you profit if the stock price goes up, taking a short position means that you profit if the price goes down. In practice, short-selling is implemented by borrowing a share and selling it for its current price, say, $100. At a later time, say, the next day, you must buy back the share and return it to the lender. If the stock price has gone down to $90, you buy it back cheaper than you sold it and earn the difference, $10 in this example. If the price has gone up, you lose money.

Dedicated short-bias managers look for companies that are going down, searching for hotels where all the rooms are empty, pharmaceutical companies with drugs that no doctors prescribe (or with new risks), or companies based on fraud or misrepresented accounting. Since stocks go up more often than they go down (called the equity risk premium), dedicated short-bias managers are fighting against the general uptrend in markets, and, perhaps for this reason, they comprise a very small group of hedge funds (anecdotally consisting of pessimistic managers).

Almost all equity long–short hedge funds and dedicated short-bias hedge funds (and most hedge funds in general) engage in *discretionary trading*, meaning that the decision to buy or sell is at the trader's discretion, given an overall assessment based on experience, various kinds of information, intuition, and so forth. This traditional form of trading can be viewed in contrast to *quantitative investment*, or "quant" for short. Quants define their trading rules explicitly and build systems that implement them systematically. They try to develop a small edge on each of many small diversified trades using sophisticated processing of ideas that cannot be easily processed using non-quantitative methods. To do this, they use tools and insights from economics, finance, statistics, mathematics, computer science, and engineering, combined with lots of data to identify relations that market participants may not have immediately fully incorporated in the price. Quants build computer systems that generate trading signals based on these relations, carry out portfolio optimization in light of trading costs, and trade using automated execution schemes that route hundreds of orders every few seconds. In other words, trading is done by feeding data into computers that run various programs with human oversight.

Some quants focus on high-frequency trading, where they exit a trade within milliseconds or minutes after it was entered. Others focus on statistical arbitrage, that is, trading at a daily frequency based on statistical patterns. Yet others focus on lower frequency trades called fundamental quant (or equity market neutral) investing. Fundamental quant investing considers many of the same factors as discretionary traders, seeking to buy cheap stocks and short sell expensive ones, but the difference is that fundamental quants do so systematically using computer systems.

While discretionary trading has the advantages of a tailored analysis of each trade and the use of soft information such as private conversations, its labor-intensive method implies that only a limited number of securities can be analyzed in depth, and the discretion exposes the trader to psychological biases. Quantitative trading has the advantage of being able to apply a trading idea to thousands of securities around the globe, benefiting from significant diversification. Furthermore, quants can apply their trading ideas with the discipline of a robot. Discipline is important for all traders, but as the saying goes,

> Have a rule. Always follow the rule, but know when to break it.

Even quants sometimes need to "break the rule," for example, if they realize that there are problems in the data feed or if sudden important events happen that are outside the realm of the models, such as the failure of the investment bank Lehman Brothers in 2008.

Quants also have the advantage of efficient portfolio construction and the ability to "backtest" strategies, meaning that one can simulate how well one would have done by following such a strategy in the past. Of course, past success does not guarantee future success, but at least it eliminates using rules that never worked. Furthermore, systematic investment reduces the effects of psychological biases, at least to a degree. The quant method's disadvantage is its reliance on hard data and the computer program's limited ability to incorporate real-time human judgment.

Whether using discretionary trading or quant methods, learning the analytical tools is useful, and this book aims to provide such tools. Full disclosure: I am a quant. That said, I believe that the methods described in this book are essential for all managers, whether discretionary or quantitative. Indeed, many serious discretionary traders often analyze the historical performance of a trading idea before implementing it in large size. For example, in my interview with Lee Ainslie, he told me how his Maverick Capital has built a quantitative system that informs their fundamental process and helps manage the risk.

Macro Strategies

If Gordon Gekko was an equity trader in the movie *Wall Street*, the Duke brothers and Eddie Murphy were macro traders in the movie *Trading Places*, using futures markets to bet on the direction of orange juice prices. I divide macro strategies into *global macro* and *managed futures*. Global macro traders bet on economy-wide phenomena around the world. They take the view that the overall stock market will go up or down, that inflation will lead to a spike in gold prices, or that emerging-market currencies will rise or collapse. Some global macro traders take large positions, as is clear from the following quote from Stanley Druckenmiller, who learned it from Georges Soros (Schwager 2008):

> When you have tremendous conviction on a trade, you have to go for the jugular. It takes courage to be a pig.

Others go for a more diversified and risk-managed approach, arguing instead,

> Bulls get rich, bears get rich, but pigs get slaughtered.

According to this saying, you can make money taking long positions (bulls) or taking short positions (bears), but if you don't control your risk (pigs), you end up going out of business. In my interview with George Soros, he explains that he too puts significant emphasis on risk management, but he feels that one should go for the jugular in the rare cases when the upside is large and the downside is limited.

The differences between these sayings reflect the great variation across global macro traders. They come from a variety of backgrounds, ranging from traders with little formal training in economics to former central bank economists. They apply a range of different approaches, some analyzing data, others following every move of central banks, yet others traveling the world for global trading ideas. Some global macro funds are thematic traders, meaning that they focus on a few themes and express each theme in terms of various trades. For instance, one theme might be that China will continue to grow at an explosive rate, and the global macro trader might express this view by buying Chinese stocks or commodities imported by China or companies or industries selling to China.

Though global macro traders are very different from one another, there are similarities. For instance, macro traders often like to express their views in a way that earns a positive carry, meaning that they earn income even if nothing changes. Hence, whether they do so intentionally or not, they often have exposure to so-called carry trades, in particular the currency carry trade. The currency carry trade involves investing in currencies with high interest rates while shorting currencies with low interest rates. This strategy earns an interest rate differential, essentially borrowing one currency at low interest and investing in another currency with a higher interest rate, but it is exposed to the risk that the relative values of the currencies can change.

Managed futures investors (also called *commodity trading advisors, CTAs*) trade many of the same securities as global macro traders: bond futures, equity index futures, currency forwards, and commodity futures. Managed futures investors often focus on finding price trends, buying instruments that are trending up, and shorting instruments that are trending down. For instance, if gold prices have been rising, a managed futures hedge fund may buy gold futures, betting that the price will continue to rise, relying on the maxim that

> The trend is your friend.

Managed futures hedge funds focus on price data, using statistical methods (managed futures quants) or using rules of thumb (technical analysis) more than they look at fundamental data. Managed futures investors then try to identify trending markets, trends that have become overextended, or snapbacks caused by countertrends. The philosophy is that trends start as people underreact to news. By the time prices catch up to fundamentals, they have been moving in the same direction for a while, and other traders may start herding into the position, leading to a delayed overreaction followed by an eventual reversion. Rather than following the news, managed futures investors focus on prices and go by the saying,

> Show me the charts, I'll tell you the news.

Risk management is central for managed futures investors, who apply a very different philosophy than the global macro view expressed by George Soros above. When managed futures investors lose money, it is often because the trend is switching direction and, in this case, they flip their position and get ready to ride the new trend.

Arbitrage Strategies

Turning to arbitrage strategies, these consist of *fixed-income arbitrage, convertible bond arbitrage*, and *event-driven investment*. Fixed-income arbitrage is based on a number of so-called convergence trades. In a convergence trade, you look for similar securities with different prices; then you buy low, sell high, and hope for convergence. Since fixed-income securities usually have a finite maturity, convergence must eventually happen, but the sooner it happens, the more profitable the trade. The biggest risk in convergence trades is that the trader is forced to unwind the trade when the price gap widens and the trade loses money. The economist (and trader!) John Maynard Keynes expressed this risk well:

> The markets can remain irrational longer than you can remain solvent.

Typical examples of fixed-income arbitrage trades include on-the-run versus off-the-run Treasury bonds, yield curve trading, betting on swap spreads, mortgage trades, futures-bond basis trades, and trades on the basis between bonds and credit default swaps (CDS).

Another classic arbitrage trade is convertible bond arbitrage. Convertible bonds are corporate bonds that can be converted into stock at a prespecified conversion ratio. A convertible bond can be viewed as a package of a straight corporate bond and a call option on the company's stock. Using option pricing techniques, the convertible bond value can be computed as a function of the company's stock price and volatility. This theoretical value of the convertible bond tends to be above the market price because convertible bonds can be very hard to sell quickly and therefore investors need to be compensated for the inherent liquidity risk.

Convertible bond arbitrage consists of buying cheap convertible bonds and hedging the risk by shorting stocks and possibly using additional hedges.

Finally, event-driven hedge funds try to exploit opportunities that arise around corporate events. The classic trade is merger arbitrage (also called risk arbitrage). In a corporate takeover, the acquirer makes a bid for the target stock above the current price to get investors to tender their shares. The stock price shoots up on the announcement but usually not all the way to the bid price. The difference reflects the risk of deal failure, but it also reflects that many investors sell their shares shortly after the announcement. Merger arbitrage managers buy the target company, typically after the announcement and after the initial price jump (unless they had the insight that this was a likely merger target in advance) and hope to earn the difference between the target stock price and the merger offer. The opposite corporate event of a merger is a spin-off or a split-off, where one company becomes two. This event also presents opportunities for event managers. Event managers trade a variety of corporate securities, not just stocks, but also corporate bonds and loans, for instance. Relative value trades across different securities issued by the same company are called capital structure arbitrage. Some event managers focus on distressed companies and may play an active role on the company's creditor committee, trying to turn the company around.

III. INVESTMENT STYLES AND FACTOR INVESTING

Although the different investment strategies are pursued in disperse asset classes by different types of managers, I nevertheless argue that there exist some pervasive investment "styles" that transcend these boundaries. I define an investment style as a method for deciding on what to buy and what to sell that can be applied broadly across asset classes and markets, as seen in Overview Table III.

The broad applicability of style investment means that it can be implemented systematically, which is called "factor investing." For instance, we study investment factors such as the value factor and the momentum factor. Whereas style investment lends itself well to factor investment, we shall see that there are many approaches—factor based and discretionary—to earning their rewards.

As a case in point, most of the managers whom I interviewed for this book use some version of value investing (buying cheap securities and selling expensive ones) and momentum investing (buying securities whose price has been rising while selling falling ones). Table I.2 includes brief quotes from each of my interviews related to value and momentum, although each of the hedge fund gurus calls it different things. As Asness's quote shows, value and momentum are clearly central in his investment strategy, and he had the insight

TABLE I.2. VALUE AND MOMENTUM EVERYWHERE

Expert Interviewed in This Book	Quotes Related to Value and Momentum
Lee Ainslie	The most common valuation metric at Maverick is the comparison of sustainable free cash flow to enterprise value [. . .] It's certainly important to be attuned to short-term expectations as well.
James Chanos	Kynikos Associates specializes in short selling, an investment technique that profits in finding fundamentally overvalued securities that are poised to fall in price. [. . .] Even if we love a position, if it's going against us, we'll trim it back.
Cliff Asness	We're looking for cheap stocks that are getting better, the academic ideas of value and momentum, and to short the opposite, expensive stocks that are getting worse.
George Soros	I developed this boom/bust theory [. . .] A bubble is when a situation moves from near-equilibrium to far-from-equilibrium. So, you've got these two strange attractors where the whole thing is an interplay between perceptions and the actual state of affairs.
David Harding	Trends are what you're looking for.
Myron Scholes	Most of the fixed-income business is a negative-feedback-type business unless you're directional, which is positive feedback, or trend following.
Ken Griffin	I started to view the markets through the lens of relative value trading.
John Paulson	The target stock runs up close to the offer price but trades at somewhat of a discount to the offer price because of the risks of failure of deal completion.

Source: Interviews in this book and statement by Chanos to the SEC, May 15, 2003.

that value and momentum strategies can be applied everywhere: in any asset class, you buy cheap assets that are trending up and short expensive assets that are coming down.[6] Soros focuses on boom–bust cycles, but, when he rides a bubble, this is essentially momentum trading, and when he decides that a bubble is bursting as the economy moves closer to equilibrium, he is a value

[6] See Asness, Moskowitz, and Pedersen (2013).

investor. Scholes talks about how fixed-income arbitrage is often based on negative-feedback trading, where one bets on mean reversion, i.e., a form of value investing, complemented by positive-feedback trading, betting on trend continuation. Ainslie and Chanos focus on fundamental value investing, but also consider short-term dynamics, which are often momentum based. Harding is one of the original systematic trend followers in the futures markets, whereas Griffin and Paulson look for relative value opportunities.

Another investment style (as seen in Overview Table III) is liquidity provision, meaning buying securities with high liquidity risk or securities being sold by other investors who demand liquidity. This investment style comes in many shapes and forms, from Griffin buying illiquid convertible bonds to earn a liquidity risk premium, to Paulson buying merger targets being dumped by investors who demand liquidity for fear of event risk, to Soros riding a credit cycle, to Asness providing liquidity through statistical arbitrage trades.

Carry trading is the investment style of buying securities with high "carry," that is, securities that will have a high return if market conditions stay the same (e.g., if prices do not change). For instance, global macro investors are known to pursue the currency carry trade where they invest in currencies with high interest rates, bond traders often prefer high-yielding bonds, equity investors like stocks with high dividend yields, and commodity traders like commodity futures with positive "roll return."

Low-risk investing is the style of exploiting the high risk-adjusted returns of safe securities. This investment style is done in several different ways across various markets. Low-risk investing can be done as a long–short equity strategy, buying safe stocks with leverage while shorting risky ones, also called "betting against beta." Low-risk investing can also be done as a long-only equity strategy, buying a portfolio of relatively safe stocks, also called defensive equity. Low-risk investing can also be applied as an asset allocation strategy called risk parity investing, and has also worked in fixed-income markets.

Lastly, quality investing is the style of buying high-quality securities, for instance, profitable, stable, growing, and well-managed companies, while shorting low-quality securities. High-quality securities naturally have higher average prices than corresponding low-quality ones, so quality investment goes hand-in-hand with value investing as investors seek securities that are cheap relative to their quality.

PART I

Active Investment

CHAPTER 1

Understanding Hedge Funds and Other Smart Money

There are many types of active investors who make markets efficiently ineffi-cient. These investors include large sophisticated pension funds with in-house trading operations, endowments, dealers and proprietary traders at investment banks, trading arms at commodity producing firms, mutual funds, proprietary trading firms, and hedge funds. In each case, the traders have slightly different contracts or profit-sharing agreements and face different political and firm-specific pressures and concerns. Since the focus of this book is the trading strategies, not the players, it would take us too far astray to discuss each of these trading set-ups in detail. However, to relate the trading strategies to real-life investors, it is worthwhile to understand the most pure-play bet on beating the market, namely hedge funds.

It is notoriously difficult to define what hedge funds are. Said simply, they are investment vehicles pursuing a variety of complex trading strategies to make money. The word *hedge* refers to reducing market risk by investing in both long and short positions, and the word *fund* refers to a pool of money con-tributed by the manager and investors. Asness has provided a tongue-in-cheek definition:

> Hedge funds are investment pools that are relatively unconstrained in what they do. They are relatively unregulated (for now), charge very high fees, will not necessarily give you your money back when you want it, and will generally not tell you what they do. They are supposed to make money all the time, and when they fail at this, their investors redeem and go to some-one else who has recently been making money. Every three or four years they deliver a one-in-a-hundred year flood. They are generally run for rich people in Geneva, Switzerland, by rich people in Greenwich, Connecticut.
>
> —Cliff Asness (2004)

Hedge funds are exempt from much of the regulation that applies to other investment companies, such as mutual funds. Hedge funds have a lot of freedom in the trading that they do, as well as limited disclosure requirements, but in exchange for this freedom, they are restricted in how they can raise money. In terms of freedom, hedge funds can use leverage, short-selling, derivatives, and incentive fees. In terms of restrictions, hedge fund investors must be "accredited investors," meaning that they need a certain amount of financial wealth and/or financial knowledge to be allowed to invest (to protect smaller, presumably less sophisticated, investors from the complexities encompassed in hedge fund strategies and risks that they may not understand). Also, hedge funds have historically been subject to a non-solicitation requirement, meaning that they cannot advertise or actively approach people for investments (although the regulation is being tightened in certain ways and loosened in others, e.g., in connection with the recent JOBS (Jumpstart Our Business Startups) Act in the United States).

Active investment has been around as long as markets have, and hedge funds have existed for more than half a century. The first formal hedge fund is believed to have been a fund created by Alfred Winslow Jones in 1949. Jones took long and short positions in stocks and reportedly earned a phenomenal 670% return from 1955 to 1965. While short-selling had been widely used long before Jones, he had the insight that, by balancing long and short positions, he would be relatively immune to overall market moves but profit from the relative outperformance of his long positions relative to his short positions. After *Fortune* magazine published Jones's results in 1966, interest in hedge funds started to grow, and in 1968 the U.S. Securities and Exchange Commission (SEC) counted 140 hedge funds. In the 1990s, the hedge fund industry saw a dramatically increased interest as institutional investors began to embrace hedge funds. In the 2000s, hedge funds with billions of dollars under management became commonplace, with total assets in the hedge fund industry reaching a peak of about $2 trillion before the global financial crisis, falling during the crisis, and since reaching a new peak.

Because of hedge fund leverage, their aggregate positions are much larger than their assets under management and, given their high turnover, their trading volume is a much larger part of the aggregate trading volume than their relative position sizes, so hedge fund trading is now a significant proportion of all trading. In an efficiently inefficient market, the amount of capital allocated to hedge funds cannot keep growing since, given a limited demand for liquidity, there is a limited amount of profit to be made and a limited need for active investment.[1]

---

[1] Pastor and Stambaugh (2012) estimate a large, but bounded, efficient size of the active management industry.

1.1. OBJECTIVES AND FEES

The objective of asset managers is to add value to their investors by making money relative to a benchmark. Mutual funds typically have a market index as a benchmark and try to outperform the market, whereas hedge funds typically have a cash benchmark (also called an "absolute return benchmark"). Hedge funds are not trying to beat the stock market but, rather, trying to make money in any environment. This is where the "hedge" part comes in. In contrast, mutual fund returns are usually benchmarked to a stock market (or bond market) index such as the Standard & Poor's 500 (S&P 500). Hence, if the S&P 500 is down 10% and a mutual fund is down 8%, it is outperforming its benchmark and applauded by its investors, whereas a hedge fund down 8% would be punished by its investors for the loss since its bets should not depend on market moves. Conversely, if the S&P 500 is up 20%, investors in a mutual fund that is up 16% will complain that it picked stocks that underperformed. Investors in a hedge fund that is truly market neutral (many are not) are satisfied that the hedged bets paid off in absolute terms. A hedge fund with returns that are independent of the market has the potential to be very diversifying to investors.

Asset managers charge fees for their investment service. Mutual funds charge a management fee (a fixed proportion of the assets), and hedge funds often also charge a performance fee. The management fee is meant to cover the manager's fixed expenses, and the performance fee is meant to strengthen the manager's incentive to perform well. The performance fee also enables the hedge fund to pay performance-based bonuses to its employees.[2]

While fees vary greatly across funds, the classic hedge fund fee structure has been "2 and 20," meaning a 2% management fee paid regardless of returns, and a 20% performance fee. For instance, if the hedge fund has a return of 12%, then the return is 10% after the management fee. The performance fee is then 20% of the 10%, that is, 2%, leaving 8% for the investors. Sometimes the performance fee is subject to a *hurdle rate*, such as the Treasury Bill rate, meaning that the hedge fund only earns performance fees on the return that exceeds the hurdle rate. However, performance fees typically do not depend on whether the fund beats the stock market return.

A hedge fund's performance fee is often subject to a *high water mark* (HWM). This means that, if the hedge fund loses money, it only starts to charge performance fees when the losses have been recovered. Just as you can see how high the water has reached by looking at the marks on the piers supporting a dock, a hedge fund keeps track of its cumulative performance and only charges performance

---

[2] The role of hedge fund incentives is studied by Goetzmann, Ingersoll, and Ross (2003), Agarwal, Daniel, and Naik (2009), Aragon and Nanda (2012), and Buraschi, Kosowski, and Sritrakul (2014).

fees when it reaches new highs. Note, however, that the HWM is investor specific. If a hedge fund gets a new investor just after suffering losses, the hedge fund can charge performance fees from the new investor as soon as it makes money (since the new investor has not incurred any losses that need to be made up).

While fees are income for asset managers, they are costs for investors. Investors should be aware of the fees they pay since fees in money management are very large, both in terms of the total amount of money paid, the fraction of the value added by the manager, and the effect of the long-term investment performance. There exist managers who track an index (explicitly or implicitly) while charging high fees, resulting in performance that underperforms the index by the fee each year, significantly hurting the long-run returns.

The fee should be viewed in relation to the amount of effective money management that the manager provides and the quality of this management. The amount of effective management can be measured as the "active risk," i.e., the volatility of the deviation from the benchmark (or tracking error). Hence, if a manager does not deviate from the benchmark, the fee should be very small. Similarly, a hedge fund manager who runs a high-risk and low-risk version of the same hedge fund typically charges a larger fee for the high-risk fund. This measure of the amount of effective management helps explain why hedge funds charge larger fees than mutual funds, namely because hedge funds effectively deliver more asset management services (since a large part of mutual fund returns is just delivering the benchmark).

To understand the importance of costs in the financial sector, consider how costs build up for a household saving for retirement. The retirement savings are managed in a pension fund with costs to pay its staff. The pension fund may hire investment consultants who charge fees to help pick the asset managers, and the asset managers charge another layer of fees. If the pension fund invests in a fund-of-funds, that adds yet another layer of fees. A final layer of costs comes from the transaction costs incurred through the turnover of the active manager (and earned by dealers and banks). Unless the fees in each layer are very competitive relative to the costs of passive management, the asset manager must add a lot of value through his trading. For an end investor to beat the market, a "double inefficiency" must exist: First, the security market must be inefficient enough that active managers can outperform, and second, the money management market must be inefficient enough that the end investor can find a money manager whose fee is below the expected outperformance.

1.2. PERFORMANCE

A number of famous hedge fund managers have produced spectacular returns, but these managers represent the best performers, not the typical hedge fund returns. Does more rigorous evidence for skill in money management exist?

This question is surprisingly hard to answer for several reasons, especially for hedge funds. First, the data on hedge fund returns are rather poor as they are available only over a limited time period and subject to important biases. To understand why, note that hedge fund databases consist of the returns of hedge funds that choose to report to the database provider. There is no comprehensive source of hedge fund returns, since their only reporting requirement is to their investors and hedge funds are often highly secretive. Hedge funds report their returns to promote themselves (remember that they are not allowed to advertise but can hope that investors will approach them if they see their track record in a database). This situation leads to several biases in the databases. First, when a hedge fund starts to report to a database, the fund reports all past returns, which are "backfilled" in the database. Since funds are more likely to start reporting after having experienced good performance, this leads to a "backfill bias": Funds that have poor performance from the beginning never make it into the database, while better performing funds are more likely to start reporting. Some databases and researchers account for this by only including returns from a certain time period after the hedge funds started reporting, disregarding the biased backfilled data. Another effect is that some hedge funds stop reporting when they experience poor performance, leading to a "survivorship bias." A bias pulling in the opposite direction arises from the fact that the most successful hedge funds often do not report to the databases. These funds value their privacy and do not need any additional exposure to clients; they may in fact be closed to new investments due to limited capacity. Hence, the databases exclude some of the most impressive track records, such as that of Renaissance Technologies.

When all these biases are taken into account, the evidence suggests that trading skill does exist among the best hedge funds and the best mutual funds, especially when considering performance before fees. Furthermore, some researchers find evidence of performance persistence, meaning that the top managers continue to be the top managers more often than not, but the persistence is not strong, and asset allocators should be careful of chasing performance, pulling money out at the bottom and investing at the peak rather than focusing on the manager's long-term record, process, and team.[3]

The evidence also suggests that the biases in many estimates of hedge fund returns are very large—beware!—these biases are not just "rounding error" but rather effects that change the perception of average returns by several percentage points. Furthermore, hedge fund returns are on average far from

---

[3] See the studies of hedge fund performance by Fung and Hsieh (1999), Malkiel and Saha (2005), Kosowski, Naik, and Teo (2007), Griffin and Xu (2009), and Jagannathan, Malakhov, and Novikov (2010) and of mutual fund performance by Kosowski, Timmermann, Wermers, and White (2006), Fama and French (2010), and Berk and van Binsbergen (2013). Berk and Green (2004) explain why large and persistent differences in manager skills may not lead to a large persistence in net returns because good managers receive large inflows and have decreasing returns to scale.

market neutral. Hedge fund indices have large correlations to equity markets, and the correlation has been growing over time. Also, hedge funds often have *negative skewness* and *excess kurtosis*, meaning that they sometimes have extreme returns, especially on the downside. Indeed, hedge funds, especially the small ones, have a high attrition rate, and the industry has been marked by some large blowups, including the failures of Long-Term Capital Management (LTCM), Bear Stearns' credit funds, and Amaranth.

Rather than looking at the performance of actual hedge funds, we can circumvent some of the issues discussed above by cutting to the chase and studying the actual trading strategies that hedge funds pursue as we do in this book. As we will see, the core strategies have worked more often than not over long time periods and worked for economic reasons of efficiently inefficient markets.

1.3. ORGANIZATION OF HEDGE FUNDS

Hedge funds are contractually organized in a number of different ways, but the typical *master–feeder* structure used by major hedge funds is illustrated in figure 1.1.

This structure is not as complicated as it first looks. The main point of the diagram is that, contractually, there is a distinction between the "fund," where the money is, and the "management company," where the traders and other employees work, even though the entire structure (or the relevant part) is often called the hedge fund for short.

An investor in a hedge fund invests in a *feeder fund*, whose sole purpose in life is to invest in the *master fund*, where the actual trades take place. (Investors in some, typically smaller, hedge funds invest directly into the master fund.) The master–feeder structure is useful since it allows the manager to focus on running a single master fund while at the same time creating different investment products (the feeder funds) tailored to the needs of the different investors. Typically, U.S. taxable investors prefer a feeder fund that is registered in the United States, while foreign investors and tax-exempt U.S. investors prefer an offshore feeder fund, established in an international financial center, such as the Cayman Islands. In addition to these tax-driven differences in where the various feeder funds are registered, feeder funds can also be used to tailor performance characteristics to different groups of investors. For instance, one can have several feeder funds denominated in different currencies, even though the underlying investments are the same. In this case, the foreign-currency-denominated feeder funds have a currency hedge in addition to their investment into the master fund. Another use of this structure is to have feeder funds at different risk levels. If the master fund has a volatility of 20% per year, one feeder fund might have the same volatility while another has half the volatility. The lower-risk feeder simply invests half its capital in

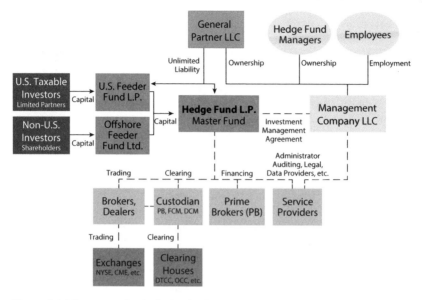

Figure 1.1. The master–feeder hedge fund structure.

a money market fund and the other half into the master fund, thus realizing half the risk.

The master fund has a pool of money, and this is where all the trades are carried out. It has an investment management agreement (IMA) with the *management company* to provide investment services, including strategy development, implementation, and trading. Hence, the management company is where all the employees work—including the traders, research analysts, operations staff, business development people, compliance, and legal personnel—and the management company is owned by the hedge fund managers. The management company trades on behalf of the fund, while the fund, and ultimately the investors, own the capital (and the hedge fund managers are typically themselves investors). The master fund is typically organized as a partnership, where the feeder funds are the limited partners, and the general partner is a company owned by the management company.

The hedge fund also contracts with agents who handle trading, custody and clearing, financing, and other services. Hedge funds trade through broker/dealers. For exchange-traded securities, brokers often merely facilitate access to exchanges, while in over-the-counter markets, dealers intermediate the hedge fund's trades. Custody is the service of "holding" the securities that the hedge fund owns, collecting dividends, keeping track of voting rights, and so on.

Clearing means doing the things that come between when the trader screams "Done!" in the phone and the trade is actually settled, that is, making sure that the shares are received or delivered and that the cash flows in the other direction. Custody and clearing are carried out by custodians, prime brokers (PBs), futures commission merchants (FCMs), and derivatives clearing merchants (DCMs). Prime brokers also provide financing for hedge funds, meaning that they provide leverage. They lend hedge funds money to buy securities worth more than their capital, and they have the securities as collateral.

Finally, hedge funds often work with a number of other service providers. A hedge fund administrator is a third party who values the positions and computes the official net asset value, auditors provide further verification of the hedge funds' assets and operations, legal advisors help structure contracts, and data vendors supply data.

1.4. HEDGE FUNDS' ROLE IN THE ECONOMY

Investors such as hedge funds often face criticism in the media. For instance, companies do not like to see their shares shorted, since this indicates a belief that the company's share price should go down. Short sellers, including hedge funds, are sometimes accused of being the source of the company's problems, though often the stock price is falling because of the company's poor business condition, and not for any other reason.

More broadly, hedge funds actually play several useful roles in the economy. First, they make markets more efficient by collecting information about businesses and impounding this information into prices through their trades. This increased efficiency can improve real outcomes for the economy, since the capital market is the tool to allocate resources in the economy. When markets are efficient, companies with good growth prospects see their share prices increase, allowing them to raise capital and finance new projects. Companies producing goods and services that are no longer needed see their share prices decrease, and the factories may be put to more productive use, possibly following a merger. In addition, CEO decisions may improve when share prices reflect more information and are more efficient and may be more prudent if active investors are monitoring them. Another useful role of hedge funds is that they provide liquidity to other investors who need to buy or sell (e.g., smooth out their consumption), need to hedge or buy insurance, or simply like certain types of securities. Finally, hedge funds provide another source of diversifying returns for their investors. In summary, hedge funds and other smart money are a natural part of an efficiently inefficient market.

CHAPTER 2

Evaluating Trading Strategies
Performance Measures

Let us first consider some simple measures that can be used to evaluate a hedge fund's overall performance or a specific strategy that the hedge fund has been using. Furthermore, these measures can be used to evaluate a strategy that a hedge fund is considering and has been simulating via a backtest, as discussed in the next chapter.

2.1. ALPHA AND BETA

The most basic measure of trading performance is, of course, the return, R_t, in a given period, t. The return is often separated into its alpha and beta. Beta is the strategy's market exposure, while alpha is the excess return after accounting for performance due to market movements. Alpha and beta are computed by running a regression of the strategy's return, $R_t^e = R_t - R^f$, in excess of the risk-free rate, R^f, on the excess return of the market, $R_t^{M,e}$:

$$R_t^e = \alpha + \beta R_t^{M,e} + \varepsilon_t$$

Here, β (beta) measures the strategy's tendency to follow the market. For example, suppose that $\beta = 0.5$. This means that if the market goes up by 10%, this strategy goes up by $0.5 \times 10\% = 5\%$, everything else being equal. For instance, if you invest half of your money in the stock market and the other half in cash, then your overall portfolio has a β of 0.5. In that case, your excess return will literally be 5% when the market goes up by 10%. More generally, your performance also depends on your idiosyncratic risk, measured by ε_t. For instance, if you only invest in biotech stocks rather than the overall market, then ε_t is the relative outperformance of your biotech stocks vis-à-vis the market. The idiosyncratic risk can be positive or negative, is zero on average, and is independent of market moves.

Knowing a strategy's beta is useful for many reasons. For instance, if you mix a hedge fund with other investments, the beta risk is not diversified away, while idiosyncratic risk largely is. Furthermore, market exposure ("beta risk") is easy to obtain at very low fees, for example, by buying index funds, exchange traded funds (ETFs), or futures contracts. Hence, you should not be paying high fees for market exposure.

Many hedge funds are (or claim to be) *market neutral*. This important concept means that the hedge fund's performance does not depend on whether the stock market is moving up or down. That is, the hedge fund has equally good potential to make money in bull and bear markets because its strategy is not simply to bet on the market going up. Mathematically, being market neutral means that $\beta = 0$.

Another use of beta is that it tells us how to *make* a strategy market neutral. Indeed, even if a strategy is not market neutral, we can make it market neutral by hedging out the market exposure, and β gives us the *hedge ratio*. Specifically, for every dollar of exposure to the hedge fund strategy, we need to short β dollars of the market. The performance of the market-neutralized strategy is then

$$\text{market-neutral excess return} = R_t^e - \beta R_t^{M,e} = \alpha + \varepsilon_t$$

Since the idiosyncratic risk ε_t is zero on average, the expected excess return of the market-neutral strategy is

$$E(\text{market-neutral excess return}) = \alpha$$

We see that the expected return in excess of the risk-free rate and the exposure to the market is given by the alpha, α. Alpha is clearly the sexiest term in the regression: It is the Holy Grail all active managers seek. Alpha measures the strategy's value added above and beyond the market exposure due to the hedge fund's trading skill (or luck, given that alpha is estimated based on realized returns).

If a hedge fund has a beta of zero (i.e., a market-neutral hedge fund) and an alpha of 6% per year, this means that the hedge fund is expected to make the risk-free return plus 6% per year. For instance, if the risk-free rate is 2% per year, the hedge fund is expected to make 8%, but the actual realization could be far above or below that, depending on the realized idiosyncratic shock.

The classic capital asset pricing model (CAPM) states that the expected return on any security or any portfolio is determined solely by the systematic risk, beta. In other words, CAPM predicts that alpha is equal to zero for any investment. Therefore, a hedge fund's search for alpha is a quest to *defy* the CAPM, to earn higher returns than simple compensation for systematic risk.

A hedge fund's true alpha and beta are estimated with significant error. Hence, if a hedge fund has an estimated alpha of 6%, how do we know whether this is luck or skill? To address this issue, researchers often look at the *t*-statistic, namely the alpha divided by the standard error of its estimate (an output of all regression analysis tools). A large t-statistic means that the alpha is large and reliably estimated, essentially because you have a long track record. Specifically, a t-statistic above 2 means that the alpha is statistically significant from zero, i.e., evidence of skill that defies the CAPM (although there can still be false positives and biases, e.g., if a manager shows only her best performing fund). A t-statistic smaller than 2 corresponds to an alpha estimate which is so noisy that it might have been achieved through luck.

We can also compute a strategy's excess return above and beyond several risk exposures, not just the market risk exposure. For instance, academics often consider the following three-factor regression model due to Fama and French (1993):

$$R_t^e = \alpha + \beta^M R_t^{M,e} + \beta^{HML} R_t^{HML} + \beta^{SMB} R_t^{SMB} + \varepsilon_t$$

where R^{HML} is the return on a value strategy and R^{SMB} is the return on a size strategy. Specifically, the high-minus-low factor (HML) goes long on stocks with a high book-to-market ratio (B/M) and shorts stocks with a low B/M. Similarly, the small-minus-big factor (SMB) goes long in small stocks and shorts big stocks. Therefore, β^{HML} measures the strategy's tendency to be tilted toward stocks with a high B/M (i.e., stocks that look cheap on this metric) and β^{SMB} measures the tilt toward small stocks. Hence, the alpha in the three-factor regression measures the excess return adjusted for market risk, value risk, and size risk. Said differently, this alpha measures the hedge fund's trading skills beyond simply taking stock market risk and tilting toward small-value stocks (which tend to outperform other stocks, on average).

2.2. RISK–REWARD RATIOS

As we have seen, a positive alpha is good while a negative alpha is bad. However, is a high positive alpha always better than a low positive alpha? Not necessarily. First, while alpha tells you the size of the market-neutral returns that a strategy delivers, it does not say at what risk. Second, alpha depends on how a strategy is scaled; for instance, a twice-leveraged strategy has twice the alpha of an unleveraged version of the same strategy. However, the quality of the strategy is what it is, so the performance measure should arguably be the same in both cases.

Risk–reward ratios resolve these issues. At a basic level, potential investors in a hedge fund want to know how the future *expected excess return* $E(R - R^f)$ compares to the risk that the hedge fund is taking. The *Sharpe ratio* (SR) is a measure of just that and is also called the risk-adjusted return. It measures the investment "reward" per unit of risk:

$$SR = \frac{E(R - R^f)}{\sigma(R - R^f)}$$

The investment reward is simply the expected excess return over the risk-free rate, that is, how much better did you do relative to putting your money in the bank? The risk is measured as the *standard deviation σ* (also called *volatility*) of your excess return. I describe below how to estimate these. Clearly, investors prefer higher SRs, as they prefer higher returns and lower risk (but their preferences might be more complex than what is captured by the Sharpe ratio when hedge funds have skewed returns and crash risk).

The SR gives the hedge fund credit for all excess returns, but we learned above that there is a difference between alpha returns and simple market exposure. The *information ratio* (IR) addresses this by focusing on the risk-adjusted *abnormal* return or, said differently, the risk-adjusted alpha:

$$IR = \frac{\alpha}{\sigma(\varepsilon)}$$

The alpha and idiosyncratic risk ε come from a regression of the hedge fund's excess return on some benchmark with excess return $R_t^{b,e}$:

$$R_t^e = \alpha + \beta R_t^{b,e} + \varepsilon_t$$

If the hedge fund has a mandate to beat a specific benchmark, then the IR is often computed without running a regression. In this case, the IR is computed simply as the expected return in excess of the benchmark, relative to the volatility of this outperformance[1]:

$$IR = \frac{E(R - R^b)}{\sigma(R - R^b)}$$

Hence, the IR measures the extent to which the strategy beats the benchmark per unit of *tracking error* risk. Tracking error is the difference between the strategy's and the benchmark's returns, and tracking error risk is the standard deviation of this difference. Many hedge funds consider their benchmark to be physical cash (money in the mattress, i.e., $R^b = 0$), so they report the IR simply as

$$IR = \frac{E(R)}{\sigma(R)}$$

which is always higher than the SR, since it does not subtract the risk-free rate. Even if many hedge funds report this number, I view it as an unreasonable number as it gives the hedge fund credit for earning the risk-free rate (and depends on the level of interest rates). The IR is almost always reported as an annualized number, as discussed further below.

Both the SR and the IR are ways of calculating risk-adjusted returns, but some traders and investors say,

---

[1] This second definition of the IR is equivalent to the first definition if we set β equal to one in the benchmark regression.

You can't eat risk-adjusted returns.

Suppose, for instance, that a hedge fund beats the risk-free rate by 3% at a tiny risk of 2%, realizing an excellent SR of 1.5. Some investors might say, "Well, it's still just 3%. I was hoping for more return." Whether this is a fair criticism or not depends on several things. First, it depends on whether the strategy's risk really is that low on a long-term basis or this period was just lucky not to have a blowup (e.g., if the hedge fund is selling out-the-money options collecting small premiums until a big market move blows it up). If we suppose that risk really is low, then the question is whether one can apply leverage to the strategy to achieve a higher return and risk. With leverage, you *can* eat risk-adjusted returns. One way to apply "leverage" is to have the investor put more money in the hedge fund, but many investors prefer not to have a large notional exposure and need ready cash. Therefore, the question is whether the hedge fund can apply leverage internally. The answer to this question is given by the *alpha-to-margin* (AM) ratio (suggested by Gârleanu and Pedersen 2011):

$$AM = \frac{\alpha}{margin}$$

The idea behind this ratio is to compute the return on a *maximally leveraged* version of a market-neutral strategy. To understand the AM ratio, note that while hedge funds can apply leverage to any strategy, there is a limit to this leverage, since hedge funds are subject to margin requirements, as discussed further in section 5.8. The maximum leverage that can be applied to a strategy is 1/margin. For instance, if the margin requirement is 10%, a hedge fund can get 10-to-1 leverage, and, in this case, the AM ratio is 10 times the expected market-neutral return. To be even more specific, if alpha is 3% per year, then the AM ratio is 30%. This means that if a hedge fund takes $100 of its capital, applies 10-to-1 leverage, and invests $1,000 in the strategy, then it has an alpha of 3% × $1,000 = $30, which is 30% of its $100 capital. The hedge fund may prefer this strategy to one trading illiquid securities that cannot be leveraged at all (margin is 100%) with an alpha of 7%. This alternative strategy has a lower AM ratio of 7%, despite its higher alpha. The AM ratio can be seen as the investment management equivalent of the return of equity (ROE) measure from corporate finance.

There is a close link between the AM ratio and the IR. The AM ratio is the reward per unit of risk (IR) multiplied by the extent to which the strategy can be leveraged, namely the risk per unit of margin equity:

$$AM = IR \times \frac{\sigma(\varepsilon)}{margin}$$

If a hedge fund strategy has a significant crash risk, volatility may not be the best risk measure. To capture crash risk, the denominator is modified in performance measures such as the risk-adjusted return on capital (RAROC):

$$\text{RAROC} = \frac{E(R - R^f)}{\text{economic capital}}$$

where *economic capital* is the amount of capital that you need to set aside to sustain worst-case losses on the strategy with a certain confidence. Hence, the denominator is the crash risk instead of day-to-day swings. Economic capital can be estimated using value-at-risk (VaR) or stress tests, concepts that we discuss in detail in section 4.2 on risk management. The Sortino ratio (S) uses downside risk:

$$S = \frac{E(R - R^f)}{\sigma^{\text{downside}}}$$

The downside risk (or downside deviation) is calculated as the standard deviation of returns truncated above some minimum acceptable return (MAR):

$$\sigma^{\text{downside}} = \sigma(R\,1_{\{R < MAR\}})$$

The MAR is often set to be the risk-free rate or zero. The indicator function in the calculation of downside risk, $1_{\{R < MAR\}}$, is the number 1 if the return is less than the MAR, and zero otherwise. Hence, the downside risk is not affected by how returns vary when they are above the MAR. Implicitly, this result is based on an assumption that investors care only (or mostly) about the downside. Therefore, the Sortino ratio assumes that investors do not care whether they make 5% in each of two years versus 1% the first year and 9% the next. In contrast, the SR is based on an assumption that investors prefer the former.

2.3. ESTIMATING PERFORMANCE MEASURES

To estimate expected returns, standard deviations, and regressions, we can use standard methods. Expected returns are estimated as the realized average return, using the available data over T time periods. Some people use geometric averages,[2]

$$\text{geometric average} = [(1 + R_1) \times (1 + R_2) \times \ldots \times (1 + R_T)]^{1/T} - 1$$

while others use arithmetic ones,

$$\text{arithmetic average} = [R_1 + R_2 + \ldots + R_T]/T$$

The geometric average corresponds to the experience of a buy-and-hold investor who neither adds capital nor takes capital out of a hedge fund. The arithmetic average is the optimal estimator from a statistical point of view, and it corresponds more closely to the experience of an investor who adds and

---

[2] For instance, mutual funds are required to report geometric averages in the United States.

redeems capital in order to keep a constant dollar exposure to the hedge fund, under certain conditions. Whether using geometric or arithmetic averages, it is important to keep in mind that any estimate of future expected returns is extremely noisy. The precision of the estimate increases with the length of the sample period, but it is difficult to estimate expected returns, even with many years of data.

The standard deviation σ can often be estimated with more precision: It is the square root of the variance σ^2, which is estimated as the squared deviations around the arithmetic average, $\overline{R}$

$$\text{variance estimate} = [(R_1 - \overline{R})^2 + (R_2 - \overline{R})^2 + \ldots + (R_T - \overline{R})^2]/(T - 1)$$

2.4. TIME HORIZONS AND ANNUALIZING PERFORMANCE MEASURES

Performance measures depend on the horizon over which they are measured. For instance, table 2.1 shows that a strategy that has an annual Sharpe ratio of 1 has very different Sharpe ratios if measured over other time horizons, such as a Sharpe ratio of 2 over a four-year period and a mere 0.06 over a trading day.

Hence, when we talk about performance measures, we need to be clear about the horizon. Furthermore, when we compare the performance of two different strategies or hedge funds, we need to make sure that the performance measures are calculated over the same time horizon. It is therefore useful to have a standard measurement horizon and, to accomplish this, performance measures are often annualized. This means that the performance measures are computed using annual data or, more commonly, using more frequent data and converted into equivalent annualized units.

To annualized expected returns, we can simply multiply them by the number n of periods per year:

TABLE 2.1. PERFORMANCE MEASURES AND TIME HORIZONS

Measurement horizon	Sharpe ratio	Loss probability
Four years	2	2.3%
Year	1	16.0%
Quarter	0.5	31.0%
Month	0.3	39.0%
Trading day	0.06	47.5%
Minute	0.003	49.9%

$$\text{ER}^{\text{annual}} = \text{ER} \times n$$

For instance, if you have measured monthly returns, you can compute the annualized return by multiplying by $n = 12$, weekly returns are multiplied by 52, and returns over trading days are multiplied by 260 (or less, depending on how holidays are accounted for). This method is natural if returns are averaged using an arithmetic average, but with geometric averages it is more natural to annualize returns taking compounding into account:

$$\text{ER}^{\text{annual}} = (1 + \text{ER})^n - 1$$

Since returns are (close to) independent over time, their variance is proportional to the time period. For instance, the annual variance is 12 times the monthly variance. More generally, the annualized variance can be computed by multiplying the measured variance by the number n of periods per year:

$$\text{var}^{\text{annual}} = \text{var} \times n$$

As a result, the standard deviation scales with the square root of the number of time periods:

$$\sigma^{\text{annual}} = \sigma \times \sqrt{n}$$

Once we have annualized each component of a risk measure, we can compute the overall annualized risk measure. For instance, to annualize a Sharpe ratio measured over n periods per year, we obtain

$$\text{SR}^{\text{annual}} = \text{ER}^{\text{annual}} / \sigma^{\text{annual}} = SR \times \sqrt{n}$$

This formula explains the SR numbers in table 2.1: The annualized SR is kept constant at 1, but as we vary the number of periods n, the measured SR varies as $\text{SR} = \text{SR}^{\text{annual}}/\sqrt{n}$. As we increase the measurement frequency n, we decrease the measured SR.

How frequently you observe profits and losses (P&L), and the corresponding SR, affects how risk is felt. If you observe P&L more frequently—for instance, if you are a hedge fund manager with a live P&L screen—then you have a lower SR between each time you look at the P&L, and the risk is more painful. One way to see why a strategy feels riskier at a frequent time scale is to calculate the probability of observing a loss over a given period. To do so, assume for simplicity that returns are normally distributed (even though that is clearly not the case in the real world). Then we can compute the probability of a loss as follows, where N is a normally distributed random variable with mean zero and a standard deviation of one:

$$\Pr(R^e < 0) = \Pr(\text{E}(R^e) + \sigma N < 0) = \Pr(N < -SR)$$

We see that the probability of losing money simply depends on the SR. The loss probabilities are reported in table 2.1 for the case of a strategy with an annualized SR of 1. We see that even for such a good strategy, the probability of a loss during a 1-minute interval is close to 50%. Hence, even when you have a great year, you probably see losses about every other minute if you are observing the P&L at that frequency. No wonder it can feel so painful.

2.5. HIGH WATER MARK

A hedge fund's high water mark (HWM) is the highest price P_t (or highest cumulative return) it has achieved in the past:

$$HWM_t = \max_{s \leq t} P_s$$

Often hedge funds only charge performance fees when their returns are above their HWM. Hence, if they have experienced losses, they must first make these back and only charge performance fees on the profits above their HWM.

2.6. DRAWDOWN

An important risk measure for a hedge fund strategy is its drawdown (DD). The drawdown is the cumulative loss since losses started. The percentage drawdown since the peak (i.e., the HWM) is given by

$$DD_t = (HWM_t - P_t)/HWM_t$$

where P_t is the cumulative return at time t (or share price).[3] In other words, the drawdown is the amount that has been lost since the peak (i.e., the HWM). If the hedge fund is currently at its peak, then the drawdown is zero, and otherwise it is a positive number. The drawdown can also be measured relative to other points in time, for example, the beginning of the year. Experiencing large drawdowns is costly and risky. In addition to the direct losses, large drawdowns often lead to redemptions from investors and concerns from counterparties, for example, prime brokers increasing margin requirements or completely pulling the financing of the hedge fund's positions. When evaluating a strategy, people sometimes consider its maximum drawdown (MDD) over some past time period:

$$MDD_T = \max_{t \leq T} DD_t$$

Figure 2.1 shows an example of a hedge fund strategy and its HWM, drawdown, and MDD.

---

[3] This drawdown formula is based on a cumulative return index P_t computed using compounding, that is, $P_t = P_{t-1} \times (1 + R_t)$. If the cumulative return index is computed by simply adding up returns (or log returns), that is, $P_t = P_{t-1} + R_t$, then the drawdown is also defined in an additive way, $DD_t = HWM_t - P_t$. Also, some investors think of drawdowns as negative numbers, so they put a minus sign in front of my definition.

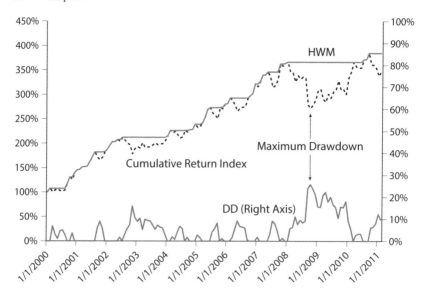

Figure 2.1. A hedge fund strategy's high water mark (HWM) and drawdown (DD).

2.7. ADJUSTING PERFORMANCE MEASURES FOR ILLIQUIDITY AND STALE PRICES

Some hedge funds may not be as hedged as they first appear. To see why, let us consider the following example. Suppose that Late Capital Management (LCM) invests 100% in the stock market but always marks to market one month late. For instance, if the stock market goes up by 3% in January, LCM will report a 3% return in February. In that case, what is LCM's stock market beta? Well, β^{LCM} will appear to be near zero, since it depends on the covariance with the market and the returns are misaligned in time:

$$\text{cov}(R_t^{LCM,e}, R_t^{M,e}) = \text{cov}(R_{t-1}^{M,e}, R_t^{M,e}) \cong 0$$

In other words, since LCM's return is last month's market return, and market returns are (close to) independent over time, LCM will appear to have a zero beta in a standard regression:

$$R_t^{LCM,e} = \alpha + \beta R_t^{M,e} + \varepsilon_t$$

The estimated values of α will be the average stock market return, which is positive (over the long term). Hence, LCM appears to be creating alpha from the perspective of the standard estimate, but does marking to market late really create value to investors? Is investing in LCM a good long-term hedge against the market? Clearly not. If you lose on your market investment, you will also lose on your LCM investment next month.

While this example is obviously unrealistic, the general lesson it teaches is more realistic than you may think. Many hedge funds invest in illiquid securities that often do not trade for days, and therefore month-end prices can be "stale." This problem can be especially severe for securities traded in over-the-counter (OTC) markets with no public price transparency, but it is also an issue for illiquid exchange-traded securities. Hence, the hedge fund returns may be based on stale price marks that do not reflect all the volatility in the market. This delay means that the co-movement with the market (beta) is mismeasured, leading to an inflated measure of alpha. We can adjust for this by regressing not just on the market return during the same period, but also during lagged time periods[4]:

$$R^e_t = \alpha^{\text{adjusted}} + \beta^0 R^{M,e}_t + \beta^1 R^{M,e}_{t-1} + \cdots + \beta^L R^{M,e}_{t-L} + \varepsilon_t$$

The alpha in this multivariate regression now accounts for stale market exposure and captures the hedge fund's value added beyond its exposure to both current and past market moves. We can then estimate the "true" all-in beta as

$$\beta^{\text{all-in}} = \beta^0 + \beta^1 + \cdots + \beta^L$$

In the example of LCM, this method will produce $\beta^{\text{all-in}} = 1$ and $\alpha^{\text{adjusted}} = 0$, thus reflecting the true (lack of) value added by this hypothetical hedge fund. This adjustment also makes a significant difference in evaluating many real-world hedge funds and hedge fund indices. We can also adjust other performance measures for the stale-price problem. For instance, to compute the adjusted information ratio, we can use the Sharpe ratio of the all-in hedged returns, $R^e_t - (\beta^0 R^{M,e}_t + \beta^1 R^{M,e}_{t-1} + \cdots + \beta^L R^{M,e}_{t-L})$:

$$\text{IR}^{\text{adjusted}} = \frac{\alpha^{\text{adjusted}}}{\sigma(\varepsilon)}$$

2.8. PERFORMANCE ATTRIBUTION

Hedge funds frequently review what factors are driving their returns, a process called performance attribution. That is, they look back over the previous quarter, say, and review which trades were the main positive return contributors and which ones detracted. This is useful both for the hedge fund's communication with its clients and for internal planning and evaluations. From the hedge fund

---

[4] This issue was pointed out by Asness, Krail, and Liew (2001), who suggested the lagged beta methodology due to Scholes and Williams (1977) and Dimson (1979).

investors' perspective, performance attribution is useful because it provides insight into the investment process, the drivers of returns, and the risk factors to which they are exposed. Internally, in a hedge fund, performance attribution can be used to determine which investment strategies appear to be working and which traders tend to make successful investments.

2.9. BACKTESTS VS. TRACK RECORDS

It is important to distinguish between performance measures that are gross versus net of transaction costs and gross versus net of fees. Whether to consider performance before or after transaction costs and fees depends on what the measure is used for. Investors clearly care about a hedge fund's performance after transaction costs and after fees—they enjoy only these net returns. A hedge fund's *track record* is its realized performance after all fees and costs over its life. Some hedge funds have different fee schedules (e.g., one option with a high management fee and no performance fee and another option with a low management fee and a high performance fee), in which case they must report the track record using the most conservative fee schedule.

Hedge funds also consider backtests of their strategies, that is, historical simulations of their performance under assumptions about how they would have behaved in the past. While investors are ultimately interested in net returns, a hedge fund might internally investigate a trading idea by first looking at the gross return in a backtest. Indeed, the hedge fund may first try to determine whether a strategy has any merit and, for this, examine whether the gross returns appear to be reliably positive. If the strategy appears to make money, the hedge fund will next consider whether the strategy survives transaction costs and, ultimately, whether it will add value for investors. While the fund's realized returns are naturally net of transaction costs, how to adjust a backtest for transaction costs is more involved. We next consider in more detail how to construct a backtest, how to account for trading costs, and how to consider a trade's leverage and financing issues.

CHAPTER 3

Finding and Backtesting Strategies
Profiting in Efficiently Inefficient Markets

No trading strategies are guaranteed to always make money, but there exist strategies that have made profits more often than losses over extensive time periods. It is important to understand *why* certain strategies can make money. One reason, of course, is luck. However, we are interested in strategies that can be expected to *continue* to make money in the future, a repeatable process that generates alpha. To find such a repeatable alpha process, one must understand the economics hiding behind the profits, or, as the saying goes,

> If you don't know who the sucker is, it's you.

While it is important to understand the economics that underlie a trading strategy, there does not need to be a true "sucker" in the game and, even if you find one, this is likely not a repeatable process. Hence, you should simply take this expression to mean that you need to understand who is taking the other side of your trade and why. If you are making money more often than not, what is motivating others to trade the other way, and will they continue to do so in the future? Remember that for every buyer, there is a seller, so someone is always taking the other side of your trades, and if you do not understand the economics of the trade, they may. As seen in figure 3.1, I believe that there are two main sources of repeatable trading profits: compensation for liquidity risk and information advantages. Figure 3.1 also shows how liquidity risk and information advantages can be decomposed further, as we discuss next. After understanding the sources of trading profits, we discuss how to backtest a new trading idea.

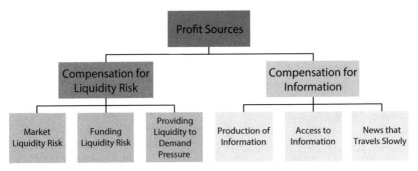

Figure 3.1. The main sources of profit for hedge fund strategies.

3.1. PRICES REFLECT AN EFFICIENTLY INEFFICIENT LEVEL OF INFORMATION

For market prices to efficiently reflect information about economic fundamentals, someone must collect the information and trade on it. That information production role is often played by hedge funds. To see why information production can be a repeatable source of profit, note first that markets cannot be perfectly efficient and always reflect all information. If they were perfect, no one would have any incentive to collect information and trade on it, and then how could markets become efficient in the first place? Markets also cannot be so inefficient that making money is very easy because, in that case, hedge funds and other active investors would have an incentive to trade more and more. The information contained in market prices must be efficiently inefficient, reflecting enough information to make it difficult to make money, but not so efficient that no one wants to collect information and trade on it (Grossman and Stiglitz 1980).

Production of information. Hedge funds produce information in many ways. They do so when they make an extensive analysis of companies and their future profit prospects, which is an information collection and processing effort called fundamental analysis. Furthermore, hedge funds seek to buy companies with strong and underappreciated business prospects, doing extensive research on consumer demands and industry dynamics. Hedge funds sometimes uncover—and short sell—fraudulent firms or firms with misstated earnings. Just as a good journalist seeks to uncover the truth and report a story first, a trader seeks to be the first to trade on new information and insights. Hedge funds may also create information more directly by providing management with ideas on how to improve the company or cut costs.

Access to information. Another source of profits is simply to have superior access to information. The most extreme example of this is illegal insider trading, when a hedge fund trades based on inside information. For example, an employee or executive at a company may provide privileged information about the firm's profits or an impending merger. Investors should stay far away from the grey area of illegal insider trading. Insider trading is unfair to other market participants and, when discovered, quickly brings down a hedge fund or other financial firm since the financial sector relies on trust. There are, however, legal situations where hedge funds can acquire proprietary data or information. For instance, it is legal to call doctors and ask what medicines they are prescribing and then trade pharmaceutical stocks based on this information.

Behavioral finance and the limits of arbitrage. A third source of profit is that news and other publicly available information simply does not always get reflected fully in the prices right away. Even though market prices certainly reflect a lot of relevant information, they don't always perfectly aggregate all information immediately. For example, when a company announces its earnings, prices move up on good news and down on bad news, but on average the price move is too small. Therefore, following good news, the price continues to drift up for several weeks after the announcement, on average, and after bad news the price drifts downward for a while, an effect called the post–earnings-announcement drift. More broadly, there is a general tendency of initial underreaction and delayed overreaction that creates trends and momentum, as discussed further in chapters 9 and 12, on quantitative equity and managed futures.

Why do these effects arise? One explanation is that some investors ("noise traders") suffer from behavioral biases and make common mistakes that push prices away from fundamentals. Why are these mistakes not corrected by the smart money? They are partly corrected, but only partly due to the limits of arbitrage (Shleifer and Vishny 1997, Shleifer 2000). Although textbook arbitrage eliminates all mispricings in theory, in the real world all "arbitrage" trades are risky, so arbitrage occurs only to a limited extent. Since arbitrage is limited by its costs and risks, arbitrage trading does not completely eliminate any mispricing; an efficiently inefficient level of mispricing persists.

So what are the real-world limits of arbitrage? First, arbitrage is often subject to *fundamental risk*, meaning that if a hedge fund buys a cheap security, say, an undervalued oil company, there is still a risk that the security will underperform due to a random event (the CEO dies in a car accident or the oil rig blows up). Second, arbitrage is subject to *noise trader risk*, meaning that if a hedge fund buys a cheap security, it might become even cheaper before the price approaches the fundamental value (De Long, Shleifer, Summers, and Waldmann 1993). This situation leads to short-term losses for the hedge fund (even if the trade was "right" ex ante), which can lead to capital redemptions, and the fund may not live to see the upside. Third, a hedge fund may try to "ride" a bubble rather than trading against it—as George Soros has done for instance during the Internet bubble—especially when the hedge fund thinks that other smart investors will delay trading against the mispricing and "pop" the bubble (Abreu and Brunnermeier 2003 and Brunnermeier and Nagel 2004). Because of these risks and the liquidity risks discussed next, hedge funds limit the size of the positions that they take and therefore competing arbitrageurs may not completely eliminate mispricings.

In summary, when you are looking for new cool trading ideas, think about whether there is information that most investors overlook, new ways to combine various sources of information, a smart way to get the information fast, or what type of information is not fully reflected in the price because of limited arbitrage.

3.2. EFFICIENTLY INEFFICIENT COMPENSATION FOR LIQUIDITY RISK

Another reason why active investors can profit is that they are compensated for taking risk. For instance, hedge funds are long in the stock market, on average, and since stock prices go up on average (called the equity premium), they are compensated for the associated market risk. However, investors can easily get exposure to the equity market, so this is beta, and not alpha (as discussed above in the chapter on performance measures). We want to understand how hedge funds can earn alpha returns as compensation for risks *other* than simple stock market exposure, importantly *liquidity risk*.

Liquidity risk consists of the risk of rising transaction costs (*market liquidity risk*); the risk of running out of cash, especially for a leveraged hedge fund (*funding liquidity risk*); and the risk of accommodating *demand pressure*. Liquidity risk is an important limit of arbitrage. Similar to the other limits of arbitrage discussed above, liquidity risk limits traders' ability to correct mispricings.

Liquidity risk is not just a limit of arbitrage, however; it affects market prices *directly* as it creates a liquidity risk premium. Said differently, the pricing of liquidity risk is a natural component of an efficiently inefficient market (whereas other limits of arbitrage only matter if some noise traders push the prices out of line in the first place). Let's see how liquidity risk affects prices.

Market Liquidity Risk

Many securities are very illiquid, meaning that they have large transaction costs. Such securities often become even more illiquid just when you need to sell, confirming the following maxim:

They'll let you in, but they won't let you out.

The risk that you cannot get out or that you will have to pay large transaction costs is called market liquidity risk. For instance, during the fall of 2008, bid–ask spreads on convertible bonds and other illiquid securities went from less than 1% to more than 5%, and in many cases dealers simply had "no bid," meaning that they would only trade if they could find a counterparty willing to take the other side.

Naturally, investors want to be compensated for taking market liquidity risk, and therefore illiquid securities are cheap and earn higher average gross returns. For instance, convertible bonds tend to be cheap relative to their theoretical value (which can be inferred from stock prices, since convertible bonds are derivatives), which is due to this market liquidity risk premium. Also, when asked how much added return Harvard's Endowment needs in private equity in return for tying up your money for five or 10 years, their CEO answered:

> We should be getting an incremental return for that illiquidity—and we call that our illiquidity premium—of at least 300 basis points annually on average over what we are expecting in publicly traded stocks.
>
> —Jane Mendillo, CEO of Harvard Management
> (*Barron's* Feb. 8, 2014)

Liquidity risk is an important reason why the standard capital asset pricing model (CAPM) does not work well in practice. Financial markets may be better approximated by the liquidity-adjusted CAPM.[1] This model says that investors care about a security i's return R^i net of its transaction cost TC^i. As a result, the CAPM should apply for net returns $R^i - TC^i$:

$$E(R^i - TC^i) = R^f + \beta^i \lambda$$

where λ is the risk premium and β^i measures the security's covariance with the net return of the overall market M,

$$\beta^i = \frac{\text{cov}(R^i - TC^i, R^M - TC^M)}{\text{var}(R^M - TC^M)}$$

The implication is that gross returns are determined by

$$E(R^i) = R^f + E(TC^i) + (\beta^{R^i,R^M} + \beta^{TC^i,TC^M} - \beta^{TC^i,R^M} - \beta^{R^i,TC^M})\lambda$$

This equation says that investors required return $E(R^i)$ is the risk-free rate plus the expected transaction cost $E(TC^i)$, plus compensation for four risks multiplied by the risk premium λ. It is natural that higher expected transaction costs lead to higher required returns, and the risk premiums are intuitive as well. The first one, β^{R^i,R^M}, is the standard market beta, which depends on the covariance between the security's own return R^i and the market return R^M. The next term means that investors require a higher return for a security

---

[1] The liquidity-adjusted CAPM is derived by Acharya and Pedersen (2005), and further evidence is provided by Pastor and Stambaugh (2003) for equities, Lin, Wang, and Wu (2011) for corporate bonds, and Sadka (2010) for hedge fund returns. Amihud and Mendelson (1986) document the effect of the level of liquidity.

with more commonality in liquidity β^{TC^i,TC^M}, that is, if its transaction cost TC^i covaries with the market transaction costs TC^M. In other words, traders do not like to hold a security whose liquidity dries up when one cannot trade many other things. The third risk premium, β^{TC^i,R^M}, implies that investors should be compensated for holding a security that becomes illiquid when the market falls, because this is often when you really need the money. The last premium, β^{R^i,TC^M}, implies that investors want to be compensated for holding securities that drop in value during a liquidity crisis.

In practice, all these forms of market liquidity risk are closely related. The main point is that traders only want to buy a security with market liquidity risk if they get compensated for it, and the way they get compensated is by buying at a low price, i.e., with a high expected return. Hence, hedge funds willing to take the risk can earn the market liquidity risk premium. Furthermore, a hedge fund with a long holding period and an ability to trade at relatively modest cost may be able to earn high net returns. Indeed, if a hedge fund can buy low due to the market liquidity risk premium while trading infrequently and smartly and also avoid forced liquidations during crises, then it will earn high returns. However, doing so involves risk, which is what the fund is compensated for. Buying securities falling in value as others are selling large positions in a liquidity spiral can often be dangerous, since it is impossible to know when the bottom has been reached. As traders say,

Don't catch a falling knife.

This liquidity–risk theory explains well the premiums earned by fixed-income arbitrage hedge funds, for instance. As we discuss in more detail later, these hedge funds often buy and sell pairs of almost identical securities: They buy a cheap illiquid security and short-sell a corresponding liquid security, earning a spread that is compensation for market liquidity risk.

The liquidity-adjusted CAPM also shows what happens during a liquidity crisis when transaction costs and liquidity risk increase: The required return increases as investors need even higher compensation for market liquidity risk, and as a result, prices drop sharply. Such liquidity crises frequently happen in specialized markets, while broad crises across markets happen around twice per decade.

While trading illiquid securities is one way to earn the market liquidity risk premium, making markets is another. As background, note that many investors want to trade immediately, and buyers and sellers are not always in the market at the same time. Hence, the order flow is fragmented and the price bounces around the fundamental value. Market makers take advantage of this—or provide a liquidity service, depending on how you see it—by taking the other side of these trades and smoothing out the price fluctuations. The term *market makers* here is meant in a general sense. For instance, high-frequency traders often effectively play the role of market makers even if they are not designated as such. The compensation for the risks associated with this liquidity service is the profit market makers make due to bid–ask spreads or market impacts.

Funding Liquidity Risk

Another important risk that a hedge fund takes is *funding liquidity risk*, that is, the risk that it cannot fund the position throughout the life of the trade. Said differently, it is the risk of being forced to unwind positions as the fund hits a margin constraint or gets uncomfortably close. Some securities are difficult to finance, since they have high margin requirements, and capital-constrained investors naturally want to be compensated for holding such "cash-intensive" securities. Therefore, required returns increase with the margin requirement, according to the margin CAPM (Gârleanu and Pedersen 2011):

$$E(R^i) = R^f + \beta^i \lambda + m^i \psi$$

where m^i is the margin requirement of security i and ψ is the compensation for tying up capital. Another implication for funding constraints and leverage constraints is that many investors prefer to buy risky securities over applying leverage to safer securities. This implication can help explain why riskier securities tend to offer lower risk-adjusted returns than safer ones within each asset class: A portfolio of risky stocks tends to underperform a leveraged portfolio of safer stocks, a portfolio of long-term Treasuries tends to underperform a leveraged portfolio of short-term Treasuries, and similarly within credit markets (Frazzini and Pedersen 2014). A similar effect holds across asset classes, giving rise to what is called Risk Parity investment (Asness, Frazzini, and Pedersen 2012).

Of course, market and funding liquidity risks are interconnected and jointly affect required returns:

$$E(R^i) = R^f + \beta^i \lambda + \underset{\text{compensation}}{\text{market liquidity risk}} + \underset{\text{compensation}}{\text{funding liquidity risk}}$$

Securities with high transaction costs and market liquidity risk tend to also be difficult to finance, and vice versa. Furthermore, these risks reinforce each other and can create liquidity spirals, as discussed in section 5.10.

Providing Liquidity to Demand Pressure

The final alpha source is the tendency of hedge funds to profit by providing liquidity to *demand pressure*. For example, if a security faces unusual buying pressure, its price is elevated, which means that its future expected return is abnormally low. Other securities may be abandoned, leading to low prices and high expected returns. In such situations, a *contrarian* trading strategy becomes profitable, effectively providing liquidity by buying low and selling high.[2]

Demand pressure arises for a number of different reasons. For instance, many of the corporate events that event-driven hedge fund managers trade on are associated with demand pressure. When a merger has been announced, the target stock jumps up on the announcement, but if the merger deal falls apart, the price will drop back down. Due to this event risk, many mutual funds and other investors sell the target stock, leading to downward pressure on the stock price. In this case, merger arbitrage hedge funds provide liquidity by buying a diversified portfolio of such merger targets. The merger arbitrage hedge funds can therefore be viewed as selling insurance against the event risk that the merger falls apart. Just as insurance companies profit from selling protection against your house burning down, merger arbitrage hedge funds profit from selling insurance against a merger deal failing.

Another source of demand pressure is that some investors want to hedge various risks. For instance, there is a large hedging demand for buying index options, especially put options, pushing up their price. Similarly, companies often create demand pressures in commodity markets when they hedge their production or output risks.

A number of institutional frictions can create demand pressures. For instance, certain investors cannot hold non–investment-grade bonds, and, as a result, when a bond is downgraded, there is a demand pressure to sell it. As another example, passive investors in commodities have traditionally held the nearest-to-maturity futures contract and, close to each future's expiration, have rolled into the next futures contract according to a specific cycle determined by the S&P GSCI index (formerly the Goldman Sachs Commodity Index), creating a demand pressure to sell the near contract and buy the far contract.

Lastly, behavioral biases can create demand pressures. Some securities may capture investors' imaginations and create a demand for their shares, while others may go overlooked. For instance, companies that interact directly with many customers may face an excess demand for their shares, such as Krispy Kreme did for a number of years, and Internet stocks before that.

In summary, you could find trading strategies by getting an edge in trading and financing illiquid securities or by trading against demand pressures.

---

[2] Demand pressure has been found to affect equity prices, e.g., in connection with stock index additions (Shleifer 1986 and Wurgler and Zhuravskaya 2002), option prices (Gârleanu, Pedersen, and Poteshman 2009), bond yields (Krishnamurthy and Vissing-Jorgensen 2012 and Greenwood and Vayanos 2014), futures prices (Keynes 1923 and de Roon, Nijman, and Veld 2000), mortgage-backed securities (Gabaix, Krishnamurthy, and Vigneron 2007), and convertible bond prices and merger spreads in connection with changes in the capital available to hedge funds and other smart money (Mitchell, Pedersen, and Pulvino 2007).

3.3. HOW TO BACKTEST A TRADING STRATEGY

Once you have a trading idea, backtesting it can be a powerful tool. To backtest a trading strategy means to simulate how it would have done historically. Of course, historical performance does not necessarily predict future performance, but a backtest is very useful nevertheless. For instance, many trading ideas are simply born bad, and this can be discovered through a backtest. For instance, suppose you have a trading idea, simulate how it would have performed over the past 20 years, and find that the strategy would never have worked in the past. Would you want to know this before you start trading? Surely, yes. Knowing this, you would be unlikely to put the trade on, and not doing so could save you a lot of money. A backtest can teach you about the risk of a strategy, and it can give you ideas about how to improve it.

Running a Backtest: Trading Rules and Beyond

To perform a backtest, you need the following components:

- **Universe.** The universe of securities to be traded.
- **Signals.** The data used as input, the source of the data, and how the data are analyzed.
- **Trading rule.** How you trade on your signals, including how frequently you review them and rebalance your positions, and the sizes of your positions.
- **Time lags.** To make the strategy implementable, the data used as input must have been available at the time it is used. For instance, if you use the gross domestic product (GDP) for any year, you must account for the fact that this number was not available on January 1 the following year; it is released with a delay. Also, if you use the closing price as a signal, it is not realistic to assume that you can trade at that same closing price (although academics often do). It is more prudent to assume that the trade is put on with a time lag, for example, using the closing price one or two days later.

While these backtest components are rather abstract when we discuss them in general, the notion of backtesting comes to life through the specific examples that we discuss in the chapters on trading strategies. Many types of trading rules exist, but let me describe two broad classes, which I call a *portfolio rebalance rule* and an *enter–exit rule*. The former starts from a *macro* view of the portfolio, and the latter builds up, trade by trade, from the *micro* level.

- **Portfolio rebalance rule.** This trading rule looks at the entire portfolio of securities and defines how it is rebalanced. This trading rule is backtested as follows. For each time period, o Determine the optimal portfolio of securities.

o Make a (paper) trade to rebalance to this portfolio.

As an example of this type of trading rule, suppose that you find the top 10% cheapest stocks by their book-to-market ratio on the last trading day of each month. You then buy an equal-weighted portfolio of these stocks and hold it for a month. Next month, you rebalance to the top 10% cheapest stocks at that time, and so on. Hence, you always have trades on and the number of securities in your portfolio is stable (it only varies if the size of your security universe changes). Another example might be that, each month, you estimate the risk and expected returns of all the securities in your universe and rebalance to the portfolio with the highest Sharpe ratio. In this example, you always have a position in each security, but the size of each security position varies over time and switches between being long and short. Note that in this case it is difficult to talk about whether any particular "trade worked" or not. You do not open a trade on IBM stock and later close it, but rather, you always have some long or short exposure to IBM that varies over time.

- **Enter–exit trading rule.** Another approach is to think in terms of discrete trades:

  o For each asset, determine when to enter a new trade and how to size the initial position.

  o Determine how the position is resized over time, depending on the circumstances.

  o Determine when to exit the trade.

For instance, if the price of gold goes above its highest value over the past 20 days (what some commodity trading advisors (CTAs) and managed futures traders call a *breakout*), then buy gold futures. Hold the position until the gold price drops below its 10-day minimum. With this kind of enter–exit rule, you may or may not have a gold position at any time. Furthermore, if you pursue this type of trading rule using many securities, you could have many or few positions on at any time, so your risk varies over time.

For all types of backtests and trading rules, we need to worry about biases and trading costs, as we discuss next.

Data Mining and Biases

Backtests typically look a *lot* better than the real-world trading performance that is realized after the trade is put on. This is to be expected for a number of reasons. First, the world is changing and trading strategies that worked in the past may no longer work as well. This could be because more people are pursuing these strategies and the competitive pressure adjusts prices and reduces profitability.[3]

Perhaps an even more important reason is that all backtests suffer from data mining biases. When I say that *all* backtests suffer from this problem, I mean that certain biases are unavoidable. For example, when you are analyzing a trading idea, you end up looking at a number of different implementations and gravitate toward one that has worked well in the past. Hence, you (consciously or subconsciously) pick this implementation of your trading idea because it has worked well in the past, but you could not have known this back then. Furthermore, some version will have worked the best in the past, perhaps just by chance, but, if this is by chance, it probably will not work well in the future, when you are actually trading on it. Or you tried the backtest because you heard someone made money on this trade, but, in this case, the backtest is biased to look good (your friend already told you!), even if this is by pure chance. These unavoidable biases mean that we should discount backtest returns and place more weight on realized returns. Furthermore, we should discount backtests more if they have more inputs and have been tweaked or optimized more.

While unavoidable biases should simply affect how we should regard backtests, there are many avoidable biases that experienced traders and researchers fight hard to eliminate. For one, it is important to have an unbiased universe of securities. For instance, if you only consider the *current* stocks in the Standard & Poor's (S&P) 500 index, then you have a biased sample. You did not know 15 years ago which stocks would be included today. Stocks often get included because they performed well, and you could not have known 15 years ago which stocks would perform well enough to be included. If you want to use the S&P 500 stocks, you should use stocks that were in the index at the time of your backtest, just as you would have done if you did the trade back then.

It is also crucial that the trading signals and trading rules be free of biases. You need appropriate time lags, as discussed above. For instance, many announcements happen after the event they are describing (first-quarter earnings are reported some time in the second quarter, and macroeconomic numbers such as the GDP and inflation arrive with a delay), and revisions of these numbers are known even later.

When parameters have been optimized or estimated, this naturally creates a bias. For instance, if expected returns have been estimated by running a regression from 1990 to 2010, and you backtest a strategy based on these parameters over the same time period, then the performance is biased to look unrealistically good. The parameters were estimated to be optimal, but you could not have

---

[3] See Harvey and Liu (2013), Harvey, Liu, and Zhu (2013), and McLean and Pontiff (2013) for measures and tests for the importance of these effects.

known this in advance, nor do you currently know the parameters that will be optimal in the future. This cheating method is called an *in-sample test*, in contrast to an *out-of-sample test*, where the parameters are estimated using data from before the simulated trading time. Out-of-sample tests are carried out in many ways: One way is to split the sample in two, pick parameters using the first sample, and simulate trading using the second. Another way is to use a "rolling" window: Each time period (say, each month), you pick parameters based on older data; you then simulate the trading over the next month, pick new parameters based on the now longer window of older data, simulate the next month of trading, and so on. Of course, the easiest way to avoid in-sample biases is to have a strategy that is simple enough that it does not rely on specific parameter values.

You should always keep in mind that the goal is to find a strategy that works in the future and *not* to have the best possible backtest. You should strive for a robust process that works even if you adjust it a little.

Adjusting Backtests for Trading Costs

Transaction costs reduce the returns of a trading strategy. A backtest is therefore much more realistic if it accounts for transaction costs. To adjust a backtest, we first need to have an estimate of the expected transaction costs for all securities and trading sizes. You can often obtain such estimates from brokers, or you can estimate the expected transaction costs, as discussed in section 5.3. Given these expected transaction costs, we can adjust the backtest in the following simple way. Each time a trade takes place in our backtest, we compute the expected transaction cost and subtract this cost from the backtest returns. For instance, if we have a monthly portfolio rebalance rule, then each month of the backtest, we do the following:

- Compute the return on the portfolio,
- Compute the new security positions and the implied trades,
- Compute the expected trading costs for every security and add them up, and
- Subtract the total expected trading cost from the portfolio return.

Adjusting a backtest for transaction costs is more important the higher the turnover of the trading strategy. Furthermore, transaction costs change the way in which you should construct your optimal trading rule and have other important implications, as discussed in section 5.1.

3.4. ON THE EQUIVALENCE OF PORTFOLIOS AND REGRESSIONS

While simulating a trading strategy with a careful backtest gets closest to reality, running regressions is another useful tool. Since a successful trading strategy is ultimately based on a signal that can predict returns, another way to test a signal is to run a *predictive regression*, that is, a regression where the future return is on the left-hand side and the signal that you know ex ante is on the right-hand side.

Sorting securities into portfolios and comparing the portfolios' relative performance is almost equivalent to looking at regression coefficients, as summarized here.

Metatheorem. Any predictive regression can be expressed as a portfolio sort, and any portfolio sort can be expressed as a predictive regression. Specifically:

(a) A time series regression corresponds to a market timing strategy.
(b) A cross-sectional regression corresponds to a security selection strategy.
(c) A univariate regression corresponds to sorting securities by one signal; a bivariate regression corresponds to double-sorting securities by two signals, allowing you to determine whether one signal adds value beyond the other; and a multivariate regression corresponds to sorting by multiple signals.

(a). To see what I mean by this, consider first a time series regression of the excess return R^e of one security, say, the overall stock market, on a forecasting variable F, say, the dividend-to-price ratio:

$$R^e_{t+1} = a + bF_t + \varepsilon_{t+1}$$

Note that the time subscript on the forecasting variable is the current time t, while the return on the left-hand side is of the future time $t + 1$, since we are trying to forecast returns with a signal we know in advance. The ordinary least square (OLS) estimate of the regression coefficient b is given by

$$\hat{b} = \frac{\sum_t (F_t - \bar{F})R_{t+1}}{\sum_t (F_t - \bar{F})^2} = \sum_{t=1}^{T} x_t R_{t+1}$$

which can be seen as the cumulative return on a long–short timing strategy, where the trading position x is given by

$$x_t = k(F_t - \bar{F})$$

Here the scaling factor $k = 1/\sum_t (F_t - \bar{F})^2$ does not affect the Sharpe ratio of the timing trade. We see that the timing trade is long in the security when the signal F_t is above its average value, $\bar{F}$, and short in the security when the signal is below its average. The timing strategy is profitable when the regression coefficient is positive and unprofitable otherwise. This result shows the close link between a regression and a timing strategy—in fact, the regression coefficient is the average profit of a timing strategy! (Furthermore, the risk-adjusted return of the strategy is closely related to the t-statistics of the regression coefficient.)

While the regression corresponds to a very specific timing strategy, we can analyze the signal's ability to time the market in many other ways. For instance, we can split the historical sample into three groups: the third of the time when the signal F had its lowest values, the third of the time when F had medium values, and the third when F was high. Based on these three subsamples, we can see whether the market, on average, had a high return when F was high and a low return when F was low.

(b). Just as timing strategies correspond to time series regressions, security selection strategies also have a regression equivalent. Security selection corresponds to a cross-sectional regression, where we have a forecasting variable F_t^i for every security i:

$$R_{t+1}^i = a + bF_t^i + \varepsilon_{t+1}^i$$

We can run this regression across *securities* at any time t. This regression gives us a regression coefficient $\hat{b}_t$ for each time period:

$$\hat{b}_t = \frac{\Sigma_i(F_t^i - \bar{F}_t)R_{t+1}^i}{\Sigma_i(F_t^i - \bar{F}_t)^2} = \sum_i x_t^i R_{t+1}^i$$

where the only difference from before is that now we are summing over securities i, not time t. This regression coefficient is the profit of a long–short security selection strategy, which is realized between time t and $t+1$. The position in security i is

$$x_t^i = k_t(F_t^i - \bar{F}_t)$$

with $k_t = 1/\Sigma_i(F_t^i - \bar{F}_t)^2$. Hence, this strategy selects a long position for securities with signals that are better than the average across securities at that time, and a short position for securities with low signals.

The overall estimate of the regression coefficient $\hat{b}$ using the Fama–MacBeth (1973) method is simply the average of all the estimates for each time period:

$$\hat{b} = \frac{1}{T} \sum_{t=1}^{T} \hat{b}_t$$

This is the average profit of the long–short trading strategy over time. The risk of the strategy is the volatility of the profits, that is, the volatility of the regression coefficients:

$$\hat{\sigma} = \sqrt{\frac{1}{T-1} \sum_{t=1}^{T} (\hat{b}_t - \hat{b})^2}$$

Therefore, the Sharpe ratio of the security selection strategy is

$$SR = \frac{\hat{b}}{\hat{\sigma}}$$

which corresponds closely to the t-statistic of the regression estimate:

$$t\text{-statistic} = \sqrt{T}\frac{\hat{b}}{\hat{\sigma}}$$

Recall that a regression coefficient is considered statistically significant if its t-statistic is above two in absolute value. We see that statistical significance corresponds to realizing a high Sharpe ratio over a long time period T. This is intuitive: A strategy is more likely to work for reasons beyond luck if it has worked well for a long time.

(c). We can also regress returns on several trading signals, say, F and G:

$$R^i_{t+1} = a + b^F F^i_t + b^G G^i_t + \varepsilon^i_{t+1}$$

In this case, the regression coefficient b^F corresponds to the profit from trading on F, given that you are already trading on G. For instance, if a hedge fund already trades on G and considers whether to trade also on F, then it is not sufficient that F make money on average. To add a strategy based on F, this signal needs to improve the overall portfolio by adding new information that is not already contained in G, without adding too much risk. The regression coefficient in the multivariate regression captures this marginal improvement. Whether a new signal adds value can also be analyzed by simply studying portfolios. In particular, if we double-sort securities by both F and G each period, then we can see whether securities with higher F values outperform securities with lower F values and almost the *same* value of G. One advantage of regressions is that it is easy to add many variables on the right-hand side, while it becomes impracticable to quadruple-sort securities.

As a final note, let me point out that timing strategies are more susceptible to biases than security selection strategies. Indeed, the time series regression corresponds to a "cheating" in-sample backtest, since the position size depends on the average forecasting variable over time $\bar{F}$, but this average was not known at the beginning of the time period. Similarly, considering whether the signal was in the top, middle, or bottom third is also cheating, because this was also not known in advance. A more correct backtest is to ask at any time whether the signal was high, medium, or low relative to the signals that had been seen up until that time (or other out-of-sample forecast methods).

Security selection strategies do not suffer from this problem: These strategies simply compare one security's signal to the average signals of other securities at that time. Hence, you do not need to know what is a typical high or low signal over time; you just need to find the securities that have better properties than others. For instance, you might go long in cheaper stocks with high ratios of book value to market value (B/M) while shorting stocks with lower B/M. To do so, you don't need to know the "fair" level of B/M; you simply need to sort stocks on this characteristic.

To summarize, in financial economics there exists a close link between regression analysis and trading strategies, or, said differently, between statistics and economics. Trading strategies are useful for practitioners to seek profits and for academics as a way to test asset pricing theories.

CHAPTER 4

Portfolio Construction and Risk Management

A hedge fund's job is to deliver the best possible risk-adjusted returns. To do so, the hedge fund must first find trades that can be expected to make money, as discussed earlier. Once several trading strategies have been identified, the investor must combine them into an overall portfolio. Portfolio construction means (i) estimating the risk that each trade involves and (ii) choosing how to size each of the positions and how to vary these position sizes over time to achieve an optimal trade-off between risk and expected return.

Active investors must put special emphasis on risk management. Risk management should be an integral part of portfolio construction and, in addition, a hedge fund should have a separate risk management team with an independent set of controls. The risk of a hedge fund portfolio changes over time for a number of reasons. First, investment opportunities vary, and people often want to invest more when the opportunities are better. Second, market risk varies over time so that the same positions can be more or less risky, depending on the circumstances. Third, the hedge fund's different bets may be more or less aligned with one another at different times. Fourth, the use of leverage means that a hedge fund cannot always "ride out" a drawdown; it must be ready to react before creditors pull their financing or investors pull their capital.

Portfolio construction should rely on continuously updated measures of risk and should ensure that the risk taken is at an appropriate level given the opportunities. The risk management overlay must simultaneously ensure that the risk never exceeds certain limits, manage the downside tail risk, and limit the risk of large drawdowns.

4.1. PORTFOLIO CONSTRUCTION

Active investors differ a great deal in their portfolio construction, with some relying on rules and intuition while others use computer algorithms to perform a formal portfolio optimization. However, there are some general principles that most successful hedge funds adhere to:

- The first principle of portfolio construction is diversification. Indeed, the saying goes that the only free lunch in finance is diversification.
- The second principle is to have position limits, which restrict the notional exposure to each security and/or its risk contribution. For example, when I have taught my class on hedge fund strategies, I have often presented MBA students with a great trade, for instance, a pure arbitrage such as one of the negative stub trades (discussed further in chapter 16, event-driven investments). Once the students have figured out the trade, I ask them to size the position, and most students invest at least 40% of their capital in the trade. The following week, we see how they would have fared. Almost every student's position blows up (except one or two students who would not do the trade at all). Indeed, simulating their margin equity shows that they could not meet their margin calls and were forced to liquidate most of their position, thus ending up with a loss, or completely broke, even when the trade finally converged. One simple and effective way to reduce the risk of being blown up by a single position—and ensure greater diversification—is to have position limits. For instance, James Chanos makes sure that all his positions are less than 5% of his net asset value (NAV), trimming positions back as they approach this limit.
- A third principle of portfolio construction is that you should make larger bets on higher conviction trades. You need to think about what trades are really promising and make sure that this is where you are taking the most risk.
- A fourth principle is that you should think of the size of a bet in terms of its risk. The magnitude of a position's risk depends both on the notional size of the position and the risk of the underlying security.
- A fifth principle is that correlations matter. For a long position, a high correlation with other longs is bad, whereas a high correlation with short positions is good. For example, Lee Ainslie prefers to have both long and short positions within each industry, thus having risk reduction through being long and short in similar securities. Furthermore, his longs are diversified across industries, thus having risk reduction through long positions with low correlations.
- The final principle is to continue to resize positions according to risk and conviction. As important as this is, many people find this unintuitive. As one student said as his simulated profit and loss (P&L) turned south: "I am in this trade with both feet, and there is no turning around now." Two simulated days later, he was out of business. Successful hedge funds don't marry their positions and don't let their bets grow large inadvertently. For instance, Lee Ainslie continues to analyze each trade's risk–reward trade-off and then decides to add or reduce its position. "Hold" is not an option. A related trader saying goes that

A trader must have no memory and forget nothing.

An investor should have "no memory" in the sense that she should do what is optimal on a going-forward basis, regardless of how she got into the current position. An investor should "forget nothing" in the sense that all his or her experiences and data should help make the best possible forecasts of risk and expected return.

Quants such as Cliff Asness use formal portfolio optimization to achieve these goals. Indeed, when trading thousands of securities around the world, you need computing power to effectively implement these portfolio construction principles. The simplest way to do this is a mean-variance approach: The goal is to choose a portfolio $x = (x^1, \ldots, x^S)$, where x^s measures the capital (i.e., the amount of money) invested in each security s. If you start with a wealth of W and choose the portfolio x, then your wealth next time period is

$$\text{future wealth} = x^1(1 + R^1) + \cdots + x^S(1 + R^S) + (W - x^1 - \cdots - x^S)(1 + R^f)$$

where $R^1, \ldots, R^S$ are the returns of the different risky investments, and the last term captures the money invested in the risk-free money market with return R^f (or the money borrowed for leverage if the sum of the risky investments is larger than the initial wealth W). The expression for the future wealth can be rewritten in terms of excess returns $R^{e,s} = R^s - R^f$:

$$\text{future wealth} = W(1 + R^f) + x^1 R^{e,1} + \cdots + x^S R^{e,S}$$

In other words, the future wealth is the current wealth W increased at the risk-free rate plus all the excess returns you make by investing in risky assets. The goal is to maximize the expected future wealth, subject to a penalty for risk as measured by variance. The portfolio optimization problem can be written using vector notation (ignoring the first term that does not depend on x) as

$$\max_x \mathrm{E}(x'R^e) - \frac{\gamma}{2}\mathrm{var}(x'R^e)$$

where γ is a risk aversion coefficient. If we write the vector of expected security excess returns as $\mathrm{E}(R^e)$ and the variance–covariance matrix as , the portfolio problem can be rewritten as

$$\max_x x'\mathrm{E}(R^e) - \frac{\gamma}{2}x'\Omega x$$

To solve this problem, we consider the first-order condition by differentiating with respect to x and setting this equal to zero:

$$0 = \mathrm{E}(R^e) - \gamma\Omega x$$

which gives the optimal portfolio

$$x = \gamma^{-1}\Omega^{-1}\mathrm{E}(R^e)$$

This optimal portfolio is characterized by taking large positions for securities with large expected returns, low variance, and low correlation to other positions.

While optimal in theory, this portfolio is often problematic in practice for several reasons (Black and Litterman 1992). First, the theoretically optimal portfolio may behave poorly in practice because the risk and expected returns are estimated with errors and often using different techniques. Using noisy risk and return estimates that come from different sources often leads the optimizer to suggest extremely large long and short positions with poor out-of-sample performance. Hence, quants try to make the portfolio optimization more "robust" in the sense that it is less sensitive to noise. To achieve a more robust portfolio, they shrink estimates of risk and expected returns, use portfolio constraints, and apply robust optimization techniques. A second problem with the basic mean-variance optimal portfolio is that real-world portfolios are often subject to a number of limits on position sizes and trade sizes, and, while these constraints can be added to the problem, they often distort the solution unless handled carefully. A third issue of a basic one-period optimized portfolio is that it does not take into account that investors trade repeatedly over time and incur transaction costs in the process, but these issues can be handled in a more sophisticated dynamic model (Gârleanu and Pedersen 2013, 2014).

Despite these challenges, portfolio optimization can be a very useful tool, but a full treatment of this topic is beyond the scope of this text. When done carefully, portfolio optimization provides a tool to reap the full benefits of diversification, to efficiently exploit high-conviction trades without excessive concentration, to systematically adjust positions based on the time-varying risk and expected return, and to minimize subjectivity in the portfolio choice.

In summary, good portfolio construction techniques can help achieve a favorable risk-return profile for a set of trading ideas. A systematic approach helps reduce a trader's own behavioral biases, that is, his tendencies to make certain mistakes. For instance, people like to hang on to their losing positions even if the reason they liked the securities no longer applies, and they like to sell winners to lock in gains even if the trade has gotten even better.

4.2. RISK MANAGEMENT

Measuring Risk

Risk can be, and should be, measured in several different ways. One straightforward and common risk measure is volatility (that is, the standard deviation of returns). Some people think that volatility only applies to normal distributions, but this is not true. What is true is that volatility does not capture well the risk of crashes for non-normal distributions. Indeed, while for normal distributions two–standard-deviation returns are uncommon and five–standard-deviation events almost never happen, this is not true for real-world hedge fund returns since they are not normally distributed. For hedge fund strategies, two–standard-deviation events are common and five–standard-deviation events certainly do happen. If this fact is kept in mind, volatility can still be a useful risk measure as long as the return distribution is relatively symmetric and without too extreme a crash risk. However, volatility is not an appropriate measure of risk for strategies with an extreme crash risk. For instance, volatility does not capture well the risk of selling out-the-money options, a strategy with small positive returns on most days but infrequent large crashes. To compute the volatility of a large portfolio, hedge funds need to account for correlations across assets, which can be accomplished by simulating the overall portfolio or by using a statistical model such as a factor model.

Another measure of risk is value-at-risk (VaR), which attempts to capture tail risk (non-normality). The VaR measures the maximum loss with a certain confidence, as seen in figure 4.1 below. For example, the VaR is the most that you can lose with a 95% or 99% confidence.

For instance, a hedge fund has a one-day 95% VaR of $10 million if

$$\text{Pr(loss} \leq \$10 \text{ million)} = 95\%$$

A simple way to estimate VaR is to line up past returns, sort them by magnitude, and find a return that has 5% worse days and 95% better days. This is the 95% VaR, since, if history repeats itself, you will lose less than this number with 95% certainty. You can estimate the VaR by looking at your past returns, but if your positions have changed a lot, this can be rather misleading. In that

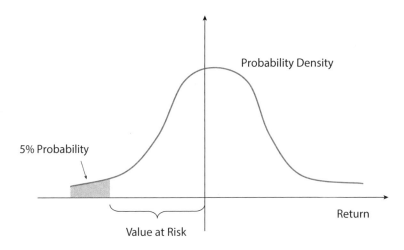

Figure 4.1. Value-at-risk.
The *x*-axis has the possible outcomes for the return, and the *y*-axis has the corresponding probability density.

case, it may be more accurate to look at your current positions and simulate returns on these positions over, say, the past three years.

One issue with the VaR is that it does not depend on how *much* you lose if you do lose more than the VaR. The magnitude of these extreme tail losses is, in principle, captured by the risk measure called the expected shortfall (ES). The expected shortfall is the expected loss, given that you are losing more than the VaR:

$$ES = E(loss \mid loss > VaR)$$

Another measure of risk is the *stress loss*. This measure is computed by performing various *stress tests*, that is, simulated portfolio returns during various scenarios, and then considering the worst-case loss in these scenarios. Such stress scenarios can include significant past events, such as the 1998 price shocks around the Long-Term Capital Management (LTCM) bailout, September 11, and the failure of Lehman Brothers, as well as imagined future events, such as the failure of a sovereign state (e.g., Greece), a large interest rate move, a large shock to equity prices, a spike in volatility, or a sharp increase in margin requirements.

While estimates of volatility and, to some extent, VaR measure the risk during relatively "normal" markets over a fixed time horizon, stress tests tell you about risk during extreme events. Indeed, volatility and VaR are statistical measures of day-to-day risk that rely on having enough data to estimate them. Stress tests explore cases where you do not have enough data to estimate the risk accurately, as well as events that can play out over several days. An important risk that may not be captured by volatility estimates is the risk of liquidity spirals, as discussed before. The point of a stress test is to make sure that positions are not so large that the hedge fund is likely to blow up in a stress event and to plan for foreseeable events, even if you cannot predict losses or give probability estimates. Of course, what actually happens during a crisis never corresponds exactly to any stress tests, but one hopes that preparing for foreseeable events will provide the discipline to survive what actually happens.

Risk Management: Prospective Risk Control

Whatever the measure of risk, risk needs to be managed. Risk management should be both prospective (i.e., controlling risk before a bad event occurs) and reactive (having a plan for what to do in a crisis). Reactive risk management is usually a form of drawdown control (discussed in detail below) and stop-loss mechanisms.

Even before you react to losses, you can manage risk prospectively. Prospective risk management comes in several forms, including diversification, risk limits, liquidity management, and tail hedging via options and other instruments.

To control risk, a hedge fund often has *risk limits*, meaning prespecified restrictions on how large a risk the hedge fund will ever take. The risk limit can be at the overall fund level and/or at the more granular level of each asset class or strategy. Hedge funds often also have *position limits* that restrict the notional exposure (regardless of how low the risk is estimated to be).

Furthermore, some hedge funds have a *strategic risk target*, meaning an average level of risk that the fund intends to take over the long term. For instance, the strategic risk target could be measured as the fund volatility, and it would often range from bondlike volatility to equitylike volatility, say, somewhere between 5% and 25% annualized volatility. The hedge fund's desired risk at a given time is sometimes called the *tactical risk target,* and the tactical risk varies around the strategic risk target, depending on the investment opportunities, market conditions, and recent performance. In particular, significant losses often drive a hedge fund to reduce positions and cut risk, that is, reactive risk management, as discussed next.

4.3. DRAWDOWN CONTROL

While prospective risk control seeks to manage the portfolio risk before losses occur, drawdown control is a reactive mechanism that seeks to limit losses as they evolve. Drawdown control is important for hedge funds using leverage because they cannot simply decide to always "ride out" a crisis. A hedge fund may therefore want to minimize the risk that its drawdown will become worse than some prespecified *maximum acceptable drawdown* (MADD), say, 25%.[1] If the current drawdown is given by DD_t, then one sensible drawdown control policy is

$$VaR_t \leq MADD - DD_t$$

The right-hand-side of this inequality is the distance between the maximum acceptable drawdown and the current drawdown, that is, the largest acceptable loss given the amount already lost. The left-hand-side is the value-at-risk, that is, the most that can be lost given the current positions and current market risk, at a certain confidence level. Hence, the drawdown policy states that the risk must be small enough that losses do not push drawdowns beyond the MADD, with a certain confidence.

If this inequality is violated, the hedge fund should reduce risk, that is, unwind positions such that the VaR comes down to a level that satisfies the inequality. Once the strategies have recovered and the drawdown is reduced, the risk can be increased again.

---

[1] This section draws from Grossman and Zhou (1993).

To make this drawdown system operational, one must choose a MADD and also the type of VaR measure to use on the left-hand side (i.e., the time period and the confidence level). This choice depends on the risk and liquidity of the hedge fund. A lower risk fund may have investors and counterparties with less tolerance for drawdowns and should therefore have tighter limits. A riskier fund, on the other hand, should have looser limits so that the drawdown system does not kick in too often in order to limit transactions costs—if you take a large amount of risk, you must live with larger drawdowns.

Drawdown control is helpful because it creates a clear plan for how to handle adversity: how much to reduce risk when you are losing money and when to do it. Without a clear plan for drawdown control, traders may have difficulty controlling their emotions during tough periods. Indeed, reducing risk after losing on a position is painful. The trader feels that a loss is being locked in if she unwinds and often prefers to try to ride out the situation—until growing losses turn into a disaster. Risk management is far from always a losing proposition, however. It can save an investor a tremendous amount, as the saying goes:

Your first loss is your least loss.

As discussed in section 5.10, prices tend to drop and rebound during a liquidity spiral where some traders are forced to unwind. Traders often end up holding onto their positions as prices fall, but eventually they have to cave and sell near the bottom as their funding dries up or panic ensues. Why are most of them selling near the bottom? Because this *defines* the bottom. When the selling is over, prices start rebounding. This logic may be what is behind the following saying:

As a trader, never panic, but if you are going to panic, panic first.

And it almost surely underlies the following poker-related maxim:

The strongest weak hand suffers the largest loss.

Using a poker analogy, one can distinguish between "strong hands" and "weak hands." Strong hands have what it takes to hold onto their positions, or even add to them at low prices. They have deep pockets and the emotional strength to live through a crisis. In contrast, weak hands must sell their positions if they incur large losses. For instance, leveraged hedge funds are weak in the sense that they can hit their margin constraint and be forced to liquidate, or their prime broker can pull the plug even before that happens. The weak hands that "panic first" and fold almost immediately suffer lower losses than the "strongest weak hands," which are forced to sell at the bottom. Of course, traders never know whether they will end up being able to ride out the crisis or be forced to liquidate, but a sound drawdown policy planned in advance without emotional stress is a good idea.

A prespecified plan for drawdown control not only helps reduce risk in a timely manner, but it can also help investors re-enter the market in time to re-coup (some of) the losses. A trader who was just forced to cut risk may be "burned" and afraid to scale the positions back up, but a systematic drawdown control system signals it is time to re-enter the market when positions have recovered sufficiently and risk has declined.

CHAPTER 5

Trading and Financing a Strategy
Market and Funding Liquidity

Implementing an investment strategy can be costly for two main reasons: (1) because of transaction costs incurred when the strategy is traded and (2) because of funding costs incurred when the strategy is leveraged.

To understand the sources of transaction costs, note first that most investors pay commissions and other direct costs on each trade. More importantly, there are several indirect transaction costs, such as the *bid–ask spread* and *market impact* costs. To understand these concepts, note first that the *bid price* is the price at which you can sell shares (because potential buyers bid this price). Similarly, the *ask price* is the price at which you can buy shares (since current owners ask for this price). The bid–ask spread arises because the bid price is below the ask price. Hence, if you buy and immediately thereafter sell one share, then you lose an amount of money equal to the bid–ask spread. Market impact costs arise if you trade a large number of shares because the process of buying many shares pushes prices up, and selling many shares pushes prices down.

Some securities have large transaction costs, and others can be traded at low cost. Securities with high transaction costs are said to be *illiquid,* in contrast to *liquid* securities, and securities with episodic spikes in transaction costs are said to have a lot of *market liquidity risk.*

Funding costs arise when a trader leverages his investments and must borrow money at a higher interest rate than the interest rate he earns on his cash holdings and short sale proceeds. Furthermore, leverage is associated with *funding liquidity risk,* that is, the risk that the trader cannot continue to finance his positions and is forced to liquidate in a fire sale.

These implementation costs—market and funding liquidity costs—are important for active investors because they eat into the profits of all trading strategies. Whereas passive unleveraged buy-and-hold investors incur only few implementation costs, an active investor may trade frequently, and the more frequent the trades, the more the investor needs to worry about the effects of transaction costs. Furthermore, the larger and more leveraged the positions a trader takes, the more important are implementation costs. Implementation costs have several implications, including affecting

(a) whether or not a strategy is profitable,
(b) which trading rule is the best,
(c) which securities to trade, and
(d) how large to scale the trade.

Whereas a high-turnover trading rule (i.e., a rule that implies frequent and/ or large trades) may be the best on paper, without taking transaction costs into account, it may be a poor trading strategy in practice. Said differently, even if returns are large *gross* of transaction costs, *net* returns may be poor. What is the best way to adjust a trading strategy in light of trading costs? This is the first topic we discuss in this chapter. We then describe how to measure transaction costs during the trade execution, how to estimate them before the decision to trade, and the implications for the capacity of a trading strategy or a hedge fund more broadly. Finally, we consider how investments are financed, the limits of leverage caused by margin requirement, and the risks of gambler's ruin and predatory trading.

5.1. OPTIMAL TRADING IN LIGHT OF TRANSACTION COSTS

In a world of perfect liquidity, you would want to trade on every idea and be willing to frequently trade in and out of large positions. However, such un-limited trading is not optimal in the real world because of transactions costs. The optimal trading policy depends on the type of market structure and trans-action costs that you face. Specifically, the optimal trading strategy depends on whether there are economies of scale in trading or not; that is, is it cheaper to split up a trade into small pieces or to trade in one large block? Said an-other way, do transaction costs increase, remain constant, or decrease with trade size? Here, I focus on these three stylized types of transaction costs and explain the market structures to which they correspond.[1]

- **Increasing transaction costs (as a function of trade size): Market im-pact.** In liquid electronic markets with small minimum tick size, such as today's equity and futures markets, the bid–ask spread and commissions

[1] This section is based on Gârleanu and Pedersen (2013), who derive the optimal trading strat-egy with increasing quadratic trading costs and trading signals with varying alpha decay values; Constantinides (1986), who considers proportional costs; Liu (2004), who considers fixed costs, among others; and Duffie, Gârleanu, and Pedersen (2005, 2007), who consider trading in over-the-counter markets.

are small for professional traders. However, the amount that can be traded at the bid or ask price is often small relative to what a large hedge fund needs to execute. Therefore, the main source of transaction costs for large traders is market impact in these markets. Since prices move more the larger position you trade, this kind of transaction cost increases with trade size. The way to deal with this type of transaction cost is to split up a trade into many small orders and trade these small orders patiently over time, as described in more detail below.

- **Constant transaction costs: Bid–ask spreads.** (Also called proportional transaction costs, since *total* transactions costs are proportional to trade size when *average* costs are constant.) This case is in between the other two. Transaction costs neither increase nor decrease with trade size; average costs simply remain constant. This happens when the main source of transaction costs is the bid–ask spread and commissions. For instance, if a trader's entire position can be executed at the bid or ask price, then there is no need to worry about market impact. This situation can happen if a market has a large tick size, so that market makers earn a lot from the bid–ask spread and, as a result, there are many market makers offering to trade large amounts at these prices.

- **Decreasing transaction costs.** In over-the-counter (OTC) markets, you often need to call a dealer on the phone to trade. It takes the dealer roughly the same amount of time to execute a small order from a retail investor and a large order from an institutional investor. That is, the dealer needs to spend time negotiating the price on the phone, finding someone who wants to take the other side of the trade or otherwise hedge the position, and so on. If the dealer charges everyone the same transaction cost as a percentage of the price, then the small orders may not be worth the time. Therefore, percentage transaction costs in these markets tend to be larger for small orders than for large orders. Hence, in these markets you do not want to split your order into little pieces but rather trade in chunks that are worth the dealer's time. Hence, you keep your position the same until it is far from your optimal position and then make a large trade to your optimal position. To execute the trade, hedge funds often call multiple dealers to get competitive bids. (Note that very large trades may start to move the price, so eventually transaction costs are also increasing in OTC markets. Hence, you should not wait until your desired trade is too large and, if it is anyway, it may make sense to split it up into large, but not very large, pieces.)

The optimal trading strategy for each of these cases is illustrated in figure 5.1. In each case, time is on the *x*-axis and the number of shares is on the *y*-axis. The solid line is the optimal number of shares in a world without transaction costs, and, naturally, this "paper portfolio" is the same in all three cases. The blue line

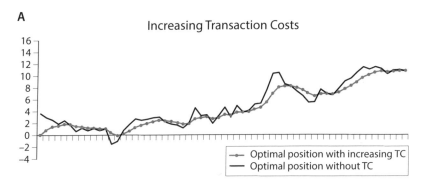

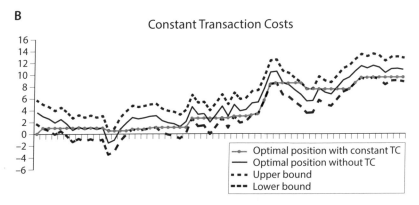

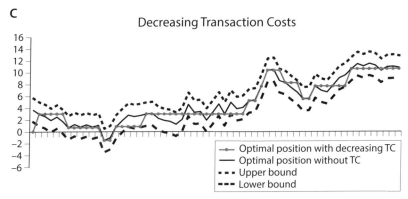

Figure 5.1. Optimal trading in three different markets.

The top panel shows the optimal trading strategy in an electronic market where the transaction costs (TC) increase in the trade size (due to market impact costs); the middle panel shows the optimal strategy in a market with constant TC (i.e., the same percentage cost for all trade sizes); and the bottom panel shows the optimal strategy in an OTC market with decreasing percentage of TC (specifically, when the dollar transaction cost is the same for all trade sizes).

with dots is the optimal position in light of transaction costs, and it differs across the three panels, since they correspond to different types of markets.

The top panel illustrates the optimal position in a liquid electronic market. It shows the optimal position with *increasing* transaction costs using the Gârleanu–Pedersen (2013) strategy. This strategy continually makes little trades toward the paper portfolio.[2] Specifically, the strategy in the figure always trades 30% toward the paper portfolio. Said differently, each time period, the new portfolio is 30% times the paper portfolio plus 70% times the existing portfolio. The optimal position thus captures most of the alpha by staying close to the paper portfolio while saving on transaction costs in two ways: (1) by trading much less than the paper portfolio, which is seen from the smoother evolution of the position size, and (2) by making many little trades to limit market impact.

The middle panel of figure 5.1 shows the optimal strategy with constant average transaction costs. In this case, there is a no-trade band around the optimal paper position, illustrated by the two dashed lines. As long as the position is inside the band, there is no trade and the position remains constant, giving rise to a horizontal segment of the blue line with dots. If the position were to move outside the band without trading, then the optimal trade would move the position to the edge of the band. Hence, the optimal strategy makes many little trades near the edge of the band, meaning that the optimal trades ensure that the portfolio never deviates too much from the paper portfolio. The width of the band depends on the size of the bid–ask spread.

The bottom panel of figure 5.1 shows the case of an OTC market where the per share transaction cost is decreasing in an extreme way: The dollar transaction is the same no matter how many shares you trade. In this case, whenever you do trade, you always trade to the optimal paper position. However, you save on transaction costs by only trading when your position gets outside a band around the optimal paper portfolio.

5.2. MEASURING TRANSACTION COSTS

There are several ways of measuring transaction costs, but three central measures are the "effective cost," the "realized cost," and the cost relative to the "volume-weighted average price." Let us consider each of these in turn.

The effective cost is the difference between the execution price and the market price before you started trading (plus any commissions paid). For buy orders, the per share effective cost, $TC^\$$, is given by

$$TC^\$ = P^{\text{execution}} - P^{\text{before}}$$

---

[2] Gârleanu and Pedersen (2013) show that this trading strategy is optimal when market impact is linear in the trade size such that the total transaction costs increase with the square of the trade size.

where $P^{\text{execution}}$ is the price you paid, on average, for all the shares you bought, and P^{before} is the mid-quote (i.e., the average of the bid and ask prices) just before you started trading. Similarly, if you are selling, your dollar transaction cost can be measured as

$$\text{TC}^{\$} = -(P^{\text{execution}} - P^{\text{before}})$$

Transaction costs are often computed as a percentage of the value, which we denote simply as TC:

$$\text{TC} = \text{TC}^{\$}/P^{\text{before}}$$

A couple of comments about this measure of transaction cost are in order. First, this trading cost measure works whether your costs are caused by a bid–ask spread or by market impact. It is simply the difference between the price at which you actually executed your trade versus the price you hoped to trade at when you started (i.e., the price you might use in a backtest). If you simply buy at the ask price, TC is half the bid–ask spread, and if you move the price, TC captures this as well. Second, if you trade over an extensive time period, then TC is measured with substantial noise. This is because prices move for many reasons that are unrelated to your own trading, which introduces noise into the execution price.

The second measure of transaction costs is the so-called realized cost. When you are buying, the realized cost can be measured as

$$\text{TC}^{\$,\text{realized}} = P^{\text{execution}} - P^{\text{later}}$$

and, similarly, when you are selling, except with the opposite sign. Here, P^{later} is the mid-price at some time after you stop trading, say after 5 minutes when prices have stabilized again. At an intuitive level, this transaction cost measure captures the fact that you experience a cost if prices always tend to drop right after you buy. This can happen because the price at which you bought was inflated because of your price pressure (or simply because you bought at the ask). Whereas the effective cost measures how much you buy above the price that prevailed *before* you entered the market, the realized cost measures how much you buy above the price that prevails *after* your order has been executed. One looks at the price impact, the other at the subsequent price reversal. If your order has a long-lasting price impact, then the effective cost is larger than the realized cost (because the price only reverses part of the way back toward its previous level). Since the market impact is also a cost, the effective cost correctly measures the difference between trading in the real world vs. hypothetical trading without costs.

The final measure of transaction costs is to compare the execution price to the so-called volume-weighted average price (VWAP). For buys, this means

$$\text{TC}^{\$,\text{VWAP}} = P^{\text{execution}} - P^{\text{VWAP}}$$

The idea behind this measure is to determine how the price at which you traded compares to the average prices at which other people traded that day.

No measure is perfect, and $TC^{\$,VWAP}$ can be both noisy and misleading. It can be misleading for the following reason: Suppose you are the only buyer in the market all day. You keep buying while others reluctantly sell at ever-higher prices. Since you participate in all trades, your average execution price is by definition *equal* to the VWAP. Hence, in this case, $TC^{\$,VWAP} = 0$, even though you clearly incurred large transaction costs. In contract, the effective cost $TC^{\$}$ would reflect a large cost, namely, the difference between the high execution price and the low price in the morning. Similarly, the realized cost $TC^{\$,realized}$ would likely measure a high cost stemming from the difference between the high execution price and the lower price that will likely prevail the next day, when the market has rebounded.

5.3. ESTIMATING EXPECTED TRANSACTION COSTS

Suppose that you have measured the transaction cost TC_i for each of many trade executions, enumerated by $i = 1, \ldots I$. These are noisy observations of the *expected* transaction costs. Assuming that the expected transaction cost is constant for all these trades, we can estimate the expected transaction cost as the average observed costs:

$$\hat{E}(TC) = \frac{1}{I}\sum_i TC_i$$

This expected transaction cost is useful in deciding which trading strategy to use, how frequently to trade, and so on. Furthermore, our estimate of expected transaction costs tells us how to adjust a backtest for transaction costs.

Of course, transaction costs differ across securities. Small stocks with low trading volume tend to have larger transaction costs than large stocks, for instance. Furthermore, as discussed above, transaction costs can depend on the trade size. Hence, in general, we want to estimate the expected transaction costs as a function of trade size, security characteristics, and market conditions.

If there are many securities, for example, the universe of U.S. stocks, people often do not estimate transaction costs separately for each stock but rather assume that transaction costs depend on security characteristics such as volatility, daily trading volume (DTV), shares outstanding, and floating shares. Transaction costs also vary over time since they depend on market conditions such as overall volatility and liquidity providers' capital and risk appetite, and whether a stock has an earnings announcement. Hedge funds try to assess transaction costs before they trade, trading off the cost of trading against the benefits. To do this, they also look at market conditions such as the current bid–ask spread and the depth of the limit order book.

Whereas the largest hedge funds often use their own proprietary trading systems and transaction cost estimates, a number of investment banks and specialized trading firms offer to execute trades efficiently using their trading systems and offer advice regarding expected transaction costs.

Let's try to get a sense for the magnitude of transaction costs for professional traders. Engle, Ferstenberg and Russell (2012) estimate average transaction costs of 8.8 basis points (bps) for NYSE stocks and 13.8 bps for NASDAQ stocks based on orders executed by Morgan Stanley in 2004. This means that, if a trader buys $10,000 worth of a NYSE stock, then the expected transaction cost is $8.8. This relatively modest cost clearly reflects that the market for U.S. large-cap stocks is very liquid, but traders still need to watch their transaction costs, especially if they frequently turn over their portfolios.

The estimated transaction costs are less for small orders, only about 4 bps. For larger orders that constitute more than 1% of the stock's typical trading volume, the estimated average trading cost is 27 bps. Transaction costs are larger for orders that are urgently executed than for those that are executed with patience.

Using live trading data from a large institutional money manager over the period 1998 to 2011, Frazzini, Israel, and Moskowitz (2012) provide transaction cost estimates in the same ballpark. In their sample of U.S. stocks in 2011, they find a median transaction cost of 4.9 bps and a value-weighted average (which gives more weight to large trades) of 9.5 bps. For global stocks, the estimated transaction costs are larger, with a median of 5.9 bps and a value-weighted average of 12.9 bps. The estimated transaction costs are naturally lower for small trades than for large trades. For trades that constitute about 10% of the typical volume, the estimated transaction costs are about 40 bps.

Transaction costs really rise if you trade more than 10% of the typical volume, so traders usually try to avoid such large trades. This rule of thumb works across time horizons: If the typical volume for a stock is 100 million shares per day, and you want to avoid trading more than 10% of the volume, then you can trade 10 million shares in one day, 20 million shares over two days, 30 million in three days, and so on, which is intuitive. Hence, the more patient you are, the more shares you can trade without a large market impact.

5.4. IMPLEMENTATION SHORTFALL: THE COSTS OF TRADING AND NOT TRADING

Above we discussed how to trade optimally in light of transaction costs, and we saw that transaction costs mean that it is generally optimal to trade less than in a world without such costs. Therefore, real-life performance differs from performance in a perfect world without transaction costs for two reasons: (i) You incur transaction costs in the real world, and (ii) you change your trading pattern to reduce transaction costs in the real world, possibly causing you to miss certain opportunities. Implementation shortfall (IS) is a measure that captures both of these costs.[3] It is the sum of the transaction cost (TC) and the opportunity cost (OC) associated with changing your trading pattern:

$$IS = TC + OC$$

The implementation shortfall IS is measured by comparing your actual live performance with the performance of a paper portfolio:

$$IS = \text{performance of paper portfolio} - \text{performance of live portfolio}$$

Here, the performance of your paper portfolio is the return of your desired portfolio if trading costs were zero. To compute the performance of the paper portfolio, you compute the return and readjust the portfolio over time as if you could trade any number of shares at the mid-quote.

The opportunity cost OC is an abstract concept that is difficult to compute directly. However, since we know how to compute transaction cost TC and we know how to compute the total implementation shortfall IS, we can infer the opportunity cost of not trading as the difference, $OC = IS - TC$.

The implementation shortfall is a useful concept for several reasons. It is important to track whether your trading ideas are being successfully implemented in practice. A hedge fund is not interested in making money in principle but in practice, and a large shortfall drives a wedge between the two. Studying your performance and implementation shortfall can help you decide whether to focus your efforts on improving your trading implementation or the strategy's alpha signals. If your shortfall is low, you should focus on improving your strategy and developing new trading ideas. In contrast, if your paper portfolio is doing well but your actual portfolio is suffering from a large shortfall, then you should focus on implementation.

How do you reduce your shortfall? By trading faster and being first to the market before it moves away from you? Or by trading more slowly and minimizing your price impact and other trading costs? To answer these questions, you must decompose your implementation shortfall into its components TC and OC. This separation allows you to analyze whether you are trading too quickly or too slowly: If you trade faster, your transaction costs rise but your opportunity costs decline. In contrast, if you trade more patiently, providing liquidity to the market, your transaction costs drop but your opportunity costs rise. How fast to trade therefore depends on the relative importance of TC and OC: Strategies in illiquid markets tend to have a large TC, implying that you optimally trade slowly, whereas strategies with a large alpha decay (i.e., the trading opportunity disappears quickly) have a large OC, implying that you optimally trade fast. Suppose you decide that the right way to reduce your IS is to increase your trading speed. How do you know whether this was a good

---

[3] This subsection is based on Perold (1988).

idea? You check whether your TC increased by less than your OC declined, making sure that your overall shortfall declined.

5.5. THE CAPACITY OF A TRADING STRATEGY OR AN ASSET MANAGER

Since transaction costs (eventually) increase with size, most trading strategies have a limited capacity (Pastor, Stambaugh, and Taylor (2014)). The more you trade on an idea, the more you move prices, and eventually the trade is no longer profitable, as illustrated in figure 5.2. The amount of capital invested in the strategy is on the x-axis. The horizontal line is the expected return without taking transaction costs into account, that is, the expected return of a portfolio trading only on paper. This line is horizontal because paper returns are the same no matter how much you invest. The upward-sloping curve is the implementation shortfall for the marginal dollar that you invest in the strategy, which increases with the number of dollars already invested. The difference between the paper return and the marginal shortfall is the net return on the last dollar invested. If we aggregate these returns, we get the total dollar profit on the strategy, indicated by the hump-shaped curve. The expected total profit rises as long as the expected paper return is above the shortfall but starts declining when marginal net returns become negative. Hence, the peak of this curve is the maximum number of dollars that can be expected to be made from this strategy. Clearly, the Sharpe ratio of the strategy's net return is higher the less you invest, so the optimal size of the portfolio is likely well to the left of the peak.

While a strategy has limited capacity, a hedge fund may have a very large capacity, since it can invest in many different strategies and markets. Nevertheless, even diversified hedge funds have capacity limits, as shown in figure 5.3. The left and right panels show two different examples of what can happen to a hedge fund's total profits when assets under management (on the x-axis) increase. In the left panel, any new assets are simply invested into the same strategies, and therefore paper returns remain constant. The shortfall initially declines, since the hedge fund can hire better traders, invest in a better trading infrastructure, gain better access to more exchanges and trading venues, and receive more favorable treatments from brokers and dealers. However, the shortfall eventually starts increasing and ultimately kills the trading strategy.

The right panel of figure 5.3 shows what happens if a hedge fund instead starts to diversify into more and more different strategies as assets grow. In this case, the shortfall only increases modestly, since the hedge fund is trading reasonably sized positions in more and more markets. However, in this case the expected paper return may start to decline as the hedge fund starts diversifying into markets and trading strategies where it lacks expertise, a behavior called "style drift." Hence, for a hedge fund to grow large, it needs to make sure that its expertise continues to grow.

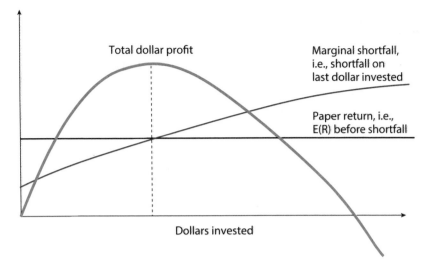

Figure 5.2. The capacity of a trading strategy.
The horizontal line is the expected return of the trading strategy gross of implementation shortfall, and the increasing line shows how the implementation shortfall rises with the number of dollars invested. Finally, the hump-shaped curve shows that total dollar profits increase at a rate equal to the difference between the two aforementioned lines.

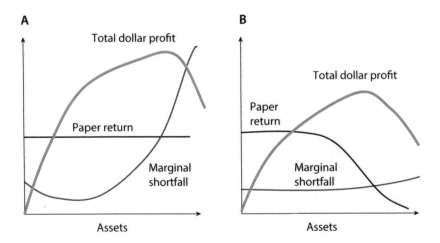

Figure 5.3. A hedge fund's capacity.
The left panel shows how a hedge fund's total profit evolves as a function of assets under management if new assets are simply invested into the same strategies. The right panel shows what happens if a hedge fund starts to diversify into strategies where it lacks expertise (called "style drift").

5.6. FUNDING A TRADING STRATEGY: DEFINITION OF LEVERAGE

Two of the biggest differences between running a paper portfolio in a backtest and running a real portfolio in a big hedge fund are (1) real-world portfolios incur transaction costs and (2) real-world portfolios need to be funded. Having covered (1) in detail, we now turn to (2). We need to understand where hedge funds get their capital from, how they access leverage, the limits of leverage due to margin requirements, and the important notion of funding liquidity risk. We first define some simple measures of leverage.

Financial leverage lets you multiply your investment performance to lift a hedge fund, just as a physical lever lets you multiply your force to lift a heavy object. Of course, leverage increases both gains and losses, so it increases the market risk by construction and introduces additional risks, such as the cost of forced deleveraging.

To leverage simply means to borrow to invest in assets worth more than all your equity capital (or to use derivatives to achieve the same thing). A hedge fund's leverage is measured as the ratio of its investments to its net asset value (NAV):

$$\text{leverage} = \text{long positions/NAV}$$

Whereas this measure ignores short positions, gross leverage adds short positions:

$$\text{gross leverage} = (\text{long positions} + \text{short positions})/\text{NAV}$$

The notion of gross leverage is implicitly based on the assumption that short positions add to risk, although shorts are in fact often hedges. In contrast, net leverage subtracts short positions (or, sometimes just the offsetting short positions):

$$\text{net leverage} = (\text{long positions} - \text{short positions})/\text{NAV}$$

Take, for instance, a hedge fund with a net asset value of $100 million, long positions worth $300 million, and short positions of $200 million. In this case, its leverage is 3, its gross leverage is 5, and its net leverage is 1. People often refer to this as 3-to-1 (or 3:1) leverage, or they say that for every dollar of net asset value, the fund is long $3 and short $2.

5.7. THE SOURCES OF LEVERAGE: A HEDGE FUND'S BALANCE SHEET

The most important part of a hedge fund's balance sheet is its equity. The equity capital naturally comes from the hedge fund's investors, including the principals running the fund. The equity capital in a particular hedge fund is called the net asset value (NAV) or assets under management (AUM), though the latter often refers to a manager's total assets across all hedge funds. A hedge fund's equity capital is not permanent since investors can withdraw their money, unlike equity capital in a regular company. Hence, in this sense, hedge funds are like open-end mutual funds, not closed-end mutual funds. However, in hedge funds, withdrawals are usually subject to initial *lock-up* provisions and *redemption notice periods*. If a hedge fund has a lock-up, then when capital is first invested, it can only be redeemed after a certain time period, for instance, one year. A redemption notice period is the amount of time in advance that investors must inform the hedge fund if they want to withdraw money. For instance, a quarterly 45-day redemption notice period means that you can only take your money out at quarter ends and only if you give notice 45 days before that time. The notice period is important for hedge funds since they often invest in illiquid securities and therefore need to trade out of positions slowly to minimize transaction costs. The notice period also makes it easier for a hedge fund to net outflows against inflows so that it does not need to trade its positions up and down too much.

What a hedge fund really wants to avoid is being forced into a fire sale, as this chapter discusses further. Redemption notice periods certainly help reduce this risk, but some hedge fund contracts even allow the fund to *suspend redemptions* or introduce so-called *gates* or *side pockets*. A gate means that only a certain fraction of a hedge fund capital can leave during any redemption period. For instance, at most 20% of the capital can pass through the gate during any quarter end. This limit helps the hedge fund avoid a fire sale, but the downside is that investors who fear that the gate will close may try to get their capital back before it is too late, which can create a "run" on the hedge fund similar to a bank run. Hence, having a gate can make it more likely that the fund will need it. Whereas gates are sometimes used by hedge funds that generally invest in illiquid but tradable securities, side pockets are used by hedge funds that own mostly liquid securities but have a subset of securities that are very illiquid. For instance, a hedge fund may place 90% of the investors' money in the "main pocket" of liquid investments and the remaining 10% in the side pocket of very illiquid investments. Investors can redeem their investment in the main pocket, but they will only get their side-pocket investment back when the fund can sell that investment in an orderly fashion.

A hedge fund's full balance sheet is illustrated in figure 5.4. The hedge fund's assets consist of long security positions, i.e., the stocks and bonds that the hedge fund owns, and various forms of cash. The liabilities are loans, equity, and short security positions. I have divided the cash and equity into groups so that the magnitudes of the various liabilities line up with the magnitudes of the corresponding assets. First, the long security positions are financed through margin loans and some of the hedge fund's equity (so these magnitudes line up as seen in the balance sheet). The margin loans mean that the hedge fund's assets can be (and usually are) larger than the fund's equity—this is the notion of

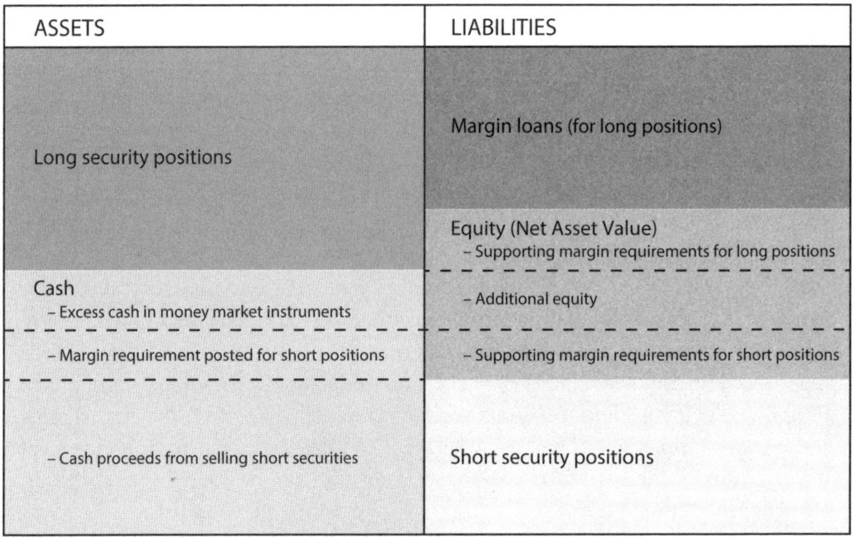

ASSETS	LIABILITIES
Long security positions	Margin loans (for long positions)
	Equity (Net Asset Value) – Supporting margin requirements for long positions
Cash – Excess cash in money market instruments	– Additional equity
– Margin requirement posted for short positions	– Supporting margin requirements for short positions
– Cash proceeds from selling short securities	Short security positions

Figure 5.4. A hedge fund's balance sheet.

leverage. To leverage long positions, hedge funds borrow using the securities as collateral. These loans against long positions are given by prime brokers or repo lenders, and they appear on the liability side of the balance sheet in figure 5.4 as "margin loans for long positions." However, a hedge fund cannot borrow the entire value of the long positions and therefore must partly use its own equity capital in "supporting margin requirements for long positions." Margin requirements are discussed in detail later.

The securities that a hedge fund has sold short are liabilities (since the hedge fund eventually needs to return these shares). The cash proceeds from the sale are assets, but they are held as collateral by the securities lender. In addition, the securities lender requires additional cash as margin requirement and, hence, the hedge fund must use equity capital "supporting margin requirements for short positions."

Lastly, the hedge fund has additional equity invested in cash instruments (e.g., money market funds, Treasury bills, or margin excess with prime brokers), as seen in the balance sheet. This additional equity makes it able to sustain losses without having to immediately liquidate positions.

Hedge funds also gain economic leverage by using derivatives and, though this economic leverage may not formally show up on the balance sheet, their notional exposures should also be considered when leverage is estimated. A small fraction of hedge funds also try to obtain unsecured bank loans or credit lines, but these are usually subject to "material adverse change" clauses and are almost never the main source of leverage.

5.8. LIMITS OF LEVERAGE: MARGIN REQUIREMENTS

How do you get leverage in the real world, that is, how can you buy assets worth more than the money you have? And how do you obtain a short position, that is, effectively own a negative number of shares? Before we delve into the institutional details, let us first look at the economics of leverage at a high level.[4]

- **Funding a leveraged long position.** Suppose that you want to buy 1 million bonds at a price of $100 per bond. You use the bonds as collateral and borrow against their value. However, you can only borrow a fraction of the value, say, $90 per bond, and not the full $100 value. The difference, 10% in this example, is called the *haircut* or the *margin requirement*. The haircut gives the lender an extra margin of safety in case the value of the bond suddenly drops and you do not want to pay the lender back. In that case, the lender can simply sell the bond and recover the loan, as long as the bond value is at least $90, that is, as long as the price drop is smaller than the haircut. Hence, to buy 1 million bonds, you do not need the full $100 million since you can fund this partly through leverage; all you need is $10 million, that is, $100 million multiplied by the 10% margin requirement.

- **Funding a short position.** If, instead, you want to short 1 million bonds, you need to proceed differently. In this case, you need to borrow securities and then sell them. Later, say, the next day, you buy the securities back and deliver them to the securities lender. Of course, you are hoping that the bond price will drop so that you can buy the bonds back cheaper than when you sold them. This way, you effectively have a negative bond position because you have sold something that you borrowed. When a hedge fund short-sells securities, its broker keeps the sale proceeds and, in addition, asks the hedge fund to post an additional margin requirement. (The broker itself may need to borrow the securities and must post 102% of the value as collateral but is likely to charge a hedge fund a higher margin requirement than 2%.)

- **How margin requirements are set.** Margin requirements are basically set to limit the lender's risk. Hence, the margin requirement must be large enough to cover the "worst-case" price move with a certain confidence. To estimate worst-case price moves, brokers use value-at-risk (VaR) and stress tests, which we discuss further in chapter 4. For a long position, this means that the probability of a drop in the price P_t greater than the margin requirement m must be low, say, below 1%:

$$\Pr\left(-\frac{P_{t+1} - P_t}{P_t} > m\right) = 1\%$$

---

[4] See Brunnermeier and Pedersen (2009) regarding margin requirements and Duffie, Gârleanu, and Pedersen (2002) regarding short-selling and securities lending.

The margin requirement is a fraction of the value of the asset, so m is between 0% and 100%. The amount of money a hedge fund needs to support its position is therefore the margin requirement m times the price P_t times the number of shares the fund buys.

If a hedge fund takes a short position, its broker will be afraid that the hedge fund will fail when the price goes *up*. If the hedge fund fails to buy back the borrowed shares, the broker needs to do so. Since the broker has the sale proceeds as well as the margin requirement, the broker can do this without using its own money, as long as the current price P_{t+1} is no greater than the sum of the sale proceeds and the margin, $P_t + m \times P_t$. The margin is set such that the probability of this event is small over some time period (e.g., 1 day or 5 days). For example,

$$\Pr\left(\frac{P_{t+1} - P_t}{P_t} > m\right) = 1\%$$

- **Funding the overall portfolio.** Since all long and short positions must be funded, a hedge fund must have enough capital to fund the sum of all positions:

$$\sum_i m_i \times P_t^i \times \text{position size}^i \leq \text{equity capital}$$

Failing to meet this requirement has led to spectacular hedge fund collapses. In fact, any financial institution must be able to fund its positions, and what brought down AIG, Lehman Brothers, and Bear Stearns was failing this inequality, that is, not being able to fund their positions.

- **Mark to market profit and loss (P&L).** Each day, a hedge fund's positions are marked to market, meaning that the value of each security is reassessed. Then the margin accounts are credited or debited for any price changes, as well as for interest payments on the borrowed capital and interest credits due on cash assets. Hence, the P&L is the return on the long positions, less the return on the short positions, plus financing:

$$\text{P\&L} = R_t^{\text{long}} \times \$\text{long} - R_t^{\text{short}} \times \$\text{short} + \text{financing}$$

The financing is the cost of the cash loan from the prime broker to support long positions (r_t^{PB}), the interest earned on the cash collateral held by the securities lender (r_t^{rebate}), and the interest earned on the additional cash in money market products (r_t^f):

$$\text{financing} = -r_t^{\text{PB}} \$\text{cash}^{\text{PB-loan}} + r_t^{\text{rebate}} \$\text{cash}^{\text{sec-lender}} + r_t^f \$\text{cash}^{mm}$$

This P&L is also the change in the hedge fund's equity capital, as is clear from the hedge fund's balance sheet in figure 5.4.

- **Interest rates and financing spreads.** A hedge fund naturally has to pay interest on the money it borrows for leverage. Furthermore, the prime broker providing the funding needs to earn a profit, leading to a *financing* *spread* between the interest that the hedge fund pays on the borrowed money and the interest it earns in the money market. Furthermore, the securities lender (sec-lender) earns a small premium for lending the shares, meaning that the cash sitting at the sec-lender earns an interest rate (called a rebate rate) that is lower than the money market rate:

$$r_t^{PB} > r_t^f > r_t^{rebate}$$

For instance, suppose that a hedge fund buys \$100 million worth of stocks, shorts \$100 million worth of stocks, and has \$50 million in margin equity. The \$100 million short sale proceeds, plus an additional 2%, stay with the securities lender and earn an interest rate called the *rebate rate*, which is typically less than the federal funds rate, say Fed funds minus 25 bps. For a difficult-to-short stock, the rebate rate can be several percentage points below the Fed funds rate, and sometimes short sellers must also pay a loan fee.

Turning to the long side of the portfolio, the remaining \$48 million in the hedge fund's margin account can be used toward financing the purchase of the long positions while the prime broker provides a loan for the remaining \$52 million. The interest rate on the loan is typically above the Fed funds rate, say Fed funds plus 30 bps. (To limit counterparty credit risk, the hedge fund might keep less cash with the prime broker and therefore need a larger loan, increasing the financing costs slightly.) The upshot of all this is that the hedge fund earns a lower interest rate on the cash backing its short sales than the interest rate on the loan that finances the long positions.

- **Margin call.** When implementing leverage or short-selling, you cannot be as laid back as a long-term unleveraged investor. You need to monitor your positions and cash levels continuously to make sure that your cash levels are above the minimum margin requirement. If a hedge fund has insufficient cash in its margin account (e.g., because of losses on its positions), it receives a margin call from its prime broker. This means that it receives notice that it needs to add cash to its account or reduce positions. If the hedge fund does not do one or the other, the prime broker will liquidate the positions. Receiving a margin call is itself a negative. Even if the hedge fund successfully adds cash, repeated margin calls are a sign of problems and can eventually lead the prime broker to terminate the arrangement or increase margin requirements. Hence, hedge funds naturally try to keep excess margin capital. (Some hedge funds have all their capital in their margin account, while others have most of their cash in a money market fund, moving it into the margin account as needed.)

The overall economics of funding a portfolio are quite general, but the specific institutional arrangements depend on the type of security. Let us briefly review the main forms of leverage, that is, the main ways that the overall economic principles discussed are put into practice.

- **Repo.** Government bonds and other fixed-income securities are usually leveraged using what is called a *repurchase agreement*, or repo for short. Economically, what a repo does is let you borrow using the bond as collateral, just as we discussed above. For instance, if you buy a bond worth $100, you can borrow $95 and let the lender hold the bond so that the lender does not have to worry about you not paying back the money, keeping a 5% haircut for safety. The repo gets its name from the fact that you formally sell the bond to the lender and, at the same time, commit to repurchasing the bond at a future time. The interest rate paid on the cash that you borrow is called the repo rate.
- **Prime brokerage (PB) of cash instruments.** Stocks are also leveraged using collateralized loans. Usually hedge funds leverage their stock portfolios using investment banks' PB service. The PB considers the hedge fund's overall portfolio of equities and determines how much capital the hedge fund needs to provide itself, called the margin requirement, and then the PB lends the hedge fund the rest. A hedge fund has an ongoing long-term relationship with its PB, and the hedge fund's portfolio is funded by one or a few PBs. In contrast, repo agreements are typically made separately for each bond, and a hedge fund often has many different repo counterparties. Other securities are also leveraged using PBs, for instance, convertible bonds, and PBs sometimes try to let the margin requirement depend on the overall portfolio (called cross-margining), though margin requirements are typically set asset class by asset class.
- **PB of OTC derivatives.** Another way to gain leverage is to buy a derivative with embedded leverage. For instance, a swap contract is constructed to have an initial market value of zero, so you might think that you can buy an unlimited number of swaps, given that they are free? Not so: If you enter into a huge swap position, you have an enormous interest rate risk, and your counterparties will worry that you will either make money or lose money, default, and never pay all the money that you lost. Therefore, hedge funds must also post margin capital when they enter into derivative contracts. PBs help hedge funds handle their OTC derivative contracts and net contracts traded with different counterparties.
- **Exchange-traded derivatives.** Finally, hedge funds can get leverage through exchange-traded futures and options. A hedge fund trades through a broker (called a futures commission merchant, or FCM) who charges the hedge fund margin requirements, and the exchange in turn charges the broker margins. The hedge fund's margins are often the same as the exchange margins, but they can, in principle, be higher or lower.

5.9. FUNDING LIQUIDITY RISK AND GAMBLER'S RUIN

A classic risk discussed in casinos and statistics books is *gambler's ruin*: the risk that you end up bankrupt despite having the odds in your favor. Suppose, for instance, that you count cards while playing blackjack. This skill gives you a small edge over the casino, but you have limited capital. Despite having the odds in your favor, you have some bad luck as the dealer draws aces, and you lose all your money. This outcome is very bad for two reasons: the obvious reason and because now you cannot exploit your edge. You lost your ability to make money from counting cards. The gambler's ruin problem goes back to Christiaan Huygens, a Dutch mathematician, astronomer, physicist, and writer, who also invented the pendulum clock, discovered the moon Titan that orbits Saturn, and made several other seminal contributions.

Gambler's ruin is also a crucial risk in investment management. Investors hope to have an edge (alpha) but have limited capital, with leverage subject to margin requirements. In investments, this risk is often referred to as *funding liquidity risk*. Whereas *market* liquidity risk is the risk that you cannot sell your securities without incurring large transaction costs, funding liquidity risk is the risk that you must sell them! Said differently, it is the risk that you are forced to sell your positions and, in the extreme, that you are forced out of the game. The costs of a funding crisis in investments are even greater than in gambling: When a hedge fund is forced to unwind its positions, it tends to be at a time when investment opportunities are *particularly* good. This is because the hedge fund's selling can depress prices and, more importantly, because forced liquidation does not happen at random times. When one hedge fund is forced to liquidate, it is more likely that other similar funds are also in trouble, which means that they may be selling similar securities and that there are therefore fewer natural buyers with ready money. This problem is especially severe due to an adverse feedback loop called a liquidity spiral.

5.10. LIQUIDITY SPIRALS: WHEN EVERYONE RUNS FOR THE EXIT

A liquidity spiral is an adverse feedback loop that makes prices drop, liquidity dry up, and capital disappear as these events reinforce each other.[5] This spiraling collapse is illustrated in figure 5.5.

The spiral starts when some kind of shock to the market causes leveraged traders to lose money. This shock leads to funding problems for some traders, who start reducing their positions. The resulting selling pressure pushes prices down, leading to further losses for all those traders with related positions. Furthermore, the market becomes more volatile and illiquid due to the order imbalances (and because these traders are the liquidity providers in normal

---

[5] Liquidity spirals were introduced by Brunnermeier and Pedersen (2009), running for the exit is discussed in Pedersen (2009), and risk management and amplification are covered in Gârleanu and Pedersen (2007).

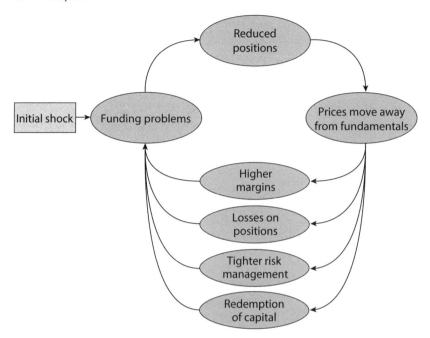

Figure 5.5. Liquidity spiral.

times). The higher market volatility and illiquidity can lead prime brokers to increase margin requirements, forcing traders to deleverage their positions. In addition, risk management considerations push traders toward reducing positions, and redemptions of capital from investors (or management) add to the funding problems. For all these four reasons, funding problems continue to grow, leading to a second round of selling, and so on, until the fire sale ends and markets can start to rebound.

A stylized price path during a fire sale is shown in figure 5.6. Prices drop sharply as traders sell, reach the bottom when the deleveraging is over, rebound as they gravitate toward fundamentals when some traders releverage and other investors arrive, and stabilize at the new equilibrium price, which is temporarily lower than before due to the exit of traders, capital, and funding.

A liquidity spiral implies that there exists a crash risk that is difficult to detect during normal trading days. Said differently, return distributions are inherently non-normal: While price changes are driven by fundamental news on most days, price changes are driven by forced selling during liquidity spirals. Liquidity spirals also change correlations across securities since, during a liquidity event, the prices of securities held by traders with funding problems start to co-move, even if their fundamentals are unrelated. Indeed, a liquidity crisis is contagious since losses in one market can lead to fire sales in other markets, hurting more traders and spreading the crisis. When a liquidity spiral

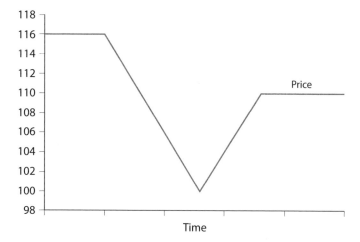

Figure 5.6. Price path during a liquidity spiral when everyone runs for the exit.
Source: Pedersen (2009) using the model of Brunnermeier and Pedersen (2005).

in one market erodes the funding of key dealers and hedge funds, liquidity dries up in other markets in which these traders are active. For instance, the global financial crisis of 2007–2009 spread in this way from the subprime market to other mortgage markets, then more broadly to credit markets, then to quantitative equity strategies, more broadly to equity markets, to currency markets, to convertible bond markets, to money markets, and then later to emerging markets, commodities markets, and beyond, as partly seen in figure 5.7.

5.11. PREDATORY TRADING

Liquidity spirals mean that forced liquidations are very costly. Another reason that forced liquidations can be very costly is predatory trading, that is, trading that exploits, or in fact induces, the need of others to reduce their positions.[6] For example, Cramer (2002, p. 182) states:

> When you smell blood in the water, you become a shark . . . when you know that one of your number is in trouble . . . you try to figure out what he owns and you start shorting those stocks.

Example. Suppose that the price of a stock X is currently $100 and that the price moves up or down $1 for every $1 million shares bought or sold. Outflow Capital Holdings (OUCH) needs to sell 10 million shares, and trader Y finds out.

---

[6] The analysis of predatory trading is from Brunnermeier and Pedersen (2005).

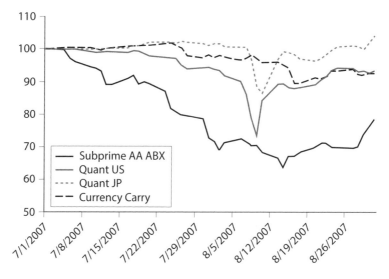

Figure 5.7. Spillover at the beginning of the global financial crisis (July 2007 to August 2007).

This figure shows how the crisis started with a decline in the subprime mortgage credit. In July 2007, quantitative long–short stock selection strategies based on value and momentum in the United States (Quant US) began to experience losses, and this subsequently spilled over to similar strategies in Japan (Quant JP). The currency carry trade experienced an unwinding in mid-August. The price series and cumulative returns have been normalized to be 100 at the beginning of July.

Source: Pedersen (2009).

What might trader Y do? Alternatively, suppose that OUCH only needs to sell if the price reaches \$99 per share. Now, what might the other trader do?

Predatory trading can arise in many different ways. For instance, it can arise when some traders use mechanical trading rules such as stop-loss orders, or during a so-called short squeeze. Prime brokers know a lot about a hedge fund's positions and funding situation and have sometimes been accused of exploiting this information:

> If lenders know that a hedge fund needs to sell something quickly, they will sell the same asset—driving the price down even faster. Goldman, Sachs & Co. and other counterparties to LTCM did exactly that in 1998.
>
> —*Business Week*, Feb. 26, 2001

Many times what looks like predatory trading really reflects the fact that other traders are trying to protect themselves, since they have similar positions and fear that they will be the next one forced to liquidate. Hence, selling as losses start to incur may simply be part of a risk management strategy.

PART II

Equity Strategies

CHAPTER 6

Introduction to Equity Valuation and Investing

Intrinsic value is an all-important concept that offers the only logical approach to evaluating the relative attractiveness of investments and businesses. Intrinsic value can be defined simply: It is the discounted value of the cash that can be taken out of a business during its remaining life.

—Warren Buffett

This part of the book describes equity strategies, also called stock selection strategies. Stock selection strategies seek to determine which stocks have high expected returns and which have low expected returns. Hedge funds then seek to buy the high-expected-return stocks and short the low-expected-return ones. Similarly, active long-only equity investors seek to overweight the high-expected-return stocks and underweight, or altogether avoid, the low-expected-return ones.

I consider three types of equity strategies: discretionary equity investments (chapter 7), dedicated short bias (chapter 8), and quantitative equity (chapter 9). Discretionary equity investment is the classic, and most common, form of equity trading, pursued by long–short equity hedge funds, active equity mutual funds, and others. Discretionary equity investment means that the traders and portfolio managers buy stocks based on their discretionary views, that is, their overall assessment of the stocks that they have analyzed. Discretionary traders perform a tailored analysis of each stock under consideration based on all kinds of information, including equity valuation models, discussions with the firms' management, competitors, intuition, and experience. Typically discretionary equity investors buy more stocks than they sell short, but the reverse is true for dedicated short bias hedge funds. Dedicated short bias hedge funds focus on findings stocks that are about to go down, looking for frauds, overstated earnings, or poor business plans. Dedicated short bias hedge funds rely on a fundamental analysis of companies in a similar way to other discretionary equity investors.

Discretionary trading can be seen in contrast to quantitative trading, which invests systematically based on a model. Both types of traders may seek lots of data and use valuation models, but whereas discretionary traders make their final trading decisions based on human judgment, quantitative investors trade systematically with minimal human interference. Quantitative investors gather data, check the data, feed it into a model, and let the model send trades to the exchanges.[1]

Quants try to develop a small edge on each of many small diversified trades using sophisticated processing of ideas that cannot be easily processed using non-quantitative methods. To do this, they use tools and insights from economics, finance, statistics, math, computer science, and engineering, combined with lots of data (public and proprietary) to identify relationships that market participants may not have incorporated in the price immediately. They build computer systems that generate trading signals based on these relations, perform portfolio optimization in light of trading costs, and trade using automated execution schemes that route hundreds of orders every few seconds. In other words, trading is done by feeding data into computers that run various programs with human oversight.

Discretionary trading has the advantages of a tailored analysis of each trade and the use of a lot of soft information such as private conversations, but its labor-intensive method implies that only a limited number of securities can be analyzed in depth, and the discretion exposes the trader to psychological biases. Quantitative trading has the advantage of discipline, an ability to apply a trading idea to a wide universe of securities with the benefits of diversification, and efficient portfolio construction, but it must rely only on hard data and the computer program's limited ability to incorporate real-time judgment.

While the three forms of equity investment have several differences, each relies on an understanding of equity valuation. As the quote above by Warren Buffett makes clear, a stock's intrinsic value is at the heart of equity valuation, as we discuss in this chapter.

6.1. EFFICIENTLY INEFFICIENT EQUITY MARKETS

Before we go into the details of deriving a stock's intrinsic value, let us recall what it is used for, namely value investing. Value investors seek to buy cheap

---

[1] Quantitative traders are close cousins to, but perform different roles than, the "sell-side quants" described in Emanuel Derman's interesting autobiography *My Life as a Quant* (2004). Sell-side quants provide analytical tools that are helpful for hedging, risk management, discretionary traders, clients, and other purposes. In contrast, quantitative traders work on the "buy-side" and build models that are used directly as a tool for systematic trading.

stocks, i.e., those with a low market value relative to the intrinsic value. Similarly, value investors short-sell expensive stocks with higher market valuations than intrinsic value.

Value investors make the market more efficient. They bring prices closer to fundamentals as they push up the prices of cheap stocks and push down the prices of expensive stocks. However, competition among value investors does not fully eliminate all inefficiencies since value investing involves fundamental risk and liquidity risk. If you buy a cheap stock for a price below the expected future profits, you can still lose money if unforeseen events harm the firm or if you are forced to sell before the stock price rises. Hence, investors need a premium for incurring these risks, leaving stocks with an efficient level of inefficiency. Said differently, the market has an efficient spread between prices and fundamentals that value investors, sometimes call their margin of safety (as discussed further below). The efficiently inefficient equity market has the property that prices can wander further from their fundamental values for illiquid stocks that are expensive to trade, volatile stocks that are risky to trade, stocks with large supply/demand imbalances, and stocks that are costly to short-sell, especially when active investors are facing reductions in capital and financing opportunities.

6.2. INTRINSIC VALUE AND THE DIVIDEND DISCOUNT MODEL

The foundation for trading equities is understanding equity valuation. The value of a stock is often called its *intrinsic value* (or *fundamental value*) to distinguish it from the market price. Whereas believers in market efficiency consider the price and the intrinsic value to be the same, believers in value investing look for stocks where the market price is cheap relative to the intrinsic value. Indeed, intrinsic value is at the very heart of value investing, as seen from the Warren Buffett quote above.

Let us consider a stock's intrinsic value V_t at a certain time t. The intrinsic value ultimately derives from the free cash that can be returned to shareholders. We will refer to these free cash flows as the "dividends" D_t, but they should be interpreted broadly as all cash returned to shareholders (including capital returned through share repurchases), less the capital that needs to be injected by shareholders (through seasoned equity offerings).

Of course, we cannot just add up dividends across different time periods because we must account for the time value of money and the uncertainty of the future cash flows. We start by considering how the value today depends on what happens over the next time period, say the next year. Today's intrinsic value depends on the next dividend D_{t+1}, the value next period, and the required rate of return k_t (also called the discount rate) over this time period.

Specifically, the current value is the expected discounted value of the dividend and value next period:

$$V_t = \mathrm{E}_t\left(\frac{D_{t+1} + V_{t+1}}{1 + k_t}\right)$$

Hence, to value a stock, we must be able to estimate the expected dividend payment next time period. We also need to decide on the required rate of return k_t, which naturally depends on the riskiness of the stock. For instance, an equity trader might estimate a stock's market beta as $\beta = 1.2$, the market risk premium as $\mathrm{E}(R^M - R^f) = 5\%$, and the current risk-free rate as $R^f = 2\%$. The trader might then use the capital asset pricing model (CAPM) to conclude that the stock's required return is $k_t = 2\% + 1.2 \cdot 5\% = 8\%$.

Lastly, to determine the intrinsic value at the current time t, it might seem that we need to estimate the intrinsic value next time period, $t+1$. However, rather than doing that, we use the valuation equation repeatedly to arrive at

$$V_t = \mathrm{E}_t\left(\frac{D_{t+1}}{1+k_t} + \frac{D_{t+2}}{(1+k_t)(1+k_{t+1})} + \cdots\right) = \mathrm{E}_t\left(\sum_{s=1}^{\infty} \frac{D_{t+s}}{\prod_{u=0}^{s-1}(1+k_{t+u})}\right)$$

This equation shows mathematically what the Buffett quote above says in words, namely that the intrinsic value is the expected discounted value of all future dividends paid to shareholders. This equation is called the dividend discount model (and it is also called the discounted cash flow model and the present value model).

Computing the intrinsic value is easier said than done, easier in principle than in practice.[2] To compute the intrinsic value, one must estimate all future dividends, all future discount rates, and the co-movement of future dividends and discount rates. To simplify this task, equity traders often assume a constant discount rate so that $k_t = k$ for all t. In this case, the valuation formula simplifies as follows:

$$V_t = \sum_{s=1}^{\infty} \frac{\mathrm{E}_t(D_{t+s})}{(1+k)^s}$$

Gordon's Growth Model

The dividend discount model can be further simplified by assuming a constant expected dividend growth. A constant dividend growth means that $\mathrm{E}_t(D_{t+s}) = (1 + g)^s D_t$, where g is the growth rate. With this assumption, the intrinsic value reduces to an intuitive expression:

---

[2] See Damodaran (2012) for an extensive description of equity valuation and financial statement analysis.

$$V_t = \frac{(1+g)D_t}{k-g}$$

The intrinsic value is naturally higher if current dividends are higher, if the dividend growth rate is higher, or if the required return is lower.

Multi-Stage Dividend Discount Models

Gordon's growth model is only appropriate for firms with a constant growth rate and, furthermore, it requires that the growth rate g be less than the discount rate k (otherwise, the denominator in Gordon's growth model would be negative, reflecting that such a high growth rate relative to the discount rate cannot be achieved in a long-run equilibrium). However, equity investors often become interested in firms that are going through unusual events, and such firms might experience several years of unusually high growth, including periods with $g > k$. Similarly, firms can experience periods of temporary contraction. In such cases, the current value of the stock can be computed as the present value of the dividends during the unusual time period plus the *terminal value*:

$$V_t = \sum_{s=1}^{T} \frac{E_t(D_{t+s})}{(1+k)^s} + \frac{P_{t+T}}{(1+k)^T}$$

Here, the terminal value P_{t+T} can be estimated by assuming a constant growth rate at that future time and using Gordon's growth model. Alternatively, P_{t+T} can be computed by assuming an industry-typical valuation ratio at that time, e.g., as 40 times $E_t(D_{t+T})$ if firms in this industry tend to trade at a price-dividend ratio of 40-to-1 (see the section on "relative valuation" below). The dividends between time t and time $t + T$ can be estimated by separately estimating all the cash flows during these years—value investors are known for spreadsheets full of such numbers. Alternatively, you can assume that the stock will experience an unusual, but constant, growth of g for the first T years. Then current value of such a stock is

$$V_t = \left(1 - \left(\frac{1+g}{1+k}\right)^T\right)\frac{(1+g)D_t}{k-g} + \frac{P_{t+T}}{(1+k)^T}$$

This equation is called the two-stage dividend discount model because the growth is assumed to have a constant rate in an initial "stage" (from time t to time $t+T$) and at another constant rate in the second stage (the time after $t+T$), which is used to compute the terminal value. (Note that this expression is positive even when the initial growth is above the discount rate, $g > k$.)

To summarize, the general idea is that valuation is based on the dividend discount model, and we can get some simple expressions by assuming a constant growth over certain time periods (based on the well-known formula for the sum of geometric series). Some equity investors take this idea further and consider three-stage and other more complex multi-stage valuation models.

6.3. EARNINGS, BOOK VALUES, AND THE RESIDUAL INCOME MODEL

For some firms, estimating dividends is difficult, for instance, because young firms tend to retain earnings for a number of years until they finally mature and start paying out dividends. More broadly, it is sometimes more natural to focus on a firm's economic earnings than its dividend payments. The two concepts are closely linked: to pay out dividends, the firm must earn profits, and earnings must ultimately be returned to shareholders to have consumption value.

To formally link earnings and dividends, we define the earnings as the net income, NI_t, and also keep track of the stock's book value, B_t. The book value is increased by the net income and reduced by capital paid out as dividends, and this key link is called the "clean surplus accounting relation":

$$B_t = B_{t-1} + NI_t - D_t$$

If we solve for dividends in the clean surplus relation and plug this expression into the dividend discount model, then we get the residual income model:[3]

$$V_t = B_t + \sum_{s=1}^{\infty} \frac{E_t(RI_{t+s})}{(1+k)^s}$$

where the *residual income*, RI, is defined as

$$RI_t = NI_t - k \cdot B_{t-1}$$

The residual income model says that the intrinsic value of the stock is equal to the book value plus the present value of the entire stream of future residual income. What is residual income? It is the amount of earnings NI_t over and above the cost of book equity, where the cost of book equity is the required return k times the level of book equity in the previous time period B_{t-1}. Naturally, residual income on any date t can be positive or negative. Residual income is

---

[3] To see this result, first note that

$$V_t = E_t\left(\sum_{s=1}^{\infty} \frac{NI_{t+s} - B_{t+s} + B_{t+s-1}}{(1+k)^s}\right)$$

Then change index on the first book value and make the appropriate adjustments to arrive at

$$V_t = B_t + E_t\left(\sum_{s=1}^{\infty} \frac{NI_{t+s} - (1+k)B_{t+s-1} + B_{t+s-1}}{(1+k)^s}\right)$$

which gives the residual income model. This version of the dividend discount model goes back to Preinreich (1938).

of course negative if the earning is negative, but residual income can also be negative with a positive earning that is smaller than the cost of capital. If the present value of all residual incomes is negative, this result corresponds to the intrinsic value being below the book value; otherwise, the intrinsic value is above the book value.

In summary, the intrinsic value is the current book value plus the present value of the additional (or residual) future profits that we expect to earn—above what could be expected based on the current book equity.

6.4. OTHER APPROACHES TO EQUITY VALUATION

Relative Valuation

Equity investors often value stocks based on the valuation of other comparable stocks. For instance, they might value a stock at $E \times P/E$, where E is the firm's earnings and P/E is the price-to-earnings ratio of comparable stocks, e.g., the average within the industry. This same method can in principle be used for any number of valuation ratios, but the important thing is that the firm's current characteristic (e.g., the current earnings E) is representative of the firm and its future prospects (not a one-year fluke number) and that the valuation ratio comes from a comparable set of stocks. Of course, relative valuation cannot tell you whether the entire stock market is over- or undervalued, but it can be informative about which stocks are expensive or cheap *relative* to others.

Implied Expected Returns

Another approach is to use the current price and the estimated future cash flows to compute each stock's "implied expected return" in the sense of its internal rate of return, also called the implied cost of capital. Based on such estimates of each stock's implied expected returns, a value investor might go long on those with high expected returns and short those with low ones.[4]

Firm Value vs. Equity Value

The same principles can naturally be used to value an entire firm (also called enterprise valuation) and its equity. Of course, the equity is worth less than the enterprise if the enterprise has debt. To value the enterprise or the equity, the

---

[4] See Hou, van Dijk, and Zhang (2012) and references therein.

key is to make sure that all inputs are "apples-to-apples." In particular, when valuing equity, one must consider the required return of the equity (which is riskier than the enterprise due to the leverage effect) and the free cash flows to equity holders (i.e., dividends). When valuing the enterprise, one must compute the present value of the free cash flows to the whole firm, that is, earnings before debt payments (but after all other cash drains, including reinvestment needs).

Similarly, when computing financial ratios, one should make sure that the numerator and denominator are apples-to-apples: If the numerator is an equity-level variable (as opposed to enterprise-level), then so should the denominator be. For instance, we consider a stock's price-to-earnings ratio, not its enterprise value-to-earnings ratio because the latter would look bad for a leveraged firm just because the interest payments reduce the earnings. Hence, with enterprise value in the numerator, the denominator should have earnings before interest expenses.

CHAPTER 7

Discretionary Equity Investing

Investment is most intelligent when it is most businesslike. . . . if a person sets out to make profits from security purchases and sales, he is embarking on a business venture of his own, which must be run in accordance with accepted business practices if it is to have a chance of success. . . . The first and most obvious of these principles is . . . "know your business" . . . A second business principle: "Do not let anyone else run your business, unless (1) you can supervise his performance with adequate care and comprehension or (2) you have unusually strong reasons for placing implicit confidence in his integrity and ability" . . . A third business principle: "Do not enter upon an operation . . . unless a reliable calculation shows that it has a fair chance to yield a reasonable profit. In particular, keep away from ventures in which you have little to gain and much to lose." . . . A fourth business rule is more positive: "Have the courage of your knowledge and experience. If you have formed a conclusion about the facts and if you know your judgment is sound, act on it—even though others may hesitate or differ."

—Benjamin Graham (1973, pp. 286–287)

Most active equity investors trade based on discretionary judgment, and many of the most successful ones swear to the principles of Graham and Dodd (1934) and Graham (1973). As is clear from the quote above, this means thoroughly analyzing a firm's business and its future profit potential, considering whether the management has the ability to deliver on this potential and the integrity to pay the profits out to shareholders, valuing the firm in relation to its price, and acting on your judgment even if it goes against conventional wisdom.

The hedge funds that use these strategies are called long–short equity funds. Long–short hedge funds seek to buy excellent stocks that trade at a discount and to short-sell bad stocks that are overvalued. They are often more long than short, perhaps because it is easier to find and implement long investments and because they may also want to earn the equity premium. Some long–short equity hedge funds are specialized in a certain area. For instance, some funds specialize in a particular industry (consistent with Graham's "know your business"), e.g., technology stocks, healthcare stocks, or commodity-related stocks. Other long–short hedge funds specialize in value investing or growth investing. The large long–short equity hedge funds are often broad, but they might consist of several specialized teams.

Discretionary equity investing is also used by active mutual funds, pension funds, sovereign wealth funds, and other traders. The main difference is that many of these investor types are long only. Hence, they will not just buy the stocks that they like, they will also overweight them relative to the benchmark, and, while they cannot short-sell stocks, they can underweight them relative to the benchmark or avoid them altogether. However, since most stocks are a very small percentage of a benchmark (often less than 1%), avoiding a stock has a much smaller effect than buying a significant position. Said differently, the short-sale constraint is often binding, so these investor types usually focus on finding good stocks rather than finding bad ones.

7.1. VALUE INVESTING

Value investing can be defined simply: it is the investment strategy of buying securities that appear cheap while possibly short-selling securities that appear expensive. The idea of value investing goes back at least to Graham and Dodd (1934). Value investing is harder than it sounds. Stocks are often cheap because there is something about them that makes investors uncomfortable, and stocks are often expensive because lots of investors love them. Value investing means going against conventional wisdom, which is never easy, avoiding (or shorting) stocks that most people love and buying those that are out of favor. Value investing takes courage, as seen from Graham's final principle in the introductory quote.

There are of course many ways to implement the general idea of value investing. The implementations of value investing differ in their definition of the intrinsic value, the typical holding period, and how the portfolio is constructed. Some value investors are patient and seek to hold their positions for the long term. They seek to buy a stock for less than the value of the future dividends that they will collect over time. Other value investors seek to buy a cheap stock and sell it over the medium term as they hope the pricing of the stock corrects itself.

One simple example of a value trade is to buy shares in a company with a lower market value than its cash holding and no debt—if you can find such a company. Is this trade a sure profit? Not if the market value is low because investors foresee that the company's management will waste the cash such that shareholders never benefit (see also Graham's second business principle). In this case, the value investor must be more active to profit from this trade, e.g., by buying enough shares to influence the management to pay out the cash as a dividend or use it productively.

Another simple implementation of value investing is to buy stocks with a high book value relative to the market value. Historically, even this very simple value strategy has been profitable, as we discuss further in chapter 9, on quantitative equity investing.

Fundamental Analysis

Value investors spend a lot of time on—you guessed it—valuation. They estimate the value of a stock using the dividend discount model in one form or another (e.g., the residual income model) as discussed above, but the difficult thing is to find the inputs to the model, not to plug them in. The process of estimating the inputs in the dividend discount model is called *fundamental analysis.*

Value investors project earnings into the future, e.g., by considering future sales growth, the evolution of the size of the overall product market in which the firm is operating, the firm's potential future market share, how profit margins will evolve based on the competitive advantage and the growth of costs, efficiency gains, and so on.

They try to figure out the best estimate of the intrinsic value in all kinds of ways. Some focus on the numbers, others on the people, yet others on the industry dynamics. The value investors who focus on the numbers analyze the accounting statements in detail, consider the evolution of the historical accounting numbers, and forecast future free cash flows.

Other value investors focus on the people, talking to the management of the firm and everyone involved in its business, such as employees, unions, customers, suppliers, and competitors. Based on these discussions, the investor seeks to determine whether the firm is well run; whether the customer base is happy, loyal, and growing; whether the firm is in a favorable competitive position; and whether costs can be controlled.

Yet other value investors focus on the industry dynamics, often specializing in a single (or a few) industries. They try to determine who is dominating an industry and whether this domination is sustainable. Which firms have the strong brand names, and who can be really profitable? Are there barriers to entry in the industry, and how easily can customers change between firms? What are the major changes that will transform the industry, for instance, technological changes, and who will benefit vs. suffer as a result of these changes? Which firms are making the key innovations, and how easily are these copied by others? How is the market share between different types of players changing?

Whereas these questions relate to the dynamics within an industry, other equity investors bet on entire industries, going long on several stocks in the same industry (or an industry index) while shorting stocks in another industry. Such investors consider which industries are about to rise or fall based on, for instance, how the macroeconomic environment will affect the various industries. This investment strategy is sometimes called "industry rotation" or "sector rotation."

Margin of Safety

When the future profits have been estimated, the value investor seeks to determine what these future profits are worth today. This is done by discounting the profits as per the dividend discount model. The value investor finally compares the estimated intrinsic value to the market value. The estimated intrinsic value is naturally sensitive to the inputs, not least to estimates of the discount rate and to growth rates. Hence, value investors often consider a range of possible estimates of the intrinsic value to consider how robust their valuation is.

> We must recognize, however, that intrinsic value is an elusive concept. In general terms it is understood to be that value which is justified by the facts, e.g., the assets, earnings, dividends, definite prospects—as distinct, let us say, from market quotations established by artificial manipulation or distorted by psychological excesses. But it is a great mistake to imagine that intrinsic value is as definite and as determinable as is the market price.
> —Graham and Dodd (1934)

Graham and Dodd (1934) therefore recommend that value investors use a *margin of safety*, that is, leave some room between the market value and the best estimate of the intrinsic value. This is illustrated in figure 7.1, which shows

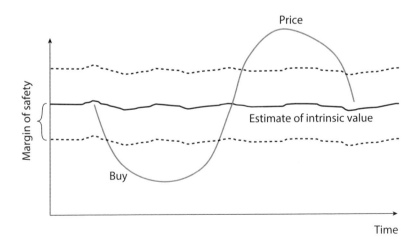

Figure 7.1. The margin of safety.

a stylized time series of a stock's price and intrinsic value. The uncertainty about the intrinsic value is indicated by the dashed "error bands" around the value, and the margin-of-safety principle means that the value investor should only buy when the price drops below the lower band.

Value Trap

"Deep" value investors go for stocks at really bargain basement prices. When you buy a stock with a very low price, for instance, a low price-to-book value, then you must always ask the following important question: Does the stock look cheap because it *is* cheap or because it deserves to be cheap? Said differently, is this stock a diamond in the rough, a cheap company that other investors somehow fail to recognize? Or, does the stock only appear to be cheap because its true fundamentals are collapsing?

> I could give you other personal examples of "bargain-purchase" folly but I'm sure you get the picture: It's far better to buy a wonderful company at a fair price than a fair company at a wonderful price.
> —Warren Buffett, Berkshire Hathaway Inc., Annual Report, 1989

Since a stock's price is the outcome of trading among thousands of people, many of them smart and successful, its price reflects a lot of information. Hence, if a stock looks cheap, there is often a reason, meaning that its growth is likely to be sub-par. The risk that a value investor ends up owning fundamentally flawed companies is called the *value trap*. For example, a bank stock may be low because the market recognizes that the bank will have to write down many of its loans. As another example, a stock can look cheap because the market realizes that the firm is subject to a lawsuit that will be very costly.

More broadly, consider a stock with an unusually low price-to-book P/B value (relative to the historical values of similar firms). Hence, by this measure, the stock looks cheap. Suppose further that you believe that the P/B will normalize over time. Does this mean that you expect to make money by buying this stock? Not necessarily—it depends on what is going to adjust, the price or the book value. If the mean-reversion of P/B is driven by a rising price, then the value investor makes money. However, the value investor may lose money if the mean-reversion of P/B is driven by a falling book value—this means that the stock experiences negative earnings that make it live up to the market's low expectations.

Investing based on P/B has been profitable on average historically, but many bets have led to losses because of the value trap. The value trap can be mitigated, at least partially, by focusing on a stock's quality characteristics, as we discuss next.

7.2. QUALITY INVESTING AND QUALITY AT A REASONABLE PRICE

One side of value investing is to look at the *price* of what you buy, and the other is to look at the *quality*. Said simply, quality investing means buying "good" companies. Quality investing can be combined with value investing, which can be called "quality at a reasonable price" (Asness, Frazzini, and Pedersen 2013).

What is a "good" company, that is, a high-quality company? Quality can be defined as characteristics for which investors should be willing to pay a higher price. Based on the dividend discount model, high quality means a high present value of future free cash flows. However, there can be many quality characteristics that can help predict future free cash flows. Following Asness, Frazzini, and Pedersen (2013), we can classify a stock's quality characteristics in four broad groups based on their version of Gordon's growth model:

$$\frac{V_t}{B_t} = \frac{E_t(NI_{t+1})/B_t \cdot E_t(D_{t+1})/E_t(NI_{t+1})}{k - g} = \frac{\text{profitability} \cdot \text{payout}}{\text{required return} - \text{growth}}$$

The left-hand side is the intrinsic value of the stock divided by its book value. We divide by book value as a normalization because otherwise differences in stocks' equity values would be mostly driven by size.

The right-hand side of the equation shows the main quality characteristics, namely those that justify a higher valuation multiple. Here, profitability (or return on equity) is defined as the profits (measured as net income, gross profits, or otherwise) per unit of book value, $E_t(NI_{t+1})/B_t$. Payout is defined as the fraction of the profits that are paid out to shareholders, $E_t(D_{t+1})/E_t(NI_{t+1})$. As above, g is the growth in profit and k is the discount rate. This way of looking at equity valuation shows that investors should be willing to pay a higher price multiple for stocks with higher growth, higher profitability, higher safety (i.e., lower required return k), and higher payout ratio.

Believers in market efficiency would agree that it is possible to identify high-quality firms, but market efficiency implies that such firms have *high prices* and *normal returns* (relative to the risk) going forward. In other words, believers in market efficiency think that high-quality firms are no better investments than low-quality firms because the market prices already reflect the quality.

In contrast, quality investors believe that it pays to identify high-quality firms since the price does not always fully reflect the quality and, therefore, the future returns are high on average. Let's discuss how quality investors trade on each quality component, namely growth, profitability, safety, and the payout ratio.

Growth: Good Growth vs. the Growth Trap

Many investors are searching for growth stocks, seeking to find the next Google, the next Apple, or the next Microsoft. Certainly, most people have heard stories of trades returning many times the original investment, and such stories are often centered around early investments in growth companies. However, stocks offering a growth dream and little current profitability can be speculative and overvalued, especially if investors project the growth too far into the future. A growth firm is only a good investment if the growth is not fully reflected in the market price.

Another pitfall to consider when investing in growth stocks is that not all types of corporate growth are value enhancing. Good growth is *sustainable* growth in *profits* that leads to growth in free cash flows. Bad growth is growth in other numbers that ultimately hurts profits.

One form of bad growth is growth in assets driven by an empire-building manager who wants to increase the scale of the firm to grow her own power and compensation, e.g., through expensive acquisitions or careless expansion. Another form of bad growth is sales growth driven by very low product prices, leading to deteriorating profit margins. Bad growth can also come in the form of temporarily improving accounting numbers by using accounting tricks that are not just unsustainable but will in fact later need to be reversed.

To see the difference between good and bad growth, consider two chains of retail shops with strong sales growth. One has increased its sales with "same-store sales growth," that is, it has increased sales in its existing shops, kept expenses constant, and increased profit margins. Clearly such same-store sales growth is good. The other retail chain has also increased sales, but this has been accomplished by buying up other retailers at premium prices. Such a strategy of asset growth, not profit growth, can often be flawed and can hurt shareholder value unless the acquisitions have special synergies or are done at very favorable prices.

Profitability and Earnings Quality

Clearly a more profitable firm is more valuable than a less profitable (or unprofitable) one. Profitability can be measured in several different ways, ranging from the reported earnings number, to measures focused on cash flows, to the "top line" gross profits (revenues minus cost of goods sold).[1] Equity investors seek to determine a company's ability to continue to make true economic profits in a sustainable way. They also look at a company's "earnings quality," meaning how reasonable a company's accounting practices are. Indeed, a company can choose to report its business activities in different ways, such as being more or less aggressive in moving items off the balance sheet, pushing expenses into the future, or recognizing revenues early using so-called accruals. Clearly, equity investors prefer a stock with

---

[1] See Novy-Marx (2013) and references therein.

higher true profits to one with similar apparent profits generated by account-ing adjustments.

Safety

A third measure of quality is safety. Investors should have a lower discount rate for safer stocks and thus be willing to pay a higher price for them, when everything else is equal. Safety can be measured using stock returns and fun-damental accounting variables, or both. The standard return-based measure is the market beta, measuring the systematic risk that the stock price will go down when the market is also down. Some equity investors also look at a stock's total volatility (or even its idiosyncratic volatility). The beta is relevant for measuring the contribution to risk in a very well-diversified portfolio, while the stock's total volatility is the risk of holding the stock in a concentrated portfo-lio. Fundamental risk measures are designed to estimate the risk of declining future profits, for instance, by considering the past variation in profitability.

Payout and Management Quality

A fourth class of quality measures focuses on how shareholder-friendly the firm is and how well managed it is. Specifically, one can look at whether profits are paid out to shareholders as dividends or share repurchases or how they otherwise benefit shareholders. In other words, does the firm's management seek to maximize shareholders' value or to extract private benefits for itself? For instance, some managers focus on generating cash for lavish perks, such as corporate jets, rather than for shareholders. Also, some managers act as "em-pire builders" who go on sprees of expensive acquisitions rather than focusing on profit growth. A sign of poor management can be that the board is packed with cronies rather than independent board members who can add value to the firm and represent the shareholders' interests. Another sign can be that the management is entrenched with a corporate governance that makes it very difficult to take the firm over by outsiders.

Of course, aside from the managers' dedication to creating value for share-holders, the quality of management more broadly is important. Investors consider whether the management has insightful and value-creating visions for the company's growth, is able to inspire and motivate employees, can cut costs, and can aim for sustainable long-run growth. Some investors seek to buy stocks with good management, others seek to buy stocks that are cheap due to poor management and then profit from improving it—this attempt to directly influence the management is called *activist investing*, as discussed further in section 7.5.

Quality at a Reasonable Price

Value investors and growth investors are often thought of as polar opposites, and sometimes they are, but at other times, they end up buying the same stocks. Figure 7.2 shows why they are often thought to be opposites. The worldview of a deep value investor, a "bargain hunter," is depicted on the top. This bargain hunter has estimated his view of the intrinsic value, which stays relatively constant over time even as the market price bounces around. Therefore, the stock will tend to look cheap to the bargain hunter when the price has fallen and this is when he will buy. Later, when the price has gone

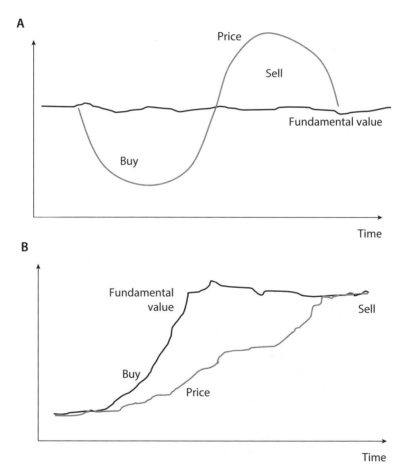

Figure 7.2. The worldviews of bargain hunters vs. growth investors.
  Panel A: Worldview of a bargain hunter.
  Panel B: Worldview of a growth investor.

up, the stock might start to look expensive to the bargain hunter and he might therefore decide to sell.

The worldview of a growth investor is depicted in the bottom panel of figure 7.2. The growth investor is trying to buy a high-growth stock with a chance of becoming the next home run. A firm that is expected to experience fast growth in the future often has already experienced growth and good news in the past and, therefore, its price has likely been on the rise. Hence, whereas the bargain hunter might be selling stocks that have been rising in value, the growth investor might be buying such stocks. Ironically, they may both feel that they act as value investors, but their views of intrinsic value are very different. The bargain hunter is (perhaps implicitly) thinking of the intrinsic value as stable, whereas the growth investor perceives that the intrinsic value has risen even faster than the price.

Who is right? Surprisingly, they may both be right on average. Historically, people who buy stocks that look cheap in the sense of having a low price-to-book value have done well. The opposite stocks—those with high price-to-book, sometimes called *growth stocks*—have consequently underperformed. However, if one sorts stocks based on certain measures of their actual growth (rather than sorting on price-to-book), then high-growth stocks have outperformed low-growth stocks. In other words, high-quality stocks have outperformed low-quality stocks, and this holds not just for growth, but also for profitability, safety, and payout/management. Given that both value investing and quality investing work, one can do even better by combining these concepts. Some equity investors seek to buy growing firms that are cheap relative to the expected growth, which is called "growth at a reasonable price" (GARP) investing. This concept can be generalized to "quality at a reasonable price" (QARP) investing, namely the strategy of buying high quality at a discounted price.

7.3. WARREN BUFFETT: THE ULTIMATE VALUE AND QUALITY INVESTOR

Warren Buffett has become one of the world's richest people based on his investment success over the past half century. How large a Sharpe ratio does it take to become the richest person in the world? Most investors guess that Warren Buffett must have realized a Sharpe ratio well north of 1 or even 2, perhaps based on Sharpe ratios promised by aggressive fund managers. The truth is that Buffett's firm Berkshire Hathaway has delivered a Sharpe ratio of 0.76 from 1976 to 2011. While this is lower than some might have expected, it is nevertheless an extremely impressive number. Buffett's Sharpe ratio is double that of the overall stock market over the same time period, which means that Buffett has delivered twice as much return per unit of risk. While some stocks or funds have clearly delivered higher Sharpe ratios over a shorter time period (which could be just luck), Buffett's Sharpe ratio is the highest of any U.S. stock or any U.S. mutual fund that has been around for at least 30 years.[2]

How has Buffett done it? Buffett is known as the ultimate value investor, but just controlling for his value exposure does not explain his alpha. However, if we also control for his focus on quality stocks, then a large part of his performance can be explained. Said differently, Buffett has been buying cheap, high-quality stocks, and such stocks have performed well in general, which helps explain Buffett's success. This finding is consistent with Buffett's own statements:

> Whether we're talking about socks or stocks, I like buying quality merchandise when it is marked down.
> —Warren Buffett, Berkshire Hathaway Inc., Annual Report, 2008

Another reason behind the magnitude of Buffett's success is his leverage. He has not only delivered a high Sharpe ratio, he has also delivered much higher absolute returns than the overall stock market, on average beating the risk-free rate by 19%, about three times the overall stock market's excess return of 6.1% per year. Berkshire's volatility of 25% is significantly higher than that of the market, in part because Buffett has leveraged his equity investments about 1.6-to-1.

Buffett's leverage comes from several sources. First, Berkshire has issued highly rated bonds at low yields, enjoying a AAA rating from 1989 to 2009. Second, Berkshire has financed about a third of its liabilities with its insurance float at an average cost *below* the risk-free rate. To understand this usually cheap and stable source of financing, note that Berkshire operates insurance and reinsurance companies and, when these companies sell insurance, they collect the premiums up front and pay a diversified set of claims later, which is like getting a loan. The efficiently run insurance firms both make a profit and help finance Buffett's investments. Third, Berkshire's liabilities also include deferred taxes (essentially an interest-free loan) and derivative contract liabilities.

7.4. HOLDING PERIODS AND CATALYSTS

Some managers buy a cheap stock with the idea of holding it for the long term. In this case, it is less important how the stock price evolves in the short term (assuming that the leverage is modest and investors do not flee). Warren Buffett sometimes takes this idea to the extreme, seeking an infinite holding period:

> when we own portions of outstanding businesses with outstanding managements, our favorite holding period is forever. We are just the opposite of

---

[2] This section is based on Frazzini, Kabiller, and Pedersen (2013).

those who hurry to sell and book profits when companies perform well but who tenaciously hang on to businesses that disappoint. Peter Lynch aptly likens such behavior to cutting the flowers and watering the weeds.

—Warren Buffett, Annual Report, 1988

There may be several reasons for this approach. First, as Buffett and Lynch point out, many investors often sell winners too quickly and hang onto losers, a phenomenon called the "disposition effect."[3] In Berkshire Hathaway's case, there might also be tax reasons since realizing capital gains would lead to taxes, which can be postponed forever as long as the holding period is forever.

On the other hand, many equity investors find it optimal to sell a stock when they think that its price has converged to its fair value or it has become expensive. Such investors view their capital as limited and want to apply that capital where its return is the highest. Hence, when a stock is no longer a great deal, they will reallocate capital to more promising investments. A common saying among traders is: "Don't get married to your position." This saying means that one should always look for the best current investments, regardless of what existing positions one happens to have, and one should not continue to hold a bad stock for fear of recognizing an error or reluctance to take profits.

Many equity investors are not only happy to take profits, they are very impatient for this to happen. Very impatient investors only buy a cheap stock if they also anticipate that a "catalyst" will make the stock price rise within a limited time horizon. Such value-and-catalyst investors seek to find cheap stocks that are about to get richer because the market is about to realize that stock's potential. For instance, if the next earnings announcement by a firm with a cheap stock will reveal that it is on a strong new course, then you have a catalyst.

Some impatient investors go even further, seeking to *create* a catalyst. For example, suppose that a hedge fund has discussed a hotel company with several of its large investors and determined that the investors appear to be overly optimistic about the prospects of the company. Placing an investigator outside of the main hotels, they determine that the hotel is largely vacant and that earnings will disappoint—so the hedge fund sells the stock short. Rather than waiting for the other investors to learn this bad news at the next earnings announcement, the hedge fund might issue a report that details their negative assessment, hoping that the stock price will drop immediately—i.e., creating their own catalyst.

7.5. ACTIVIST INVESTING

Another way to create a catalyst is to engage actively in a discussion with the firm's board, as activist investors do. Activist investing means buying shares in a company that could be worth more with better management and then trying

---

[3] See Shefrin and Statman (1985) and Frazzini (2006).

to affect the decisions of the firm. When an investor has bought more than 5% of the shares in a U.S. stock, he must make a so-called "13D filing," where he reports his position size and declares whether he intends to be active. The mere presence of an activist investor can send a message to management to get their act together. Furthermore, the activist investor may make specific suggestions to the management or board, e.g., by sending a letter suggesting a replacement of the management, changing certain board members, giving cash back to shareholders, cutting costs, or selling assets that are worth more elsewhere and focusing on the remaining firm. The activists can also try to get more direct influence by seeking a seat on the board, engaging in a "proxy fight" (i.e., creating a referendum on a specific proposal, e.g., at the annual meeting, where shareholders can authorize someone to act as their proxy and vote their shares), or trying to take over the company.

7.6. TRADING ON FLOWS AND SENTIMENT

Rather than looking at a stock's fundamental value and quality characteristics, some equity investors focus on technical drivers of price changes based on order flow or try to anticipate investor sentiment. Large orders can move prices because they may reflect information or because liquidity providers must be enticed to take the other side of the trade. Hence, if a trader can predict that a large order will hit the market, e.g., a large buy order from a pension fund, then they may try to trade ahead of this flow. In other words, they may try to buy before order flow pushes price upward, although such "front-running" can be illegal, especially if done by a broker who takes advantage of information about its clients. Alternatively, a trader might try to take advantage of the subsequent price reversal, short-selling the stock when its price has been pushed up in order to profit as the price comes back down—as opposed to front-running, this trading activity actually helps the pension fund, which sends the large order because it reduces the price impact.

Some hedge funds buy a stock even if they think it is overvalued, betting that the stock is about to get even more expensive. Some investors claimed to pursue this strategy during the Internet bubble of the late 1990s, for instance.[4] This form of trading activity contributes to price bubbles. It is based on the so-called "greater fool theory," meaning that the investors may acknowledge that it is a foolish stock to buy, but this is fine as long you can sell at an even higher price to a greater fool. Of course, this activity cannot go on forever; bubbles eventually burst, and it is hard to predict when, so this is a risky strategy.

A clearly illegal form of trading seeks to push others to *become* greater fools, namely "pump and dump" schemes, where a trader might buy a stock

---

[4] See, e.g., Cramer (2002).

and create a hype around it to drive the price up. Such price manipulation hopefully only exists in small corners of the market because of regulation and because competitive forces in the liquid securities markets make such schemes difficult and unprofitable.

7.7. INTERVIEW WITH LEE S. AINSLIE III OF MAVERICK CAPITAL

Lee S. Ainslie III is the managing partner of Maverick Capital Management, LLC, an investment management firm focusing on global equities. Before founding Maverick in 1993, Ainslie was a managing director of Tiger Management Corporation, the famous hedge fund founded by Julian Robertson, which gave rise to several successful "Tiger Cub" funds of which Maverick is one of the most prominent. Ainslie received a B.S. in systems engineering from the University of Virginia and an M.B.A. from the University of North Carolina.

LHP: *How did you get started as an investor?*

LA: I have been fascinated by stocks ever since I became a member of a high school investment club when I was in eighth grade in Virginia. After engineering school, I went to business school, and Julian Robertson was on the board of that school. I was fortunate to be asked to work with the board on a couple of issues, and as a result I got to know Julian. Occasionally, we would discuss stocks, and to my pleasant surprise one day he asked me to consider working at Tiger. That was my introduction to the hedge fund business.

LHP: *Great. What is your investment process?*

LA: To oversimplify, we are really trying to look out two or three years in every industry in which we invest, trying to identify who's winning and losing, and, perhaps most importantly, recognize the discrepancies between our view and the view of the markets.

We have a very deep and thorough process. I think we're unusual in that our typical ratio of primary positions to investment professionals is roughly four to one, which allows an uncommonly deep level of due diligence. Our process is less about suddenly recognizing a new potential investment that we then investigate, but rather more about constantly updating our strategic views of every industry in which we invest and looking for changes in that competitive landscape that may present new opportunities.

LHP: *Can you give some examples of what you might be looking for in a company? What are some characteristics you like to see in a long position, let's say?*

LA: First and foremost, we focus on the quality of management. We work hard to evaluate the management team's desire to create shareholder value, their competitive drive, their intellect, and ability to execute. Management is top of list.

Second is the quality of the business. This includes the persistence of cash flow streams, the drivers and sustainability of growth, and a strong understanding of the competitive dynamics within an industry. It may sound cliché, but we invest a great deal of time talking to competitors, suppliers, and customers—as well as interacting with as many members of management throughout different divisions and different locations around the world as we can.

Finally, valuation. I think part of the art of being a successful investor is to be very comfortable with a number of different valuation methodologies and to recognize which approach is the most appropriate or most meaningful in a different circumstance. Having said that, the most common valuation metric at Maverick is the comparison of sustainable free cash flow to enterprise value.

LHP: *How do you know if a company's favorable characteristics are already in the price?*

LA: Well, I'm not sure we ever really know for sure, but by talking to folks on both the sell-side and buy-side we try to develop an understanding of consensus expectations. Often valuation itself can give real insight into true expectations as well. And, as mentioned, we try to understand the discrepancies between our view and the view of the market. Just ten years ago, developing a decent understanding of consensus estimates was rather straightforward, but it's not nearly as simple today. So we invest a lot of time to develop a thoughtful view of the intrinsic value of a company and then compare and contrast our perspective to how the market is valuing different companies.

LHP: *Which perspective is more useful: To try to estimate a company's performance over the next year or two—say, the next earnings announcement—and compare one's view to the expectation in the market vs. estimating the stock's overall fundamental value and comparing it to the market price?*

LA: It's certainly important to be attuned to short-term expectations as well. For companies in which we invest, we try to have a strong understanding of what investors are expecting each quarter for a number of different key metrics. However, we are typically much more focused on looking out over the next several years and far less concerned with short-term results. Trading around quarterly results is just not what our research process is geared towards. We need to be attuned to short-term results just to avoid short-term mistakes, but I believe we're much more likely to be successful on a consistent basis by understanding how longer term competitive dynamics will play out. In our way of thinking, the odds of making the right investment decision improve the further out we look.

LHP: *For short positions, are you there just looking at the opposite of what's a good long position or are there different types of things you look for?*

LA: A bit of both. For most of our shorts, the investment process is essentially a mirrored process of what we're doing on the long side. We're looking for some combination of unsustainable fundamentals, incompetent management teams, or illogical valuations—preferably all three! We also have a bucket of really idiosyncratic shorts, for instance, we occasionally find companies that we believe have materially misrepresented themselves.

LHP: *How do you assess when is the right time to buy and when is the right time to get out of the position?*

LA: It's purely driven by the discipline of making sure our portfolio is always focused on the opportunities we judge to be the most attractive. In the utopian world, every single day we would consider the return we think we can achieve in every one of our positions, how much risk we need to take to achieve that return, and how that risk-return profile compares to every other investment opportunity that we have. So if something is being bought or sold, that typically means we have concluded that another investment is more attractive at that point in time than a current investment. Of course, this is all easier in theory than in practice, but that's our mindset.

We are very focused on looking forward, not backwards. At what price we have previously bought or sold a security should not be relevant to our evaluation of the attractiveness of that stock from current prices.

This approach of exiting a position when it is no longer as compelling as other opportunities means that we often are selling stocks that we still believe offer meaningful upside. However, if that investment is no longer one of our most compelling, then we redeploy that capital into a stock that is.

LHP: *Do you use quantitative methods for portfolio construction?*

LA: We have actually developed a very robust quantitative research effort, which I think is unusual for a fundamentally oriented investment firm. All of our investment decisions are primarily driven by fundamental considerations, but our quantitative research effort has helped us in many different ways. In terms of portfolio construction, our quantitative effort plays a critical role in our decisions regarding the sizing of individual positions, factor exposures, and the risk profile of the portfolio.

One of the unexpected benefits of incorporating quantitative approaches into our investment process is that it has both demanded and enabled a disciplined fundamental process that is very thorough and consistent across industry sectors and regions. Most of our quant work is very dependent upon the bottoms-up research and conclusions of our investment team. So we recognized early on that we had to take steps to ensure these fundamental inputs were very reliable, which has really improved our research process—a very nice unintended consequence.

LHP: *Why do you think you beat the market, and who takes the other side?*

LA: First of all, I think we're fortunate to have an unusually talented investment team. Our investment team is quite deep but also very experienced as the average investment professional has over a decade of investment or industry experience, the majority of which has been spent at Maverick. So while that ratio of four investments per professional that I previously mentioned is a huge advantage, the talent of each professional, which is obviously harder to quantify, is the more critical factor in our success.

The fact that we are completely indifferent to index weightings gives us a meaningful advantage as well. A significant portion of the capital invested in the markets is invested in a manner that is very aligned with the relevant weightings to an index, typically on a cap-weighted basis. At Maverick, we are blissfully ignorant of a particular stock's or sector's weighting in any index—all we care about is the attractiveness of an investment on a risk-return basis.

Last but not least, I think stability has been a big advantage for us over the years. We've enjoyed stability of both our investment team and our investor base, which really does allow us to invest with a longer term horizon. The vast majority of the capital we manage is attributable to profits we have generated for our investors, and most of the capital we manage has been invested in Maverick for more than ten years. We're relatively unconcerned with short-term swings in our performance because we're confident that our investors share our longer term perspective. Finally, the stability of our portfolio is very helpful; on the long side, our average holding period is over a year. For the hedge fund world, that's an unusual time frame that allows us to get to know our companies and their management teams quite well. Management teams appreciate investors that act as long-term partners instead of short-term traders.

LHP: *So, if certain stocks are out of favor, other investors might recognize it, but they might not want to buy if they think that they need to hold it for a long period to make the profit?*

LA: Yes, and, going back to your earlier question about the time frame over which you're comparing your expectations to those of the rest of the world, I think that many hedge funds are just looking out one or two quarters. By being focused longer term, we are operating in a less competitive landscape. Further, over the long term, fundamentals have to play a bigger role as markets eventually recognize true underlying values, and the shorter term illogical dislocations become less relevant.

LHP: *Warren Buffett has said that he likes to hold forever. Would you also go to that extreme?*

LA: No. I have a great respect for Warren Buffett and agree with the vast majority of his philosophies. But this is one tenet that I've always disagreed with because I believe in our portfolio we have a responsibility to invest our capital as effectively and efficiently as we can day in and day out. If you're holding a stock forever, by definition there will be periods of time when there are more attractive uses for your capital. The approach of "Too bad—I'm wedded to this stock." does not allow an investor to free up that capital to redeploy it in a more attractive opportunity. While we may still respect the management team and still believe the company will do well, if we have identified an investment that we believe is more compelling, then we will redeploy our capital.

LHP: *What makes a person a good investor, e.g., what do you look for when you hire?*

LA: First and foremost is integrity. We've now been in business for over twenty years, and over that time we have worked awfully hard to develop a reputation we're very proud of. If any member of our team were ever to make an unethical decision, all that effort can be unwound overnight. This is a pretty amazing industry in that we can pick up the phone, call a brokerage firm, and invest hundreds of millions of dollars given the broker's confidence that when we place that order, we will fulfill our obligation. I'm not aware of other businesses that work this way. Likewise, our investors will not entrust their capital with us unless they have complete confidence that we will consistently put their interests first and conduct ourselves in an appropriate manner at all times. I think one of the factors that some firms may overlook when evaluating people is personal integrity because even a junior person can make a decision that can have a dramatic impact on the reputation of your firm.

Number two, dedication. This is a very, very competitive business. There is a significant amount of brainpower chasing similar opportunities. At the end of the day, working more intelligently and working harder tends to have a high correlation to success.

We're looking for folks who can think creatively and develop a differentiated point of view. Investing is not a skill where you can simply complete a checkpoint process or crank through one particular methodology and automatically come to the correct conclusion. The ability to develop a fresh perspective on an investment thesis or recognize a different angle to evaluate an investment is critical to being a successful investor over time.

People skills play a significant role. It's important for us to develop strong relationships, not just with the management teams of the companies we invest in, but also with their competitors, suppliers, and customers. Those that have stronger people skills are more likely to be successful in developing those dialogues and more likely to understand when different individuals are not being as forthright as you would hope.

Finally, a very strong competitive streak is crucial. For virtually everyone here, one of the aspects we really enjoy about being in this business is that we recognize that everyone is keeping score. We strive to develop a reputation that we're proud of and that is driven both by how we conduct ourselves and, of course, by the performance we deliver to our investors.

LHP: *Is there a specific trade that has been important to your career?*

LA: Our general counsel only allows us to talk about losing trades. So here is a trade that was indeed important to my career, but it's not something I'm proud of. If you go back to 1994, there were a couple of important software trends in place. One was the adoption of Microsoft Windows 3.1, which was a real breakthrough in terms of the usability of operating systems. Secondly, the first meaningful gaming platform war developed between Sega and Nintendo, which was intensified by the introduction of the Sony PlayStation later that year. We had the belief that both of these developments would spur significant software sales for both PCs and gaming. At the time, there were two retailers that dominated this space, Babbage's and Software Etc. They were primarily mall-based retailers of software. We thought each may represent interesting investments given these two strong secular trends, and, as we were doing our work trying to understand the dynamics between the two, they decided to merge. The company that they formed was called NeoStar.

This was now a very compelling investment in my mind. In addition to these tremendous tailwinds, there were huge potential synergies in putting these two businesses together in terms of reducing the competitive dynamics in pricing, closing stores that directly competed with one another, and by improving the bargaining positions with their suppliers given their newfound scale. As I look back, I still think it's fair to say that we were right on all the above.

Unfortunately, despite these tremendous opportunities, the company went bankrupt in less than two years. Why did they go bankrupt? Recall that when you asked me what we look for in potential investment that the top of my list was management. In this case, management ended up getting into a battle of egos between the two sides—not atypical in these situations—regarding who was going to get what responsibility, what title, etc. Management made shockingly poor buying decisions, essentially double-ordering in the chaos of the merger, so the inventory levels ended up being wildly inappropriate. Management did a very poor job of executing on some of the synergies that should have been rather easy to realize. Management leveraged up the balance sheet to a degree that proved unsustainable. I could go on, but you probably get the idea.

So despite getting many of the very important fundamental factors correct, management ended up bankrupting what should have been a great opportunity. Fortunately, we didn't ride this ship all the way down, but we rode it down far enough still to be a painful memory. The only silver lining is the experience was a very important lesson that there's so much more to evaluating a stock than just understanding the large secular trends and what looks to be a great opportunity on paper. The ability and decisions of management can trump all other considerations.

LHP: *In your core fund, you tend to be a bit more long than short and vary that net exposure over time. How do you think about that timing decision?*

LA: To be clear, we have different long–short funds with different levels of gross and net exposure and therefore different risk-return profiles. I believe you're referring to our flagship fund, in which we typically target net exposure around 45%.

The net exposure does vary, but it's usually between 30% and 60%. The variation is driven first and foremost by our view of the relative attractiveness of our long and short portfolios. While we do invest a great deal of time to understand macroeconomic factors and consider risks in the market, such perspectives only have a limited influence on our exposures. With that tight range of net exposure, we are unlikely to have a significant impact on our performance through such market-timing decisions. That's very much on purpose. Timing decisions are very difficult to get right on a sustainable basis. Maverick's core fund is designed to maintain a balance of longs and shorts within every region in which we invest and within every industry in which we invest, such that macro considerations—whether it be the performance of the markets, sector rotations, etc.—should never have a big influence on our success. Indeed, our success, or lack of success, is driven by our ability to generate alpha through security selection—again, on purpose, because that's the skill in which we have the greatest confidence in our abilities.

CHAPTER 8

Dedicated Short Bias

We like to have Murphy's Law working for us.

—James Chanos

Whereas most equity investors focus on buying stocks, a small group of hedge fund managers focus on short-selling. While dedicated short bias managers go more short than long, they often rely on the same techniques as other equity investors, namely fundamental analysis.

The focus on short-selling makes these managers zoom in on all the potential problems that firms might have. Hence, dedicated short bias managers look for stocks with materially overstated earnings, aggressive accounting methods, and incomprehensible statements in SEC filings. When they find such signs of a potential "cover-up," they try to dig deeper into what is actually going on. They also try to investigate whether firms are engaged in outright fraud.

In addition to such misbehaving firms, dedicated short bias managers also search for well-intending firms with fundamentally flawed business plans. This could be firms with an interesting technology but no sustainable way to make profits or firms based on technology that is becoming obsolete, e.g., as happened to Nokia and BlackBerry when the iPhone came out. They might also look for firms that rely on excessive use of credit and are about to get into trouble.

Short-selling is far more challenging than buying stocks for a number of reasons, as we will discuss in detail. Perhaps for this reason, the short sellers have a particular reputation:

> Short sellers are odd people. Most of them are ambitious, driven, antisocial, and single minded. As individuals, they are not very likely to own a Rolex watch or a Presidential springer spaniel or any other symbolic trapping of success; they are likely to have a wry slightly twisted sense of humor. As a group, short sellers like to disagree, and they like to win against big odds. Typically, they have an axe to grind, a chip on the shoulder. As in the general

population, some of them are cretins and some are not, but they are all
smarter (most of them, in fact, are intellectual snobs) and more independent
than most people. Contrary to popular wisdom, they do not form a cabal and
bash stocks senseless. They normally are secretive and slightly paranoid.
And they are frequently irreverent in their regard for business leaders and
icons of Wall Street.

—Staley (1997, pp. 25–26)

8.1. HOW SHORT-SELLING WORKS
AND WHY IT CAN BE DIFFICULT

Everyone knows what it means to buy 100 shares in IBM, but what does it
mean to short-sell 100 shares? At an abstract level, it means to own *minus*
100 shares! Short-selling is the opposite of buying a stock; it is a bet that the
stock price will fall. Hence, if the price of IBM goes up by 10%, investors who
bought the share will earn 10% while traders who shorted it will lose 10%.
Conversely, if IBM drops 10%, investors who bought the stock will lose 10%
while traders who shorted it will earn 10%.

In practice, short-selling is done as follows: Suppose that Fidelity owns
shares in IBM and the hedge fund Short Capital wants to sell it short. Then
Short Capital borrows (via its broker) a share from Fidelity, promising to return
the share the next day. Short Capital then sells the share in the market for, say,
$100. The next day, the market price has dropped to $98, and Short Capital
buys the share back and returns it to Fidelity. (Of course, it will not be the exact
same share, but shares are fungible, so this does not matter.) In this example,
Short Capital made $2, profiting from the drop in the price of IBM. Fidelity is
no worse off than it would have been without lending the security, and, in fact,
they are better off too as they made a small loan fee as we discuss next.

The description above leaves out a few important details. First of all, when
Short Capital sells the IBM share, it does not get to pocket the $100 that the
sale raises; that is, Short Capital cannot use this money for other trades. Quite
to the contrary, Short Capital must leave this money with its broker and, furthermore, must leave some additional margin equity. Hence, short-selling does
not free up capital; it uses capital. The reason for this is that the security lender,
Fidelity in this example, needs to be ensured that it will get its share back.
Therefore, when Fidelity lends its share, it receives cash collateral in exchange.
If the security borrower does not return the share, Fidelity can use the cash
collateral to buy the share back in the market. To be able to buy the share back
even if it appreciated in value, Fidelity receives cash collateral that is higher
than the initial market value of IBM—and the extra cash corresponds to a margin requirement for Short Capital.

When Short Capital returns the IBM share, Fidelity returns that cash plus interest (at a rate called the rebate rate). If the interest rate is lower than the money market interest rate, then Fidelity earns a premium because it can invest the cash at a higher rate than it pays for it. Such a low interest rate translates into an implicit cost for Short Capital, which is called a "loan fee" (and sometimes it literally is a fee). Hence, short-selling is not exactly the opposite of buying because shorting is associated with a loan fee. However, for about 90% of the stocks in the United States, the loan fee is small, typically around 0.10–0.20% annualized. For the remaining 10% of hard-to-borrow stocks, the loan fee varies from about 1% annualized, to several percent, up to 50%, which would be an enormous loan fee.[1]

Loan fees are usually close to zero because the number of lendable shares is in principle infinite, as the same share can be re-used many times. As a result, the short interest can in principle be larger than the number of shares outstanding, although such a large short interest almost never arises in equity markets (but it regularly happens for U.S. Treasury bonds). To understand this, consider the example of Short Capital borrowing the share from Fidelity and selling it in the market. Suppose that a mutual fund run by Vanguard buys the share. Then Vanguard might lend the share to another hedge fund, which sells it short again. The share is then bought by another investor, who might in turn lend it, and so on. Regardless of how many times a share has been lent, it is always held by someone who could lend it again, so if everybody wants to earn a positive loan fee by lending and if there were no frictions in this process, the loan fee would be driven to zero. However, not all investors lend their shares, and there can be significant search frictions in this process, leading to positive loan fees sometimes.[2]

Shorting is not always possible. First of all, short-selling of shares is banned in some countries or banned for some stocks for some periods in others. For instance, many countries banned short-selling of financial stocks during the global financial crisis. Even if short-selling is legal, it requires that one can find a share to borrow. While this is usually the case, it isn't always possible—and it is usually particularly difficult when short sellers really want to do it. Indeed, the securities lending market is driven by its own supply and demand issues, so when the demand for borrowing shares is high relative to the supply of lendable shares, the loan fee rises and it becomes more difficult to locate the shares.

The potential difficulty in locating a share also means that short-selling is subject to a risk called "recall risk." Indeed, short sellers often want to keep

---

[1] The size of loan fees is studied by D'Avolio (2002) and Geczy, Musto, and Reed (2002).
[2] This process and the equilibrium loan fee are modeled by Duffie, Gârleanu, and Pedersen (2002).

their short position on for several days, weeks, or months. To do this, they often borrow the share for just one day and then "roll over" the securities loan each day, meaning that they keep extending the contract with the lender for another day after making mark-to-market adjustments. In some cases, they make a "term loan," meaning that they immediately agree to borrow the share for a longer period, say a week. In any event, the short seller often wants to keep her position on when the securities loan is due (e.g., because the stock price still has not gone down or has even gone up). The short seller then risks that the lender will not extend the stock loan and that it is difficult to find another share. In this case, the securities lender recalls the share—and, hence, the short seller faces recall risk. If the short seller does not send back the share that has been recalled, the lender can enforce a "buy in" by buying the share itself using the cash collateral.

When short sellers are forced to close their short positions, they are forced to buy the share back and, when many short sellers do this simultaneously, the stock price can be driven up—a "short squeeze." A short squeeze feeds on itself: As the buying drives the price up, more short sellers may be forced to close their positions as they cannot make their margin calls, leading to further buying, higher prices, and more margin calls.

There are two reasons why short sellers face margin calls when stock prices rise. First, their positions are marked to market each day, so if a stock price increases from $100 to $105, then short sellers must pay $5 per share shorted. Second, when prices move against a short seller, the dollar value of the position increases, leading to higher margin requirements (since margins are typically a fixed percentage of value). For instance, if the margin requirement is 20%, then margin requirement goes from $20 per share to $21 per share in the above example. In contrast, when prices move against an investor with a leveraged long position—i.e., prices drop—then the position size decreases. Hence, such a long investor faces a mark-to-market payment but a reduction in the margin requirement.

In addition to these "technical" reasons why short-selling can be difficult, short-selling is also difficult simply because it is less intuitive for most people and because it is up against the general headwind that stocks go up more often than they go down on average (i.e., the equity premium is positive). For instance, shorting a stock that goes up by less than the overall market is in principle a successful trade, but it may not feel that way. In other words, such a trade has positive alpha to the market and makes money if it is hedged, but it loses money if seen in isolation.

In summary, short-selling can be difficult as it requires locating a lendable share, it requires posting margin collateral, it is associated with a loan fee, and it evolves recall risk and funding liquidity risk (the risk that you run out of capital before the trade converges).

8.2. SHORT SALE FRICTIONS MEAN
THAT COMPANIES CAN BE OVERVALUED

Dedicated short bias managers sell short to profit from stocks being overvalued. If short sellers could do so without all the costs and risks discussed above, the market clearing price would incorporate both the views of pessimists and optimists, thus reflecting more information. The difficulties in shorting, however, make it harder to express negative views, opening the potential for stocks to be overvalued in an efficiently inefficient way.

To understand the effect of short sale frictions, suppose that people have different opinions about a stock: Some are very optimistic, and others are skeptical. If short-selling is difficult, the skeptics will simply have a zero position in the stock, focusing their investments on other stocks. The optimists will naturally buy the stock, pushing up the price (especially if they ignore that there might be skeptics with negative views that are not being reflected in the price). Hence, the market price could end up being too high relative to the average view of the company's fundamentals. Furthermore, a too-high current price means that future returns will be low.

This process of stock price overvaluation can be significantly amplified when investors start to speculate in the future forecasts of other investors, rather than focusing on the company's fundamentals. The phenomenon of investors focusing on forecasting the forecast of others is called the "Keynesian Beauty Contest" because of the following quote:

> ... professional investment may be likened to those newspaper competitions in which the competitors have to pick out the six prettiest faces from a hundred photographs, the prize being awarded to the competitor whose choice most nearly corresponds to the average preferences of the competitors as a whole; so that each competitor has to pick, not those faces which he himself finds prettiest, but those which he thinks likeliest to catch the fancy of the other competitors, all of whom are looking at the problem from the same point of view. It is not a case of choosing those which, to the best of one's judgment, are really the prettiest, nor even those which average opinion genuinely thinks the prettiest. We have reached the third degree where we devote our intelligences to anticipating what average opinion expects the average opinion to be. And there are some, I believe, who practice the fourth, fifth and higher degrees.
>
> —John Maynard Keynes (1936)

The idea is that investors focus on what the stock price will be tomorrow—driven by the average opinion of buyers tomorrow—rather than the long-term intrinsic value of the stock. Focusing on the opinions of future buyers could still lead to an efficient market since the future buyers should also care about the fundamentals (as should the buyers even further into the future to whom they will eventually sell). However, Keynes's point is that the process can go off track when investors ignore fundamentals and buy a stock simply based on the view that others will drive the price higher. This process could be self-fulfilling as long as every fool can sell to a greater fool, but eventually this process must come to an end as stock prices revert to fundamentals. Let us see how in a specific example.

Speculative Bubbles: An Example

Consider the market for stock A, a cyclical firm that depends on the macro environment. All investors agree that, next year, it is equally likely to be a boom or a recession. There exist two types of investors, type 1 and type 2, who differ in their views on how cyclical the stock really is. Type 1 investors believe that the company will be worth 80 in a recession and 120 in a boom. Given that these are equally likely, they value the stock at 100 (ignoring risk premiums).

Type 2 investors believe that the stock is more cyclical. They think that the value in a recession will be only 60, but the value in boom will reach 140. Given that these scenarios are equally likely, type 2 investors also value the stock at 100.

Suppose that short-selling is impossible and that the price is always set by the most optimistic investors. What is the current price? Given that all investors agree that the intrinsic value is 100, this would seem the obvious guess. However, let's first consider what the price will be next year.

In a recession, type 1 investors will be most optimistic about the firm; they will buy the stock and drive the price to 80. In a boom, type 2 investors are the most optimistic and the price will be 140. Given that a recession and boom are equally likely, the current price will be $(80 + 140)/2 = 110$. Hence, all investors are willing to pay 110, more than the 100 that everyone agrees the stock is worth! For instance, type 1 investors might think that in a recession the stock is worth 80 and, in a boom, I can sell the stock to the type 2 investors, who will overvalue it at 140. Both types of investors expect to sell to a greater fool in some scenario. The resulting speculative bubble of 10% in this example could be significantly higher if we considered the dynamics over many time periods, not just 1 year, so that investors would forecast higher degrees of others' forecasts.[3]

---

[3] Miller (1977) discusses how short sale frictions can lead to overvaluation, and Harrison and Kreps (1978) model the speculative dynamics.

Loan Fees and Stock Valuation in an Efficiently Inefficient Market

The overvaluation in the example above was driven by the combination of short sales being impossible and speculative behavior. In practice, short-selling is in fact possible in most countries, but there are costs and frictions associated with short-selling, as we have discussed. Limited short-selling creates an extra supply of shares that can reduce bubbles, mitigating the bubble effects discussed earlier.

However, the short-selling cost also has a surprising effect: The short seller's cost of borrowing a share is a source of *income* for the optimistic owner of the stock who lends it out. The owner may therefore be willing to pay more for the stock in reflection of this securities-lending income than he would have if everything else were equal. In other words, capitalizing the loan fee can contribute to the higher stock prices—and the high stock price contributes to short sellers' willingness to pay a loan fee. Hence, as short interest builds up in stocks with significant divergence of opinions, prices and loan fees may suddenly become very high, but eventually loan fees come down as shorting demand has been satisfied and prices revert toward fundamentals.[4]

Evidence on the Return of Highly Shorted Stocks

There exists significant evidence that stocks can become overvalued and that a high demand for short-selling is associated with low subsequent returns for the stock. Stocks with high short interest (i.e., with a high number of shares currently being shorted) have low subsequent return.[5] Furthermore, stocks with high lending fees have low future returns—both the gross returns that abstract from the loan fee and even the return net of the loan fee. This is especially so when the high loan fee is driven by an increase in the demand for shorting. Cohen, Diether, and Malloy (2007) find that an increase in shorting demand is associated with a 3% negative abnormal return for the stock in the following month, consistent with the idea that short sellers can identify overvalued stocks, which subsequently fall in price.[6]

There is also evidence that short sellers can identify misbehavior by firms, for instance, the short interest rises around negative fundamental events, such as SEC enforcement actions for earnings manipulation and earnings restatements that lead to shareholder lawsuits.[7]

---

[4] For the equilibrium price and loan fee with speculation, see Duffie, Gârleanu, and Pedersen (2002).

[5] Desai, Ramesh, Thiagarajan, and Balachandran (2002).

[6] See also Jones and Lamont (2002).

[7] Dechow, Sloan, and Sweeney (1996) and Griffin (2003).

8.3. FIRMS VS. SHORT SELLERS: IS SHORT-SELLING GOOD OR BAD FOR SOCIETY?

Management in many companies does not like to have their shares shorted. They feel that it is a vote of no confidence, and they are afraid that short sellers will drive down the stock price. Managers sometimes try to fight short sellers in various ways. For instance, they may take actions to make shorting difficult such as stock splits or distributions specifically designed to disrupt short-selling or try to coordinate with shareholders to withdraw shares from the stock lending market. Sometimes managers even accuse short sellers of crimes, suing them or requesting that the authorities investigate their activities.

For instance, when David Einhorn (who runs the hedge fund Greenlight Capital) criticized Lehman Brothers for covering the full extent of its troubles before the failure in 2008, Lehman fought back:[8]

> For the last several weeks, Lehman has been complaining about short sellers. When management teams do that, it is a sign that management is attempting to distract investors from serious problems.
>
> —David Einhorn

Policy makers and the general public also sometimes want to fight short sellers:

> Policymakers and the general public seem to have an instinctive reaction that short selling is morally wrong. Short selling has been characterized as inhuman, un-American, and against God (Proverbs 24:17: "Do not rejoice when your enemy falls, and do not let your heart be glad when he stumbles"). Hostility against short selling is not limited to the United States. In 1995, the Finance Ministry in Malaysia proposed mandatory caning as the punishment for short sellers.
>
> —Lamont (2012)

Lamont (2012) further documents how the U.S. Congress held hearings in 1989 on the problems with short-selling, during which a representative described short-selling as "blatant thuggery." During the hearings, however, an SEC official testified that

> many of the complaints we receive about alleged illegal short selling come from companies and corporate officers who are themselves under investigation by the Commission or others for possible violations of the securities or other laws.
>
> —Ketchum and Sturc (1989)

---

[8] See Mallaby (2010), p. 352.

During the hearings, officials from three firms testified against short sellers, and, paradoxically, their testimony provided evidence to the general point by the SEC official. Indeed, after their testimonies, the presidents of two of these three firms were prosecuted for fraud (for the third firm, the SEC determined that the company had made materially false and misleading statements but that the evidence was insufficient to prosecute).

Many people forget that there are significant benefits of short-selling. First of all, short-selling can make a market more efficient by allowing both positive and negative opinions to be expressed in the market. When your grandmother buys a stock, who protects her from buying a worthless piece of paper marketed by a malicious firm? Who helps ensure that the price she pays corresponds to the aggregate view of what the stock is expected to be worth? Well, this is what an efficient market is supposed to ensure, but a market does not become efficient by itself—investors need to be able to trade on their insights, positive and negative.

> To enjoy the advantages of a free market, one must have both buyers and sellers, both bulls and bears. A market without bears would be like a nation without free press. There would be no one to criticize and restrain the false optimism that always leads to disaster.
> —Bernard Baruch, testimony before the Committee on Rules, House of Representatives, 1917

Furthermore, short-selling comes with other benefits. It allows hedging. It makes markets far more liquid, reducing investors' transaction costs. Short-selling makes markets more liquid by making market prices more informative, by increasing turnover, and by allowing market makers to provide liquidity on both sides of the market while hedging their risks.

Hence, overall allowing short-selling is clearly the right decision as short-selling is for the better. Does this mean that short-selling can never be associated with misbehavior? Of course not. If short sellers are trying to manipulate the market, this is clearly wrong and illegal, but price manipulation is wrong and illegal both when traders are buying and when they are short-selling—so this is not specific to short-selling (e.g., "pump and dump" is price manipulation on the long side). A particular regulatory concern is that bears short-sell a stock in order to push the price down and that the low price itself will kill the firm—i.e., short-selling kills a firm that would otherwise be in good shape. For instance, a low stock price could make it more difficult to issue shares or borrow. This concern is particularly relevant for bank stocks where the idea is that short-selling drives down the price, and this result creates a run on the bank, eventually leading to real troubles for the bank. While this concern may occasionally have some relevance, there is little evidence for this mechanism, and, at best, it would imply a temporary short sale ban of financial stocks during severe crisis, as has been implemented in several countries. That said, such stories are often used in connection with scapegoating short sellers.

Some investors in a stock are also annoyed with short sellers and may decide not to lend their shares. This decision is often irrational. When an investor lends his share to a short seller, the share is sold in the market, which could drive down the price, but, when the share is returned to the lender, it must be bought back, which could drive up the price. Hence, for a long-term investor, the argument cannot be that shorting drives down the price, for this is at most a temporary effect. Also, the argument cannot be that the short sellers discover negative facts about the stock because this information will come out sooner or later anyway, and it should be better for the value of the stock to stop the management's misbehavior early rather than late. If the investor thinks that the short sellers are right, maybe she should sell her shares rather than holding them without lending them out. Furthermore, not lending the shares means that the investor does not earn the loan fees.

In conclusion, short sellers take the difficult side of making markets efficient, going against conventions, against the upbeat pitches of firms and equity analysts, against the headwind of the equity premium, and against the loan fees. They contribute to price discovery and help society allocate capital to the most productive firms.

8.4. CASE STUDY: ENRON

Enron Corporation was an apparently highly successful energy and commodities company, which *Fortune* magazine named "America's Most Innovative Company" each year from 1996 to 2000. Enron employed approximately 20,000 people, and its market capitalization reached $60 billion, about 70 times its earnings, in the beginning of 2001. On December 2, 2001, however, Enron went into bankruptcy, causing a major scandal. The scandal was not caught by Enron's auditor, Arthur Andersen, and the scandal ultimately led to the dissolution of one of the world's five largest accounting firms. The short seller James Chanos became famous for spotting early the issues with Enron. Here, we hear his version of the Enron story (from his statement to the U.S. Securities and Exchange Commission, May 15, 2003), and we will hear more from him in the interview in the next section.

My involvement with Enron began normally enough. In October of 2000, a friend asked me if I had seen an interesting article in the *Texas Wall Street Journal*, which is a regional edition, about accounting practices at large energy trading firms. The article, written by Jonathan Weil, pointed out that many of these firms, including Enron, employed the so-called "gain-on-sale" accounting method for their long-term energy trades. Basically, "gain-on-sale" accounting allows a company to estimate the future profitability of a trade made today and book a profit today based on the present value of those estimated future profits.

Our interest in Enron and other energy trading companies was piqued because our experience with companies that have used this accounting method has been that management's temptation to be overly aggressive in making assumptions about the future was too great for them to ignore. In effect, "earnings" could be created out of thin air if management was willing to push the envelope by using highly favorable assumptions. However, if these future assumptions did not come to pass, previously booked "earnings" would have to be adjusted downward. If this happened, as it often did, companies wholly reliant on "gain-on-sale" accounting would simply do new and bigger deals—with a larger immediate "earnings" impact—to offset those downward revisions. Once a company got on such an accounting treadmill, it was hard for it to get off.

The first Enron document my firm analyzed was its 1999 Form 10-K filing, which it had filed with the SEC. What immediately struck us was that despite using the "gain-on-sale" model, Enron's return on capital, a widely used measure of profitability, was a paltry 7 percent before taxes. That is, for every dollar in outside capital that Enron employed, it earned about seven cents. This is important for two reasons; first, we viewed Enron as a trading company that was akin to an "energy hedge fund." For this type of firm, a 7 percent return on capital seemed abysmally low, particularly given its market dominance and accounting methods. Second, it was our view that Enron's cost of capital was likely in excess of 7 percent and probably closer to 9 percent, which meant from an economic point of view, that Enron wasn't really earning any money at all, despite reporting "profits" to its shareholders. This mismatch of Enron's cost of capital and its return on investment became the cornerstone for our bearish view on Enron and we began shorting Enron common stock in November of 2000 for our clients.

We were also troubled by Enron's cryptic disclosure regarding various "related party transactions" described in its 1999 Form 10-K, as well as the quarterly Form 10-Qs it filed with the SEC in 2000 for its March, June and September quarters. We read the footnotes in Enron's financial statements about these transactions over and over again and we could not decipher what impact they had on Enron's overall financial condition. It did seem strange to us, however, that Enron had organized these entities for the apparent purpose of trading with their parent company, and that they were run by an Enron executive. Another disturbing factor in our review of Enron's situation was what we perceived to be the large amount of insider selling of Enron stock by Enron's senior executives. While not damning by itself, such selling in conjunction with our other financial concerns added to our conviction.

Finally, we were puzzled by Enron's and its supporters' boasts in late 2000 regarding the company's initiative in the telecommunications field, particularly in the trading of broadband capacity. Enron waxed eloquent about a huge, untapped market in such capacity and told analysts that the present value of Enron's opportunity in that market could be $20 to $30 per share of Enron stock. These statements were troubling to us, because our portfolio already contained a number of short ideas in the telecommunications and broadband area based on the snowballing glut of capacity that was developing in that industry. By late 2000, the stocks of companies in this industry had fallen precipitously, yet Enron and its executives seemed oblivious to this fact. And, despite the obvious bear market in pricing for telecommunications capacity and services, Enron still saw huge upside in the valuation of its own assets in this very same market, an ominous portent.

Beginning in January 2001, we spoke with a number of analysts at various Wall Street firms to discuss Enron and its valuation. We were struck by how many of them conceded that there was no way to analyze Enron, but that investing in Enron was instead a "trust me" story. One analyst, while admitting that Enron was a "black box" regarding profits, said that, as long as Enron delivered, who was he to argue.

In the spring of 2001, we heard reports, later confirmed by Enron, that a number of senior executives were departing from the company. Further, the insider selling of Enron stock continued unabated. Finally, our analysis of Enron's 2000 Form 10-K and March 2001 Form 10-Q filings continued to show low returns on capital as well as a number of one-time gains that boosted Enron's earnings. These filings also reflected Enron's continuing participation in various "related party transactions" that we found difficult to understand despite the more detailed disclosure Enron had provided. These observations strengthened our conviction that the market was still over-pricing Enron's stock.

In the summer of 2001, energy and power prices, specifically natural gas and electricity, began to drop. Rumors surfaced routinely on Wall Street that Enron had been caught "long" in the power market and that it was being forced to move aggressively to reduce its exposure in a declining market. It is an axiom in securities trading that no matter how well "hedged" a firm claims to be, trading operations always seem to do better in bull markets and to struggle in bear markets. We believe that the power market had entered a bear phase at just the wrong moment for Enron.

Also in the summer of 2001, stories began circulating in the marketplace about Enron's affiliated partnerships and how Enron's stock price itself was important to Enron's financial well-being. In effect, traders were saying that Enron's dropping stock price could create a cash-flow squeeze at the company because of certain provisions and agreements that it had entered into with affiliated partnerships. These stories gained some credibility as Enron disclosed more information about these partnerships in its June 2001 Form 10-Q, which it filed in August of 2001.

To us, however, the most important story in August of 2001 was the abrupt resignation of Enron's CEO, Jeff Skilling, for "personal reasons." In our experience, there is no louder alarm bell in a controversial company than the unexplained, sudden departure of a chief executive officer no matter what "official" reason is given. Because we viewed Skilling as the architect of the present Enron, his abrupt departure was the most ominous development yet. Kynikos Associates increased its portfolio's short position in Enron shares following this disclosure.

The effort we devoted to looking behind the numbers at Enron, and the actions we ultimately took based upon our research and analysis, show how we deliver value to our investors and, ultimately, to the market as a whole. Short sellers are the professional skeptics who look past the hype to gauge the true value of a stock.

8.5. INTERVIEW WITH JAMES CHANOS OF KYNIKOS ASSOCIATES

Jim Chanos is the founder and managing partner of Kynikos Associates LP, the world's largest exclusive short-selling investment firm. Chanos opened Kynikos Associates LP in 1985 to implement investment strategies he had uncovered while beginning his Wall Street career as a financial analyst with Paine Webber, Gilford Securities, and Deutsche Bank. His celebrated short sale of Enron shares was dubbed by Barron's "the market call of the decade, if not the past fifty years." Chanos received his BA in economics and political science in 1980 from Yale University.

LHP: *How did you get started as a short seller?*

JC: One of the first big companies I looked at as a securities analyst was Baldwin United. It was really more a matter of chance that I was asked to look at that company by my boss, and that we stumbled upon what ultimately proved to be a big fraud.

LHP: *So following on this successful call, you decided to focus on the short side?*

JC: Yes, because I felt that one of the lessons of that episode was that it's very difficult to do the research on overvalued firms, so not many people do it, but there was value added. Many people contacted us after Baldwin to get our research, so I felt that there was an unserved part of the marketplace.

LHP: *Can you tell me about your investment process?*

JC: We have a different approach than most hedge funds. Most hedge funds have an approach where the portfolio manager is at the top and a group of junior analysts are below. The typical model is that the portfolio manager pressures the junior analysts to go get ideas, bring them in, process them, and show them to the portfolio manager, who will pick and choose. We don't like that business model because it puts a lot of responsibility at the junior level and, if something goes wrong, the junior person does not have an incentive to pass on the relevant information.

Here, the senior partners, particularly myself and two other heads of research, are the ones who first come up with the ideas. We then send the idea down to our staff for processing and a recommendation. The recommendation could be "It looks like a good short," but most of the time, it is "No, there is an explanation to what you thought was happening—it's all okay." This is a better business model because it puts the economic ownership and the intellectual ownership up at the same level—at the top.

LHP: *What are the steps from an idea to knowing that you should short this?*
JC: There's a whole process. The first step is: Can we borrow the shares? Because if you can't borrow the shares, you can't do the trade.

Assuming we can borrow the stock, then we start with the bull case: Why do people like this company? We assign the stock to the appropriate analyst who will then begin talking to sell-side analysts, get all the research reports that are out on the company, and begin to understand the story, as much as he or she can. At the same time, we begin looking at the financials, breaking out comparable companies in the same industry. And after a week or two, we'll prepare an internal memo that lays out why it is a good short or not.

When we have formed a hypothesis, we talk to the bulls and ask them to debunk it. We will have them in here for lunch, and sometimes we'll have our story up on the white board. "Here's why we're negative on China. Where are we wrong? Where do you see that we're wrong?" Finally, after a few weeks of the initial idea, the senior partners discuss the case and make a decision.

LHP: *And are there some key numbers that you focus on?*
JC: Yes, but we're a little leery of any one number because companies can game numbers. But it's hard to fudge return on capital, where you look at operating income to total net business assets. If a company is showing a declining return on capital, usually something is going wrong. Or a very low return on capital with high growth, like Enron was.

LHP: *What about insider selling and departures?*
JC: Yes, we are always looking at those, and if you see both, you've really got a red flag.

LHP: *Are there other red flags?*
JC: If you can't understand the disclosures, usually there's a reason for that. If you read a company's 10-K two or three times and are still not able to figure out how they make money, there's a reason for that. They're trying to intentionally not tell you—keep it obfuscated. So the nature of a company's disclosure is also important to us.

LHP: *Do you rely on red flags or can you usually find a smoking gun?*

JC: Well, you can't always get a smoking gun. And that's the problem. I mean taking a position in the market is not a criminal court of law, so it's not based on evidence "beyond a shadow of a doubt." The market is more like a civic court, based on the "preponderance of evidence." Often you don't see the smoking gun even in the best shorts, until very much at the end. To use the Enron example, we had a pattern of a lot of questionable things, but we did not think it was a fraud.

LHP: *I heard that you don't tend to visit companies, hire detectives, or talk to ex-employees.*

JC: Yes. Well, first of all, we don't tend to visit companies because we're not going to be invited. People know who we are. But when we need information from a company, it's not that hard to get. Companies do conference calls. We do have good relationships with the sell-side brokers, so that if we have a question about a number, we can usually get it answered. Furthermore, access to management is one of the most overrated things you have, in that if management is telling you something that they're not telling anyone else, they're breaking the law, under Regulation FD [Fair Disclosure]. The management is just going to tell you the same exact story they tell every other investor, which is in every bullish research report and in every presentation on their website. Further, you get a false sense of security—if the CEO is telling it to you, so therefore it must be true. That's number one.

Number two, in terms of talking to ex-employees and hiring private detectives—we think that gets into a real grey area. Again, even ex-employees can have fiduciary responsibilities to their company. So having an ex-employee tell you corporate secrets is probably a violation of securities law. We stay as far away as possible from anything that could be material non-public information.

LHP: *What about talking to competitors?*

JC: Yes, we do sometimes talk to competitors and industry people to get a sense of how the businesses work and industry trends.

LHP: *How do you know whether the negative information is already reflected in the price?*

JC: Well, that's a really good question. How much negative information is already out there? Is it already reflected in the stock price? Is it time to cover your short, if all the negative news is out? We don't know; it's a judgment call.

LHP: *Can you give examples of some of the more memorable short sales that you did?*

JC: Obviously Enron was a story that put us on the map, and it was an interesting short story. I think that being short a number of the Drexel Burnham stocks back in the late eighties was also an interesting situation on the short side, including the junk bond companies Integrated Resources and First Executive. More recently, some of the real estate companies.

Our biggest loser was America Online, which we shorted in 1996, I think, and basically covered in 1998, when the stock was up eightfold. We shorted it because we believed that the company was not properly accounting for its marketing costs. It then took a big bath write-off in '96, and people said, "Okay. Everything must be fine." We simply pointed out that the big write-off meant that they were never profitable, and our view was that they probably never would be. But we underestimated the power of the Internet and the euphoria of retail investors, who just didn't care. And because it was an Internet stock and one of the Internet leaders, the stock just kept going up and up and up. Fortunately, it was never more than a one percent position for us. So we kept trimming it back, even as it kept doubling. But having said that, we probably lost five, six, seven percent over two years on the position. While not a disaster, certainly you never want to see a short go up eightfold against you. This trade underscores the risk of the short side, and it taught us a lesson on how to size positions in volatile stocks. You can never be too big in the volatile stocks; you need to have more names to diversify your risk.

LHP: *Can you talk about the difficulties of short-selling, and how you try to overcome them?*

JC: There are lots of difficulties to short-selling. I mean the market generally goes up. You have to borrow the share. You have less advantageous tax treatment. No one likes you. But all of them, I think, create the opportunity, that's the flip side.

LHP: *Do you think that the "mechanical" obstacles to short-selling or the behavioral ones are most important?*

JC: It's a great question because, when I first started doing this, I thought that being short would just be the mirror image of going long. I don't believe that anymore. I believe that there's a behavioral aspect of shorting that's very difficult for most people, and this is the most important effect.

Wall Street exists to sell securities to people. So most of the stuff you're going to hear all the time is positive. Buy recommendations. I come in every morning, and I check my BlackBerry. Of our 50 domestic stocks, probably 10 of them are going to be commented on that morning by someone, raising earnings estimates, going from "buy" to "strong buy," the CEO is on CNBC, there's a takeover rumor, or whatever it might be. Ninety-nine percent of the time, it's just noise with no new information, but it's a positive drumbeat.

When you're short, that drumbeat is negative reinforcement. You're coming in every day and being told, "You're wrong. You're wrong. You're wrong. You're wrong. This company's going to do well because of this, this, and this." And most people just say, "Life's too short. I don't need this. I don't want to hear this about my shorts every day. I'd rather be long and just hear the positive, happy things every day." Human beings are human beings. Even most hedge fund managers worry much more about their short positions, and some very, very good traditional long managers are terrible short sellers.

So I think that good short sellers are born, not made, quite frankly. I never used to think that. But I do think that now, after 30 years of doing this. That is, you have to have some mental makeup that allows you to just drown out that positive noise, disregard it, and just focus on your work, your facts, and your conclusions, based on that.

LHP: *So were you born in such a way that the positive hype is only making you want to short more?*

JC: I don't know about that. I mean there's a difference between drowning out noise and being stubborn. You want to be aware of what's being said, so that you're not missing something important—that one percent of the time where something has changed, and you need to know it and get out of the way. So you just don't dig in your heels.

LHP: *There is also the asymmetry that stocks can only drop to zero, but there's no limit to how far they can go up.*

JC: Yes, they can go up to infinity, but I've always said, "I've seen many more go to zero than infinity."

LHP: *Do you have only short positions in your fund?*

JC: We have two groups of funds. Our main institutional product is the short-only funds, and those are just pure short. We also have a small traditional long and short hedge fund, called the Kynikos Opportunity Fund.

LHP: *How do you manage risk and construct your portfolio?*

JC: At any given time, we have about 50 stocks, domestic or abroad. We size the positions based on volatility, based on borrow, and based on industry exposure. We construct a portfolio with an eye toward return and risk. And we have a rule that no one position can ever be more than five percent of the value of the fund. Plus, we're never leveraged. With 50 positions, the average position is two percent, a large position for us is three percent, and a small position is one percent. Even if we love a position, if it's going against us, we'll trim it back, like we did with America Online.

LHP: *Why do you think that people are often critical of short sellers?*

JC: Part of the reason is that there are a lot of misunderstandings about it. People start with the idea: How can you sell something you don't own? And then once you start down that path, it's much harder to get people to think about it, in the form of the marketplace. But then I point out to them that insurance is a giant short-selling scheme. Much of agriculture is a giant short-selling scheme. You're selling forward what you don't have yet, with the idea that you will replace it later at a profit. When an airline sells you an advance purchase ticket, they're short-selling you a seat. All kinds of business are done on a short sell basis, where you get money up front, and you get the goods or services later.

People often make the analogy that short-selling is like taking fire insurance out on someone else's house, but there is an important difference. The difference is that if you imagine a person taking insurance out on someone else's house, then you're making the next leap of faith that the person is going to commit arson. So, the analogy implies that a short seller is going to do something criminal to make the stock price go down—and that's the fallacy. Anybody, long or short, who knowingly spreads false stories about a company is guilty of securities fraud.

LHP: *Hearing about the actual people—like you—might help demystify short-selling.*

JC: That's one of the reasons why I've been more public than other short sellers. When you're anonymous, it's easy then for people to think the worst of you and to just extrapolate. But when you actually put a human face behind the story and say, "This is why we do this, and these are the kinds of companies we're looking for, and this is why it's important to the marketplace to have people with a negative viewpoint, as well as a positive viewpoint, so people can make their own decisions." I think then people understand it a lot easier. The marketplace is ultimately a reflection of information, and to limit people to only expressing positive views is crazy.

LHP: *So short sellers play the role of collecting information in the financial markets?*

JC: Exactly. Of the major financial frauds of the past 25 years, almost every single one of them has been uncovered by an internal whistle blower, a journalist, or a short seller. Not outside auditors. Not outside counsel. Not law enforcement. It's almost always someone who has a vested interest or a guilt complex internally. Short sellers help uncover important information.

CHAPTER 9

Quantitative Equity Investing

I think that good quant investment managers . . . can really be thought of as financial economists who have codified their beliefs into a repeatable process. They are distinguished by diversification, sticking to their process with discipline, and the ability to engineer portfolio characteristics.

—Cliff Asness (2007)

Quantitative equity investing—quant equity, for short—means model-driven equity investing, performed, for instance, by equity market neutral hedge funds. Quants codify their trading rules in computer systems and execute orders with algorithmic trading overseen by humans.

There are several advantages and disadvantages of quantitative investing relative to discretionary trading. The disadvantages are that the trading rule cannot be as tailored to each specific situation and it cannot be based on "soft" information such as phone calls and human judgment. These disadvantages may be diminishing as computing power and sophistication increase. For instance, quant models may analyze transcripts of a firm's conference calls with equity analysts using textual analysis, looking at whether certain words are being frequently used or doing more complex analysis.

The advantages of quantitative investing include, first, that it can be applied to a broad set of stocks, yielding significant diversification. When a quant has constructed an advanced investment model, this model can be simultaneously applied to thousands of stocks around the world. Second, the quant's modeling rigor may largely overcome the behavioral biases that often influence human judgment, perhaps those very biases that create the trading opportunities in the first place. Third, the quant's trading principles can be backtested using historical data. Quants view data and scientific methods as central to investing:

> We are misguided when we exalt ourselves by insisting that the psychology of the marketplace and of man are unknowable. The sciences of man are

now emerging from the Dark Ages. Economics and psychology stand today at Koestler's watershed just as astronomy did in the time of Tycho Brahe. Our superstition, blind belief, and ignorance are being swept away forever by the scientific accumulation and analysis of data. There will be predictability in the affairs of men.

—Thorp and Kassouf (1967)

Quantitative equity can be subdivided into three types of trades: fundamental quant, statistical arbitrage (stat arb), and high-frequency trading (HFT), as seen in table 9.1. These three types of quant investing differ along several dimensions, including their intellectual foundation, their turnover, their capacity, how trades are determined, and the extent to which they can be backtested.

Fundamental quantitative investing seeks to apply fundamental analysis—just like discretionary traders—but does so in a systematic way. Fundamental quant is therefore based on economic and finance theory along with statistical data analysis. Given that prices and fundamentals change only gradually, fundamental quant typically has a turnover of days to months and has a high capacity (meaning that a lot of money can be invested in the strategy) also due to significant diversification.

Stat arb seeks to exploit relative mispricings between closely related stocks. Hence, it is based on an understanding of arbitrage relations and statistics, and its turnover is typically faster than that of fundamental quants. Due to the faster trading (and perhaps fewer stocks with arbitrage spreads), stat arb has a smaller capacity.

TABLE 9.1. THREE TYPES OF QUANTITATIVE INVESTING

	Fundamental Quantitative Investing	Statistical Arbitrage	High-Frequency Trading
Based on	Economics, finance, statistics	Arbitrage relations, statistics	Statistics, engineering, information processing
Turnover	Days to months	Hours to days	Instances to hours
Capacity	Higher	In between	Lower
Who determines trade	Strategy	Strategy, but some orders may not be filled	Market
Backtest	Reliable	Transaction-cost estimate essential	Heisenberg uncertainty principle of finance

Finally, HFT is based on statistics, information processing, and engineering, as an HFT's success depends partly on the speed with which they can trade. HFTs focus on having superfast computers and computer programs and co-locating their computer at the exchanges, literally trying to get their computer as close as possible to the exchange server, using fast cables, etc. HFTs have the fastest turnover of their trades and naturally have the lowest capacity.

The three types of quants also differ in the way trades are determined: Fundamental quants typically determine their trades ex ante, stat arb traders determine their trades gradually, and HFTs let the market determine their trades. More specifically, a fundamental quant model identifies high-expected-return stocks and then buys them, almost always getting their orders filled; a stat arb model seeks to buy a mispriced stock but may terminate the trading scheme before completion if the prices have moved adversely; finally, an HFT model may submit limit orders to both buy and sell to several exchanges, letting the market determine which ones are being hit. This trading structure means that fundamental quant investing can be simulated via a backtest with some reliability; stat arb backtests rely heavily on assumptions on execution times, transaction costs, and fill rates; while HFT strategies are often difficult to simulate reliably so HFTs must also rely on experiments.

HFT is subject to what one could call the Heisenberg uncertainty principle of finance. In physics (quantum mechanics), the Heisenberg uncertainty principle states that there is a limit to the precision with which one can know a particle's position and momentum because the act of observing disturbs the particle. Analogously, one cannot simulate with precision the timing and price of execution of a limit order because the act of submitting the order changes the market dynamics.

9.1. FUNDAMENTAL QUANTITATIVE INVESTING

Fundamental quants trade on factors such as value, momentum, quality, size, and low risk. They use information similar to that used by discretionary traders, but they effectively try to "teach" a computer what a great equity analyst does and then apply this methodology across thousands of stocks around the world in a systematic manner.

Fundamental quant investing can be applied both in a long-only and long–short context. In fact, given that quant models often have views on all stocks in the investment universe, these views can be naturally applied in several contexts such as long–short market-neutral hedge fund strategies, 130/30 long-biased strategies, and long-only benchmark-driven strategies. The underlying building block is the same, namely the quantitative estimates of which stocks have high expected returns, which ones have low expected returns, and a risk model. The long–short hedge fund portfolios are often combinations of several "factors," meaning that long–short portfolios that are regularly rebalanced to bet on a specific phenomenon. At the same time, these factors are useful representations of which stocks have high vs. low expected returns and therefore are also useful for the other types of quant equity investing. We start by considering the value factor, which captures the return to quant-style value investing.

Value Investing, Quant Style

Quants perform value investing by systematically computing a measure related to a stock's fundamental value (the present value of future free cash flows) and comparing it to the stock's current market value. Quants then buy value stocks—those with high ratios of fundamental value to market value—and sell those with the opposite characteristics.

One might think that such a strategy only works if it is based on an extremely good measure of the fundamental value, one that contains more information than the market price. This intuition is not correct in general, though, which might be surprising. The reason is that prices depend not only on expected future cash flows but also on how these are discounted, that is, prices reflect expected returns. Said simply, value investing works because the price equals the expected cash flows divided by the expected return—so, flipping this equation around, the expected return is cash flows divided by price. Hence, value investing may work for any variable that can reasonably be used to normalize the price.

As a case in point, value investing has worked historically even for very simple measures of value such as a stock's book to market (*BM*), that is, the ratio of the book value of equity to the market value of equity.[1] Of course, the book value is a somewhat simplistic measure of the fundamental value with all the issues related to accounting variables (including that it is backward looking, not forward looking), but it nevertheless serves as a useful scaling variable for market values.

Based on variation in stock's expected returns, value stocks are likely to be those with high expected returns, which could either be driven by rational compensation for risk, by institutional frictions, or by behavioral reasons. Some economists (e.g., Keynes 1936, Shiller 1981, and Lakonishok, Shleifer, and Vishny 1994) have argued that stocks vary excessively, which creates opportunities for value investors:

---

[1] Studies of the relation between book to market and expected returns go back to Stattman (1980). An even simpler measure of value is the return over the past five years, where value stocks are taken to be those with a low past five-year return (De Bondt and Thaler 1985).

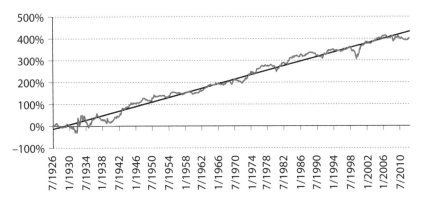

Figure 9.1. Cumulative performance of the value factor HML, 1926–2012.
The figure shows the cumulative sum (i.e., without compounding) of the long–short value factor HML constructed based on stocks' book-to-market ratios.

> day-to-day fluctuations in profits of existing investments, which are obviously of an ephemeral and nonsignificant character, tend to have an altogether excessive, and even absurd, influence on the market
>
> —John Maynard Keynes (1936)

Value investing has worked on average historically, as seen in figure 9.1, which plots the cumulative returns to the high-minus-low (HML) factor of Fama and French (1993). HML goes long on the 30% stocks with the highest book-to-market scores—i.e., the cheapest stocks by this measure—and shorts the 30% most expensive stocks.[2] By being balanced long and short, the return of HML captures the outperformance of cheap stocks relative to expensive stocks, thus eliminating any direct effect of overall market movements. Over this time period, HML has delivered an average excess return of 4.6% per year with an annual volatility of 12.3%, corresponding to a Sharpe ratio of 0.4.

Value investing also works based on other value measures such as earnings-to-price, dividends-to-price, and cash flows-to-price, and it can be refined further by considering the quality of a stock as discussed below.

Value strategies have also worked across regions and asset classes. Value strategies have worked in global stock markets, including in the United Kingdom, continental Europe, and Japan, and they have worked in other asset classes, such as commodities and currencies (Cutler, Poterba, and Summers

---

[2] Fama and French (1993) construct such long–short portfolios separately among small and large stocks, respectively, and then take the average of these two portfolios. This construction seeks to reduce size effects in the HML factor.

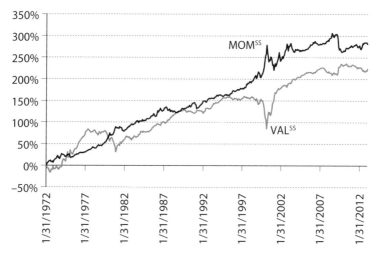

Figure 9.2. Performance of global value and momentum stock-selection strategies, 1972–2012.

The graphs show the cumulative sums of monthly returns of the value and momentum strategies across the United States, United Kingdom, continental Europe, and Japan (Asness, Moskowitz, and Pedersen 2013).

1991 and Asness, Moskowitz, and Pedersen 2013). Interestingly, value strategies in different regions and asset classes tend to be positively correlated, suggesting a common global systematic risk factor, which could be consistent with a risk-based explanation for value investing. As seen in figure 9.2, the returns to value investing are negatively correlated with another important quant equity strategy, namely momentum investing, which we discuss next.

Stock Momentum: Quant Catalysts

Momentum investing means buying recent winners and short-selling recent losers. Specifically, the strategy plotted in figure 9.2 considers each stock's performance over the most recent year (leaving out the most recent month, as discussed further below) and goes long on the stocks that had the highest returns while shorting those that had the lowest returns. As seen in the figure, momentum has worked quite well, historically producing an even higher return than value investing, at least before transaction costs.[3]

---

[3] Momentum profits were first documented by Jegadeesh and Titman (1993) and Asness (1994). Theories of initial underreaction and delayed overreaction have been proposed by Barberis, Shleifer, and Vishny (1998), Daniel, Hirshleifer, and Subrahmanyam (1998), and Hong and Stein (1999). For more on the relation to catalysts, see the interview with Cliff Asness in this chapter.

The strong performance of momentum investing means that stocks that have been outperforming over the past 12 months tend to continue to outperform over the following month. It is hard to justify momentum with a rational risk premium because the high turnover of momentum would imply that a stock's risk characteristics should quickly and frequently change. Perhaps a more appealing story is that stocks exhibit an initial underreaction to news and then perhaps a delayed overreaction. It may be surprising that both underreaction and overreaction can drive momentum profits, but here is why: First, good news today leads to a price increase today, but, if price initially underreacts, then the price must continue to go up in the future—i.e., producing momentum. Second, if prices have been going up for a while and investors start to jump on the bandwagon leading to a delayed overreaction, then this further adds to the momentum.

Another way to conceptualize the momentum is to think of it as a quant measure of equity catalysts. Recall, as discussed in chapter 7, that discretionary equity investors are often looking for stocks that have value plus a catalyst, meaning cheap stocks where the market is about to recognize their potential. Such a catalyst can make the value bet pay off quickly as the stock price rises, rather than the equity analyst having to wait for his profit until the company actually delivers on its potential with all the risks that comes with waiting. High-momentum stocks are stocks that have been outperforming and, therefore, may be increasingly popular among investors. Combining value and momentum investing is a powerful cocktail since these strategies are negatively correlated and, therefore, the combination delivers higher risk-adjusted returns than either one does alone. A stock that has favorable value and momentum characteristics is a cheap stock on the rise, which has a better chance of continuing its trend than an average momentum stock (because it is still cheap) and a better a chance of delivering on its value (because potential investors are starting to recognize it).

Quality Investing: Systematizing Graham and Dodd

Just as momentum investing is a natural complement to value investing, so is quality investing (but for a different reason). Quality investing is the strategy of buying high-quality stocks. High-quality stocks can be defined as stocks that are profitable, growing, stable, and well managed, as discussed in section 7.2. Different investors might have different views of each of these quality components, but considering a variety of such quality measures, Asness, Frazzini, and Pedersen (2013) find that quality factors have delivered positive excess returns on average for both U.S. and global stocks and for both small and large stocks.

Quality investing buys "good" stocks that deserve a higher-than-normal price (or price-to-book ratio) and short-sells "bad" stocks that deserve to be cheap. In contrast, simple value factors short-sell the expensive stocks (whether or not the expensiveness is justified by the stocks' quality characteristics) and buys the cheap ones (whether or not they deserve to be cheap). Hence, quality investing complements simple value investing and, indeed, quant value and quality factors tend to be negatively correlated.

Combining value and quality factors gives rise to a strategy that can be called "quality at a reasonable price," which has higher risk-adjusted returns than each component alone. Combining quality, value, and momentum yields an even stronger strategy that buys upward-trending stocks that are cheap relative to their quality and shorts falling stocks that are expensive.

Betting against Beta and Low-Risk Investing

The classic capital asset pricing model (CAPM) says that a security's expected excess return should be proportional to its beta, $E(r_t^i - r^f) = \beta^i E(r_t^M - r^f)$. Hence, if stock A has a beta of 0.7 and stock B has twice the beta of 1.4, then stock B should have twice the excess return on average. However, the CAPM does not hold empirically as the average returns of low-beta stocks is almost as high as the average return of high-beta stocks. In the lingo of the CAPM, the security market line (SML) is too flat empirically, as seen in figure 9.3.

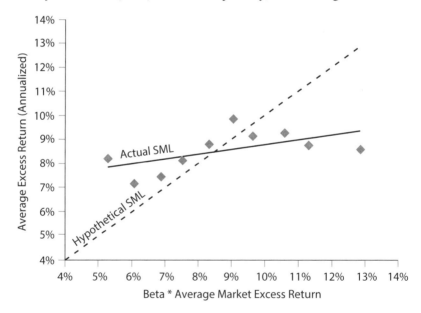

Figure 9.3. The security market line is too flat relative to the CAPM.

The figure plots ten dots corresponding to ten U.S. stock portfolios sorted by their ex ante beta, 1926 to 2010. The horizontal axis shows the CAPM-predicted return for each portfolio, i.e., its ex post realized beta multiplied by the market risk premium, $\beta^i E(r_t^M - r^f)$. The vertical axis plots each portfolio's actual average excess returns, corresponding to $E(r_t^i - r^f)$. The 45-degree line is the hypothetical SML implied by the CAPM.

What should you do if the data do not fit the theory? Reject the theory or exploit that the financial market doesn't behave as it "should." But how could you exploit the flat security market line? Well, the safe stocks are the ones that have high returns compared to what the CAPM says they should. Said differently, the safe stocks have positive alpha and the risky stocks have negative alpha.

So, you should probably buy the safe stocks and short-sell the risky ones. Does that make money? No, not if you buy $1 of safe stocks and short $1 of risky ones. As seen in figure 9.3, the five portfolios with the riskiest stocks have slightly higher average returns than the five safest portfolios. However, buying safe stocks and shorting risky ones also would not be a market-neutral portfolio because, by construction, the long side is much safer than the short side.

To have a market-neutral portfolio, you need to buy about $1.4 worth of safe (i.e., low-beta) stocks and short-sell $0.7 worth of risky (high-beta) stocks. This portfolio *does* make money because it exploits the fact that, while safe and risky stocks have similar average returns, the safe stocks have significantly higher Sharpe ratios. This portfolio exploits the differences in Sharpe ratios by leveraging the safe shorts and deleveraging the risky ones so that both the long and short sides of the portfolio have a beta of 1. The portfolio is called a "betting against beta" (BAB) factor. The BAB factor for U.S. stocks has realized a Sharpe ratio of 0.78, as seen in figure 9.4. As also seen in the figure, the BAB factor has had positive performance in most global stock markets as well as in the credit markets, bond markets, and futures markets.

One reason that low-risk investing has worked is that many investors face leverage constraints or are simply afraid of the risks that comes with leverage. Therefore, investors looking to pick up a higher return might buy risky securities rather than applying leverage to a portfolio of safe securities. This behavior pushes up the prices of risky stocks—and high prices mean low returns. This behavior simultaneously lowers the demand for safe stocks, lowering their prices and increasing their expected returns. Hence, a modified CAPM equilibrium arises in which the security market line is flatter due to leverage-constrained investors buying the risky stocks while less constrained investors leverage the safer stocks. This BAB theory can therefore explain why mutual funds and individual investors (who might be leverage constrained or averse) hold stocks with betas above one on average while Warren Buffett and leveraged buyout (LBO) investors apply leverage to safer stocks on average.[4]

There are also several other forms of low-risk investing. Some long-only investors buy safe stocks without shorting risky stocks. This method should

---

[4] The flat security market line was first documented by Black, Jensen, and Scholes (1972). The idea that leverage constraints can explain this phenomenon was pioneered by Black (1972, 1992) and extended by Frazzini and Pedersen (2014), who found evidence in several asset classes and in the portfolios of mutual funds, individuals, Warren Buffett, and LBO deals. Asness, Frazzini, and Pedersen (2014) studied BAB factors within and across industries. Clarke, de Silva, and Thorley (2013) consider other forms of low-risk investment.

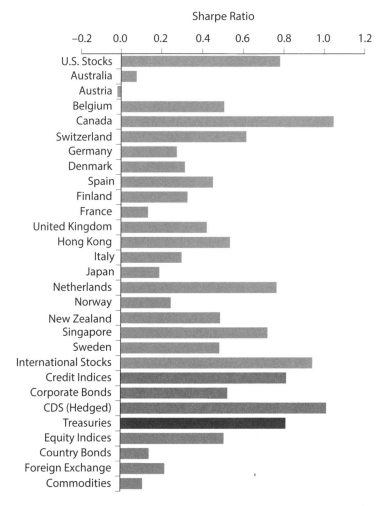

Figure 9.4. Sharpe ratios of betting against beta portfolios.
Source: Frazzini and Pedersen (2014).

earn an average return just below the overall market return with a significantly lower risk, thus realizing a higher Sharpe ratio. Rather than focusing on low-beta stocks, other investors focus on stocks with low total volatility, low idiosyncratic volatility, low earnings volatility, high-quality stocks, or seek to construct the minimum-variance portfolio.

A low-risk portfolio constructed without regard to industries or sectors tends to overweight stocks in non-cyclical industries such as utilities, retail, or tobacco stocks. However, these industry bets are not the main reason that low-risk investing works. In fact, low-risk investing has historically worked both for investing across and within industries. Figure 9.5 shows BAB factors

Sharpe Ratio

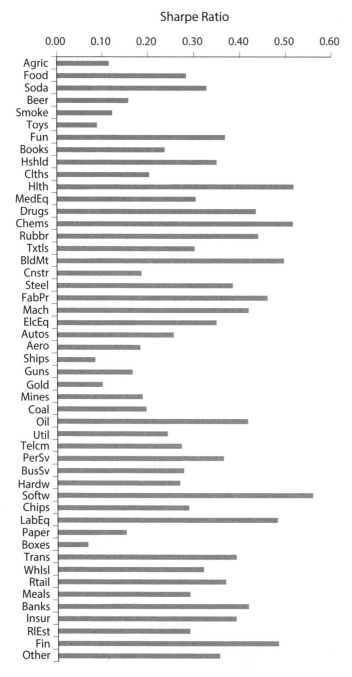

Figure 9.5. Betting against beta strategies within each U.S. industry, 1926–2012.
Each bar plots the Sharpe ratio of a BAB strategy within an industry.
Source: The data are based on Asness, Frazzini, and Pedersen (2014).

constructed within each industry in the United States. For example, the BAB factor for utility stocks goes long on a leveraged portfolio of the safer utility stocks while shorting the riskier utility stocks. Remarkably, low-risk investing has worked within each industry in the United States.

Quant Portfolio Construction

Quants apply their models across hundreds or even thousands of stocks. This diversification eliminates most of the idiosyncratic risk, meaning that firm-specific surprises tend to wash out at the overall portfolio level and any single position is too small to make a significant dent in the performance.

By being equally long and short, an equity market neutral quant portfolio also eliminates the overall stock market risk. Some quants try to achieve market neutrality by making sure that the dollar exposure on the long side equals the dollar value of all the short positions. However, this method only works if the longs and shorts are equally risky. Hence, quants also try to balance to market beta of the long and the short side. Some quants try to be both dollar neutral and beta neutral.

Quants also often eliminate (some) industry risk. For each industry, they may go long on the "good" stocks in the industry while shorting the "bad" ones, thus being neutral to the overall movement in the industry. For instance, figure 9.5 shows the performance of industry-neutral BAB factors, which can be combined into an overall industry-neutral factor. This industry-neutral portfolio construction can create a higher Sharpe ratio for two reasons. First, it eliminates industry risk. Second, it may pick "good" stocks more accurately because the portfolio is constructed by comparing industry peers, which is often a more meaningful comparison. If a factor also works for selecting industries—as momentum does, for instance—then quants may both bet on within-industry momentum and across-industry momentum, controlling the amount of risk arising from each bet.

When a quant has eliminated (most of) the idiosyncratic risk, market risk, and industry risk, then what risk is left? No risk at all? Surely not. The risks that are left are the risks associated with the factors that the quant wants to bet on. If a quant is betting on value, for instance, her portfolio risk is that the value factor performs poorly. A value-based portfolio loses if cheap stocks get cheaper and expensive stocks get more expensive or if the "cheap" stocks turn out not to be cheap relative to their deteriorating fundamentals. Hence, like all leveraged investors, quants face the risk of a liquidity spiral like the one that happened in the 2007 quant event, as we discuss later.

While we have discussed the general tricks of quant investing, there are many differences in the specifics of quant portfolio construction. Some quants seek to control the volatility of their portfolios, whereas others keep a constant notional exposure. Some try to tactically time which factors are more likely to work at any time, and others keep a constant weight on each factor. Quants also differ in how they get from each stock's signal to its weight in the portfolio. Academic factors traded only on paper often buy the top 10% stocks with the most favorable characteristics while shorting the bottom 10%, rebalancing the paper portfolio each month. This strategy leads to a large turnover and is therefore rarely used in practice. Quants try to estimate the relation between the signal value and the expected return and construct the portfolio and the rebalancing strategy that maximizes performance after transaction costs.

The Quant Event of 2007

In August 2007, a major event played out for quant equity strategies, although the event was largely hidden to outsiders. To "see" the event, one must look through the lens of a typical quant's diversified long–short portfolio at a high frequency.[5] I experienced the dramatic event first hand as discussed in the preface.

In June and July 2007, many banks and some hedge funds started to experience significant losses due to the ripple effects of the developing subprime credit crisis. These losses led some firms to start reducing risk and raise cash by selling liquid instruments such as their stock positions, hurting the returns of common stock-selection strategies. The money markets started breaking down, and some banks strapped for cash closed down some of their trading desks, including quant equity proprietary trading operations. Simultaneously, some hedge funds were experiencing redemptions. For instance, some funds of funds (hedge funds investing in other hedge funds) hit loss triggers and were forced to redeem from the hedge funds they were invested in, including quants.

While the subprime credit crisis had little to do with the stocks held by quants, quant liquidation meant that high-expected-return stocks were being sold and, to close short positions, low-expected-return stocks were being bought. Of course, the various quants had very different models, but there was nevertheless overlap in which stocks were considered high expected returns—after all, they were all chasing the same thing, namely high returns.

These liquidations started to hurt the quant value strategy in July and more so in August. The value strategy was also hurt by money being pulled out of stocks that were potential leveraged buyout (LBO) candidates because of the reduced access to leverage. These were stocks that LBO firms considered cheap based on strong value and cash flow characteristics, and, since quants typically consider similar characteristics, this hurt value strategies. Value strategies were

---

[5] This section is based closely on Pedersen (2009). See also Khandani and Lo (2011).

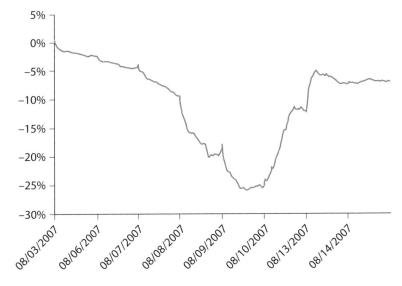

Figure 9.6. The quant equity event of August 2007.
The graph shows the simulated cumulative return to a long-short market-neutral
value and momentum strategy for U.S. large-cap stocks, scaled to 6% annualized
volatility during the period August 3–14, 2007.
Source: Pedersen (2009).

also hurt because the cheap stocks on the long side had more leverage and
therefore more sensitivity to widening credit spreads.

On Monday, August 6, 2007, a major deleveraging of quant strategies began.
Figure 9.6 shows a simulated cumulative return to an industry-neutral long–
short portfolio based on value and momentum signals. As discussed above,
fundamental quants also use many other factors, and not all were affected, but
many have some exposure to value and momentum. Also, certain statistical
arbitrage strategies that rely on price reversals were affected by the liquidity
event due to the unusual amount of price continuation (not shown in the graph).

The figure shows that the portfolio incurs substantial losses from Monday, August 6, through Thursday, August 9, as quants were unwinding, and then recovers
much of its losses on Friday and Monday as the unwinding ended and some
traders may have reentered their positions. The smoothness of the graph is note-
worthy. It is not an artifact of drawing the graph by connecting a few dots—the
graph uses minute-by-minute data. The smoothness is due to a remarkable short-
term predictability arising from the selling pressure and subsequent snapback.
For instance, the strategy was down 90% of the ten-minute intervals on Tuesday,
August 7. This predictability provides strong evidence of a liquidity event, as it is
statistically significantly different from the behavior of a random walk.

Notice the magnitude of the losses in figure 9.6. The simulated strategy loses about 25% from Monday to Thursday, and it has been scaled to have an annualized volatility of about 6% using a well-known commercial risk model. If you interpret this volatility naïvely, it means that the strategy should, with a certain confidence, be able to lose up to about 12% *in a year*. In this event, it lost twice that in just four days!

Considering the four-day volatility of $6\% \times \sqrt{4/260} = 0.74\%$, the strategy's loss is more than thirty standard deviations. The thirty standard deviations must be interpreted correctly. This number does not mean that this was a thousand-year flood and can never happen again. It means that the event was a liquidity event, not based on stock fundamentals, and that this risk model does not capture liquidity risk and the endogenous amplification by the liquidity spirals. Indeed, most of the time stock price fluctuations are driven primarily by economic news about fundamentals, but during a liquidity crisis, price pressure can have a large effect. Hence, the distribution of stock returns can be seen as a mixture of two distributions: shocks driven by fundamentals mixed with shocks driven by liquidity effects. Since fundamentals are usually the main driver, conventional risk models are calibrated to capture fundamental shocks, and liquidity tail events are not well captured by such models. Hence, the result of 30 standard deviations means that the event is statistically significantly different from a fundamental shock and, hence, must have been driven by a liquidity event.

What do you do when you are in the middle of a liquidity spiral? Well, first you must figure out whether your losses are indeed due to a liquidity spiral or fundamental losses. The difference is important because a liquidity spiral eventually ends, most likely with a snapback, whereas fundamental losses might continue and have no reason to be reversed. Figure 5.6 in chapter 5 shows a stylized price path during a liquidity spiral when everyone is running for the exits and prices drop and rebound (based on a model that I had published two years before the quant event with Markus Brunnermeier).[6] There is a striking similarity between the stylized figure 5.6 and the plot of actual market prices in figure 9.6: Both graphs go down smoothly, go back up smoothly, and, finally, level off below where they started. This drop and rebound in prices is the signature of a liquidity spiral, a signature that is also seen in many other liquidity events, such as the flash crash discussed later.

Clearly, the quant event was a liquidity spiral when considering all the evidence until Thursday (see the calculation above), but when did this become clear? Well, in real life nothing is ever crystal clear except with hindsight, but quants had a good idea already on Monday. First, the losses seemed too large and too smooth during the day to be explained by other factors. Second, while there were fundamental drivers of losses for value investing in July, the total losses of value

---

[6] Brunnermeier and Pedersen (2005, 2009).

plus momentum were becoming hard to explain and now economic fundamentals seemed to be improving for the stocks that were held long relative to the stocks that were shorted in this portfolio. In fact, while the simulated portfolio was losing enormous sums, equity analysts were upgrading their recommendations of its long positions relative to its shorts, again suggesting that the losses were liquidity driven, not due to fundamentally bad bets. Third, the co-movements across stocks behaved anomalously and also suggested a liquidity spiral. For instance, even though momentum is normally negatively correlated to value, these strategies suddenly became positively correlated. Said differently, stocks started moving in sync just because they might be held by quants even if they were not fundamentally linked. Fourth, the events this Monday followed other alarms bells that had already started ringing in July and the first week of August.

Having identified a liquidity spiral, what should you do? You have several options: (a) partially liquidate the portfolio, which frees up cash, reduces risk, but contributes to the adverse price moves, incurs transaction costs, and gives up part of the upside when the liquidity spiral turns; (b) rotate the portfolio toward the more idiosyncratic factors that were not affected by the unwinding, which would also incur transaction costs, give up upside, but not free up any cash; (c) stay the course; (d) add to the position, betting that the turnaround is near; or (e) not just liquidate the portfolio but also flip it around, incurring large transaction costs in a big bet that the unwinding would continue for a long time and a bet that goes against all the factors that you normally believe in.

Different quants took different strategies, and the best action depended on the leverage of the fund, the financing of the leverage (including the margin requirements and the risk that the margin requirements would change), the amount of free cash, the risk of the portfolio, and the size and liquidity of the portfolio. An unleveraged long-only stock portfolio faces no risk of forced liquidation by creditors (however, investors might redeem their assets, but this tends to happen more slowly), so such portfolios can better wait out the crisis or even add to the exposure of the most affected factors. In contrast, a highly leveraged portfolio cannot sustain large losses without managing the risk and therefore you need to carefully reduce positions and free up cash to avoid getting a margin call and avoid doing so too late. With larger and more illiquid portfolios, you must take into account that such risk management takes more time. When you see that the liquidation is about to end, you must be ready to quickly increase the position to earn as much of the reversal as possible. Indeed, as seen in figure 9.7, the portfolio finally raged back the other way on Friday, making enormous sums of money and profiting about three-quarters of the day's ten-minute intervals.

It is important to remember that the quant event happened during a relatively calm period for the overall stock market. The stock market was *up* 1.5% during the week of the quant event, and it was up year-to-date through July and August. Hence, the quant event was hidden from the general market because it could only be seen through the lens of a quant portfolio.

Figure 9.7. Deviation from parity for Unilever's dual-listed stocks.

The figure shows the percentage spread between the prices of Unilever NV and Unilever PLC computed as PNV/PPLC − 1, where the adjusted prices are expressed in common currency.

In 2008, the liquidity problems spread much more broadly around the economy and, in September 2008 a truly systemic liquidity crisis unfolded around the bankruptcy of Lehman Brothers. Ironically, the value/momentum quant equity strategies performed relatively well during 2008.

9.2. STATISTICAL ARBITRAGE

Statistical arbitrage (stat arb) strategies are also quantitative, but they are usually less based on an analysis of economic fundamentals and more based on arbitrage relations and statistical relations.

Dual-Listed Shares: Siamese Twin Stocks

Some stocks are joined at the hip in the sense that their fundamental values are economically linked. A classic example is when two merging companies in different countries decide to retain separate legal identities but function economically as a single firm through an "equalization agreement." The merged entity has dual-listed shares in the sense that both its former shares continue to be listed on the respective exchanges.

For instance, the Unilever Group originated from the 1930 merger of the Dutch Margarine Unie and the British Lever Brothers. Unilever still consists of two different companies, Unilever NV, which is based in the Netherlands and has shares traded in euros, and Unilever PLC, which is based in the United Kingdom and has its shares traded in British pounds at the London Stock Exchange. While the prices of NV and PLC follow each other closely, there is often a significant spread between the two, as seen in figure 9.7.

In globally integrated and efficient financial markets, the stock prices of the twin pair should move in lockstep and always be at parity. In practice, however, there are deviations from parity, as seen for Unilever and other twin stocks. Each stock moves partly with its own market.

Multiple Share Classes

Another stat arb trade based on closely linked securities arises when the same firm issues different share classes, such as A shares vs. B shares or ordinary shares vs. preference shares. Often B shares have fewer voting rights than A shares but the same rights to dividends. Similarly, preference shares may have the same rights to payments but fewer control rights (although preference shares are often debtlike securities). Furthermore, there is sometimes a significant difference in the liquidity in the different share classes. The differences in voting right and liquidity can lead to very significant spreads between the share classes. For example, figure 9.8 shows the price discount of BMW's preference shares relative to the regular shares, a discount that varies over time and has been large for long time periods.

Trading on the spread across share classes is not a perfect arbitrage, not just because the spread can widen but also because corporate events can lead to a different treatment of the different share classes. For instance, an activist

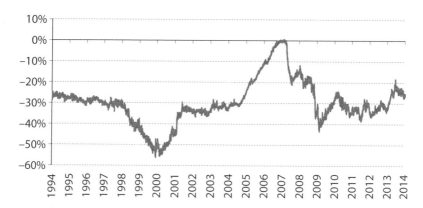

Figure 9.8. The price discount of BMW preference shares relative to the ordinary shares.

investor might propose corporate actions that affect the share classes differently, e.g., differential share repurchases. On the other hand, many corporate events can also lead to a collapse of the spread, e.g., this may happen if the company is taken over.

Efficiently Inefficient Arbitrage Spreads: The Case of Twin Stocks

Stat arb traders trade on the discrepancy between twin stocks. This practice reduces the arbitrage spreads, but competition between stat arb traders often does *not* entirely eliminate the spread. Trading on these spreads requires a constant monitoring of the market from identifying mispricing in the first place, understanding the contractual rights of the different types of shares, and executing the trade. The trade execution involves transaction costs and often currency risk that needs to be hedged.

The arbitrage spread would be zero in a perfectly efficient market, so nonzero spreads provide clear evidence of market inefficiencies. The spreads are efficiently inefficient, however, in the sense that spreads are larger when the arbitrage trade is riskier and more costly to implement and when arbitrage capital is more scarce. As a further sign of efficiently inefficient pricing of liquidity risk, it is often the less liquid shares that trade at discounts, particularly when the liquidity premium is high.

As an example of the efficiently inefficient market, consider the arbitrage spreads between local Unilever shares trading in Europe relative to their counterparts trading in the United States as American depositary receipts (ADRs). The ADR for Unilever NV trades very close to the actual price of the NV, often within 0–2% (depending on how well you synchronize the prices) and, similarly, the ADR for Unilever PLC trades very close to the actual price of PLC. However, the ADR trades at significant spreads to each other, just as the ordinary NV and PLC shares do. Why is this?

The ADRs trade at close prices to the regular shares because the arbitrage spread reflects a relatively simple arbitrage. This is because the ADR and the ordinary shares are fungible in the sense that one can be exchanged for the other (similar to the way in which exchange traded funds (ETFs) can be created and redeemed). In contrast, if you buy a share of NV and short a share of PLC, these positions cannot be netted—you must hold both positions until their prices converge, potentially tying up capital for a long time.

The arbitrage spread between the ADRs closely follows the arbitrage spread of the ordinary shares. However, as seen in figure 9.9, the spread tends to be slightly smaller for the ADRs. This difference is likely because the ADR arbitrage is a slightly simpler strategy since both ADRs are traded in U.S. dollars, so no currency hedging is needed. The smaller ADR spread thus represents another sign of efficiently inefficient markets.

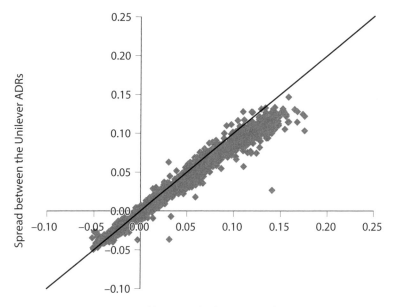

Figure 9.9. The arbitrage spreads of ADRs vs. the local shares of Unilever.
The horizontal axis shows the arbitrage spread of the ordinary shares of Unilever NV vs. PLC, and the vertical axis shows the arbitrage spread of the corresponding ADRs, 2000–2013. The graph also shows the 45-degree line. The fact that most points lie between the horizontal axis and the 45-degree line reflects that the ADR spread tends to be smaller since it corresponds to an easier arbitrage.

Pairs Trading and Reversal Strategies

In addition to finding dual-listed stocks and closely related share classes, stat arb traders also look for stocks that simply behave similarly in a statistical sense without any explicit arbitrage link.[7] One such strategy is *pairs trading*, where stat arb traders look for pairs of highly correlated stocks, identify situations when their prices move apart, and bet on a convergence by buying the stock that lags behind and shorting the one rising more.

Pairs trading is a bet on price reversals. Stat arb traders also make broader bets on price reversals. Such broader reversal strategies do not consider pairs of stocks but simultaneously consider a larger universe of stocks and seek to

---

[7] See Gatev, Goetzmann, and Rouwenhorst (2006) for pairs trading and Nagel (2012) on reversal trades and their relation to liquidity and volatility.

buy those that lag behind and those that have gotten ahead of the market. The simplest type of reversal strategy is to buy stocks that have experienced the lowest return over the past days and short those that had the highest return. More sophisticated reversal strategies (also called *residual reversal* strategies) seek to estimate each stock's expected return in light of its characteristics and the returns of other stocks with similar characteristics, and then bet that the residual between the stock's actual return and its expected return will revert.

Index Arbitrage and Closed-End Fund Arbitrage

Finally, stat arb traders pursue strategies that seek to arbitrage the difference between a "basket security" and its components. For example, they try to arbitrage the difference between stock index futures and the prices of the underlying stocks, the discrepancies between futures and an ETF, the difference between the ETF and its constituents, and the difference between a closed-end mutual fund and its underlying stock holdings. These arbitrage spreads tend to be small given that the strategies can be implemented with limited risk, with the exception of the closed-end funds, where large arbitrage spreads can arise. These trades often require very sophisticated trading infrastructure to minimize the transaction costs and limit execution risk, given the many legs of the trade as well as minimal funding costs if spreads are tight.

9.3. HIGH-FREQUENCY TRADING: EFFICIENTLY INEFFICIENT MARKET MAKING

HFTs trade many different strategies; some provide liquidity, and others demand liquidity.[8] When HFTs provide liquidity in today's electronic markets, they essentially serve the same role as the old-fashioned market makers and the specialists on the floor of the New York Stock Exchange.

Liquidity would be almost unlimited and bid–ask spreads virtually zero in a perfectly efficient market in which all investors are always present in the market and have the same information. However, as we have seen, markets are not perfectly efficient and liquidity problems are everywhere. To understand the basic economics of market making in an efficiently inefficient market, note that most investors do not follow the markets constantly, they occasionally decide to trade, and then they often want to trade immediately. Hence, the natural buyers and the natural sellers do not arrive in the market at the same time and,

---

[8] Jones (2013) provides an overview of HFT, a review of the flash crash, and a list of relevant references. Budish, Cramton, and Shim (2013) analyze the HFT trading arms race.

even when they do, they sometimes go to different exchanges, so the order flow is fragmented. This behavior means that the market price bounces around the "equilibrium price" (that is, the price that would prevail if all the buyers and sellers were present in the market simultaneously) and the price would bounce around a lot more if it weren't for the market makers (and here I am using the term "market makers" generally, including liquidity-providing HFTs). That is, when an excess of buyers show up in the market, the price is pushed up, and when the sellers show up, the price is pushed down.

Market makers provide a service, namely liquidity (or immediacy). That is, when more sellers arrive to the market than buyers, market makers stand ready to buy the excess supply. Market makers hold the securities in inventory until the natural buyers arrive, satisfying the buyers' demand by unloading the inventory.

Market makers charge a price for the liquidity service. This price is the profit of the market maker and the transaction cost of the natural buyers and sellers. Specifically, market makers earn profits due to the bid–ask spread and due to market impact, i.e., buying low and selling high as the price bounces around. This is similar to the profits earned by a grocery store with a markup between what it pays for the groceries and what it sells them for. The grocery store needs to earn a markup large enough to be compensated for paying its employees, rent, freight costs, and the cost of capital, but in a competitive market, the markup should be no greater than that. Similarly, market makers need compensation for the costs associated with liquidity provision and, the more competitive the market, the more liquid the market.

In addition to the costs of setting up a large trading infrastructure, market makers face the risk of losing money because they are trading against informed investors. Indeed, if there is selling pressure in the market (leading the market makers to be net buyers), this could either be because of order fragmentation or because the equilibrium price has actually changed—and market makers are never sure which one it is. In the former case, market makers buy low and then sell high when the price rebounds, earning a profit. In the latter case, market makers buy low and sell even lower when they realize that the price pressure was not a temporary effect but rather an expression that the fundamental value has declined (and sellers might have known something that the market maker didn't know). Hence, to be profitable, market makers need to keep adjusting to the market conditions. When news arrives, they need to immediately adjust their orders. Indeed, limit orders provide the market with free "options" to trade whenever the true value has changed.

Conceptually, market makers in electronic markets work as follows. They seek to determine the equilibrium price of a stock and submit a limit order to buy at a price just below the equilibrium price and a limit order to sell at a price just above it. They constantly update their estimates of the optimal order placement based on other orders arriving to the market for this stock and other stocks, and then they frequently cancel orders when the equilibrium price changes and submit new ones. Furthermore, market makers must manage inventory risk, making sure to shade orders to encourage the market to diminish their positions and hedge market and industry exposures.

HFT also pursues many other strategies than liquidity provision and, in fact, by some estimates they initiate trade with marketable orders more often than their limit orders are hit passively. For example, HFTs exploit short-lived relative mispricing across related securities similar to the stat arb strategies discussed above. Some HFTs also have strategies that seek to hit "stale" limit orders, including the limit orders submitted by other HFTs. For instance, if a news announcement increases the value of a stock, the HFT will immediately hit (i.e., buy from) a limit order to sell near the old equilibrium price. Simultaneously, liquidity-providing HFTs immediately try to cancel their stale orders.

HFTs engage in an "arms race" against each other where being fast is not important per se but being *faster* is very important. Indeed, there are only so many stale limit orders, so only the fastest HFTs get to hit them. On the flip side, to reduce the risk of being exposed to adverse selection, an HFT needs to be able to cancel its own limit orders before they become stale and are hit by other HFTs.

Some HFTs may also try to identify and exploit large orders that are broken up into smaller trades and traded over hours or days. For example, if you are seeking to buy a large stock position, try to submit a limit order to buy the same number of shares each minute, right at the minute, and see what happens to your execution (relative to an execution where you split up the order more finely and more randomly and execute at more random times).

The Flash Crash of 2010

On May 6, 2010, dramatic market events occurred in the U.S. stock market that came to be known as the flash crash. From the morning, the market was dropping on large trading volume and volatility due to rising fears about the ongoing European debt crisis.

At 2:32 p.m., the Standard & Poor's 500 (S&P 500) stock market index was down 2.8%. The limit order book was thinning due to the heightened volatility and because some exchanges were experiencing data delays and other data problems. When traders in electronic markets start to question the data quality, it is as if they cannot "see," and being afraid to trade blindly, they naturally scale back their orders or even pause trading altogether.

At this time, a mutual fund (reportedly, Waddell & Reed Financial, Inc.) submitted a very large order to sell 75,000 e-mini S&P 500 futures (about $4.1 billion worth). Such a large order rarely hits the market; in fact, it had only happened twice over the previous 12 months, one of which was by the same mutual fund. The last time this mutual fund had executed a similar sized order, it had done so over the course of several hours, but on the day of the flash crash, the selling mutual fund decided to have the order executed with an algorithm over just 20 minutes. Over the next 13 minutes, the market dropped 5.2% in value, an enormous move over such a short time period, as seen in figure 9.10.

HFTs initially provided liquidity. They were net buyers as the market was dropping, but, at 2:41 p.m., HFTs turned around and became net sellers, perhaps to reduce their inventory risk, but throughout the event, HFTs were mainly buying and selling to each other as documented by the CFTC and SEC:

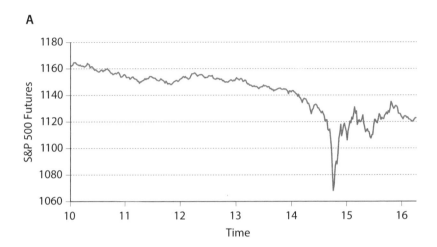

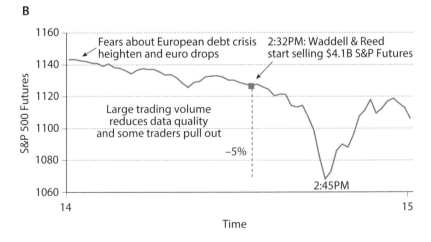

Figure 9.10. The flash crash of May 6, 2010.

Still lacking sufficient demand from fundamental buyers or cross-market arbitrageurs, HFTs began to quickly buy and then resell contracts to each other—generating a "hot-potato" volume effect as the same positions were rapidly passed back and forth. Between 2:45:13 and 2:45:27, HFTs traded over 27,000 contracts, which accounted for about 49 percent of the total trading volume, while buying only about 200 additional contracts net.[9]

CFTC and SEC continues:

At 2:45:28 p.m., trading on the E-Mini was paused for five seconds when the Chicago Mercantile Exchange ("CME") Stop Logic Functionality was triggered in order to prevent a cascade of further price declines. In that short period of time, sell-side pressure in the E-Mini was partly alleviated and buy-side interest increased. When trading resumed at 2:45:33 p.m., prices stabilized and shortly thereafter, the E-Mini began to recover.

When the price of the S&P 500 neared the bottom, its liquidity dried up in the sense that the depth in limit order book almost completely vanished. Furthermore, the liquidity crisis in the S&P 500 spilled over to many other markets, partly because traders were arbitraging the relative mispricings that arose due to the falling S&P 500. Relative-value traders started buying the S&P 500 while shorting other securities, thus depressing prices in other markets (while supporting the S&P 500). First, ETFs were hit, and then many individual stocks. Some stocks experienced highly unusual trades as their limit order books were wiped out, and market orders started hitting "placeholder bids" at extreme prices, including a trade at $0.01 for Accenture. The most extreme trades were later canceled, however.

The role of HFTs in the flash crash was not so much what they did but what they didn't do, namely provide unlimited liquidity. However, the failure of market makers to provide liquidity in the face of overwhelming one-sided demand pressure, confusion about market prices, and increasing risk has always been a problem. For example, old-fashioned market makers in NASDAQ stocks and in over-the-counter markets have been known to take their phones off the hook when markets have gone off the cliff, e.g., in the 1987 stock market crash. Also, half a century before the flash crash of 2010, a similar event occurred that came to be known as the "Market Break of May 1962." This event was also investigated by the SEC and, as in the flash crash, the SEC found that the "lateness of the NYSE tape and the size of the price declines on the NYSE prompted some over-the-counter dealers to withdraw as market makers in certain securities."[10]

---

[9] U.S. Commodities and Futures Trading Commission and Securities and Exchange Commission (2010).

[10] U.S. Securities and Exchange Commission (1963).

9.4. INTERVIEW WITH CLIFF ASNESS
OF AQR CAPITAL MANAGEMENT

Cliff Asness is a cofounder and managing principal at AQR Capital Management, a global investment management firm built at the intersection of financial theory and practical application. One of the original quant investors, Asness has also written a large number of influential and award-winning articles. Before cofounding AQR, he was a managing director and director of quantitative research at Goldman Sachs Asset Management. He earned two B.S. degrees from the University of Pennsylvania and his Ph.D. and MBA from the University of Chicago, where he wrote his dissertation, one of the very early studies of momentum investing, establishing the type of momentum strategy still most commonly studied in academia today, as Prof. Fama's student and teaching assistant.

LHP: *Your Ph.D. dissertation had seminal research on momentum, reversal, and statistical arbitrage—how did that come about?*
CSA: Being present at the University of Chicago when my two advisors, Gene Fama and Ken French, were doing their research on value and size, I first thought I would write some extension of value investing. I spent a lot of time with the data, and I kind of ran across this weird result that stock returns have strong momentum (measured over the last twelve months, leaving off the most recent month). The momentum effect was about as strong as value investing, in fact, even stronger in gross returns. I hadn't seen this result in the academic literature (though it turned out that two researchers at UCLA were looking at something similar at the same time, minus that skipping the last month part), so I was pretty excited, but also nervous. Gene was a big believer in efficient markets, so the thought that I would write a thesis for him on something that was on the surface so inconsistent with market efficiency was a bit scary. I recall telling him about these findings, fully expecting him to send me back to the drawing board, but his response was "If it is in the data, pursue it!" That was a great moment for me and my respect for Gene.

Another thing I found while mucking around with the data was that the most recent month was associated with reversal. I thought that was cool, but I wasn't fully sure how implementable it was. It turns out that effect was the seeds of what many successful stat arb traders have been able to build around, and I gave up on it too soon. It is my personal "fish story," that is, the one that got away . . .
LHP: *Was there a moment when you realized that your momentum result was a significant finding?*
CSA: For me, probably the key moment in my dissertation was when I extended the sample back to 1926. As you know, the only cure for data mining

is an out-of-sample test, so I wanted to see if my findings held up during another time period. I was initially doing all my analysis using the same data as Fama–French from 1963 to 1990, but it suddenly dawned on me that there existed data from 1926. Fama–French only used data starting in 1963 because they didn't have companies' book values earlier than that. This is really obvious, but I just said, "Wait a second. I do have price data from 1926, and unlike them my stuff doesn't need book values, so why am I limiting myself to their sample period?" So I basically ran my stuff from '26 to June of '63. This became one of the "famous regressions in my life"; yes, I know not many people have that category (and it's only famous to me). It just worked perfectly on pristine data that hadn't been looked at yet. The momentum effect was strong, the most recent month's strong reversal was there, and the longer term reversal also worked pre-1963. That was a very exciting moment for me as a twenty-three-year-old. I was like, "Holy crap, it works!" That said, I had no idea momentum would play such a large role in academia. I just wanted to graduate.

LHP: *When I was in graduate school at Stanford, my professors discouraged internships on Wall Street, referring to the tragedy that happened to Chicago, where their best Ph.D. students left academia, following a "corrupting" star student to go to Wall Street. I think it's been called Chicago's "lost generation." Can you tell me about that?*

CSA: Ha! Well, for many years afterwards, I kept hearing from my academic friends that Gene was mad at me for leaving academia. I guess it made it worse that a whole bunch of my Chicago Ph.D. classmates came with me when I left. My response was always, "Really???" and their response was, "No, not really. . . ." Well, Gene trained me to be a good empiricist, so after this happened enough times I realized there was probably something to it. But I always tried to think of it as a compliment, and Gene and I are on very good terms today.

LHP: *So, why did you decide to leave for Wall Street?*

CSA: I absolutely loved the work that I was doing when I was at Chicago. But I went to graduate school straight from college, so I have to admit that I did have a little nagging question about what the real world would be like. Also, my best friend from college went to Goldman Sachs and was telling me that I owe it to myself to at least see what it's like. So I decided to try a summer at Goldman. It turns out that summer never ended! I started out as a fixed-income trader. So by day I traded bonds, and by night I worked on my thesis, which was on stocks. After a short time, Goldman decided it needed a quantitative research group that covered both stocks and bonds, and they asked me to start that up. The mandate for the group was quite broad, and it struck me that here was an opportunity for me to be able to do all the fascinating things I was working on in school, and I would work with the rigor of an academic, but in a more applied setting. That was really appealing to me.

LHP: *What were the most difficult steps in the transition from studying markets academically to using the research to trade real money?*

CSA: First, there was learning how the real world works, all the broker relationships, and so on. Then you quickly see the importance of transaction costs and portfolio construction. It's not that academics don't know about these things, but when you're doing it for real money, playing with "live ammunition" as they say, it ups the ante. For instance, you realize that, if you want to run a reasonably large amount of money, you can't go as deep into small cap as you'd like, where transaction costs are too large. You can't run a very high turnover strategy, etc. Also, one of the biggest adjustments was having to convince people that you can really do it. I will tell you the hurdle for people letting you play with live ammo, their ammo, can be very different from the hurdle to writing a successful paper. I was a twenty-five-year-old geek at Goldman Sachs, saying, "Give me money; this quant stuff seems to work." For example, they made us go present our work to Abby Cohen the then, and still, Goldman markets guru. I respect Abby, but she was a very different kind of analyst than we were. But we did it, she got it, and gave us the thumbs up.

LHP: *What else is different in the real world?*

CSA: Well, the single biggest difference between real world and academia is—this sounds over scientific—time dilation. I'll explain what I mean. This is not relativistic time dilation as the only time I move at speeds near light is when there is pizza involved. But to borrow the term, your sense of time does change when you are running real money. Suppose you look at a cumulative return of a strategy with a Sharpe ratio of 0.7 and see a three-year period with poor performance. It does not faze you one drop. You go: "Oh, look, that happened in 1973, but it came back by 1976, and that's what a 0.7 Sharpe ratio does." But living through those periods takes—subjectively, and in wear and tear on your internal organs—many times the actual time it really lasts. If you have a three-year period where something doesn't work, it ages you a decade. You face an immense pressure to change your models, you have bosses or clients who lose faith, and I cannot explain the amount of discipline that you need.

LHP: *Warren Buffett's Berkshire Hathaway stock return has a Sharpe ratio of about that magnitude.*

CSA: Yes, and he had some periods of losses too, of course—some of them fairly horrific. A Sharpe ratio of 0.7 can make a lot of wealth, but it still loses a fair amount of times and sometimes for multiple years in a row. I got lucky—this is probably the single biggest luck in my professional life, that the first couple of years were very good for our process. We made a lot of money in the first two years with great risk-adjusted returns. If the first couple of years were bad, I'd probably be doing something else; that's just how this business works. It's a good process, and it has worked over time, including the full "out of sample period" since my dissertation ended, so I don't feel this piece of good luck was at all unfair (of course I don't!), but navigating through the inevitable bad times is the single biggest change of mind-set you have to make leaving academia.

LHP: *Yes, when you started your quant group at Goldman Sachs, you were a young guy with triple digit returns, on track to become a Goldman Sachs partner—so why did you walk away from that to start a new firm?*

CSA: That wasn't an easy decision. We were doing well at Goldman, and they treated us great. But if you projected forward, the path at Goldman would be very different than the path as an independent firm. For me, success would increasingly look like becoming more a part of senior management at a very large firm. The path on our own might keep me closer to research, which has always been my passion. A couple of catalysts pushed me to make the decision. One was that a fellow Chicago Ph.D. classmate who worked for me at the time left to start his own hedge fund, and his initial success got my competitive juices flowing. Second, a Goldman colleague from another group, David Kabiller, also started making the case that we could successfully do this on our own. He almost had more confidence in us than we did—and lots of business ideas. So a year later, I left with John Liew and Bob Krail (also fellow Chicago Ph.D. classmates and the two most senior members of my team), about half the rest of the team in total, and David to start AQR. I should say the people who stayed at Goldman to run our old group were an all-star team themselves, too.

LHP: *So you decided to take the chance and start AQR.*

CSA: Yes, we had an easier time raising money than we expected and in fact had to turn back about half of the subscriptions. However, we had no idea what was coming around the corner. Those young and cocky Goldman Sachs quants were about to eat humble pie for a long stretch!

LHP: *You are referring to the tech bubble?*

CSA: Correct. Actually, our first month, August 1998, was good despite that the market was collapsing and LTCM and many other hedge funds were getting into trouble. We were running very different strategies, and we made money. Then things turned south. To understand why, recall that two very important investment themes underlying our trading strategies are value and momentum—we used other strategies too and have developed many new ones over the years, but these are still important. The tech bubble was a period when value was strongly out of favor and momentum helped, but not nearly enough. It turns out we timed the launch of our business and our first fund right before the start of the tech bubble, literally just before the start of its really crazy phase. Remember the idea behind time dilation I mentioned before? Our tough start lasted about 18 months, but it felt like a lifetime.

LHP: *How did investors react to the tough start?*

CSA: Many of our investors stuck with us, especially those who really understood our process, and we showed them lots of evidence that the Internet valuations didn't make sense and that, going forward, our investments looked even better. Of course, while many did, not every investor stuck with us. One of the frustrating things about this business is how sensitive many investors are to short-term performance—in both directions, we've been the beneficiaries also. Many investors have a tendency to pile into investment strategies or managers who have recently had good performance, and they flee at the first sign of trouble, or, even worse, stick around a bit and get out at the worst possible time when it feels like it's been losing forever, but statistically it's not even that shocking. The problem with this behavior is that, if you poorly time the entry and exit of these strategies, you are not able to take advantage of the fact that these strategies make money over the long run. I shouldn't whine too much; it's probably why some of the strategies exist in the first place and don't get arbitraged away as easily as some might assume, but it's hard to keep that perspective at times. In any case, the investors who stuck with us really got rewarded when the Internet bubble burst in 2000 and the following years.

LHP: *Let's shift gears a bit and talk about your approach to quantitative investments. So how do you pick stocks?*

CSA: Well, everyone has secrets, but I'll share a few of the most basic ideas: As I mentioned before, at the simplest level and leaving out a fair amount, we're looking for cheap stocks that are getting better, the academic ideas of value and momentum, and to short the opposite, expensive stocks that are getting worse. Our models are a lot subtler than that today, including other themes, and more sophisticated ways to ferret out cheapness and momentum, but while we've been striving to improve things for a long time now, the core principles remain the same after 20 years.

Further, while my dissertation was on equities, we extended the research to bonds (remember, I was a bond trader), currencies, commodities, and several other asset classes.

LHP: *What are the differences/similarities between quantitative and discretionary investment?*

CSA: I think good judgmental managers are often looking for the same things we are—cheap stocks with a catalyst as to why they won't remain cheap, and vice versa for shorts. In fact, for a long time I used to think we did something very different, until I realized that "catalyst" and "momentum" share a lot in common and so do quants and more discretionary managers. In fact, be it for rational or irrational reasons, I think this is the type of management, quant or judgmental, that adds value over time. The big difference between quants and non-quants comes down to diversification, which quants rely on, and concentration, which judgmental managers rely on. But what we tend to like or dislike in general is actually fairly similar.

A discretionary manager gets to intimately know the companies they invest in. We don't, but our advantage is that we can apply our trading philosophy to thousands of stocks at the same time. If the philosophy works, it's very hard for us to lose over time given that we spread the risk over so many stocks. Of course, as implied earlier, it's very easy to lose for a while even if you're right! Even if a discretionary manager knows a company very well, the CEO can still turn out to be a philandering embezzler, so you have that stock-specific randomness if you only hold a few stocks. And no matter how well you know something, there is still just a chance you're wrong.

LHP: *What are the main benefits of quant investment?*

CSA: Quantitative investors can process a lot of information. We look at many more stocks and many more factors than is easily done by discretionary stock pickers. Further, we apply the same investment principles across stocks, backtest our strategies, and follow our models with some discipline.

LHP: *Do you always follow the models?*

CSA: Discipline is important. We do not think we're more immune to psychological biases than others, but following the models helps. If we followed them with less discipline, we run the serious risk of reintroducing the exact biases we are trying to exploit! For instance, if people run from stocks with any problems, making value stocks too cheap and attractive buys long-term, if we use our judgment to selectively override our models, perhaps we undo precisely the bet we want to make, in order to make ourselves more "comfortable"? Discipline is not always easy, by the way. It's really hard to stick to a strategy. But when people cave and disregard their models, they seem to usually do this within an hour and a half of the worst possible time to cave. Admittedly, that's not a quant study, but it's been my experience. The difficulty of sticking to the models is part of why they work.

LHP: *How do you determine whether a new trading factor is good?*

CSA: We have a lot of trading factors, as you know, ranging from a number of more sophisticated value and momentum factors to factors based on altogether different signals. We've been working on this for 20 years, and all the additions and changes to our model had to pass a number of tests. First, it has to make some sense. Then, unlike a judgmental manager, we have to test it. It has to survive a number of out-of-sample tests. For instance, does a trading signal work in all countries? Across time periods? Does it work after the time when it was first discovered? If applicable, does it work in different asset classes? Also, we test the economics of the idea, not just the return performance. If the idea is that a factor predicts earnings and therefore returns, we test whether it in fact does predict earnings, not just returns. We also focus keenly on whether the performance survives transactions costs.

LHP: *In your view, what are the main reasons that these strategies work?*

CSA: You know, there are three possible reasons a strategy may have worked in the past: One is random chance. I don't believe that's it (I better not!). I think we're fairly rigorous, and we've tested our stuff in a hundred places including 20 years out of sample from when first discovered. So for our core strategies at least, I'm very certain it is not just random chance, but you still have to list that as a possibility; not to is just intellectually dishonest. Two is that our strategies may work because we're picking up a risk premium: What we are long is riskier than what was short, and we're getting paid for that. The last possibility is that what we're doing is something that is a bit of a free lunch, that is, a market inefficiency brought on presumably by other investors acting irrationally or with a "behavioral bias." Frankly, over time, I drifted more toward the latter, but not as far as most of the active management world. Free lunch, by the way, sounds too great since you still have to work really hard to collect it using sophisticated portfolio optimization techniques and suffer through those periods where it doesn't work for a while. So I think in some places we're picking up disciplined risk premiums that are not very correlated with long-only markets, which means, if someone doesn't have those in their portfolio, they should add them. In other places, I think we're taking advantages of human biases and we're trying to be disciplined and determined about it, taking the other side of some common psychological trait or institutional constraint that influence security prices.

PART III

Asset Allocation and Macro Strategies

CHAPTER 10

Introduction to Asset Allocation
The Returns to the Major Asset Classes

Design of a portfolio involves at least four steps: deciding which asset classes to include and which to exclude from the portfolio; deciding upon the normal, or long-term, weights for each of the asset classes allowed in the portfolio; altering the investment mix weights away from normal in an attempt to capture excess returns from short-term fluctuations in asset class prices (market timing); and selecting individual securities within an asset class to achieve superior returns relative to that asset class (security selection)

—Brinson, Hood, and Beebower (1986)

Macro investing deals with an investor's overall asset allocation, that is, how much to invest in equities, bonds, and the other major asset classes. This macro investment goal can be separated into two components:

(1) The long-term *strategic asset allocation* policy. For example, the Norwegian sovereign wealth fund (Norges Bank Investment Management) has had a *benchmark portfolio* (also called *policy portfolio*) of about 60% global equities and 40% global bonds.

(2) The reallocations around the long-term weights based on current market views, called *tactical asset allocation* or *market timing*. For example, a pension fund that views the equity market as especially attractive may decide to temporarily increase its equity weight. As another example, a macro hedge fund may have a zero strategic asset allocation to the equity market so its entire investment strategy is to go long and short markets based on its tactical views. However, even a market-neutral hedge fund may use asset allocation techniques to manage its relative allocations across its various trading strategies.

These macro investment decisions should be viewed in contrast to security selection, e.g., stock selection. Whereas macro investment deals with how much to allocate to each overall market or asset class, security selection deals with finding the best securities within a market.

Macro investors are concerned with the overall market developments and economic conditions such as whether inflation is rising, economic growth, which countries are doing well, global trade, and other global trends such as political changes. Macro investors are often considered "top-down," meaning that they begin by analyzing the overall economic conditions, decide which markets and sectors are likely to perform well, and then decide what securities to use to implement these macro views. Investors focused on security selection, on the other hand, are considered "bottom-up," meaning that they find securities that they like and the overall asset allocation falls out as a result. For instance, if a security selector finds a lot of attractive stocks in Brazil, he may end up with a large weight on Brazilian equities, perhaps without an explicit view on the aggregate Brazilian market.

This chapter first discusses frameworks for strategic and tactical asset allocation. Then it describes the fundamental sources of returns for each of the major asset classes.[1] Return drivers and global macro trading strategies that exploit them are discussed more in chapter 11, which also considers how central banks, the macro economy, and other factors affect global asset markets. Chapter 12 then describes managed futures investing, which is focused on trend-following strategies.

10.1. STRATEGIC ASSET ALLOCATION

Large institutional investors often first decide on their long-run strategic asset allocation, that is, the desired typical portfolio consistent with the investment goals around which one can implement tactical bets and security selection views. This strategic asset allocation is crucial to the success of pension funds, endowments, and other investors. The strategic allocation is sometimes called the policy portfolio or the benchmark portfolio.

The strategic asset allocation of large institutional investors is naturally focused on market risk premiums, specifying the allocation to equities (equity risk premiums), government bonds (term premiums), corporate bonds and other risky debt (credit risk premiums), illiquid and real assets such as real estate, forestland, and infrastructure (liquidity risk premiums), as well as the cash reserves. The strategic asset allocation may also include allocations to alternative risk premiums, such as the styles discussed in this book (value, trend-following, liquidity, carry, low-risk, and quality premiums) or in terms of

---

[1] See also Ilmanen (2011) for an excellent overview of the historical returns to the major asset classes and analysis of expected return drivers.

active investment strategies (e.g., hedge fund allocations across equity, macro, and arbitrage strategies). There are naturally many ways to choose the strategic allocation. Here we consider several methods, namely passive asset allocation, constant rebalanced asset allocation, liquidity-based asset allocation, and risk-based asset allocation.

For a hedge fund that is market neutral on average, the strategic allocation can simply be viewed as a flat investment in the market, but hedge funds often use these asset allocation techniques to size their bets across strategies. For instance, a multi-strategy hedge fund must decide on its allocation across the different equity strategies, arbitrage strategies, and macro strategies and how to vary the allocations over time.

Passive Asset Allocation

The only truly passive portfolio is the market portfolio. The market-weighted asset allocation means that you invest 45% in equities if equities have a total market capitalization that is 45% of the market capitalization of the entire investment universe under consideration, e.g., stocks, government bonds, credits, and real assets.

The market portfolio is passive in two unique ways: First, the market portfolio implies minimal trading. When stocks increase in value, your allocation to stocks naturally increases and, simultaneously, the market portfolio weight for stocks increases correspondingly, so you need not trade to maintain your passive market allocation. You only need to trade when there are new securities issued or when you need to increase or decrease your overall investment (e.g., due to fund flows).

Second, investing in the market portfolio is "macro consistent" in the sense that everyone can do it. If you buy the market allocation, you are not assuming that someone else is the "sucker" with a worse asset allocation. In other words, the market portfolio is consistent with an equilibrium in the spirit of the capital asset pricing model (CAPM).

Constant Rebalanced Asset Allocation

A constant rebalanced portfolio is a portfolio that regularly rebalances to constant portfolio weights, for instance, 60% in stocks and 40% in bonds. This strategy sounds passive since the portfolio weights are constant, but it is not passive in the sense of the two criteria above: It requires frequent rebalancing, and not everyone in the market can do it.

The 60/40 portfolio has gained popularity among pension funds, perhaps because it implies a value trade in its asset allocation. When stocks increase in value, their weight rises above 60%, leading the 60/40 investor to sell some shares. Conversely, when stock prices fall, the investor buys equity shares. The famous manager of the endowment of Yale University, David Swensen, recommends such portfolio rebalancing:

> Rebalancing represents supremely rational behavior. Maintaining portfolio targets in the face of market moves dictates sale of strong relative performers and purchase of poor relative performers. Stated differently, disciplined rebalancers sell what's hot and buy what's not. . . . When markets make extreme moves, rebalancing requires substantial amounts of courage . . . owners of private assets face a particular challenge in rebalancing activity.

> —David Swensen (2000)

Liquidity-Based Asset Allocation

As is clear from the quote above, Swensen recognizes the difficulty in rebalancing illiquid allocations. The ultimate illiquid assets are private assets or investments in private equity, which are often difficult or impossible to sell. Such illiquidity not only affects the rebalance frequency and drift away from the strategic asset allocation, it also affects the ability to withdraw capital. Hence, short-term investors who may need to withdraw capital at short notice must limit their exposure to assets with high liquidity risk. For instance, mutual funds with daily redemption notice periods must be able to sell their assets quickly and therefore cannot invest in illiquid private assets. Hence, the asset allocation across assets of differing liquidity must depend on the investors' holding period and financing. Therefore, long-term investors with stable financing can earn a liquidity premium from their ability to invest in illiquid assets (Amihud and Mendelson 1986).

Risk-Based Asset Allocation and Risk Parity Investing

While many investors think about how many dollars to invest in each asset class (or, equivalently, what fraction of the capital should be allocated to the asset class), other investors think instead in terms of risk. They consider how much risk they should take in each asset class.

To understand the motivation for risk-based asset allocation, consider first an investor deciding between cash and a single risky asset, say equities. As discussed in chapter 4, portfolio theory stipulates that an optimal amount of money invested in a risky asset, x, is proportional to the ratio of expected excess return $E(R^e)$ to the variance σ^2:

$$x = \frac{1}{\gamma} \frac{\mathrm{E}(R^e)}{\sigma^2} \tag{10.1}$$

where the factor of proportionality depends on the risk aversion γ. This means that the portfolio risk is given by

$$\text{portfolio risk} = \sigma \times x = \frac{1}{\gamma} \frac{\mathrm{E}(R^e)}{\sigma} = \frac{1}{\gamma} \mathrm{SR} \tag{10.2}$$

This portfolio risk is measured in terms of the amount of money that is at risk. For instance, if you invest $x = \$100$ million with an annual volatility of $\sigma = 10\%$, then the standard deviation of your profit or loss over the next year will be $\$10$ million. Equation 10.2 shows that this portfolio risk should be driven by the Sharpe ratio, SR. That is, you should have a large portfolio risk when you have a good investment with a high SR and take little risk when your SR is low.

If the Sharpe ratio is expected to be relatively stable, then the investor should seek a stable risk exposure, implying a smaller dollar exposure when risk rises and a higher dollar exposure when risk goes down. Said differently, if the SR is constant, then the desired portfolio risk is also constant, and so the notional exposure $x = $ desired risk$/\sigma$ varies inversely proportionally to asset volatility σ.

This idea can also be applied across asset classes. To do this, one must estimate the Sharpe ratio for each asset class and allocate risk budgets accordingly. *Risk parity investment* is based on the idea that the different major asset classes—equities, bonds, credits, and real assets (commodities and inflation-linked securities)—have similar Sharpe ratios. With this starting point, traditional asset allocations seem inefficient since a large fraction (more than 80%) of the overall risk comes from a single source, namely equities. Instead, a risk parity asset allocation means that each asset class contributes more equally to the portfolio risk. One simple way to do this is to let the portfolio weight of each asset class be inversely proportional to its risk. More sophisticated risk parity allocations take into account the correlations across asset classes.

An unleveraged risk parity allocation has a much smaller risk than traditional asset allocations since it allocates more of its capital to the least risky asset classes. Hence, to achieve a high expected return, leverage is needed. This leverage could be both a risk and a reason for the higher historical risk-adjusted returns delivered by risk parity allocations.

Asness, Frazzini, and Pedersen (2012) argue that many investors are averse to leverage, preferring instead to overweight risky asset classes that may deliver high unleveraged returns such as equities. This behavior raises the Sharpe ratio of the safer asset classes in equilibrium, creating an opportunity for investors who are willing to use leverage or who accept low expected returns at even lower levels of risk. In other words, the traditional equity-dominated asset allocation may be efficiently inefficient for investors with leverage constraints, while less constrained investors can leverage the more efficient tangency portfolio.

10.2. MARKET TIMING AND TACTICAL ASSET ALLOCATION

Market Timing

Market timing means choosing the size of the overall long or short position in a market. For instance, an investor seeking to time the equity market asks herself whether she thinks that stocks in general are going to go up or down. The timing decision can be based on both qualitative and quantitative inputs. It might be based on views on what the central bank is doing or the investor's interpretation of the recent indicators from economic news releases (e.g., the employment situation).

Market timing rules can be analyzed using regressions and backtests (as also discussed in chapter 3). To be specific, let us consider how one might time the equity market based on the dividend yield. To understand why this might work, recall that equity returns consist of the dividend yield plus the capital appreciation:

$$R_{t+1} = \underbrace{\frac{D_{t+1}}{P_t}}_{\substack{\text{dividend} \\ \text{yield}}} + \underbrace{\frac{P_{t+1} - P_t}{P_t}}_{\substack{\text{price} \\ \text{appreciation}}} \tag{10.3}$$

The dividend yield can usually be well estimated in advance, especially for a broad equity index. For example, let us consider the dividend yield based on the past year's dividend (which of course is already known) as a proxy for the expected future dividend, $DP_t = D_t/P_t$. The price appreciation is of course hard to predict, but the dividend yield may still be a useful market timing signal for the overall equity return. To examine this timing ability, consider the following predictive regression:

$$R^e_{t+1} = a + b \, DP_t + \varepsilon_{t+1} \tag{10.4}$$

On the left-hand side, we have the excess stock return over the money market rate, $R^e_{t+1} = R_{t+1} - R^f$. We consider the excess return because market timing is ultimately not just a question about whether equities will make money; it is a question of whether they will make *more* money than a risk-free investment. Note that the dividend yield on the right-hand side, DP_t, is measured at time t whereas the excess return on the left-hand side is measured at time $t + 1$ as this is a predictive (i.e., market timing) regression. In other words, the regression seeks to determine whether knowing the dividend yield in advance is helpful in predicting the future excess return.

What does the regression coefficient b mean? Clearly, a coefficient of zero means that the dividend yield is not helpful as a predictor. This would be consistent with the random walk hypothesis, which states that nothing should be able to predict excess returns (except perhaps by chance). A positive b coefficient indicates that the predictor may be useful (if it is robust and large enough as discussed below), while a negative coefficient implies that the predictor potentially works backward, meaning that you should short the market when the predictor is high.

When the predictor is the dividend yield, we can also interpret the magnitude of the b coefficient. In particular, a naïve benchmark is that $b = 1$. This means that, if the dividend yield is one percentage point larger, then the stock return is also expected to be one percentage point larger. In other words, the dividend yield predicts the stock return because it is part of the stock return (as seen in equation 10.3), but it does not predict the price appreciation.

In contrast, the random walk hypothesis $b = 0$ means that the price appreciation is expected to be low when the dividend yield is high, such that the overall expected equity return is independent of dividend yields. Perhaps the truth lies somewhere between these benchmarks? The data suggest otherwise.

I run this regression from 1926 to 2013 with U.S. monthly data, where the monthly excess return is annualized by multiplying by 12 to make it comparable to annual dividends (the result is almost the same with 1-year forward returns, but the t-statistics must be estimated in a more complex way with overlapping data).[2] The time series of the dividend yield is plotted in figure 10.1. We see that the dividend yield has varied significantly over the century, is highly persistent, and has been lower during the recent decades than earlier in history, reflecting higher equity valuations. The predictive regression yields

$$R^e_{t+1} = -5.3\% + 3.3 \times DP_t + \varepsilon_{t+1} \tag{10.5}$$

We see that the estimated b coefficient is in fact greater than one! In words, a high DP not only means that you earn a high dividend yield, it also means that you expect to earn a larger-than-normal price appreciation. This is actually intuitive since a high dividend yield means that equities are likely cheap and therefore have a high expected price appreciation. A one percentage point higher dividend yield translates into a 2.3 percentage point higher estimated expected price appreciation such that the total equity premium increases by 3.3 percentage points. The t-statistic of the estimate is 2.8, indicating that the coefficient appears significantly different from zero,[3] but the estimated standard error of 1.2 also means that the coefficient could really be anywhere between $3.3 - 2 \times 1.2 = 1$ and $3.3 + 2 \times 1.2 = 6$, a wide range.

The estimated coefficients imply that the equity premium varies significantly as the dividend changes over time. For instance, the lowest observed dividend

[2] The dividend yield data are from Shiller's website, http://www.econ.yale.edu/~shiller/data .htm.

[3] The regression coefficient is subject to a bias due to the highly persistent regressor, as shown by Stambaugh (1999), which reduces the statistical significance of the predictive regression coefficient.

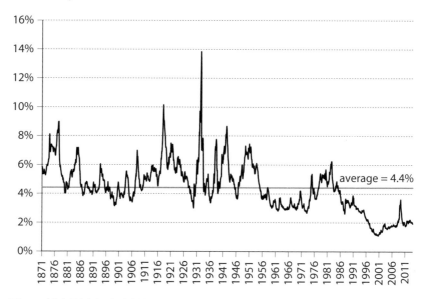

Figure 10.1. Dividend yield in the United States, 1871–2013.
Source: Robert Shiller's data, http://www.econ.yale.edu/~shiller/data.htm.

yield of 1.1% happened in 2000 during the height of the Internet bubble. Based on the regression estimates, this translates into an equity premium of $E_t(R^e_{t+1})$ $=-5.3\% + 3.3 \times 1.1\% = -1.6\%$. The highest observed dividend yield of 13.8% happened during the stock market trough of 1932, implying an equity premium of 41%.

How could you trade on the insights that come out of this regression? Let us consider a simple backtest. Table 10.1 shows that when the dividend yield has been high, the annualized market return in the following month has been high on average, 11.2%. During periods of low dividend yield, the subsequent market return has been lower. This can be viewed as a backtest of the strategy to invest only when the dividend yield is high (or low). Investing only at those times would have given much of the market return at a lower risk and, if one had used leverage at those times, this strategy could in principle have outperformed the market at the same average risk over the full period, although the

TABLE 10.1. MARKET EXCESS RETURN CONDITIONAL ON THE DIVIDEND YIELD

	DP_t above Its Median	DP_t below Its Median
Market excess return $t + 1$	11.2%	4.2%
Market volatility $t + 1$	21.6%	15.3%

improvement in Sharpe ratio is modest. One could further test more complex timing strategies, e.g., a linear scaling of the market exposure as a function of the dividend yield (consistent with the linear regression).

Out-of-Sample vs. In-Sample

Both the regression and the backtest above suffer from a serious problem: They were not known at the beginning of the time period in 1926! To make a timing strategy, an investor needs to decide on three things: (1) what is the predictor? (2) is the current level of the predictor high or low? and (3) how does variation in the predictor translate into future predicted returns?

Each of these steps is difficult to do in real time, and backtests are often subject to biases with respect to some or all of them. First, choosing the predictor is not easy, and backtests often tend to look at variables that have worked in the past, a selection bias as they may not work in the future. Second, knowing whether a predictor is high or low is based on limited historical evidence or guidance from judgment and economic theory. This is easy, however, in an in-sample (i.e., cheating) backtest, but in 1932 investors did not know that this dividend was at an all-time high compared to the *next* 80 years, and in 2000 investors did not know that the dividend yield would not get any lower in the next decade (even if judgment might have suggested that these values were extreme). Third, it is naturally difficult to estimate how the level of the predictor translates into predicted returns, e.g., the regression coefficient is estimated with significant error even with a hundred years of data.

To backtest a timing strategy in a realistic way, one must consider the out-of-sample performance, that is, the return that could have been achieved with the information available at the time (as discussed further in chapter 3). Studying the out-of-sample performance of a range of different predictor variables for the U.S. equity premium, Welch and Goyal (2008) find that most of these market timing models fare poorly.

Clearly, timing the market is incredibly difficult—it is a single bet with close to even odds. For macro investing to have a chance at success, it must either start with a strong strategic asset allocation and make modest tactical tilts or diversify across many timing strategies. In chapter 12, we see that a simple trend-following timing strategy has performed well when diversified across fifty-some equity, bond, currency, and commodity markets.

Tactical Asset Allocation

As discussed above, market timing means deciding the allocation to one risky market, say the equity market, which is implicitly a trade-off between cash and equities. Deciding among multiple markets is called tactical asset allocation.

The classic tactical asset allocation decision is how to set the relative weights among cash, equities, and bonds.

Global tactical asset allocation (GTAA) is an even more wide-ranging macro investment strategy. Here, the goal is not just to decide on the allocation across asset classes but also to consider the various global markets. For instance, should you invest in the overall equity market index in the United States, Japan, the United Kingdom, Canada, Brazil, or Australia? Or should you go long on some of these equity indices while shorting others? With GTAA, the distinction between asset allocation and security selection starts to blur, since, for example, a GTAA investor can be seen as selecting to be long on the Brazilian and Australian stock markets and to short the U.K. and Canadian stock markets. In the next chapter, we discuss how global macro investors make these decisions.

10.3. UNDERSTANDING THE RETURNS OF THE MAJOR ASSET CLASSES

To decide on strategic asset allocations and how to change these allocations tactically, it is important to understand the returns of each of the major asset classes. Here we consider both the long-term return drivers and how expected returns change over time.

What Drives Equity Returns

At the most basic level, equity returns consist of two components, the dividend yield and the capital appreciation as seen in equation 10.3. The realized price appreciation is, of course, impossible to know in advance, and even the *expected* price appreciation is difficult to estimate. To better understand the drivers of price appreciation, it is useful to further decompose the equity return based on the price-dividend ratio, $PD_t = P_t/D_t$:

$$R_{t+1} = \underbrace{\frac{D_{t+1}}{P_t}}_{\substack{\text{dividend} \\ \text{yield}}} + \underbrace{\frac{D_{t+1} - D_t}{D_t}}_{\substack{\text{dividend} \\ \text{growth}}} + \underbrace{\frac{PD_{t+1} - PD_t}{PD_t}}_{\substack{\text{valuation} \\ \text{change}}} + \underbrace{\frac{D_{t+1} - D_t}{D_t} \cdot \frac{PD_{t+1} - PD_t}{PD_t}}_{\substack{\text{small} \\ \text{adjustment}}} \qquad (10.6)$$

We see that an equity investor earns three types of returns (plus a small adjustment, which is often ignored): First, you simply collect dividends.[4] The higher the dividend, the higher the return. Importantly, the dividend should be seen in relation to what you paid for the stock, and this ratio is called the *dividend yield*. Hence, the dividend yield could be high simply because the market

---

[4] The dividend yield should in principle include all the payments to equity owners less their capital infusions, that is, net share buybacks should be included in dividends.

price of the stock is low. A typical dividend yield is 2%, but there is a lot of variation over time across firms, with some currently paying nothing to shareholders (and possibly issuing shares) and a small fraction paying more than 8%.

Second, you earn equity returns if the stock's dividends grow over time. This dividend growth naturally sets you up for higher future dividend income, but the return may be more immediate than that: If the price-dividend ratio remains unchanged, then a 4% increase in dividends results in a 4% increase in the price—i.e., a capital appreciation of 4%. What dividend growth is to be expected? First, since firm profits are earned in nominal terms, earnings and dividends tend to rise with inflation. Hence, an inflation of 2% tends to raise earnings and dividends by 2%. Furthermore, if the company participates in normal economic growth (say, growth of GDP per capita), this could lead to a real dividend growth rate of around 2%, although the historical real dividend growth rate has been below the overall economic growth (perhaps because of growth due to new firms) of around 1.5%. The sum of these numbers results in a total nominal dividend growth rate of around 3 to 4%, say 3.5%.

Third, you earn equity returns—positive or negative—from a change in valuation. For instance, if the market is currently paying a 50-to-1 price-dividend ratio for stocks and then mean-reverts to 40-to-1 (half way toward its long-run mean around 30), then you lose 20% of the equity value. Conversely, increases in the price-dividend ratio lead to capital appreciation. Hence, capital appreciation can be driven by higher dividends at the same valuation or by higher valuation of the same dividends.

Lastly, the equity return has a small adjustment term, which arises when both the valuation and dividends change in the same time period. For instance, if dividends grow by 5% and the valuation grows by 8%, then the adjustment term is only $5\% \times 8\% = 0.4\%$, a marginal effect (which reflects that the new dividends also benefit from the higher valuation). Hence, this term is often ignored.

What is the long-term return on equities? Well, over the long term, the valuation cannot grow or fall forever, so long-run returns arise primarily from dividend yield and dividend growth. Hence, a typical stock with a 2% dividend yield and a 3.5% dividend growth rate has an expected return of 5.5% over the long term.

We can further compute the *equity premium*, that is, the expected return on equities in excess of the risk-free rate. The equity premium is important because it tells by how much equities are expected to beat cash and it should be viewed as the current market compensation for the risk in equities. Of course, the equity premium depends both on the expected equity return and the current risk-free interest rates. Given that the current interest rates are near zero, this means that the equity premium is also about 5.5%, under the same assumptions as above. A more typical nominally risk-free interest rate might be around 3 to 4%, that is, a 1 to 2% real rate plus 2% inflation. With an interest rate of 3%, the equity premium would only be 2.5% under the maintained assumptions, but of course, all these numbers are subject to significant uncertainty.

The historical U.S. equity premium over cash has been about 7 to 8% per year from 1926 to 2013, but it has been lower in most other countries. This high historical U.S. equity premium can be decomposed as follows: The historical average dividend yield was 3.9%, almost double its current value. The dividend growth rate was 4.6%, higher than my estimate above due to higher historical inflation of about 3%. The price appreciation due to valuation change has been substantial, 2.4%, due to the increase in the price-dividend ratio (and to a convexity effect associated with arithmetic averages of returns with time-varying valuation ratio).[5] The average adjustment term is small (about 0.15%). The average risk-free rate has been 3.5%, implying a low average real rate. These numbers explain the historical equity return of $3.9 + 4.6 + 2.4 = 11\%$ and the equity premium of $11 - 3.5\% = 7.5\%$. Given the current higher equity valuation, the historical equity premium does not appear sustainable in the future. Price-dividend ratios cannot rise forever—on the contrary, the valuation level may mean-revert over time, leading to even lower equity returns than estimated above.

Finally, equity returns can also be understood in terms of the earnings yield, that is, the ratio of earnings (or, net income NI) to the price:

$$R_{t+1} = \underbrace{\frac{NI_{t+1}}{P_t}}_{\substack{\text{earnings} \\ \text{yield}}} + \underbrace{\frac{P_{t+1} - (P_t + NI_{t+1} - D_{t+1})}{P_t}}_{\substack{\text{price} \\ \text{surplus}}} \tag{10.7}$$

If we consider this relation in terms of book values, then the second term is zero (called the "clean surplus accounting relation") as discussed in chapter 6. For market values, the second term need not be zero as the market value can vary for a number of reasons, but the *expected* value of this term is approximately equal to the inflation rate under certain conditions that apply mostly for mature firms.[6]

$$E_t(R_{t+1}) \cong \underbrace{\frac{E_t(NI_{t+1})}{P_t}}_{\substack{\text{earnings} \\ \text{yield}}} + \underbrace{i}_{\text{inflation}} \tag{10.8}$$

Hence, the expected earnings yield can be viewed as a simple measure of the expected *real* return of a stock or an entire stock market. This can be seen

---

[5] The equity premium is calculated as 12 times the arithmetic average of monthly excess returns over T-bills using the value-weighted stock price index from Ken French's website, mba.tuck.dartmouth.edu/pages/faculty/ken.french/. The average geometrically compounded return is 1.4 percentage points lower, around 6.3% over cash.

[6] To see why the expected price surplus could be equal to inflation, suppose that (a) the real market value of assets in place at time $t + 1$ is expected to remain unchanged, such that the nominal value is expected to grow to $(1 + i)P_t$, and (b) the retained earnings $NI_{t+1} - D_{t+1}$ are invested in zero NPV projects (e.g., cash or other securities). Then the time $t + 1$ market value P_{t+1} equals $(1 + i)P_t + NI_{t+1} - D_{t+1}$, yielding a price surplus equal to i. To see why this relation might not hold, consider a firm that currently has zero earnings and zero dividends and whose value derives from the chance that earnings suddenly become large in the future (at time $t + 2$ or later). Such a firm will have a zero earnings yield and an expected price surplus equal to its required return.

informally by subtracting inflation from both sides of equation 10.8. A more correct way to adjust for inflation (the difference matters only for countries with high inflation) is to define the real return R_{t+1}^{real} by $(1 + R_{t+1}) = (1 + R_{t+1}^{real})(1 + i_t)$, which together with equation 10.8 gives

$$E_t(R_{t+1}^{real}) \cong \underbrace{\frac{E_t(NI_{t+1}/(1+i))}{P_t}}_{\text{adj. earnings yield}} \tag{10.9}$$

Here, the real expected return is seen to be the earnings yield, where the numerator has been inflation adjusted. Indeed, for the earnings yield to be truly inflation neutral, earnings and prices should both be measured in terms of time-t dollars, which is why the earnings term in the numerator is inflation adjusted.

Investors often compare the earnings yield with the bond yield (called the "Fed model," although the Fed does not use this as a model for equity valuation), but this comparison ignores the notion that the earnings yield is a measure of *real* returns, whereas bond yields are measures of *nominal* returns (Asness 2003). Intuitively, real stock returns are not affected by inflation since inflation raises future earnings and prices, whereas inflation reduces the real value of bonds with fixed nominal coupons.

To apply this earnings-yield method to real data, note that the average earnings yield in the United States has been about 7% from 1926 to 2013, close to the real return of equities. Indeed, the price surplus has been about 3.6%, close to (but slightly above) the realized inflation of ca. 3%. Hence, equation 10.8 has worked decently over this sample. The sum of the two parts gives the total nominal equity return, which has been around 11%.

At the end of 2013, the earnings yield was about 5.5%, which suggests an expected nominal equity return of about 7.5%, assuming an inflation rate of 2%. This estimate is higher than the 5.5% derived based on equation 10.6, which is partly due to the cyclically high earnings. Using a cyclically adjusted earnings yield of 4.3% implies a nominal expected equity return of 6.3%, broadly consistent with the number derived from equation 10.6. The cyclically adjusted earnings can be computed in the spirit of Shiller's cyclically adjusted price earnings (CAPE) ratio, that is, by taking a 10-year average of inflation-adjusted earnings.

Bond Returns

A bond's return over the long term—here, interpreted as the time to maturity—is equal to its yield to maturity.[7] This long-term return can be compared to the expected return of rolling over a cash investment in the money market. Hence,

---

[7] This statement is true by definition if we think of the return as the internal rate of return. If coupon payments are reinvested until maturity, then there is reinvestment risk.

a bond has a positive expected long-run excess return if its yield is greater than the expected average overnight interest rate over its life. The bond yield can also be compared to the expected inflation over its life as investors should seek high *real* expected returns.

Bond returns are discussed in more detail in chapter 14. As explained in that chapter, a bond's one-period holding return can be written as its current yield to maturity YTM_t minus the modified duration $\bar{D}$ times the change in yield:

$$R_{t+1} \cong \underbrace{\text{YTM}_t}_{\text{yield}} - \underbrace{\bar{D}(\text{YTM}_{t+1} - \text{YTM}_t)}_{\substack{\text{capital} \\ \text{appreciation due} \\ \text{to yield change}}} \tag{10.10}$$

Hence, a bond's short-run return depends both on its yield and its expected yield change. As discussed in chapter 14, the yield change can be predicted by the roll down on the yield curve, that is, by assuming that the bond's expected yield next period will equal the current yield on such shorter term bonds (recall that a bond becomes more short term as time passes). The expected yield change based on roll down assumes an unchanged yield curve, which has historically been a good assumption on average. Of course, yields fluctuate a lot over time, and one-period returns are dominated by these changes, which reflect surprising shocks to growth, inflation, or monetary policy. The yield change can also be predicted by other factors, e.g., by assuming that yields mean-revert to their long-term averages or by considering expected central bank policy actions as discussed further in chapter 11.

Credit Returns

The return of a fixed-coupon corporate bond faces both interest-rate risk and the credit risk that the company might default and pay back less than the face value. The pure *credit return* can be derived by hedging out the interest-rate component, that is, by going long on a corporate bond and short on a government bond of the same duration. This credit return corresponds approximately to the return of a credit default swap (CDS). The credit return depends critically on the so-called *credit spread*,[8] defined as the difference between the yield on the corporate bond and the yield on the duration-matched government bond, $s_t = y_t^{\text{corporate}} - y_t^{\text{government}}$. Using equation 10.10 for both the corporate and government bond and adjusting for default losses, we get the following relation for credit returns:

---

[8] For corporate bonds with embedded options or mortgage-backed securities with prepayment risk, the discussion applies if one uses the option-adjusted spread rather than the simple credit spread.

$$R_{t+1}^{corporate} - R_{t+1}^{government} \cong \underbrace{s_t}_{\substack{\text{credit} \\ \text{spread}}} - \underbrace{\bar{D}(s_{t+1} - s_t)}_{\substack{\text{valuation and} \\ \text{rating risk}}} - \underbrace{L_t}_{\substack{\text{loss from} \\ \text{default}}} \qquad (10.11)$$

We see that the expected credit return is given by the credit spread, less the duration times the expected change in the credit spread, and less the expected default losses. Naturally, a higher credit spread leads to a higher return, everything else being equal.

A narrowing of the credit spread is associated with capital appreciation as seen in equation 10.11. In contrast, a widening credit spread leads to losses. Hence, the short-run risk of a corporate bond is not just that it defaults but also that the credit spread changes due to changes in the perceived default risk, e.g., related to a downgrading of the credit rating ("rating risk"). If a corporate bond is held to maturity, then the long-run return does not depend on the intermediate changes in valuation; rather, it depends on whether the investor receives the principal. Indeed, as seen in the last term of equation 10.11, credit returns are reduced by default-induced losses. The expected loss due to default is the product of the risk of default and the loss in the event of default.

Over the long run, credit returns are therefore approximately the credit spread minus the average loss rate. Over a 10-year holding period, the cumulative default probability of investment-grade bonds is about 4%, that is, about 0.4% per year (highest in the end of the holding period where the bonds may have been downgraded). The loss in default (i.e., one minus the recovery rate) differs across bonds, depending on whether they are senior or subordinated and whether they are secured or unsecured. Senior unsecured corporate bonds have an average loss in default of around 60%, that is, an average recovery rate of around 40%. Hence, the average annual loss from actual defaults of investment-grade bonds over a 10-year holding period has historically been small, around $0.60 \times 0.4\%$ = 0.24% per year. Given that investment-grade bonds have had yield spreads around 1%, their long-run excess returns have been around $1 - 0.24\% = 0.76\%$. Of course, the yield spread and default risk are higher for lower rated bonds, but, broadly speaking, for investment-grade bonds the yield spread has been several times larger than the expected default loss.

For speculative-grade corporate bonds, the loss rate becomes closer to half the credit spread. The 10-year cumulative default probability is about 30%, that is, about 3% per year for speculative-grade bonds. With a similar assumption on recovery rates as above, the average annual loss from defaults of speculative bonds has historically been around $0.60 \times 3\% = 1.8\%$ per year. The credit spread for speculative-grade bonds varies dramatically, from less than 1% to well into the double digits, but a spread number corresponding to the estimated default loss could be 5%, say, leading to an expected excess return of $5 - 1.8\% = 3.2\%$ per year.[9]

[9] The average default rates and recovery rates are from Moody's Investor Services, "Corporate Default and Recovery Rates, 1920–2010."

Currency Returns

Let us next consider return on investing in foreign currency and, for concreteness, we do this from the perspective of a U.S. investor such that the local currency is dollars. Suppose that the investor starts with $1, converts this into $1/S_t$ foreign currency units (where S_t is the spot exchange rate measured in number of dollars per unit of foreign currency, e.g., dollars per yen), invests the money at the foreign money market interest rate R_t^{f*}, and considers the dollar value next time period $t + 1$ when the spot exchange rate is S_{t+1}. This strategy gives a currency return of

$$R_{t+1} = \underbrace{\frac{1+R_t^f}{S_t}S_{t+1} - 1 = R_t^{f*}}_{\text{carry}} + \underbrace{\frac{S_{t+1}-S_t}{S_t}}_{\substack{\text{currency}\\\text{appriciation}}} + \underbrace{R_t^{f*}\frac{S_{t+1}-S_t}{S_t}}_{\substack{\text{adjustment}\\\text{term}}} \qquad (10.12)$$

Naturally, the currency return is the sum of the foreign interest earned—i.e., the carry—and the currency appreciation (plus a small adjustment that disappears with continuous compounding). Empirically, exchange rate changes over time are hard to predict, and therefore the foreign interest rate gives a simple measure of the expected short-run return of the currency.[10] This idea forms the basis of the currency carry trade, as discussed further below.

To get an idea of the long-run return of a currency, note that purchasing power parity (PPP) holds approximately in the long run. That is, while the real price of a car is not exactly the same in different countries, the prices tend to converge in the long run. This happens more quickly for items that are easy to ship, like an iPhone, and more slowly for goods that are hard to ship. The convergence may not happen at all for goods that are associated with significant service costs if the labor costs differ persistently across countries. For example, the price of a haircut in Denmark and Kenya are not likely to converge any time soon.

Let us understand the return implications of assuming that the PPP holds in T years (where T could be 5 years, for instance, depending on the expected speed of convergence). To do this, let's denote the exchange rate consistent with the PPP by S_t^{PPP}. Given an average expected cumulative domestic inflation rate of i from year t to year $t + T$ and an expected foreign inflation of $i*$, the PPP exchange rate evolves as follows:

$$S_{t+T}^{PPP} = \frac{1+i}{1+i*} S_t^{PPP} \qquad (10.13)$$

---

[10] The uncovered interest rate parity (UIP) conjectures that higher foreign interest rates should be associated with lower future changes in exchange rates, but the UIP does not hold empirically. Said differently, the currency carry trade has worked on average as high interest rates have not been associated with average future depreciation.

If we assume that the PPP holds in year T, then the exchange rate will converge to S_{t+T}^{PPP}. Therefore, the long-run expected currency appreciation is $S_{t+T}^{PPP} - S_t$, which depends on the current deviation from the PPP and the expected inflation rates. We can use this relation to derive an intuitive formula for the expected currency return. It is useful to consider the excess return above the domestic return $R_{t,t+T}^f$ of a risk-free investment from t to $t + T$ (either the expected return of rolling over money market investments or the return of a T-year bond). The cumulative long-run currency excess return from year t to $t + T$ can now be written as

$$E_t(R_{t,t+T} - R_{t,t+T}^f) \cong \underbrace{R_{t,t+T}^{f*} - R_{t,t+T}^f}_{\substack{\text{interest-rate} \\ \text{differential}}} + \underbrace{i - i^*}_{\substack{\text{inflation} \\ \text{differential}}} + \underbrace{\frac{S_t^{PPP} - S_t}{S_t}}_{\substack{\text{current} \\ \text{cheapness} \\ \text{relative to PPP}}} \quad (10.14)$$

Alternatively, if the valuation is assumed to converge halfway toward parity, then the last term should be divided by two.

If we want an expression of the expected return *per year* (rather than cumulative returns over the T years) as a function of *annualized* interest rates and annualized inflation rates, then a similar expression arises if we use continuously compounded returns:

$$E_t(R_{t,t+T} - R_{t,t+T}^f) \cong \underbrace{R_{t,t+T}^{f*} - R_{t,t+T}^f}_{\substack{\text{interest-rate} \\ \text{differential}}} + \underbrace{i - i^*}_{\substack{\text{inflation} \\ \text{differential}}} + \underbrace{\frac{\log(S_t^{PPP}) - \log(S_t)}{T}}_{\substack{\text{current} \\ \text{cheapness} \\ \text{relative to PPP}}} \quad (10.15)$$

This means that a currency has a high long-run expected return if it has a high interest rate, a low expected inflation, and is currently cheap relative to the PPP. Each of these three effects is intuitive. A high interest rate means that putting money into that country will earn a high local nominal return. A low inflation rate means that the high nominal return will also be a high real return or, viewed differently, the low inflation will likely lead to a currency appreciation. Finally, if the currency is currently cheap, an investor will earn the appreciation as the valuation normalizes.

For instance, suppose that the Australian dollar has an interest rate which is 3 percentage points higher than the U.S. rate, the Australian inflation rate is 1 percentage point higher than the U.S. one, and the Australian dollar is 5% more expensive relative to the United States based on PPP. Then under the assumptions that these rate differences will continue for five years and that the valuation will go to parity over the period, then the long-run expected return is $3\% - 1\% - 5\%/5 = 1\%$ per year.

The expected return can also be written in terms of real interest rates:

$$E_t(R_{t,t+T} - R_{t,t+T}^f) \cong \underbrace{R_{t,t+T}^{f,\text{real}*} - R_{t,t+T}^{f,\text{real}}}_{\substack{\text{real} \\ \text{interest-rate} \\ \text{differential}}} + \underbrace{\frac{\log(S_t^{PPP}) - \log(S_t)}{T}}_{\substack{\text{current} \\ \text{cheapness} \\ \text{relative to PPP}}} \quad (10.16)$$

CHAPTER 11

Global Macro Investing

The whole world is simply nothing more than a flow chart for capital.
—Paul Tudor Jones

The term *global macro* is used for a type of hedge funds that pursue a variety of different investment strategies. Global macro investors look for opportunities all over the world and in all asset classes, often use long-term, "big-picture" themes to drive positions, and are sometimes willing to take large, unhedged bets. Macro investors closely follow central banks, consider macroeconomic links, and incorporate both financial and non-financial information, such as political, technological, and demographic trends.

Global macro hedge funds typically invest in overall market indices, making a directional bet on an entire market or making relative-value bets across markets. For example, whereas an equity long–short manager might bet that Ford will outperform Toyota, a global macro manager might bet that the overall auto industry will thrive, that the U.S. auto industry (or broader stock market) will outperform the Japanese one, or that the dollar–yen exchange rate will drop.

Macro traders look at a variety of markets, including global equity indices, bond markets, currency markets, and commodity markets. Macro managers base their decisions to go long or short based on a variety of themes ranging from the *carry* of a position, their view of the likely central bank actions, their analysis of the macroeconomic environment, selecting good vs. bad countries based on the relative pricing and trends across global markets, and specific overarching themes, as we discuss in this chapter.

Global macro hedge funds use different methods to gain confidence in their investment views. Some travel the world evaluating countries by talking to central banks, local government officials such as representatives from the ministry of finance, firms, journalists, and politicians (in the government or the opposition). Such macro traders try to assess where the economy is going, the general sentiment, the likely political and policy changes, and the country's trade prospects. While some *discretionary macro hedge funds* find such local knowledge so important that they set up local offices around the world, others find this loose talk to be mostly noise and rely instead on hard data, historical precedence, thorough research, and other information; the most extreme example of the latter is the *systematic macro hedge funds* and *systematic global tactical asset allocation funds*, which trade based on quantitative models.

11.1. CARRY TRADES

A classic macro trade is the currency carry trade: Invest in currencies with high interest rates while selling currencies with low interest rates. For instance, in January 2012, Australia had an interest rate of about 4% and Japan had an interest rate of close to 0%. Hence, you could borrow 100 yen in Japan at 0% interest, exchange the yen into about 1 Australian dollar, and then earn an interest rate of 4% per year. If you hold this position for a year, then you will have A\$1.04 at the end of the year and still owe ¥100. If the exchange rate remains about 0.01A\$/¥, then we can exchange the money back to ¥104, repay the loan, and cash in our profit of ¥4. This is *not* a guaranteed profit, however. If the exchange rate moves, the profit can quickly turn to a loss. Think about what type of currency move will make you lose money, and what type will make a profit even greater than ¥4.

The return that you earn if the exchange rate does not change—4% in this example—is called the carry. A *carry trade* means investing in instruments with higher carry and shorting instruments with lower carry.

Economists used to believe that high-interest currencies would tend to depreciate and that this depreciation would exactly offset the high interest rate on average. Under this hypothesis (called the "uncovered interest rate parity"), the carry trade would not make any money on average. However, this theory is clearly rejected by the data (as academics have concluded), meaning that the carry trade has historically made money (as macro traders have experienced). Indeed, high-interest currencies neither depreciate nor appreciate significantly on average in developed markets.[1] In other words, currency moves sometimes reduce the carry trade profit and sometimes add to the profit, and these profits and losses roughly balance out on average.

The currency carry trade is characterized by having many small profits and episodic large losses, as traders say:

The carry trade goes up by the stairs and down by the elevator.

---

[1] In emerging markets, macro investors often look at each country's real interest rate, that is, the nominal interest rate minus the inflation rate.

This return pattern is evident if you simply look at the time series of the Aussie–yen exchange rate (check yourself). Therefore, exploiting the carry trade has risk, especially if the trade is leveraged. For instance, a macro trader might decide to leverage the Aussie–yen trade three times to earn a carry of $3 \times 4\% = 12\%$, but this method would expose him to large potential losses if the Australian dollar suddenly depreciated sharply.

The idiosyncratic currency risk can be diversified away by investing in a number of high-interest currencies while shorting several low-interest currencies, but diversification does not cure the risk of carry-trade crashes since during so-called "carry-trade unwinds," most high-interest-rate currencies fall together. This is seen in figure 11.1, which shows the distribution of the quarterly profits from a currency carry trade. The peak of the distribution is above zero, indicating that the carry trade makes money more often than not, while the hump to the left indicates the not-so-unlikely risk of large losses on a diversified carry trade. The carry-trade unwind often happens during times of economic disruptions when markets are illiquid, traders need funding, and risk aversion rises. (See Brunnermeier, Nagel, and Pedersen (2008) for details.)

This risk leads macro traders to ponder when they should get out of the carry trade. When liquidity starts to dry up and risk increases, perhaps it is time to unwind the carry trade before others do so? Timing this is not easy; the fickle behavior of many traders may be exactly what leads to carry unwinds when everyone runs for the exit at the same time. This is an example of the liquidity spirals discussed more generally in section 5.10.

Macro traders must also be aware of currencies that are pegged or managed by the central bank. Indeed, if a currency is pegged, the carry trade may look like a perfect arbitrage until the peg breaks, at which time the carry trade gets crushed. This is called a "peso problem" because of the experience with the

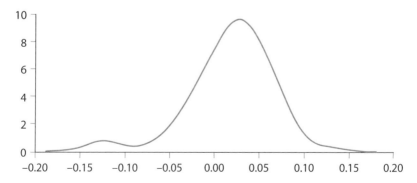

Figure 11.1. The distribution of quarterly excess returns from the currency carry trade. Source: Brunnermeier, Nagel, and Pedersen (2008).

Mexican peso in the 1970s. Macro traders are therefore often reluctant to base their investment in a managed currency on its carry. If they believe that a currency band is stable, they may bet on mean-reversion, buying the currency as it nears its lower bound and selling it close to its upper bound.

More dramatically, macro traders may bet that a currency peg will break, as George Soros famously did when he "broke the Bank of England" in 1992. This is a story often told, but let me mention here that such a trade has a *negative* carry. Said differently, the carry trade will be positioned in the opposite direction. To defend a currency under attack, the central bank must raise the local interest rate (as the Bank of England did in 1992). This move induces a negative carry for someone shorting the currency, but this negative carry is more than offset if the currency breaks quickly and violently.

While the currency carry trade is the most famous carry trade, macro traders can in fact trade on carry in every asset class. The concept of carry can be defined generally as the amount you will earn if prices stay the same. Hence, a carry trade generally means investing in securities with high carry while short-selling securities with low carry. Here are some examples of carry trades:

- **Currency carry trade:** As discussed above, this trade means investing in high-interest currencies while shorting low-interest ones. Typically, macro traders get currency exposure using foreign exchange (FX) forward contracts, though less liquid futures markets also exist. Hedge funds would rarely implement the trade in the cash market (i.e., actually borrowing money in one country and exchanging it to another currency), but multinational banks can do this.
- **Bond carry trade:** A bond's carry is its yield-to-maturity in excess of the financing rate. For example, a 10-year Japanese government bond has a high carry if the Japanese yield curve is steep. Some macro investors trade on bond carry across countries, buying bonds in countries with high carry while shorting bonds in countries with low carry. Such trades can be implemented with cash bonds (financed in repo), bond futures, or interest-rate swaps.
- **Yield-curve carry trade**: Macro investors also trade bonds of different maturities within the same country. This is called a yield-curve trade. Chapter 14 provides more sophisticated measures of bond carry (that include a so-called roll-down effect) and discusses in more detail how to implement bond and yield-curve trades.
- **Commodity carry trade:** The carry of a commodity futures contract is the amount of money one makes if the spot commodity price does not change. As the futures price expires at the spot price, this can be calculated directly from the current futures prices. The commodity carry arises due to convenience yield for producers who need physical

inventory and due to futures price distortions from commodity index investors. The commodity carry trade invests in high-carry commodities against low-carry ones. Another carry trade is to invest in different futures contracts on the same commodity such as buying a crude futures contract that expires in December while shorting a lower carry crude contract that expires in March. (This is similar to the yield-curve carry trade for bonds.)

- **Equity carry trade**: The carry of an equity is its dividend yield, so an equity carry trade is to invest in equity futures with high dividend yields while shorting ones with low dividend yield. (Value investors also look at dividend yield, so, for equities, carry is closely related to value.)
- **Credit carry trades**: In credit markets, the carry is sometimes taken to be simply the yield spread over risk-free bonds. Hence, a credit carry strategy of buying higher yielding bonds while shorting lower yielding ones is naturally exposed to substantial credit risk.

The performance of carry trades in different global markets is reported in table 11.1 based on estimates from the 1980s to 2011 by Koijen, Moskowitz, Pedersen, and Vrugt (2012). We see that each of these carry trades has performed well historically. The carry trades in different asset classes have a low correlation and, as a result, a diversified carry trade that invests in all of the four asset classes has an impressive Sharpe ratio of 1.4 (before transaction costs and other costs). Hence, macro traders may not just love buying high-carry securities because it feels good and is intuitive but also because carry predicts returns on average.

While some macro traders trade explicitly on carry, others focus on different investment themes. Some macro traders combine various methods, for instance, focusing on other themes while also paying close attention to their position's carry, trying to implement their trading idea in a way that has a positive carry. Such macro traders often end up being exposed to the carry trade even when this is not the main objective.

TABLE 11.1. PERFORMANCE OF CARRY TRADES ACROSS GLOBAL MARKETS

	Currency Carry Trade	Bond Carry Trade	Commodity Carry Trade	Equity Carry Trade	Diversified Carry Trade
Sharpe ratio	0.6	0.8	0.5	0.9	1.4

Source: Koijen, Moskowitz, Pedersen, and Vrugt (2012).

11.2. CENTRAL BANK MONITORING

Macro traders pay tremendous attention to central banks. Why? Well, because that's where the money is (to paraphrase Willie Sutton). Central banks control short-term interest rates, which has implications across all markets. For example, the interest rate determines the currency carry and bond prices. Therefore, macro investors monitor central banks, trying to predict their next move. Is the central bank about to raise interest rates or lower them? If the central bank is about to lower rates, how large will the rate cut be: 25 basis points (bps), 50 bps, or more? Will the central bank signal a hawkish or dovish stance that will change the market's expectations about future rate changes? Will it implement unconventional monetary policies, such as lending facilities or quantitative easing (i.e., buying long-term bonds) or increase the strength of such programs (e.g., buying more bonds per month or "tapering" such a purchase program)?

To answer these questions, macro traders seek to understand each central bank's objectives and policy constraints and to analyze the same economic data as the central bank. Central bank objectives differ across countries. In the United States, the Federal Reserve has a "dual mandate" of price stability and maximum employment. This dual mandate can be summarized by saying that the Fed sets the nominal interest rate R^f approximately according to the Taylor rule (Taylor 1993):

$$R^f = 4\% + 1.5 \times (\text{inflation} - 2\%) + 0.5 \times \text{output gap} \qquad (11.1)$$

where the output gap is the "percentage deviation of real GDP from its target," meaning whether output is above or below its potential. One can simply think of the output gap as unemployment, more specifically, whether unemployment is below its "natural" level arising from job search delays and other things.[2]

The Taylor rule reflects that the Fed would like to keep inflation at 2% and the output gap at zero. In that case, the Fed sets a nominal interest rate of 4%, corresponding to a real interest rate (R^f—inflation) of 2%. If inflation rises above 2%, then the Fed raises nominal interest rates more than 1-for-1 (called the "Taylor principle"). Specifically, if inflation rises to 3%, then the Fed increases the nominal rate to 5.5%. Hence, the real interest rate goes up to 2.5%,

---

[2] If one replaces the output gap with unemployment in the Taylor rule equation, then one must naturally also adjust the coefficients. To do this change, one can use the empirical relation (called Okun's law) that the output gap is approximately equal to minus 2 times unemployment less the "natural rate of unemployment" (NAIRU). With a NAIRU of approximately 5% in the United States, this gives a Taylor rule of $R^f = 4\% + 1.5 \times (\text{inflation} - 2\%) - (\text{unemployment} - 5\%)$. Note that empirically estimated Taylor rules differ significantly across time periods and countries. For instance, the constant term implies an average real rate of 2%, although the real rate has been significantly lower over a longer historical period.

and this rise in the real rate is meant to cool the economy, bringing inflation back down toward its target. Similarly, a negative output gap, i.e., high unemployment, results in lower interest rates that stimulate the economy.

The Taylor rule is only an approximation of the actual behavior of the Fed, and several other parameter choices and extensions have been suggested, though none perfectly match the Fed's actual choices. For instance, macro economists have noted that the Fed often acts with a certain amount of inertia, preferring to raise interest rates only gradually.

Other central banks, such as the European Central Bank (ECB), have a single objective of price stability, that is, to keep inflation relatively constant (often around 2%). Countries with a pegged exchange rate must also use their monetary policy to achieve the exchange-rate objective, raising interest rates when the currency is falling in value and lowering interest rates when it is rising. Increasingly, central banks also have a financial stability goal.

Global macro traders obsess about central bank actions for two reasons. First, and most importantly, central bank actions move asset prices, and it is rewarding to be positioned correctly for the next central bank action. Second, central banks are active in the money markets, bond markets, and currency markets, and since they are *not* trading to maximize profit, their actions sometimes give rise to trading opportunities.

So how do macro investors trade based on their views on monetary policy? The simplest way is to buy bonds or interest rate futures if they think the central bank is lowering rates, and go short if they think the central bank is raising rates. They might also speculate on the slope of the yield curve since a central bank rate hike raises short-term interest rates more than long-term interest rates, thus flattening the yield curve. Macro traders might also bet on future central bank actions using forward-interest-rate markets.

Understanding central bank actions is also useful for currency trading. When the interest rate goes up, the carry improvement may attract capital and lead to currency appreciation. Foreign exchange markets are affected more directly by central banks when they actively intervene, buying or selling currency. Predicting such interventions and their timing is difficult, but some general patterns may emerge. If central banks generally try to dampen exchange-rate swings, then exchange rates move only slowly toward their new fundamentals, creating trends in currency markets that macro traders can exploit as discussed below in section 11.4.

Example: The Greenspan Briefcase Indicator

Many macro traders were religiously following Alan Greenspan when he was the chairman of the Federal Reserve. Perhaps for this reason, he made intentionally ambiguous statements using language that was dubbed "Fedspeak." (Chairman

Bernanke, in contrast, believed that transparency is more helpful.) Traders monitored Greenspan's every move, especially on the days when the Federal Open Market Committee (FOMC) would decide on the new interest rate target.

As he walked to work on such a day, traders would already have figured out (e.g., based on the Taylor rule or recent Fedspeak) whether interest rates were heading upward or downward, leaving open the question: Will the Fed change the interest rate or leave it unchanged? The answer lay inside Greenspan's briefcase, invisible to traders. However, the thickness of the briefcase held the answer, or so the thinking went: A thick briefcase meant lots of argument, leading to a rate change. A thin briefcase meant keeping interest rates the same. Hence, Greenspan's briefcase was carefully watched (e.g., on live TV) when he walked into the Federal Reserve on FOMC days. Supposedly, in later years, Greenspan had his briefcase transported into the Fed hidden in the trunk of a car on such days, leaving Greenspan to stroll to work, arms free.

11.3. TRADING ON ECONOMIC DEVELOPMENTS

The Holy Grail for global macro traders is to know where the economy is moving. In particular, they want to know whether economic growth will be strong or slow and whether inflation is picking up or calming down. The combination of growth and inflation determines the economic environment, as illustrated in table 11.2.

If growth is strong and inflation high, the economy is doing well but may be "overheating," leading the central bank to increase interest rates. Hence, in such an environment, bond prices drop and macro investors anticipating this eventuality sell bonds short. While the yield curve may be steep in the early stages of an overheated economy, central bank actions are likely to flatten the curve over time as the policy interest rate is raised.

Stocks should do well in an overheated economy as growth fuels their profit and inflation does not affect their value (since their earnings will grow with inflation and thus keep their real value). Also, credit default swaps should fare well, while corporate bonds should see falling credit spreads, but prices will be dragged down by their interest-rate exposure.

TABLE 11.2. FOUR ECONOMIC ENVIRONMENTS DEPENDING ON GROWTH AND INFLATION

	Strong Growth	**Slow Growth**
High inflation	Overheated	Stagflation
Low inflation (or deflation)	Goldilocks	Lost decade

In a "Goldilocks" economy, not-too-hot and not-too-cold, both stocks and bonds can do well. Volatility might be falling, lowering option prices, but we must be aware that the calm will not last forever.

Stagflation is a central bank's nightmare because fighting the inflation with higher interest rates means further hurting the stagnating economy. Stocks suffer due to the poor growth prospects, and bonds suffer due to inflation. Commodities and Treasury inflation-protected securities (TIPS) may do well, at least in nominal terms, due to their inflation protection, and gold prices may also benefit from a flight to quality.

In a "lost decade" with low inflation and slow growth, bond yields are likely to fall, meaning that bond prices rise. For example, after the global financial crisis of 2008–2009, bond yields started falling and, while some investors repeatedly noted that yields could now only go up, bonds yields kept falling. Similarly, Japanese bond yields kept falling through the 1990s and, to a lesser extent, the 2000s.

Global macro hedge funds analyze the economic environment and make directional investments based on their analysis. Macro investors also consider relative-value trades, comparing different countries' relative growth and inflation developments. Such traders bet on which asset classes in which countries will outperform and which will underperform as we discuss further in section 11.4. First, we need to explore what determines the state of the economy.

The state of the economy is determined by aggregate supply and demand, and we consider their respective underlying drivers. There are several competing models in modern macroeconomics, but I focus on a simple model that captures the ideas that many macro traders and policy makers have in mind when they think about economic questions.

What Drives Aggregate Supply?

Macro economists want to determine a country's aggregate supply of output, i.e., the gross domestic product (GDP), often referred to with the symbol Y. This output is produced by the country's labor (L) and capital (K). The labor L refers to the number of people who work. A country's physical capital K refers to its machines, plants, natural resources, computers, trucks, and infrastructure that are put to use. The output supplied can be thought of as using production function F:

$$Y = \text{TFP} \times F(K,L) \tag{11.2}$$

where TFP is the total factor productivity, which measures how good the technology is, how well educated and skillful the population is, and how efficiently capital and people are allocated to the most productive sectors.

In the long run, that is all there is to it: Output is what the country can produce with the people and machines that it has. Prices and wages adjust to ensure that supply equals demand, and long-run GDP simply depends on the labor, capital, and production technology. Hence, macro traders look at population growth, education, investment, and technological innovation to determine long-run growth.

Short-run economic fluctuations are more complex, however. In the short run, a central determinant of aggregate supply is the employment rate. The labor used in production L depends not only on the country's overall available labor force but also on what fraction of the people actually work. Unemployment means fewer hands adding to the country's output. Similarly, output depends on the utilization rate of capital, meaning whether machines are idle or running at full speed.

Short-run economic dynamics are therefore closely connected to unemployment, and unemployment is related to inflation. The "Phillips curve" states that, in the short run, inflation increases with employment (as well as with expectations about future inflation). Since the supply of output increases with employment, output supply is also positively related to inflation in the short run, and this relation is represented as the aggregate supply (AS) curve in figure 11.2.

So why might inflation be positively related to employment? This may be because nominal wages are "sticky" in the short term, meaning that it takes time to change people's salary expectations and to renegotiate salaries. With sticky wages, higher-than-expected price inflation for output goods implies that firms earn higher profits and therefore hire more people. Said differently, if nominal wages stay relatively constant while output prices increase surprisingly, then real wages decline, and firms want to hire. Therefore, (unexpected) inflation tends to be positively related to employment and supply in the short term. (In the long term, expectations adjust to the level of inflation such that wages follow suit, implying that permanently higher inflation has no effect on supply, at best.)

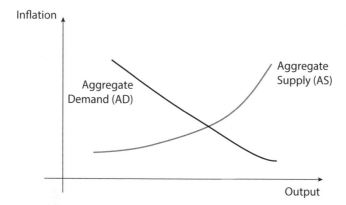

Figure 11.2. Short-run aggregate supply and demand curves.

What Drives Aggregate Demand?

In the short run, output depends on demand as well as supply. To link aggregate demand to inflation, modern economists first consider the behavior of central banks as discussed in section 11.2.[3] Since central banks want to control inflation, higher inflation leads to higher real interest rates. This is seen from the Taylor rule in equation 11.1.

How then does the interest rate affect demand? To see this, note that the aggregate demand for output (Y) consists of demand from consumption (C), investment (I), government spending (G), exports (X), less imports, (M):

$$Y = C + I + G + X - M \tag{11.3}$$

To figure out how demand depends on interest rates, consider first the determinants of private consumption, C. A lower interest rate increases private spending because it makes it cheaper to borrow (e.g., to take a car loan or credit card loan) and less attractive to save for the future. Private spending also depends on income and expectations about future income. Since income equals output Y, a multiplier effect can enhance the interest-rate sensitivity of consumption.

A lower interest rate also increases real investment I. This is because firms find it profitable to construct new plants and machines when they can be financed at a lower rate. Government spending, exports, and imports are relatively insensitive to interest rates, but they constitute possible demand shocks (e.g., due to changes in trade patterns as discussed later).

In conclusion, a lower interest rate raises aggregate demand (which is called the investment–saving curve or IS curve). Furthermore, recall that lower inflation leads to lower interest rates. Putting these two insights together explains why lower inflation leads to higher aggregate demand, as seen in the AD curve in figure 11.2.

Supply and Demand Shocks Determine Growth and Inflation

Short-run output and inflation are determined as the equilibrium point where aggregate supply meets demand in figure 11.2. Macro investors are not satisfied with understanding the current state of the economy, however; they want to know what happens *next*. They want to figure out whether economic growth will rise or slow down and whether inflation is about to pick up or quiet down.

[3] This section is based on a version of an IS-MP model, that is, the combination of an investment-savings (IS) relation and the central bank's monetary policy (MP) function. The MP function replaces the so-called LM curve (liquidity preference and money supply curve) in the traditional IS-LM model.

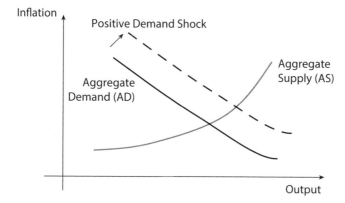

Figure 11.3. The effect of a positive demand shock.

These changes are what move asset prices, and macro investors want to be positioned correctly for the next big move.

To figure out what happens next, macro economists must consider the shocks that are about to hit the economy and what effects they will have. One possibility is a positive demand shock, as illustrated in figure 11.3. Suppose, for example, that aggregate demand increases because of stronger consumer confidence or monetary easing (i.e., an interest rate below the level prescribed by the Taylor rule). As seen in figure 11.3, this increase raises both output and inflation, leading

TABLE 11.3. SUPPLY AND DEMAND SHOCKS GENERATE FOUR TYPES OF ECONOMIC ENVIRONMENTS

	Strong Growth	**Slow Growth**

High inflation	Positive demand shocks:
	    Stronger consumer confidence
	    Monetary easing
	    Easier access to credit
		Negative supply shocks:
		    Higher oil prices
		    Depreciating capital
		    Inefficient use of capital or trade

Low inflation (or deflation)	Positive supply shocks:
	    Lower oil prices
	    Better technology
	    Labor market more global or more skilled
		Negative demand shocks:
		    Weaker consumer confidence
		    Money tightening
		    Worse access to credit

to rising stock prices and falling bond prices. Hence, if a macro investor anticipates rising aggregate demand—or anticipates that rising demand is more likely
than reflected in current prices—then she might buy stocks and short-sell bonds.

Alternatively, the demand shock can be negative, or the shock could come
from the supply side. A supply shock (i.e., a change in the supply of goods for
the same output prices) can be driven by a change in oil prices, technological
innovation, or change in the labor market. These shocks correspond to up/
down movements in the AS/AD curves, and the effects of these four types of
shocks are illustrated in table 11.3.

Interestingly, we see that these demand and supply shocks are what generate
the four economic environments from table 11.2. Demand shocks can generate
an overheated economy or a lost decade, while supply shocks can generate Goldilocks or stagflation. Macro investors thus ponder the relative likelihood of supply and demand shocks when deciding on directional trades across asset classes.

The various types of supply and demand shocks occur over different time
scales as some macro events drive the short-term dynamics (within a year),
others affect the medium-term economic environment (1–5 years), and yet others determine the long-run growth (5+ years). The typical short-term demand
shocks include changes in the consumer spending rate, changes in monetary
policy, and changes in access to consumer credit (credit boom vs. banking
crisis). Short-run supply shocks include changes in prices of natural resources,
especially energy prices.

In the medium run, supply shocks can arise from changes in capital. Capital
improvements are due to successful investments, including foreign direct investment (FDI). If a country fails to invest enough, its capital stock decreases
as it depreciates and becomes obsolete. One driver of investment is how low
the real interest rate is, which depends in part on the inflation risk premium
(i.e., stable inflation is best) and the rule of law. Also, supply shocks can arise
from changes in labor-market frictions (sticky wages, search frictions, and
rigid labor laws), product-market frictions (sticky prices and anticompetitive
corporate measures), and capital-market frictions (market and funding illiquidity) leading to unemployment and lower capital utilization. For instance, a systemic banking crisis slows growth because the ability to finance projects is a
driver of investment. In the long run, output depends on supply factors such as
technological progress and population growth.

11.4. COUNTRY SELECTION AND OTHER GLOBAL MACRO TRADES

There are no limits to the kinds of trades that global macro hedge funds might
consider. Here we consider some of the key trades based on relative-value
country selection, momentum, trade flows, and political events.

Value and Momentum in Global Markets

As discussed in chapter 9, value and momentum strategies have worked well in individual equity markets over the past century. Such strategies are also pursued by global macro investors, though in very different macro markets. Macro momentum investing means buying markets that have outperformed, while shorting markets that have underperformed. For example, a global manager might buy equity indices in countries that are trending upward while shorting equity futures in countries that are lagging. The simplicity of this strategy makes it easy to generalize across markets.

Macro value investing means buying cheap markets while shorting expensive ones. For instance, a manager might compare the overall pricing of an equity market with where she thinks the fundamental value is. Of course, estimating fundamental value can be challenging, and there are many ways to approach it. Here is a simple way to think about value investing for several of the major global asset classes based on Asness, Moskowitz, and Pedersen (2013):

- **Global equity index value trade**: For equity indices, one can use the same techniques as in valuing individual equities. In other words, if you can value each of the stocks, just add up their value to get the fundamental value of the index and compare it to the overall price. One simple measure is the price-to-book ratio for the overall market (or other valuation ratios). Hence, one macro value trade is to buy "cheap" equity indices in countries with low price-to-book ratios while shorting equity indices with high ones.
- **Currency value trade**: For currencies, one measure of value can be derived using purchasing power parity (PPP). PPP says that goods should cost the same in all countries. Hence, if a burger (or a diversified basket of goods) costs more in euros than in US$, then the euro should fall in value going forward, resulting in a short-euro value bet.[4] A simpler way to trade on currency value is to trade on long-term reversal, betting that currencies that have experienced large real appreciation (over five years, say) will eventually see a partial reversal of this move.
- **Global bond value trade**: A bond value trade is buying and selling 10-year bonds across countries globally. One measure of value is the real bond yield, that is, the yield minus the local inflation rate. Another simple measure is the current yield minus where the yield used to be for that country, focusing on long-run reversal. More sophisticated value measures would take into account each country's risk of default (government

---

[4] Especially for emerging markets, the PPP comparison should be adjusted for the Balassa–Samuelson effect that prices of non-tradable goods are systematically lower in poorer countries. For example, a haircut cannot easily be exported, and it is likely to remain cheaper in a poorer country even if iPad prices converge.

debt, current account, and so on), the risk of future inflation, and global investment flows.

- **Commodity value trade**: Measuring the fundamental value of a commodity is difficult because it depends on a host of supply and demand factors. The simplest commodity value trade is to use long-run reversal (which also works in all the other asset classes), betting that commodities that have risen exceptionally in value will underperform those that have risen less.

Asness, Moskowitz, and Pedersen (2013) examine such global value and momentum trades in global equity, currency, bond, and commodity markets. Figure 11.4 plots the performance over time and reports the Sharpe ratios and correlations. The figure also shows the "combo" strategy of using both value and momentum signals together. As seen in the figure, value and momentum have worked in each of the asset classes. It is a testimony to the strength of these investment philosophies that they work both in individual equity markets and macro markets.

Value and momentum are highly negatively correlated. This makes sense because they are somewhat opposite trading ideas: One buys what looks cheap while the other buys what is trending upward (and may have become expensive

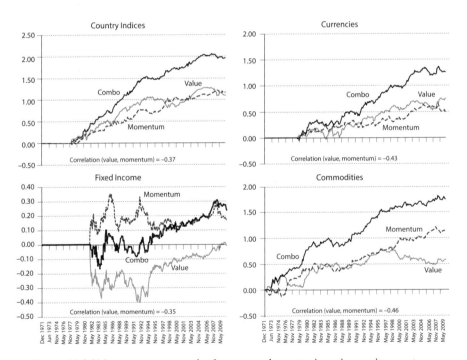

Figure 11.4. Value, momentum, and val-mom-combo strategies using equity country indices, currencies, fixed income, and commodity markets.
Source: Asness, Moskowitz, and Pedersen (2013).

as a result). However, value and momentum are not exact opposites since momentum looks at the short-run while value looks at the long run, and, as a result, both can make money on average. The strong negative correlation between value and momentum means that it is powerful to combine them as seen from the performance of the combo strategy. Many macro traders do just one or the other, however, as it is unintuitive to look for a cheap country that is trending upward—by definition you are missing the bottom.

Global Trade Flows and Terms of Trade

Global trade can be an important determinant of economic activity and exchange rates, especially for a small country. A country that exports more than it imports experiences buying pressure of its currency, which can lead to currency appreciation, especially if the buying pressure suddenly increases. Furthermore, the export sector fuels the domestic economy. Hence, some global macro investors try to predict changes in trade flows based on the new events that affect the relative supply and demand of exports and imports.

One important indicator is a country's terms of trade, which measures the prices of the goods that a country exports relative to the prices of the goods that the country imports. For instance, suppose that South Africa exports diamonds and imports mining machines. If the price of diamonds rises relative to the price of machines, this is an improvement of South Africa's terms of trade.

Macro traders may both track changes in terms of trade and try to predict their various implications. The increase in diamond prices will boost exports and create demand for the South African rand (ZAR), everything else being equal. While the diamond industry benefits, the exchange rate appreciation hurts other parts of the local economy, e.g., wine and textile exporters (a phenomenon called the "Dutch disease").

The trade surplus is the major determinant of the current account surplus (which also includes interest income from foreign assets and foreign aid). A country's current account surplus corresponds to its net increase in foreign assets, called a capital outflow. Capital flows and trade flows are therefore closely linked, and shocks to either can be important for exchange rates. For example, a country can experience strong capital inflows that push the exchange rate upward, leading to trade deficits.

Political Events and Regulatory Uncertainty

Changes in trade flows and terms of trade can influence exchange rates, but they can also work the other way. Sometimes countries try to influence their exchange rate to increase exports, and macro investors like to be attuned to such developments.

More generally, political events can be important for global macro developments. Countries may change their trade relations in various ways, opening or closing markets, imposing tariffs, imposing explicit or implicit trade barriers, and some countries face embargos due to strained intergovernmental relations.

The most extreme outcome of political events is a war, but more often macro traders look at more mundane new policies and legislation. They try to predict the consequences of the new legislation, e.g., which sectors will benefit and which sectors will be harmed.

11.5. THEMATIC GLOBAL MACRO

Some global macro traders focus on a few "big ideas" that they call "themes." They believe that certain macro events will be important drivers of economic events in the future and then try to find various ways of profiting if the theme indeed plays out.

For instance, some global macro traders might believe that China's growth will outpace what people expect. They might therefore buy Chinese stocks, buy commodities, especially those that China imports heavily, buy stocks in commodity-producing countries such as Australia, and possibly sell bonds if they believe that inflation will ensue. Another theme might be that China is instead in a bubble, leading the macro trader to take the opposite positions.

Yet another thematic global macro manager might believe that global warming is coming, buying carbon rights and windmill companies, or that oil production cannot keep up with demand, leading to rising energy prices.

Recently, an important theme has been systemic risk in the financial sector and sovereign credit risk. Some macro traders may focus on the likelihood that countries with large government debt will default or have inflation or that uncertainty and money growth will result in rising gold prices. Try to think of your own themes and create ways to trade on them.

11.6. GEORGE SOROS'S THEORY OF BOOM/BUST CYCLES AND REFLEXIVITY

George Soros is one of the most successful investors of all times. In addition to being a successful investor, he is a philanthropist, opinion maker, and philosopher. Soros has developed a theory of boom/bust cycles and reflexivity, as he describes in the following excerpt from a recent lecture.[5]

Let me state the two cardinal principles of my conceptual framework as it applies to the financial markets. First, market prices always distort the

---

[5] Soros (2010), "Financial Markets," in *The Soros Lectures*, PublicAffairs, New York.

underlying fundamentals. The degree of distortion may range from the negligible to the significant. This is in direct contradiction to the efficient market hypothesis, which maintains that market prices accurately reflect all the available information. Second, instead of playing a purely passive role in reflecting an underlying reality, financial markets also have an active role: they can affect the so-called fundamentals they are supposed to reflect.

There are various pathways by which the mispricing of financial assets can affect the so-called fundamentals. The most widely traveled are those that involve the use of leverage—both debt and equity leveraging. The various feedback loops may give the impression that markets are often right, but the mechanism at work is very different from the one proposed by the prevailing paradigm. I claim that financial markets have ways of altering the fundamentals and that the resulting alterations may bring about a closer correspondence between market prices and the underlying fundamentals.

My two propositions focus attention on the reflexive feedback loops that characterize financial markets. I described the two kinds of feedback, negative and positive. Again, negative feedback is self-correcting, and positive feedback is self-reinforcing. Thus, negative feedback sets up a tendency toward equilibrium, but positive feedback produces dynamic disequilibrium. Positive feedback loops are more interesting because they can cause big moves, both in market prices and in the underlying fundamentals. A positive feedback process that runs its full course is initially self-reinforcing in one direction, but eventually it is liable to reach a climax or reversal point, after which it becomes self-reinforcing in the opposite direction. But positive feedback processes do not necessarily run their full course; they may be aborted at any time by negative feedback.

I have developed a theory about boom-bust processes, or bubbles, along these lines. Every bubble has two components: an underlying trend that prevails in reality and a misconception relating to that trend. A boom-bust process is set in motion when a trend and a misconception positively reinforce each other. The process is liable to be tested by negative feedback along the way. If the trend is strong enough to survive the test, both the trend and the misconception will be further reinforced. Eventually, market expectations become so far removed from reality that people are forced to recognize that a misconception is involved. A twilight period ensues during which doubts grow and more people lose faith, but the prevailing trend is sustained by inertia. As Chuck Prince, former head of Citigroup said: "As long as the music is playing, you've got to get up and dance. We're still dancing." Eventually a point is reached when the trend is reversed; it then becomes self-reinforcing in the opposite direction.

Let me go back to the example I used when I originally proposed my theory in 1987: the conglomerate boom of the late 1960s. The underlying trend is represented by earnings per share, the expectations relating to that trend by stock prices. Conglomerates improved their earnings per share by acquiring other companies. Inflated expectations allowed them to improve their earnings performance, but eventually reality could not keep up with expectations. After a twilight period the price trend was reversed. All the problems that had been swept under the carpet surfaced, and earnings collapsed. As the president of one of the conglomerates, Ogden Corporation, told me at the time: I have no audience to play to.

The chart below is a model of the conglomerate bubble. The charts of actual conglomerates like Ogden Corporation closely resemble this chart. Bubbles that conform to this pattern go through distinct stages: (1) inception; (2) a period of acceleration, (3) interrupted and reinforced by successful tests; (4) a twilight period; (5) and the reversal point or climax, (6) followed by acceleration on the downside (7) culminating in a financial crisis.

The length and strength of each stage is unpredictable, but there is an internal logic to the sequence of stages. So the sequence is predictable, but even that can be terminated by government intervention or some other form of negative feedback. In the case of the conglomerate boom, it was the defeat of Leasco Systems and Research Corporation in its attempt to acquire Manufacturer Hanover Trust Company that constituted the climax, or reversal point.

Typically, bubbles have an asymmetric shape. The boom is long and drawn out; slow to start, it accelerates gradually until it flattens out during the twilight period. The bust is short and steep because it is reinforced by the forced liquidation of unsound positions. Disillusionment turns into panic, reaching its climax in a financial crisis.

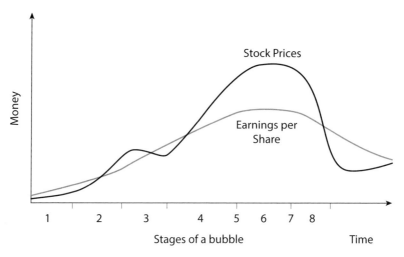

Figure 11.5. Soros's theory of boom/bust cycles and reflexivity.
Source: Soros (2010).

The simplest case is a real estate boom. The trend that precipitates it is that credit becomes cheaper and more easily available; the misconception is that the value of the collateral is independent of the availability of credit. As a matter of fact, the relationship between the availability of credit and the value of the collateral is reflexive. When credit becomes cheaper and more easily available, activity picks up and real estate values rise. There are fewer defaults, credit performance improves, and lending standards are relaxed. So at the height of the boom, the amount of credit involved is at its maximum and a reversal precipitates forced liquidation, depressing real estate values.

Not all bubbles involve the extension of credit; some are based on equity leveraging. The best examples are the conglomerate boom of the late 1960s and the Internet bubble of the late 1990s. When Alan Greenspan spoke about irrational exuberance in 1996, he misrepresented bubbles. When I see a bubble forming I rush in to buy, adding fuel to the fire. That is not irrational. And that is why we need regulators to counteract the market when a bubble is threatening to grow too big; we cannot rely on market participants, however well informed and rational they are.

Bubbles are not the only form in which reflexivity manifests itself. They are just the most dramatic and the most directly opposed to the efficient market hypothesis; so they do deserve special attention. But reflexivity can take many other forms. In currency markets, for instance, the upside and downside are symmetrical so that there is no sign of an asymmetry between boom and bust. But there is no sign of equilibrium either. Freely floating exchange rates tend to move in large, multi-year waves.

The most important and most interesting reflexive interaction takes place between the financial authorities and financial markets. While bubbles only occur intermittently, the interplay between authorities and markets is an ongoing process. Misunderstandings by either side usually stay within reasonable bounds because market reactions provide useful feedback to the authorities, allowing them to correct their mistakes. But occasionally the mistakes prove to be self-validating, setting in motion vicious or virtuous circles. Such feedback loops resemble bubbles in the sense that they are initially self-reinforcing but eventually self-defeating. Indeed, the intervention of the authorities to deal with periodic financial crises played a crucial role in the development of a "superbubble" that burst in 2007–2008.

It will be useful to distinguish between near-equilibrium conditions, which are characterized by random fluctuations, and far-from-equilibrium situations, in which a bubble predominates. Near-equilibrium is characterized by humdrum, everyday events that are repetitive and lend themselves to statistical generalizations. Far-from-equilibrium conditions give rise to unique, historic events in which outcomes are generally uncertain but have the capacity to disrupt the statistical generalizations based on everyday events. The rules that can guide decisions in near equilibrium conditions do not apply in far-from-equilibrium situations. The recent financial crisis is a case in point.

Uncertainty finds expression in volatility. Increased volatility requires a reduction in risk exposure. This leads to what John Maynard Keynes called "increased liquidity preference." This is an additional factor in the forced liquidation of positions that characterizes financial crises. When the crisis abates and the range of uncertainty is reduced, it leads to an almost automatic rebound in the stock market as the liquidity preference stops rising and eventually falls. That is another lesson I have learned recently.

11.7. INTERVIEW WITH GEORGE SOROS OF SOROS FUND MANAGEMENT

George Soros is the chairman of Soros Fund Management. One of the first and most successful hedge fund managers ever, he has been running his funds since 1973. He became known as "The Man Who Broke the Bank of England" when he made around $1 billion by short-selling the British pound during the 1992 U.K. currency crisis. Soros is also a prolific writer and has developed a theory of reflexivity. He was born in Budapest in 1930, survived the Nazi occupation of Hungary during World War II as well as the postwar imposition of Stalinism, fled to England, and graduated from the London School of Economics in 1952.

LHP: *I have the impression that you have an incredible sense of the sentiment in the market, the prevailing biases, what regulators are considering, and what market participants are thinking. How did you get that insight?*

GS: Over the years, I've developed a theory about markets. At one time, my theory was very different from the prevailing view. I focused on what I considered important in anticipating the future, rather than evaluating the present. I also noted interplay between politics and economics. So I considered actions by governments very important. At times, macro changes were important; at other times they were not. I looked at markets at various levels. There were times when I focused on the macro. At other times, I focused on a particular industry or company. It was an ever-changing game. I liked to say that I wasn't the best at playing the market by any particular set of rules, but I was particularly attuned to changes in the rules. That's really, I would say, what set me apart.

LHP: *Can you describe how you were so attuned to those changes in the rules of the game?*

GS: It was a constant process of learning. I talked to a lot of people. The markets were evolving. I look at markets not as timeless but changing with time. I view the markets as a historical process. My own involvement is an evolutionary process. My views are not timeless, but very time-bound.

LHP: *Can you describe the evolution of your market involvement?*

GS: The financial markets have changed dramatically since the end of the Second World War. Early on, they were very regulated. Currencies were regulated. Credit markets too. Take the banking system. I participated in the evolution of the banking system from the moment that it became interesting as an investment, which was in 1972. I wrote a paper called "The Case for Growth Banks." At the time, bank shares were practically not traded. I felt this was about to change, and it did change in 1973, and there was a case for growth banks. Regarding emerging markets—in the early days they were not emerging, they didn't exist! So, in the course of my history, I actually participated in the emergence of markets—let's say, opening up the Swedish stock market. It was totally isolated and totally frozen.

LHP: *Can you give an example of a macro trade you did and explain how you got the idea and how you convinced yourself that you had conviction on the trade?*

GS: Well, the most convincing thing, I suppose, is my coming out of retirement, or semiretirement, to take an active role in anticipation of the financial crisis of 2008. I was largely withdrawn and out of date in my knowledge of the markets, but I believed there was a big macro development which was going to swamp other factors. I felt that I had to protect the estate that I had acquired over the years, and, you know, my money was being invested by others. It was a pretty large fund, where the positions tended to be on the long side so I opened a macro account where I hedged, basically, the positions of others and took positions that were net/net short.

LHP: *How did you get conviction that this was going to be a major financial crisis before the market had recognized it?*

GS: Well, because I had developed this boom/bust theory. Call it a theory of bubbles. I've written books about it. I published a book in '98 when I said I thought that markets were about to collapse, *The Crisis of Global Capitalism.* The prediction turned out to be false; the markets didn't collapse.

LHP: *Well, it took a few more years.*

GS: The authorities managed to contain the problem in 1998. You had Long-Term Capital Management, and it was a pretty serious situation, which was saved by Bill McDonough, the head of the Federal Reserve in New York. He put the players in one room and said, "You've got to do something!" And then they saved the day. So, we survived '98. But by allowing what I call this super bubble to develop, it grew larger and finally exploded in 2008. In 2006, I published a book, *The Age of Fallibility,* where I had a very short section that previewed what was coming. In 2006, it was clear to me that it was coming. Even if it wasn't clear when exactly it would come.

LHP: *Right—you have this consistent record of understanding these boom/ bust cycles. At a high level, I understand what you mean, but it might not be* *obvious to someone like me to know where we are in that cycle in any kind of situation.*

GS: It wasn't obvious to me, either. That's the whole point, you see. A bubble is when a situation moves from near-equilibrium to far-from-equilibrium. So, you've got these two strange attractors where the whole thing is an interplay between perceptions and the actual state of affairs. You've got these two functions, the cognitive function and the participative function, and the interplay between them is reflexivity.

LHP: *If I understand your investment process correctly, you're comfortable positioning yourself both to profit from a boom, even as it pushes us farther away from the equilibrium state, and also positioning yourself to profit from the bust that happens as we move closer to the near-equilibrium state.*

GS: Yes.

LHP: *So, then how do you know when to switch from one to the other?*

GS: I don't know. My theory doesn't tell me, because it's actually unknowable, because it's not predetermined. It's determined by the actions and the attitudes of market participants and regulators. As a general rule, I would say that I've usually underestimated how far from equilibrium a situation can become. For instance, we lost a lot of money in 2000 when we thought that the IT bubble was collapsing, yet it had another revival.

LHP: *But as an investor, you must decide when to position yourself long versus short. Are there some signs you look for to make that switch?*

GS: Well, we're looking. We know that it's going to swing, but we don't know when.

LHP: *How did you think about what's going to be the next move of Volcker or Greenspan or other policy makers?*

GS: Well, it depends. Each—each occasion was different.

LHP: *Was it putting yourself in their place?*

GS: Well, yes. Naturally.

LHP: *I would like to understand how you size your positions. In* The Alchemy of Finance, *you say: "I was willing to risk only gains, not my capital. This gave the fund its own momentum: picking up speed when the wind was behind us and trimming sails in stormy weather." But, you have also emphasized taking very large positions when you have great conviction.*

GS: Well, I take very large positions only when there is an asymmetry. For instance, betting against the European exchange rate mechanism was a low-risk bet. By taking a very large position, I wasn't taking a large risk. That was also the case when John Paulson took a very large position against subprime mortgages because there was a disparity between the risk and the reward—he learned that from reading my book.

LHP: *What are the typical situations with very favorable risk–reward ratios?*

GS: There are many situations where there is a disparity between risk and reward. When you've got a fixed currency system, for instance. If a currency is fixed so it can only fluctuate within, say, a 2% band, then your downside risk in taking a short position is 2%, okay? However, if it breaks, then it can move much further. So, if you only have a 2% risk, you can take a large position.

LHP: *And do you tend to reduce risk after losses and increase risk after gains?*

GS: Well, generally speaking, you should not risk a significant part of your capital. Therefore, if you have a good run and you're making a lot of profit, you can risk your profits more than you can risk your capital.

LHP: *You've invested both in developed markets and emerging markets. Is there something different about investing in emerging markets?*

GS: Yes, but then the emerging markets themselves change. So, let's say Brazil was an emerging market, but now it's got quite a lot of substance to it and is no longer behaving the way it used to.

Also, emerging markets in the early years emerged because people in America decided to invest. So foreign investors were dominating. And that, in itself, created a boom/bust situation, because the entrance of foreign investors created additional demand, which outweighed the domestic demand. So shares were revalued.

But foreign investors were just as liable to be attracted by this rapid appreciation as they were likely to be pushed to dump it when it went against them. So they were an external influence, and their entry and exit created a boom/bust sequence.

LHP: *Finally, would you say that there is a specific experience that shaped you as an investor?*

GS: The formative experience of my life was growing up in Nazi-occupied Hungary. That's when I learned the difference between normal and far-from-equilibrium. In normal conditions, you play by normal rules, but in the German occupation, being a Jew, it was not normal. Because, you know, the Germans were killing normal citizens because they were Jewish; that's not normal. So, you have to recognize that.

LHP: *So do you also imply that it's important as an investor to be able to face strong adversity and have the discipline to continue through tough periods?*

GS: Right. All that. When the performance of a stock doesn't correspond to your prediction, then something is wrong, and you need to identify what that is. And one of the things that can be wrong is your hypothesis. So you have to be constantly reexamining what it was that you believed in when you bought the stock.

CHAPTER 12

Managed Futures
Trend-Following Investing

Cut short your losses . . . and let your profits run on.

—David Ricardo (1772–1823)

. . . big money was not in the individual fluctuations but in . . . sizing up the entire market and its trend.

—Jesse Livermore

David Ricardo's imperative, which has survived two centuries, suggests an attention to trends.[1] Trends are also at the heart of the century-old statement by the legendary trader Jesse Livermore, and trends continue to play an important role for active investors. The traders who are most directly focused on trend-following investing are the managed futures hedge funds and commodity trading advisors (CTAs). Such funds have existed at least since Richard Donchian started his fund in 1949, and they have proliferated since the 1970s when futures exchanges expanded the set of tradable contracts. BarclayHedge estimates that the CTA industry has grown, managing approximately $320 billion as of the end of the first quarter of 2012.[2]

[1] Ricardo's trading rules are discussed by Grant (1838), and the quote attributed to Livermore is from Lefèvre (1923).

[2] This chapter is based closely on Hurst, Ooi, and Pedersen (2013), "Demystifying Managed Futures," *Journal of Investment Management* 11(3), 42–58. I thank my co-authors Brian Hurst and Yao Hua Ooi for their collaboration. The time series momentum methodology largely follows Moskowitz, Ooi, and Pedersen (2012) and is related to cross-sectional momentum, discussed in chapters 9 (quantitative equity) and 11 (global macro). See Fung and Hsieh (2001) for an early contribution on the characteristics of CTAs, Baltas and Kosowski (2013) for further analysis of CTAs in light of time series momentum, and Hurst, Ooi, and Pedersen (2014) for more than a century of evidence on time series momentum.

Managed futures returns can be largely understood by simple, implementable trend-following strategies—specifically time series momentum strategies. This chapter provides a detailed analysis of the economics of these strategies and applies them to explain the properties of managed futures funds. Using the returns to time series momentum strategies, we analyze how managed futures funds benefit from trends and how they rely on different trend horizons and asset classes, and we examine the role of transaction costs and fees within these strategies.

Time series momentum is a simple trend-following strategy that goes long on a market that has experienced a positive excess return over a certain look-back horizon and goes short otherwise. We consider 1-month, 3-month, and 12-month look-back horizons (corresponding to short-term, medium-term, and long-term trend strategies) and implement the strategies for a liquid set of commodity futures, equity futures, currency forwards, and government bond futures.

Trend-following strategies only produce positive returns if market prices exhibit trends, but why should price trends exist? We discuss the economics of trends based on initial underreaction to news and delayed overreaction as well as the extensive literature on behavioral biases, herding, central bank behavior, and capital market frictions. If prices initially underreact to news, then trends arise as prices slowly move to more fully reflect changes in fundamental value. These trends have the potential to continue even further due to a delayed overreaction from herding investors. Naturally, all trends must eventually come to an end as deviation from fair value cannot continue indefinitely.

We find strong evidence of trends across different look-back horizons and asset classes. A time series momentum strategy that is diversified across all assets and trend horizons realizes a gross Sharpe ratio of 1.8 with little correlation to traditional asset classes. In fact, the strategy has produced its best performance in extreme up and extreme down stock markets. One reason for the strong performance in extreme markets is that most extreme bear or bull markets historically have not happened overnight but have occurred over several months or years. Hence, in prolonged bear markets, time series momentum takes short positions as markets begin to decline and thus profits as markets continue to fall.

Time series momentum strategies help explain returns to the managed futures universe. Like time series momentum, some managed futures funds have realized low correlation to traditional asset classes, performed best in extreme up and down stocks markets, and delivered alpha relative to traditional asset classes.

When we regress managed futures indices and manager returns on time series momentum returns, we find large R-squares and very significant loadings on time series momentum at each trend horizon and in each asset class. In addition to explaining the time variation of managed futures returns, time series momentum also explains the average excess return. Indeed, controlling for time series momentum drives the alphas of most managers and indices below zero. The negative alphas relative to the hypothetical time series momentum strategies show the importance of fees and transaction costs. Comparing the relative loadings, we see that most managers focus on medium- and long-term trends, giving less weight to short-term trends, and some managers appear to focus on fixed-income markets.

12.1. THE LIFE CYCLE OF A TREND

The economic rationale underlying trend-following strategies is illustrated in figure 12.1, a stylized "life cycle" of a trend. An initial underreaction to a shift in fundamental value allows a trend-following strategy to invest before new information is fully reflected in prices. The trend then extends beyond fundamentals due to herding effects and finally results in a reversal. We discuss the drivers of each phase of this stylized trend, as well as the related literature.

Start of the Trend: Underreaction to Information

In the stylized example shown in figure 12.1, a catalyst—a positive earnings release, a supply shock, or a demand shift—causes the value of an equity, commodity, currency, or bond to change. The change in value is immediate, shown by the solid line. While the market price (shown by the dashed line) moves up as a result of the catalyst, it initially underreacts and therefore continues to go up for a while. A trend-following strategy buys the asset as a result of the initial upward price move and therefore capitalizes on the subsequent price increases.

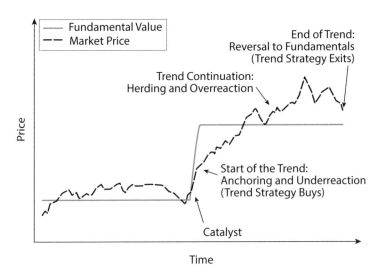

Figure 12.1. Stylized plot of the life cycle of a trend.
Source: Hurst, Ooi, and Pedersen (2013).

At this point in the life cycle, trend-following investors contribute to the speeding up of the price discovery process.

Research has documented a number of behavioral tendencies and market frictions that lead to this *initial underreaction*:[3]

i. **Anchor-and-insufficient-adjustment.** People tend to anchor their views to historical data and adjust their views insufficiently to new information.

ii. **The disposition effect.** People tend to sell winners too early and ride losers too long. They sell winners early because they like to realize their gains. This creates downward price pressure, which slows the upward price adjustment to new positive information. On the other hand, people hang on to losers because realizing losses is painful. They try to "make back" what has been lost. Fewer willing sellers can keep prices from adjusting downward as fast as they should.

iii. **Non-profit-seeking activities.** Central banks operate in the currency and fixed-income markets to reduce exchange-rate and interest-rate volatility, potentially slowing the price adjustment to news. Also, investors who mechanically rebalance to strategic asset allocation weights trade against trends. For example, a 60/40 investor who seeks to own 60% stocks and 40% bonds will sell stocks (and buy bonds) whenever stocks have outperformed.

iv. **Frictions and slow moving capital.** Frictions, delayed response by some market participants, and slow-moving arbitrage capital can also slow price discovery and lead to a drop and rebound of prices.

The combined effect is for the price to move too gradually in response to news, creating a price drift as the market price slowly incorporates the full effect of the news. A trend-following strategy will position itself in relation to the initial news and profit if the trend continues.

Trend Continuation: Delayed Overreaction

Once a trend has started, a number of other phenomena exist which may extend the trend beyond the fundamental value:[4]

i. **Herding and feedback trading.** When prices have moved in one direction for a while, some traders may jump on the bandwagon because

---

[3] References are: i. Edwards (1968), Tversky and Kahneman (1974), and Barberis, Shleifer, and Vishny (1998); ii. Shefrin and Statman (1985) and Frazzini (2006); iii. Silber (1994); and iv. Mitchell, Pedersen, and Pulvino (2007) and Duffie (2010).

[4] References are for i. Bikhchandani, Hirshleifer, and Welch (1992), De Long, Shleifer, Summers, and Waldmann (1990), Graham (1999), Hong and Stein (1999), and Welch (2000); ii. Wason (1960), Tversky and Kahneman (1974), and Daniel, Hirshleifer, Subrahmanyam (1998); iii. Vayanos and Woolley (2013).

of herding or feedback trading. Herding has been documented among equity analysts in their recommendations and earnings forecasts, in investment newsletters, and in institutional investment decisions.

ii. **Confirmation bias and representativeness.** These heuristics show that people tend to look for information that confirms what they already believe and to look at recent price moves as representative of the future. This attitude can lead investors to move capital into investments that have recently made money and conversely out of investments that have declined, both of which cause trends to continue.

iii. **Fund flows and risk management.** Fund flows often chase recent performance (perhaps because of i. and ii.). As investors pull money from underperforming managers, these managers respond by reducing their positions (which have been underperforming), while outperforming managers receive inflows, adding buying pressure to their outperforming positions. Furthermore, some risk-management schemes imply selling in down markets and buying in up markets, in line with the trend. Examples of this behavior include stop-loss orders, portfolio insurance, and corporate hedging activity (e.g., an airline company that buys oil futures after the oil price has risen to protect the profit margins from falling too much, or a multinational company that hedges foreign exchange exposure after a currency moved against it).

End of the Trend

Obviously, trends cannot go on forever. At some point, prices extend too far beyond fundamental value and, as people recognize this, prices revert toward the fundamental value and the trend dies out. As evidence of such overextended trends, extended price moves that have occurred over 3–5 years tend to partly be reversed.[5] The return reversal only reverses part of the initial price trend, suggesting that the price trend was partly driven by initial underreaction (since this part of the trend should not reverse) and partly driven by delayed overreaction (since this part reverses).

12.2. TRADING ON TRENDS

Having discussed why trends might exist, we now demonstrate the performance of a simple trend-following strategy: time series momentum. We construct time series momentum strategies for 58 highly liquid futures and currency forwards

[5] Such long-run reversal exists for time series momentum strategies (Moskowitz, Ooi, and Pedersen 2012) and also in the cross section of equities (De Bondt and Thaler 1985) and the cross section of global asset classes (Asness, Moskowitz, and Pedersen 2013).

from January 1985 to June 2012—specifically 24 commodity futures, 9 equity index futures, 13 bond futures, and 12 currency forwards. To determine the direction of the trend in each asset, the strategy simply considers whether the asset's excess return is positive or negative: A positive past return is considered an "up trend" and leads to a long position; a negative return is considered a "down trend" and leads to a short position.

We consider 1-month, 3-month, and 12-month time series momentum strategies, corresponding to short-, medium-, and long-term trend-following strategies. The 1-month strategy goes long if the preceding 1-month excess return was positive and goes short if it was negative. The 3-month and 12-month strategies are constructed analogously. Hence, each strategy always holds a long or a short position in each of 58 markets.

The size of each position is chosen to target an annualized volatility of 40% for that asset.[6] Specifically, the number of dollars bought/sold of instrument s at time t is $40\%/\sigma_t^s$ so that the time series momentum (TSMOM) strategy realizes the following return during the next week:

$$\text{TSMOM}_{t+1}^{X-\text{month, Asset}-s} = \text{sign}(\text{excess return of } s \text{ over past } X \text{ months})\frac{40\%}{\sigma_t^s}R_{t+1}^s$$

Here, σ_t^s is the ex ante annualized volatility for each instrument, estimated as an exponentially weighted average of past squared returns. This constant-volatility position-sizing methodology is useful for several reasons: First, it enables us to aggregate the different assets into a diversified portfolio that is not overly dependent on the riskier assets—this is important given the large dispersion in volatility among the assets we trade. Second, this methodology keeps the risk of each asset stable over time, so that the strategy's performance is not overly dependent on what happens during times of high risk. Third, the methodology minimizes the risk of data mining given that it does not use any free parameters or optimization in choosing the position sizes.

The portfolio is rebalanced weekly at the closing price each Friday, based on data known at the end of each Thursday. We therefore are only using information available at the time to make the strategies implementable. The strategy returns are gross of transaction costs, but we note that the instruments we consider are among the most liquid in the world. Below we consider the effect of transaction costs and the use of different rebalance rules. Academics often consider monthly rebalancing, but it is interesting to also consider higher rebalancing frequencies, given our focus on explaining the returns of professional money managers who often trade throughout the day.

---

[6] Our position sizes are chosen to target a constant volatility for each instrument following the methodology of Moskowitz, Ooi, and Pedersen (2012). More generally, one could consider strategies that vary the size of the position based on the strength of the estimated trend. For example, for intermediate price moves, one could take a small position or no position and increase the position depending on the magnitude of the price move.

Figure 12.2 shows the performance of each time series momentum strategy in each instrument. The strategies deliver positive results in almost every case, a remarkably consistent result. The average Sharpe ratio (excess returns divided by realized volatility) across assets is 0.29 for the 1-month strategy, 0.36 for the 3-month strategy, and 0.38 for the 12-month strategy.

12.3. DIVERSIFIED TIME SERIES MOMENTUM STRATEGIES

Next, we construct diversified 1-month, 3-month, and 12-month time series momentum strategies by averaging returns of all the individual strategies that share the same look-back horizon (denoted $TSMOM^{1M}$, $TSMOM^{3M}$, and $TSMOM^{12M}$, respectively). We also construct time series momentum strategies for each of the four asset classes: commodities, foreign exchange, equities, and fixed income (denoted $TSMOM^{COM}$, $TSMOM^{FX}$, $TSMOM^{EQ}$, and $TSMOM^{FI}$, respectively). For example, the commodity strategy is the average return of each individual commodity strategy for all three trend horizons. Finally, we construct a strategy that diversifies across all assets and all trend horizons that we call the diversified time series momentum strategy (denoted simply TSMOM). In each case, we scale the positions to target an ex ante volatility of 10% using an exponentially weighted variance–covariance matrix.

Table 12.1 shows the performance of these diversified time series momentum strategies. We see that the strategies' realized volatilities closely match the 10% ex ante target, varying from 9.5% to 11.9%. More importantly, all the time series momentum strategies have impressive Sharpe ratios, reflecting a high average excess return above the risk-free rate relative to the risk. Comparing the strategies across trend horizons, we see that the long-term (12-month) strategy has performed the best, the medium-term strategy has done second best, and the short-term strategy, which has the lowest Sharpe ratio of the three strategies, still has a high Sharpe ratio of 1.3. Comparing asset classes, commodities, fixed income, and currencies have performed a little better than equities.

Figure 12.2. Performance of time series momentum by individual asset and trend horizon.

This figure shows the Sharpe ratios of the time series momentum strategies for each commodity futures (dark grey), currency forward (light grey), equity futures (light blue), and fixed-income futures (dark blue). We show this for strategies using look-back horizons of 1 month (A), 3 months (B), and 12 months (C).

Source: Hurst, Ooi, and Pedersen (2013).

A. 1-Month TSMOM

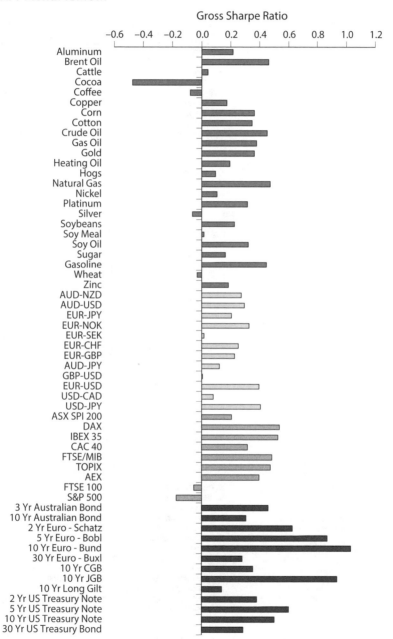

B. 3-Month TSMOM

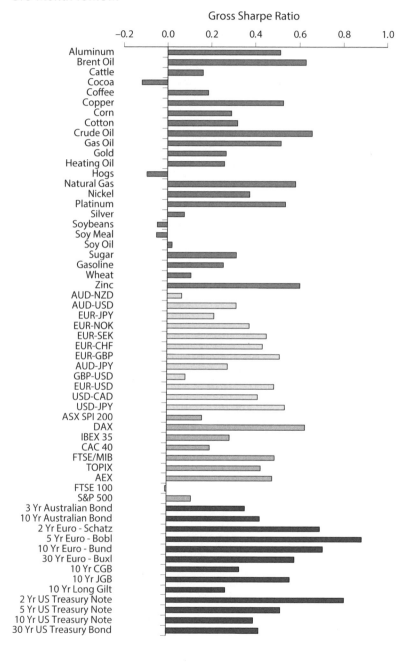

C. 12-Month TSMOM

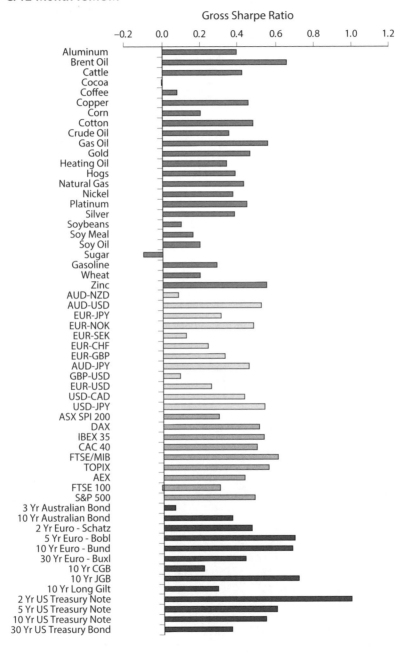

Gross Sharpe Ratio

TABLE 12.1. PERFORMANCE OF TIME SERIES MOMENTUM (TSMOM) STRATEGIES

Panel A. Performance of TS-Momentum across Asset Classes

	Commodities TSMOM	Equities TSMOM	Fixed-Income TSMOM	Currencies TSMOM	Diversified TSMOM
Average Excess Return	11.5%	8.7%	11.7%	10.49%	19.4%
Volatility	11.0%	11.1%	11.7%	11.9%	10.8%
Sharpe Ratio	1.05	0.78	1.00	0.87	1.79
Annualized Alpha	12.1%	6.8%	9.0%	10.1%	17.4%
t-Stat	(5.63)	(3.16)	(4.15)	(4.30)	(8.42)

Panel B. Performance of Time Series Momentum across Signals

	1-Month TSMOM	2-Month TSMOM	12-Month TSMOM	Diversified TSMOM
Average Excess Return	12.0%	14.5%	17.2%	19.4%
Volatility	9.5%	10.2%	11.3%	10.8%
Sharpe Ratio	1.26	1.43	1.52	1.79
Annualized Alpha	11.1%	13.3%	14.4%	17.4%
t-Stat	(6.04)	(6.70)	(6.74)	(8.42)

Notes: This table shows the performance of time series momentum strategies diversified within each asset class (Panel A) and across each trend horizon (Panel B). All numbers are annualized. The alpha is the intercept from a regression on the MCSI World stock index, Barclays Bond Index, and the GSCI commodities index. The t-statistic of the alpha is shown in parentheses.

Source: Hurst, Ooi, and Pedersen (2013).

In addition to reporting the expected return, volatility, and Sharpe ratio, table 12.1 also shows the alpha from the following regression:

$$\text{TSMOM}_t = \alpha + \beta^1 R_t^{\text{Stocks}} + \beta^2 R_t^{\text{Bonds}} + \beta^3 R_t^{\text{Commodities}} + \varepsilon_t$$

We regress the TSMOM strategies on the returns of a passive investment in the MSCI World stock market index, the Barclays U.S. aggregate government bond index, and the S&P GSCI commodity index. The alpha measures the excess return, controlling for the risk premiums associated with simply being long in these traditional asset classes. The alphas are almost as large as the excess returns since the TSMOM strategies are long–short and therefore have small average loadings on these passive factors. Finally, table 12.1 reports the

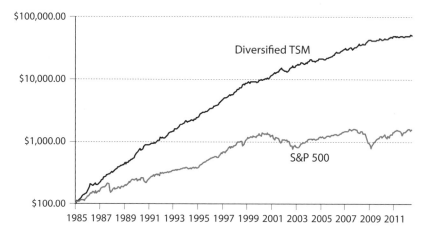

Figure 12.3. Performance of the diversified time series momentum strategy and the S&P 500 index over time.

The figure shows the cumulative return gross of transaction costs of the diversified TSMOM strategy and the S&P 500 equity index on a log scale, 1985–2012.

Source: Hurst, Ooi, and Pedersen (2013).

t-statistics of the alphas, which show that the alphas are highly statistically significant.

The best performing strategy is the diversified time series momentum strategy, with a Sharpe ratio of 1.8. Its consistent cumulative return is seen in figure 12.3, which illustrates the hypothetical growth of $100 invested in 1985 in the diversified TSMOM strategy and the S&P 500 stock market index, respectively.

12.4. DIVERSIFICATION: TRENDS WITH BENEFITS

To understand this strong performance of time series momentum, note first that the average pairwise correlation of these single-asset strategies is less than 0.1 for each trend horizon, meaning that the strategies behave rather independently across markets so one may profit when another loses. Even when the strategies are grouped by asset class or trend horizon, these relatively diversified strategies also have modest correlations. Another reason for the strong benefits of diversification is our equal-risk approach. The fact that we scale our positions so that each asset has the same ex ante volatility at each time means that, the higher the volatility of an asset, the smaller a position it has in the portfolio, creating a stable and risk-balanced portfolio. This is important because of the wide range of volatilities exhibited across assets. For example, a five-year U.S. government bond futures typically exhibits a volatility of around 5% a year, while a natural gas futures typically exhibits a volatility of around 50% a year. If a portfolio holds the same notional exposure to each asset in the portfolio (as some indices and managers do), the risk and returns of the portfolio will be dominated by the most volatile assets, significantly reducing the diversification benefits.

The diversified time series momentum strategy has very low average correlations to traditional asset classes. Indeed, the correlation with the S&P 500 stock market index is –0.02, the correlation with the bond market as represented by the Barclays U.S. aggregate index is 0.23, and the correlation with the S&P GSCI commodity index is 0.05. This low average correlation hides the fact that the strategy can at times be highly correlated to the market, but these correlations are offset on average by other times when the strategy is negatively correlated to the market.

Trend-following investing has performed especially well during periods of prolonged bear markets and in sustained bull markets, as seen in figure 12.4. Figure 12.4 plots the quarterly returns of time series momentum against the quarterly returns of the S&P 500. We estimate a quadratic function to fit the relation between time series momentum returns and market returns, giving rise to

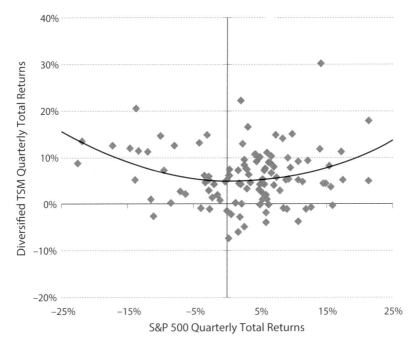

Figure 12.4. Time series momentum "smile."
This graph plots quarterly non-overlapping hypothetical returns of the diversified time series momentum strategy vs. the S&P 500, 1985–2012.
Source: Hurst, Ooi, and Pedersen (2013).

a "smile" curve. The estimated smile curve means that time series momentum has historically done the best during significant bear markets or significant bull markets, performing less well in flat markets. To understand this smile effect, note that most of the worst equity bear markets have historically happened gradually. The market first goes from "normal" to "bad," causing a TSMOM strategy to go short (while incurring a loss or profit depending on what happened previously). Often, a deep bear market happens when the market goes from "bad" to "worse," traders panic, and prices collapse. This leads to profits on the short positions, explaining why these strategies tend to be profitable during such extreme events. Of course, these strategies do not always profit during extreme events. For instance, the strategy might incur losses if, after a bull market (which would get the strategy positioned long), the market crashed quickly before the strategy could alter its positions to benefit from the crash.

12.5. TIME SERIES MOMENTUM EXPLAINS ACTUAL MANAGED FUTURES FUND RETURNS

We collect the returns of two major managed futures indices, BTOP 50 and DJCS Managed Futures Index,[7] as well as individual fund returns from the Lipper/Tass database in the category labeled "Managed Futures." We highlight the performance of the five Managed Futures funds in the Lipper/Tass database that have the largest reported "Fund Assets" as of 06/2012. While looking at the ex post returns of the largest funds naturally biases us toward picking funds that did well, it is nevertheless interesting to compare these most successful funds to time series momentum.

Table 12.2 Panel A reports the performance of the managed futures indices. We see that the index and manager returns have Sharpe ratios between 0.27 and 0.88. All of the alphas with respect to passive exposures to stocks, bonds, and commodities are positive, and most of them are statistically significant. We see that the diversified time series momentum strategy has a higher Sharpe ratio and alpha than the indices and managers, but we note that time series momentum index is gross of fees and transaction costs while the managers and indices are after fees and transaction costs. Furthermore, while the time series momentum strategy is simple and subject to minimal data mining, it does benefit from some hindsight in choosing its 1-, 3-, and 12-month trend horizons—managers experiencing losses in real time may have had a more difficult time sticking with these strategies through tough times than our hypothetical strategy.

---

[7] These index returns are available at the following websites: http://www.barclayhedge.com /research/indices/btop/index.html; http://www.hedgeindex.com/hedgeindex/secure/en/index performance.aspx?cy=USD&indexname=HEDG_MGFUT

TABLE 12.2. UNDERSTANDING THE PERFORMANCE OF MANAGED FUTURES

Panel A. Performance of Managed Futures Indices and Top Funds

	BTOP 50	DJCS MF	Manager A	Manager B	Manager C	Manager D	Manager E
Begin date	Jan. 30, 1987	Jan. 31, 1994	Apr. 30, 2004	Oct. 31, 1997	May 31, 2000	Mar. 29, 1996	Dec. 31, 1998
Average excess return	5.2%	3.2%	12.4%	13.3%	11.8%	12.3%	8.1%
Volatility	10.3%	11.7%	14.0%	17.7%	14.8%	17.2%	16.4%
Sharpe Ratio	0.50	0.27	0.88	0.75	0.80	0.72	0.49
Annualized Alpha	3.5%	1.1%	10.7%	9.3%	8.5%	9.4%	5.1%
t-Stat	(1.69)	(0.41)	(2.15)	(2.05)	(2.05)	(2.22)	(1.17)

Panel B. Time Series Momentum Explains Managed Futures Returns

	1-Month TSMOM		3-Month TSMOM		12-Month TSMOM		Intercept (annualized)		R^2	Correl. to Diversified TSMOM
DJCS Managed Futures	0.26	(3.65)	0.56	(7.69)	0.23	(3.86)	−8.8%	(−4.58)	0.58	0.73
BTOP 50	0.27	(4.87)	0.56	(9.00)	0.08	(1.78)	−6.6%	(−4.24)	0.53	0.69
Manager A	0.39	(2.85)	0.59	(4.51)	0.31	(2.69)	2.8%	(0.80)	0.54	0.73
Manager B	0.66	(5.00)	0.35	(2.56)	0.47	(4.03)	−0.8%	(−0.23)	0.46	0.66
Manager C	0.55	(4.93)	0.52	(4.47)	0.25	(2.55)	0.6%	(0.19)	0.55	0.72
Manager D	0.50	(4.54)	0.80	(6.85)	0.22	(2.25)	−3.6%	(−1.19)	0.57	0.70
Manager E	0.35	(3.32)	0.70	(6.42)	0.48	(5.29)	−6.0%	(−2.09)	0.64	0.78
% Positive Betas, all MF Funds in Lipper/ Tass DB	76%		78%		76%					

Notes: Panel A shows the performance of managed futures indices and the five largest managed futures managers in the Lipper/Tass database as of June 2012. All numbers are annualized. The alpha is the intercept from a regression on the MCSI World stock index, Barclays Bond Index, and the GSCI commodities index. Panel B shows the multivariate regression of managed futures indices and managers on time series momentum returns by trend horizon. *T*-statistics are reported in parentheses. The bottom row reports the percentage of all funds in the Lipper/Tass database with positive coefficients. The right-most column reports the correlation between the managed futures returns and the diversified TSMOM strategy.

Source: Hurst, Ooi, and Pedersen (2013).

Fees make a significant difference, given that most CTAs and managed futures hedge funds have historically charged at least 2% management fees and 20% performance fees. While we cannot know the exact before-fee manager returns, we can simulate the hypothetical fee for the time series momentum strategy. With a 2-and-20 fee structure, the average fee is around 6% per year for the diversified TSMOM strategy, although this high fee is due to the high simulated performance of the strategy. Furthermore, transaction costs are on the order of 1 to 4% per year for a sophisticated manager, possibly much higher for less sophisticated managers, and higher historically. Hence, after these estimated fees and transaction costs, the Sharpe ratio of the diversified time series momentum strategy would historically have been near 1, still comparing well to the indices and managers, but we note that historical transaction costs are not known and are associated with significant uncertainty.

Rather than comparing the performance of the time series momentum strategy to those of the indices and managers, we want to show that time series momentum can explain the strong performance of managed futures managers. To explain managed futures returns, we regress the returns of managed futures indices and managers (R_t^{MF}) on the returns of 1-month, 3-month, and 12-month time series momentum:

$$R_t^{MF} = \alpha + \beta^1 TSMOM_t^{1M} + \beta^2 TSMOM_t^{3M} + \beta^3 TSMOM_t^{12M} + \varepsilon_t$$

Panel B of table 12.2 reports the results of these regressions. We see the time series momentum strategies explain the managed futures index and manager returns to a large extent in the sense that the R-squares of these regressions are large, ranging between 0.46 and 0.64. The table also reports the correlation of the managed futures indices and managers with the diversified TSMOM strategy. These correlations are large, ranging from 0.66 to 0.78, which provides another indication that time series momentum can explain the managed futures universe.

The intercepts reported indicate the excess returns (or alphas) after controlling for time series momentum. While the alphas relative to the traditional asset classes in Panel A were significantly positive, almost all the alphas relative to time series momentum in Panel B are negative. Even though the returns of the largest managers are biased to be high (due to the ex post selection of the managers), time series momentum nevertheless drives these alphas to be negative. This is another expression in which time series momentum can explain the managed futures space and is an illustration of the importance of fees and transaction costs. Another interesting finding that arises from Panel B is the relative importance of short-, medium-, and long-term trends for managed futures funds.

In summary, while many managed futures funds pursue many other types of strategies besides time series momentum, our results show that time series momentum explains the average alpha in the industry and a significant fraction of the time variation of returns.

12.6. IMPLEMENTATION: HOW TO MANAGE MANAGED FUTURES

We have seen that time series momentum can explain managed futures returns. In fact, this relatively simple strategy has realized a higher Sharpe ratio than most managers, at least on paper. This result suggests that fees and other implementation issues are important for the real-world success of these strategies. Indeed, as mentioned above, we estimate that a 2-and-20 fee structure implies a 6% average annual fee on the diversified time series momentum strategy run at a 10% annualized volatility. Other important implementation issues include transaction costs, rebalance methodology, margin requirements, and risk management.

To analyze the effect of how often the portfolio is rebalanced, figure 12.5 shows the gross Sharpe ratio for each trend horizon and the diversified time series momentum strategy as a function of rebalancing frequency. Daily and weekly rebalancing perform similarly, while the performance trails off with monthly and quarterly rebalancing frequencies. Naturally, the performance falls more quickly for the short- and medium-term strategies as these signals change more quickly, leading to a larger alpha decay.

As mentioned, the annual transaction costs of a managed futures strategy are typically about 1 to 4% for a sophisticated trader, possibly much higher for less sophisticated traders, and higher historically given higher transaction costs in the past. Transaction costs depend on a number of things. Transaction costs

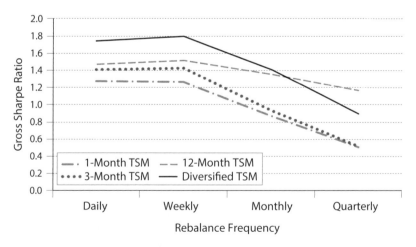

Figure 12.5. Gross Sharpe ratios at different rebalance frequencies.
This figure shows the Sharpe ratios gross of transaction costs of the 1-month, 3-month, 12-month, and diversified time series momentum strategies as a function of the rebalancing frequency.

increase with rebalance frequency if the portfolio is mechanically rebalanced without transaction-cost optimization (although more frequent access to the market can also be used to source more liquidity) and transaction costs are higher for short-term trend signals than long-term trends. Hence, larger managers—for whom transaction costs play a more important role—may allocate a larger weight to medium- and long-term trend signals and relatively lower weight to short-term signals.

To implement managed futures strategies, managers must post margin to counterparties, namely the futures commission merchant and the currency intermediation agent (or currency prime broker). The time series momentum strategy would typically have margin requirements of 8–12% for a large institutional investor and more than double that for a smaller investor. Hence, time series momentum is certainly implementable from a funding liquidity standpoint as it has a significant amount of free cash.

Risk management is the final implementation issue that we discuss. Our construction of trading strategies is systematic and already has built-in risk controls due to our constant-volatility methodology. This position sizing controls the risk of each security by scaling down the position when risk spikes up. Furthermore, it achieves a risk-balanced diversification across securities at all times. Lastly, some managed futures managers use drawdown control, further seek to identify overextended trends to limit the losses from sharp trend reversals, and try to identify short-term countertrends to improve performance in range-bound markets.

12.7. INTERVIEW WITH DAVID HARDING OF WINTON CAPITAL MANAGEMENT

David W. Harding is the chairman and chief executive officer of Winton Capital Management, a global investment manager focusing on managed futures investments. Before founding Winton Capital, Harding co-founded Adam Harding and Lueck (AHL) in 1987, one of the first systematic trend-following CTAs in Europe, which was subsequently bought by the Man Group and remains one of the cornerstones of the FTSE-listed company.

> **LHP**: *How did you become interested in managed futures investment in the first place?*
> **DWH**: I started at a stockbroker called Wood Mackenzie in London in 1982 after leaving Cambridge with a degree in natural sciences, specializing in theoretical physics. I was a trainee in the fixed interest area, and within the first month of my starting, the London Financial Futures Exchange— LIFFE—started. The first contracts on LIFFE were bond futures, so I took the opportunity to be posted onto the floor of the exchange. This way, I got

interested in futures and charting and applying statistical programming to futures at the beginning of my career, when I was 21 years old.

LHP: *How did you decide that you wanted to apply statistical techniques to that market, as opposed to what other people were doing at the time?*

DWH: I was looking at long strings of numbers going up and down and drawing charts. I was trained as a scientist, and I had learned a lot in my physics degree about methods of analyzing data—for example, Fourier analysis—and I couldn't help but wonder if this could be applied to these time series.

LHP: *Is there a specific incident that set the course for your career?*

DWH: I spent two years in the mid-'80s drawing charts by hand every day, which is a very laborious process. That certainly gave me a lot of time to look at time series. When you press a button on your computer and a chart appears, you don't interact with the data in a very detailed way. Whereas if you draw these graphs day by day by hand, you reflect on the empirical nature of the data more deeply. So, I would say that period I had at Sabre Fund Management had a big impact on my feeling about the non-randomness of the data.

LHP: *Was there a particular property of the charts that caught your attention?*

DWH: Trends. Trends are what you're looking for. Trends are what technical analysis exists to try to foretell and forecast. People see trends in the data because there are trends in the data, and people are reasonably good at seeing trends in the data.

LHP: *Can you talk about your investment process? How is it today, and how did you get there?*

DWH: We study data about markets and look for evidence in the data for when the odds of the market moving up or down aren't exactly 50/50. We place bets when the odds are in our favor.

LHP: *You determine whether the odds are not 50/50 through extensive research and then trade through a systematic process, correct?*

DWH: Yes, exactly. We trade in lots of markets at the same time, putting positions on and taking them off. It's all coded into a computer program because it's a more complicated pattern than any individual trader can manage.

LHP: *What are the pros and cons of model-driven investment versus trading on someone's instincts or a human's assessment based on softer pieces of information?*

DWH: The pro is intellectual rigor, discipline. It's an evidence-based approach, so you're demanding fairly hard-edged scientific evidence before risking money.

The main disadvantage, I would say, is that you can't take into account all factors. If something's never happened before, then your research can't tell you anything about it.

LHP: *Does your research suggest that it's better to have the same type of model for every instrument, or is it better to have a very specific model for each one?*

DWH: If you have very different models for very different markets, then you encounter problems with overfitting of data.

LHP: *Do you think these opportunities arise because traders make systematic errors that are similar across all the different markets?*

DWH: I'll answer that in an oblique way by saying there is a theory, much beloved of academics, that markets are efficient, and that they perfectly discount all future information.

In its most extreme form, it says not only that markets discount the future, but they accurately reflect all fundamentals of economies and everything that's known about companies and so on and so forth, and they synthesize this information into completely perfect prices.

This theory would be laughable if it wasn't so widely believed in. It's come out of valuing options and modeling diffusion processes: price movement as a diffusion using the Brownian motion and the heat equation. That is a good approximation for modeling short-term options, but to extend that to the idea that there is this perfect matrix of prices that reflects everything perfectly is putting too much weight on a small base of evidence, as they say in science.

LHP: *So how do your models exploit that markets are not perfectly efficient?*

DWH: Markets are social institutions and reflect all sorts of phenomena that you'd expect such social institutions to reflect. They reflect certain things about the price formation process, and one of those is, obviously, the tendency of markets to serially correlate because ideas catch on slowly and spread, and fevers develop and people get over-optimistic and become disappointed.

LHP: *Are there some circumstances or events that illustrate the value of managed futures?*

DWH: We tend to make money out of surprises, and people are very bad at foreseeing surprises. If you just look at the history of the last hundred years, I mean, the First World War came out of a clear, blue sky. Talk about the efficient market theory. Bond yields and stock prices didn't move on July 25th, 1914, or July 23rd, 1914, despite the assassination of Franz Ferdinand a month before. They had no idea what was going to come. So the market didn't efficiently discount the First World War. Then we had the Communist Revolution in Russia—efficient market theory didn't get that. Same with the Second World War, Hitler, the arms race, the invention of computers. It's just been one thing after another in terms of completely surprising the markets—and I'm not even touching on the last 20 years, the collapse of the banking system, and so on.

LHP: *So how do managed futures or trend following benefit from surprises?*

DWH: There are obviously large surprises in human history, continually. But there are also small surprises which affect one market.

LHP: *But for an investor to benefit from a surprise, it cannot be a complete surprise; it would have to show up in prices before it happened; that is, it would have to unfold gradually.*

DWH: Well, I guess that you're right. Luckily, most surprises do unfold gradually. To preserve the ridiculous idea of efficient market theory, all surprises would have to be instantaneously discounted, but this is just not possible. The collapse of the banking system unfolded with a sickening series of events over time, so the stock market fell by 50% over the space of a year, and trend-following systems worked well.

LHP: *Yes. Do you think that trend-following investment tends to push a price toward the fundamental or away from it?*

DWH: I don't think it's really very easy to pin down the fundamental value of something. The idea of fundamentals suggests that there is an equilibrium price at which the market will clear. But, of course, the world isn't in equilibrium. It's changing all the time, isn't it? You shouldn't really say there's a fundamental value, but a spectrum of possible fundamental values, and trend following probably moves prices around within the range of possible values.

LHP: *Do you think that having more managed futures investors will tend to eliminate trends, or make trends stronger?*

DWH: I can only give you an unsatisfactory answer, which is I think it'd probably change the autocorrelation spectrum of price data. In other words, it will change the nature of trends, somewhat.

LHP: *Some people say that managed futures have tail-hedging properties. Do you agree?*

DWH: I'm relatively uncomfortable with that concept. Over the last 20 years commodity trading advisors have tended to do well when stock markets go down. But CTAs can have a strong positive correlation to the stock market at some times and a strong negative correlation at others because the biggest sector they trade is stock indices. If there happens to be a substantial decline in stocks when we happen to be long, then we won't have tail hedging properties at all. We'll have tail exacerbating properties.

The best diversification you get from investing in a CTA is investing with somebody who doesn't have a view about the future. And since most investment consists of people telling you what their view about the future is, it's a novel idea to invest with somebody who doesn't have a view about the future.

LHP: *How important is it to keep changing one's investment approach and continuing to do research?*

DWH: There are no final and immutable truths in financial markets. If you think you've found the answer and all you have to do is implement it forever, then you are ultimately doomed. To be competitive, you've got to work hard and keep at it and keep going all the time.

LHP: *Nevertheless, are there certain signals or parts of your model that you've implemented that you sort of came up with in the '80s and you still use today?*

DWH: Yeah, definitely there are. Because we trade relatively slowly, our models are not in a state of perpetual revolution. We're changing things gradually and doing long-term research, which leads to, perhaps, more changes in the models as the years pass.

LHP: *When you allocate to different asset classes, is that also based solely on research or is there any judgment in whether you put more weight on commodities versus equities, and so on?*

DWH: It's more or less a research question, but there is no uniquely accurate answer. A lot of our research gives very imprecise answers, in contrast to what people think. But you have a set of expected returns, a set of variance matrices, a set of transaction costs, and there is obviously some way in which to turn those into some sort of an optimal portfolio.

LHP: *You've said that trend following is an "agnostic" form of investment— can you explain what you mean?*

DWH: Yes. Trend following contains many less embedded assumptions than other types of investments. We don't take a view on what's going to happen next year and the year after and the year after. We don't take a view on whether China is going to boom or bust. For example, we don't take a view on whether there's going to be an ongoing scarcity of commodities. There are people very busily setting up their portfolios with the absolute certainty that there's going to be a terrific scarcity of commodities over the next 10 or 20 years, because it's so obvious to them that, you know, the number of people is increasing, blah, blah, blah. But they weren't doing that 10 years ago. In other words, they do it after prices have already risen for 10 years. I'd have a lot of respect for them if they'd done it before prices had risen for 10 years. That is a rather weak form of trend following. It's trend following by accident.

A lot of what goes on in the investment world is fighting yesterday's battles.

PART IV

Arbitrage Strategies

CHAPTER 13

Introduction to Arbitrage Pricing and Trading

In Wall Street the old proverb has been reworded: "Give a man a fish and you feed him for a day. Teach him how to arbitrage and you feed him forever." (If, however, he studied at the Ivan Boesky School of Arbitrage, it may be a state institution that supplies his meals.)

—Warren Buffett, Annual Report, 1988

In academic textbooks, arbitrage refers to a guaranteed profit achieved by simultaneously buying low and selling high. More specifically, a textbook arbitrage is to buy one security and sell another more expensive security (or a portfolio of securities), where the security you buy yields the same or better cash flows than the one you sell. In theory, an arbitrage trade never requires any cash and delivers positive profits at some point in time with positive probability.

Such academic arbitrage trades almost never exist in the real world, but this does not stop practitioners from using the word arbitrage for trades that buy and then sell almost the same securities at attractive relative prices. I use the word *arbitrage* in the practitioner sense. While buying low and selling high can often be expected to be profitable, it almost always requires a cash outlay (e.g., for margin requirements), the trade can lead to significant losses before it converges, and there is often a non-trivial risk that the arbitrage link is broken such that the trade never converges. As we will see, arbitrage opportunities arise as compensation for liquidity risk and deal risk in connection with corporate events, convertible bonds, and fixed-income markets, and they present an interesting window into the workings of financial markets. Said differently, arbitrage is the most direct symptom of efficiently inefficient markets.

13.1. ARBITRAGE PRICING AND TRADING: A GENERAL FRAMEWORK

An important insight in finance is that competition is a strong force that tends to eliminate arbitrage opportunities. Therefore, many models in finance impose the so-called "no-arbitrage condition" that arbitrage never exists.

Arbitrage is the Holy Grail of finance. I am reminded of the movie *Indiana Jones and the Last Crusade,* where Harrison Ford plays an archeology professor who tells his students to

forget any ideas you've got about lost cities, exotic travel, and digging up the world. We do not follow maps to buried treasure and *X* never, ever marks the spot.

However, in the rest of the movie, he proceeds to do all of that in search of the Holy Grail. Similarly, finance professors tell their students to

forget any ideas you've got about easy money, exotic options, and arbitraging the world. We do not follow math to buried treasure and arbitrage never, ever exists.

But outside the classroom, finance professors often run around chasing arbitrage opportunities. Fortunately, the arbitrage pricing theory not only tells you how to price securities in the absence of arbitrage, it also tells you how to exploit arbitrages if they do exist.

Simply using the no-arbitrage condition and frictionless markets, we get a beautiful theory of relative asset pricing: A security can be "priced by arbitrage" in the sense that we can compute its fundamental value based on the value of other related securities. Arbitrage pricing can be done in the following three ways (of increasing complexity):

1. If two securities have the same payoffs, they must have the same value.
2. If a portfolio has the same payoff as a security, then the value of the security is equal to the price of the portfolio, which is called a *replicating portfolio.*
3. If a self-financing trading strategy has the same final payoff as a security, then the value of the security is equal to the initial cost of the strategy. A self-financing strategy, also called a *dynamic hedging strategy,* is a trading strategy that is rebalanced over time in a way that does not require money in or out of the pocket, except in the beginning and in the end.

If we can find a way to replicate a security—with another security, a replicating portfolio, or a dynamic hedging strategy—then we know what the security's value is. If the security is trading at a different market price, then we can make the arbitrage trade, which is supposed to eliminate the mispricing.

Indeed, if the security price is lower than the replication cost, then we buy the security and sell the replicating portfolio. Buying the security pushes its price up, so doing the arbitrage contributes to eliminating the opportunity.

Similarly, if the security price is higher than its value, then we short-sell the security and buy the replicating portfolio. The trick is to find out how to replicate a security. We discuss below how to do this for options and, in the chapters that follow, we consider many other arbitrage trades.

In the real world, traders face transaction costs and funding costs, which means that arbitrage trades involve costs and are almost never risk free. With transaction costs, we cannot determine an exact fundamental value using the no-arbitrage condition, but we can find an upper and lower bound for the value. The three types of arbitrage arguments above are increasingly influenced by frictions. While the arbitrages of types 1 and 2 involve buy-and-hold strategies, type 3 requires dynamic trading, which involves much higher transaction costs. Therefore, arbitrage relations based on type 3 can more easily break down in an efficiently inefficient market.

The strength of an arbitrage relation also depends on whether it has a natural convergence time. Suppose for instance that the same security is traded on two different trading venues. If the shares are fungible in the sense that you can buy shares at one exchange and sell them at the other exchange, then arbitrage is super easy and the trade converges as soon as you can hit "buy" on the one exchange and "sell" on the other. Since this type of arbitrage is easy, it almost never happens in the real world and, if it does happen, it only lasts for a split second. The situation is different, however, if the shares are not fungible. For instance, dual-listed companies such as Unilever trade at two different exchanges, but the shares bought at one exchange cannot be sold at the other exchange. In this case, there is no natural convergence time and relative mispricings can persist over long time periods.

13.2. OPTION ARBITRAGE

Arbitrage pricing is especially useful for valuing *derivative* securities, that is, securities with a payoff that depends on the price of another security. The other security is called the *underlying* (security), and we denote its price by S_t.

An important class of derivatives is options. There are several types of options, most notably *call options* and *put options*. Call options give the right, but not the obligation, to buy an underlying asset at a fixed price, called the exercise price (or strike price), X. Put options give the right to sell the asset at a fixed price. European options can only be exercised at the time of expiration, whereas American options can be exercised any time up until expiration.

If the current price of an underlying stock S_t is above the strike price X, then a call option is said to be in-the-money (i.e., you get money if you exercise).

If the stock price is below the strike, then the call option is out-of-the-money, and, if $S_t = X$, then the option is at-the-money.

At expiration, a call option is worthless if it is out-of-the-money and worth $C_t = S_t - X$ if it is in-the-money. Similarly, a put option is worth $P_t = X - S_t$ if it is in-the-money, and otherwise it is worthless. Before expiration, options are never worthless as long as there is a chance that the underlying security price moves in-the-money before expiration.

Options are used for a number of reasons, importantly because they offer embedded leverage.[1] Indeed, buying a call option is similar to buying a stock, financed partly with a loan of X. For the same number of dollars, you can buy many more call options than stocks, so for the same dollar investment, the upside potential is far greater with options. Of course, risk and return are related, and options are also much more likely to lose all their value than stocks.

Put-Call Parity for European Options

The prices of calls and put options are closely related. This can be seen with a simple arbitrage argument. You can create a "synthetic" stock by buying a European call option, shorting a European put option with the same strike price X, and putting enough money in the bank to have X at the option expiration time T years from now. Since the price of a synthetic stock must be equal to the price of an actual stock, we get the classic put-call parity:[2]

$$C_t - P_t + \frac{X}{(1 + r^f)^T} = S_t$$

The put-call parity usually holds well in the real world because, if it didn't, it would open a relatively easy arbitrage trade. Indeed, to arbitrage deviations from the put-call parity involves a buy-and-hold trade with a given convergence time, namely the expiration of the options. One exception is when the stock is difficult to sell short, in which case the right-hand side can be larger than the left-hand side.

Option Arbitrage Trading in the Binomial Model

Let us see how to derive the value of a call option written on a stock that does not pay dividends—and how to trade on potential arbitrage opportunities. The

---

[1] See Frazzini and Pedersen (2013).

[2] This version of the put-call parity requires that the stock does not pay any dividends before the option expiration. Otherwise, one must subtract the present value of the dividends on the right-hand side.

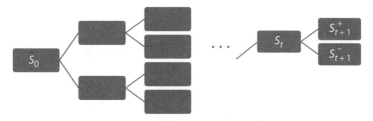

Figure 13.1. Binomial tree for the evolution of the stock price.

methodology is much more general, however, as it works for almost any deriv-ative on almost any underlying asset.[3] We start by assuming that the stock price evolves over time in a "tree," as seen in figure 13.1. The tree always has two branches, meaning that each time period the stock price can go up or down. Since there are several time periods before expiration time, there are many possible final stock prices.

To compute the initial value of the option, we need to compute the option value in the whole tree, starting from the back. The final scenarios correspond to the expiration time of the option, so the option value is simply the exercise value, that is, the greater of zero and $S - X$.

To see how we compute the option price at earlier times, consider any time period t, where we want to compute the option value C_t. We take as given the current stock price S_t, the possible stock prices (S_{t+1}^+ and S_{t+1}^-) in the next time period, and the option values in the scenarios where the stock price moves up or down, denoted by C_{t+1}^+ and C_{t+1}^-, respectively.

In order to find the value of the option, we need to find a portfolio of the stock and cash that replicates the option. The number of stocks in the dynamic hedging strategy is called the hedge ratio (or delta) Δ_t, and the amount of money in the money market is denoted by b_t. The goal is to determine Δ_t and b_t such that the hedging strategy matches the value of the option regardless of whether the stock price goes up or down:

$$\Delta_t S_{t+1}^+ + b_t(1 + r^f) = C_{t+1}^+$$

$$\Delta_t S_{t+1}^- + b_t(1 + r^f) = C_{t+1}^-$$

Solving these two equations with two unknowns gives the correct hedge ratio:

$$\Delta_t = \frac{C_{t+1}^+ - C_{t+1}^-}{S_{t+1}^+ - S_{t+1}^-}$$

---

[3] For American-type derivatives, one should check at every "node" in the tree whether exercise is optimal, but early exercise is not optimal for call options written on non-dividend-paying stocks in a frictionless market.

and the corresponding money market investment

$$b_t = \frac{C_{t+1}^- S_{t+1}^+ - C_{t+1}^+ S_{t+1}^-}{(S_{t+1}^+ - S_{t+1}^-)(1 + r^f)}$$

The option price is now given by the current value of the hedging strategy, $C_t = \Delta_t S_t + b_t$. With some simple algebra, the option price can be shown to be

$$C_t = \frac{qC_{t+1}^+ + (1 - q)C_{t+1}^-}{1 + r^f}$$

where $q = \frac{1 + r^f - S_{t+1}^-/S_t}{(S_{t+1}^+ - S_{t+1}^-)/S_t}$ is a number between zero and one, which is called the "risk neutral probability" of the stock price moving up. We see that the option price can be derived as a simple present value calculation as if the probability of an up move is equal to q and as if the investors are risk neutral. The existence of risk-neutral probabilities is a general property of arbitrage pricing. The risk premium is hidden in the risk-neutral probability in the sense that the real probability of an up move is usually larger than the risk-neutral probability, so that securities are priced as if up moves are less likely than they actually are.

Given that we have found the option value C_t in each scenario at time t, we can use the same technique again to find the option value at time $t-1$, and so on until we have the initial option value. This method also shows how to replicate the option payoff with a dynamic hedging strategy using stocks and risk-free securities, that is, how to choose the hedge each time period depending on the stock price.

Hence, if the option's market price differs from its value, we know how to implement the arbitrage trade. For example, if the option price is $2 above its value, we short-sell the option and hedge it by implementing the dynamic strategy. In principle, this arbitrage trade initially earns us the $2 mispricing, and subsequently we have completely offsetting payoffs.

Traders do make this type of trade in the real world, but things are often more complex. First, traders typically cannot immediately pocket the $2 because of margin requirements. Second, even if a trader implements his hedge perfectly such that his portfolio is worth the same as the option at the time of expiration (such that he earns $2 in *every* final scenario), he might face temporary losses before expiration if the option suddenly becomes even more mispriced. Third, the stock does not exactly evolve in a tree, so the hedge can never be perfect.

Arbitrage Trading Based on Implied Volatility: The Black–Scholes–Merton Formula

If we have more and more scenarios in the binomial model (or write the model in continuous time), the option price converges to the celebrated

Black–Scholes–Merton[4] formula for the price C_t of a European call option with strike price X:

$$C_t = S_t e^{-\delta T} N(d_1) - X e^{-r^f T} N(d_2)$$

where δ is the dividend yield, r^f is the risk-free rate, T is the time to expiration, $d_1 = (\ln(S_t/X) + (r - \delta + \sigma^2/2)T)/(\sigma\sqrt{T})$ and $d_2 = d_1 - \sigma\sqrt{T}$.

The numbers d_1 and d_2 depend on σ, which is the stock's volatility, that is, the annualized standard deviation of the stock return. A key insight from the Black–Scholes–Merton model is that option prices depend crucially on this volatility. If the volatility is higher, then the corresponding option price is higher.

This insight also means that, for any option price C_t, there exists a corresponding volatility σ that justifies the price in the sense that, if we plug this σ into the Black–Scholes–Merton formula, then the formula spits out the right price. This level of stock volatility is called the *implied volatility*.

According to the Black–Scholes–Merton model, the implied volatility of all options on the same underlying stock should be the same, namely the stock's true volatility. Therefore, option prices can be more easily compared by looking at their implied volatilities. If one option has a higher implied volatility, it is more expensive relative to its fundamental Black–Scholes–Merton value— and a candidate for short-selling. Option arbitrageurs look to short-sell options with implied volatility above their assessed true volatility and buy options with implied volatility below the true volatility.

Of course, it must be recognized that the option's market price can differ from the model-implied fundamental value because of a possible arbitrage opportunity, or because the model is wrong, or because the estimate of the true volatility is wrong, or some combination of these things. Clearly, the Black–Scholes–Merton model rests on strong assumptions that are not satisfied in the real world. In particular, real stock prices can suddenly jump and the volatility varies over time, features that are not captured by the standard Black–Scholes–Merton model (but can be captured in extensions of the basic model). Such potential jumps in the stock price can explain why implied volatilities tend to be higher for out-of-the-money put options, especially for index options, a tendency called the implied volatility "smirk." Hence, this smirk is not just an arbitrage opportunity but also a reflection of a real crash risk.

As in the binomial model, we can derive the option replicating portfolio in the Black–Scholes–Merton model. If a hedge fund short-sells an option, it will hedge its position by buying Δ_t shares, where

---

[4] See Black and Scholes (1973) and Merton (1973), for which Myron Scholes (whom we meet in the interview in chapter 14) and Robert C. Merton won the Nobel Prize in 1997. (The Nobel Prize is not given posthumously, and Black passed away in 1995.)

$$\Delta_t = \frac{\partial C_t}{\partial S_t} = e^{-\delta T} N(d_1)$$

Since Δ_t is changing over time, the hedge fund must keep adjusting the number of shares held, which is called dynamic hedging. Hedge funds usually adjust their hedges at least daily.

13.3. DEMAND-BASED OPTION PRICING

In the real world, option prices depend not only on arbitrage relations but also on supply and demand conditions. Many investors want to buy insurance against severe stock market crashes, leading to an excess demand for put options on stock indices. Furthermore, demand for embedded leverage on the market with finite downside also leads to demand for options. This demand would not push up the price of options if competitive intermediaries could arbitrage options perfectly as in the Black–Scholes–Merton model, but in the real world, intermediaries face significant costs and risks when implementing option arbitrage trades. Therefore, demand pressure can move option prices. Hence, just as people pay more for car insurance than the actuarial risk of a car crash, investors often pay more for market "insurance" than the Black–Scholes–Merton model-implied option price. Banks and hedge funds take the other side of this trade, making an expected profit, but not a certain arbitrage profit, as the option prices adjust to an efficiently inefficient level.[5]

---

[5] Bollen and Whaley (2004) find evidence that option demand moves option prices and Gârleanu, Pedersen, and Poteshman (2009) present a model of demand-based option pricing with consistent evidence.

CHAPTER 14

Fixed-Income Arbitrage

Trading on fixed-income arbitrage is like picking up nickels in front of a
steamroller.

—Saying among traders

The global fixed-income markets are vast in terms of the value of outstanding
bonds, the turnover of these bonds, and the size of the related derivatives markets. The most important fixed-income market is the government bond market,
followed by the markets for corporate bonds and mortgage bonds. The key
derivatives markets include bond futures, interest-rate swaps, credit default
swaps, options, and *swaptions,* which give the option to enter into an interest-
rate swap.

   Almost all bond prices depend heavily on the risk-free interest rate, so there
is significant co-movement among bond yields and bond returns. Therefore,
fixed-income arbitrage traders often trade on the relative value among fixed-
income securities to exploit price differences among closely related securities. The close connection between the securities means that a lot of the risk
is hedged away by going long and short. However, the limited risk and the
competition among fixed-income arbitrageurs imply that the relative price discrepancies between bonds are usually small in an efficiently inefficient market.
Hence, to achieve high returns, fixed-income arbitrage traders often need to use
a significant amount of leverage. Such highly leveraged arbitrage trades can
earn moderate profits when the relative price discrepancies converge ("picking up nickels"), interrupted by occasional dramatic losses when many fixed-
income arbitrageurs are forced to simultaneously deleverage their positions in
a fire sale (the "steamroller").

   An example of a classic fixed-income arbitrage trade is to sell short newly
issued *on-the-run* bonds against long positions in older *off-the-run* bonds.
Other classic trades include yield curve trades called *butterflies*, swap spread
trades, mortgage trades, and fixed-income volatility trades.

Before we get into the details of these trades, we first consider the fundamentals of bond yields and bond returns. The collection bond yields across all maturities are called the "yield curve" or the "term structure of interest rates." Fixed-income arbitrage traders are obsessed with the yield curve. We discuss how the yield curve is characterized by its level, slope, and curvature, where the level is set by the central bank, and the slope and curvature are determined by expected future central bank rates and risk premiums. We discuss how to understand each of these elements of the term structure and how to trade on them.

14.1. FIXED-INCOME FUNDAMENTALS

Bond Yields and Prices

Bond prices and bond yields are two sides of the same coin. Given a bond's price P, its *yield to maturity* (YTM) is the internal rate of return if you hold the bond to maturity. Conversely, given a bond's YTM, its price is the discounted value of the future coupons C and face value F at this discount rate:

$$P_t = \sum_{\text{coupon dates } t_i} \frac{C}{(1 + \text{YTM})^{t_i - t}} + \frac{F}{(1 + \text{YTM})^{T - t}} \tag{14.1}$$

Here, t is the current time, T is the maturity time, and, hence, $T - t$ is the time to maturity.

The Yield Curve

The collection of the yields of bonds of all maturities is called the yield curve or term structure of interest rates, as seen in figure 14.1.

Sometimes there are several government bonds with the same maturity but different coupon rates. For instance, there might be a newly issued 10-year bond and an "old" 10-year bond issued 20 years ago, originally as a 30-year bond. These bonds often have slightly different yields due to their different coupons (and different liquidity as discussed further in the section on on-the-run vs. off-the-run). So which yield are we plotting at the 10-year point in figure 14.1? To clarify this question, fixed-income traders often look at the term structure of *zero-coupon* bond yields, i.e., the yield on a bond where $C = 0$ so that its entire value comes from the face value, which is paid at a *single* point in time. Traders observe zero-coupon bonds both by looking at the prices of such traded bonds and by inferring the zero-coupon bond yields from the prices of coupon bonds. Indeed, a coupon bond can be viewed as a portfolio of zero-coupon bonds—one for each coupon payment and one for payment of the face value. Hence, coupon bond values can be derived from zero-coupon bond yields, and vice versa.

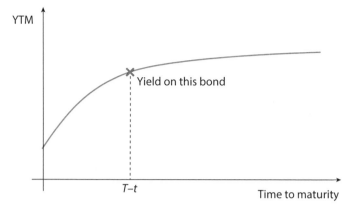

Figure 14.1. The yield curve, also called the term structure of interest rates.

Bond Returns and Duration

Having understood bond prices and bond yields, we just need to understand bond returns—i.e., how much money one can make in percentage from holding a bond. For instance, fixed-income traders sometimes make or lose fortunes on long-term bonds when interest rates just move fractions of a percent—but why do long-term bond prices react more to yield changes than bonds of shorter maturity? Intuitively, long-term bond prices react more to changes in yield because they need to earn this yield over a longer time period so that the effect is compounded. Let us analyze bond returns in more detail.

If you hold a bond to maturity, your return will be the bond's YTM when you bought it (assuming that the cash flows can be reinvested at YTM). What is the bond return over a shorter holding period, say from t to $t + 1$? The holding period return over a single time period is

$$\text{bond return}_{t,t+1} = \frac{P_{t+1} + \text{possible coupon}}{P_t} - 1 \qquad (14.2)$$

If the bond's YTM stays the same, then the short-term holding period return is exactly equal to the YTM (regardless of whether a coupon is paid or not). Hence, the bond return deviates from the YTM if and only if its yield changes. Because coupon payments and face-value payments are fixed, only changes in yield cause these fixed payments to have greater or lesser value. A bond's price moves in the opposite direction of its yield, as seen in equation 14.1; rising yields means falling prices, and vice versa. Hence, the price sensitivity to yield changes is negative, and its absolute value is called the duration, D:

$$D_t = -\frac{\partial P_t}{\partial \text{YTM}_t} \frac{1 + \text{YTM}_t}{P_t} \qquad (14.3)$$

By the magic of fixed-income mathematics, the duration can be shown (by differentiating equation 14.1) to be equal to the weighted-average time to maturity of all the remaining cash flows (coupons and face value)

$$D_t = \sum\nolimits_{\text{coupon and maturity dates } t_i} (t_i - t) w_{t_i} \tag{14.4}$$

where each weight w_{t_i} is the fraction of the bond's present value being paid at that time

$$w_{t_i} = \frac{\text{cash flow}_{t_i}}{(1 + \text{YTM})^{t_i - t} P_t} \tag{14.5}$$

Equation 14.4 explains the term "duration": D_t is a weighted average of the times $t_i - t$ to the remaining cash flows. For instance, the duration of a 5-year zero-coupon bond is naturally equal to its time to maturity, 5. The magic is that D_t is also given by equation 14.3, that is, it also tells us how sensitive a bond price is to changes in its yield. Hence, equations 14.3 and 14.4 together tell us that the prices of longer term bonds are more yield sensitive than those of shorter term bonds.

With this definition of duration, we can compute the price change ΔP that occurs with a sudden change in yield, ΔYTM_t:

$$\frac{\Delta P_t}{P_t} \cong -\frac{D_t}{1 + \text{YTM}_t} \Delta \text{YTM}_t = -\bar{D}_t \Delta \text{YTM}_t \tag{14.6}$$

Here, the last equality introduces the "modified duration," $\bar{D}_t = D_t / (1 + \text{YTM}_t)$. Rather than looking at a sudden shock, we can also use this duration logic to write an intuitive expression for the bond return over a time period from t to $t + 1$. If the YTM stays the same over this time period, then the bond return equals the YTM (which can be seen by combining equations 14.1 and 14.2). If the YTM changes, then this yield change leads to an additional effect given via the modified duration (computed next time period at the current yield):

$$\text{bond return}_{t, t+1} \cong \text{YTM}_t - \bar{D}_{t+1} (\text{YTM}_{t+1} - \text{YTM}_t) \tag{14.7}$$

If the yield rises as in figure 14.2, then the bond return will be reduced during this period, as seen in equation 14.7. If this happens, however, then the expected return going forward will be higher, as the bond now earns a higher yield. Indeed, if a zero-coupon bond is held to maturity, its return will still average its original YTM.

Yield and Return of a Leveraged Bond

Traders are often interested in their excess return over the risk-free rate and, correspondingly, a bond's yield above the short rate. Indeed, bonds are often leveraged, that is, bought with borrowed money (where the bond is used as

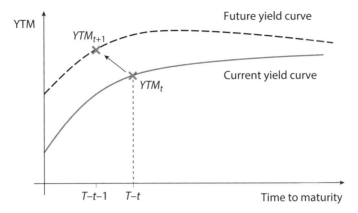

Figure 14.2. Bond returns and changes in the yield curve.

collateral) and the bond's excess return is effectively the return of such a leveraged position.

When an arbitrageur borrows against a bond in a *repo* transaction, she must pay an interest rate called the *repo rate* (see section 5.8 on margin requirements). Hence, the yield on this leveraged position is $YTM_t - repo_t$, as illustrated in figure 14.3. Most government bonds have almost the same repo rate, which is called the *general collateral (GC) repo rate*. An arbitrageur who owns a bond that is viewed as particularly attractive collateral can borrow at a lower repo rate. In this case, the bond is said to be *on special*, and the discount in its repo rate is called its *specialness*:

$$repo_t = GC_t - specialness_t \qquad (14.8)$$

A bond's repo rate changes over time. This variation is primarily driven by changes in the GC repo rate, which in turn is driven by central bank monetary policy. The bond's repo rate is also driven by changes in the specialness due

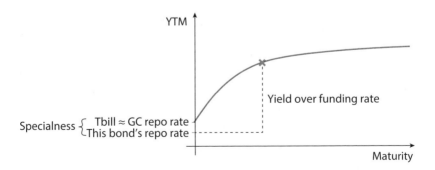

Figure 14.3. The yield of a leveraged bond.

to changes in the bond market's liquidity characteristics. If the bond is held to maturity, the investment will make money if and only if the YTM at the time of purchase is greater than the average repo rate over the life of the bond. The return on a leveraged bond is calculated as before, except that we now subtract the financing rate:

$$\text{leveraged bond return}_{t,t+1} \cong \text{YTM}_t - \text{repo}_t - \bar{D}_{t+1}(\text{YTM}_{t+1} - \text{YTM}_t) \quad (14.9)$$

Immunization

Fixed-income arbitrage traders often want to be hedged with respect to the risk of changes in the level of interest rates, i.e., to parallel up or down moves in the yield curve. To hedge this risk, traders make sure that the total duration in dollars of their long positions (i.e., number of securities held long, x^{long}, multiplied by modified duration, and multiplied by the value, $x^{\text{long}} \bar{D}^{\text{long}} P^{\text{long}}$) matches the total duration of their short positions ($x^{\text{short}} \bar{D}^{\text{short}} P^{\text{short}}$). This so-called immunization implies that an immediate parallel shift in the yield curve is hedged. In particular, if $\Delta \text{YTM}^{\text{long}} = \Delta \text{YTM}^{\text{short}}$, where Δ indicates change, then the resulting profit or loss (P&L) is approximately zero:[1]

$$\text{P\&L}^{\$} \cong -x^{\text{long}} \bar{D}^{\text{long}} P^{\text{long}} \Delta \text{YTM}^{\text{long}} + x^{\text{short}} \bar{D}^{\text{short}} P^{\text{short}} \Delta \text{YTM}^{\text{short}} = 0 \quad (14.10)$$

Convexity

We have seen that, when bond yields change, bond prices respond in the opposite direction and the magnitude is approximately given by modified duration times yield change. However, this is only an approximation, and it works best for small changes in yield. We can use convexity to improve the approximation:

$$\frac{\Delta P_t}{P_t} \cong -\bar{D}_t \Delta \text{YTM}_t + \tfrac{1}{2}\text{convexity}_t (\Delta \text{YTM}_t)^2 \quad (14.11)$$

Convexity is defined as the second derivative of the bond price with respect to yield changes and can also be written using the weights w_{t_i} given in equation 14.5:

$$\text{convexity}_t = \frac{\partial^2 P_t}{\partial (\text{YTM}_t)^2} \frac{1}{P_t} = \sum_{\text{coupon and maturity dates } t_i} \frac{(t_i - t)(t_i - t + 1)}{(1 + \text{YTM}_t)^2} w_{t_i} \quad (14.12)$$

---

[1] This equation is the result of applying equation 14.6 for both the long positions and the short positions since $\text{P\&L}^{\$} = x^{\text{long}} \Delta P^{\text{long}} - x^{\text{short}} \Delta P^{\text{short}}$.

Since the bond return involves the convexity multiplied by the *squared* yield change—a positive number—having a large positive convexity on the long investments is a good thing when yields change. For a long–short trader, it can be desirable to have a larger convexity on the long positions than on the short positions because this means that changes in yield lead to profits. In chapter 15, we discuss how convertible bond traders profit from convexity (which is also called gamma trading).

What Yield Changes Are Already Priced In? Forward Rates

Fixed-income investors often have a sense of the direction of interest rates. For instance, if the short-term interest rate is already at zero, chances are that it will be rising. Does this mean that one should sell short on bonds? Not necessarily, because bond yields already reflect this expectation, at least to some extent. You should only sell short on bonds if you think that bond yields will rise faster or further than what is priced in. How do you know what is priced in, though?

To answer to this question, we want to determine the future yield on a bond that will make you break even if you invest today. This rate is called the *forward rate* (or the *break-even rate*). Before we define the forward rate, we start with zero-coupon bond yields y_t^T at the current time t for bonds on any maturity T. The forward rate $f_t^{s,T}$ at some future time s of a bond that matures at time T is given by "the break-even condition":

$$(1 + y_t^T)^{T-t} = (1 + y_t^s)^{s-t}(1 + f_t^{s,T})^{T-s} \qquad (14.13)$$

In words, this means that the return on investing in a bond that matures at time T (the left-hand side of the equation) must equal the return of investing in a shorter term bond that matures at time s and reinvesting the money at the forward rate (the right-hand side of the equation). Suppose that at time t, you buy the long-term bond that matures at time T. If the bond's future yield at time s turns out to be equal to the forward rate, then your return from t to s will have equaled the risk-free return, y_t^s. If the bond future yield is lower, its price will have risen and your return will be higher. Hence, fixed-income traders will buy a bond if their expectations of future yields are below the forward rates implied by the yield curve. The forward rate can be solved as

$$f_t^{s,T} = \frac{(1 + y_t^T)^{(T-t)/(T-s)}}{(1 + y_t^s)^{(s-t)/(T-s)}} - 1 \qquad (14.14)$$

The forward rate can also be seen as a future yield that can be locked in today. The forward rate can in principle be locked in by buying the bond that matures at time T while shorting the same dollar amount of the bond that matures at time s.

Fixed-income traders use forward rates in two ways: First, they compute the whole forward yield curve at some time in the future, say in one year.[2] They look at this yield curve to see if it is consistent with their views on future yields and trade on any potential discrepancies. For instance, a trader might buy a 10-year bond today if he thinks that the 1-year forward yield of a 9-year bond yield appears too high.

Second, fixed-income traders compute the path of expected short-term interest rates at many times in the future.[3] They consider whether this path is consistent with their views on central bank policy, as we discuss in more detail next.

14.2. WHAT DETERMINES YIELDS? THE ECONOMY AND THE CENTRAL BANK

The central bank sets the overnight interest rate. This is the central element of monetary policy. As discussed in more detail in chapter 11, most central banks set the overnight interest rate to control inflation and to achieve high employment (i.e., economic growth). Hence, when inflation is going up, the central bank tends to increase the interest rate to cool the economy and to bring inflation back to its target. Similarly, when the economy is overheating, the central bank raises the interest rate. On the flip side, the central bank lowers the interest rate in a recession with falling inflation and slowing growth.

The overnight interest rate affects all other interest rates (which is part of what is called the monetary transmission mechanism). To see how this works, consider the return of holding a bond from time t to maturity T. In fact, let's look at the hold-to-maturity return of a *leveraged* bond position, which can also simply be viewed as the bond's excess return:

$$\text{leveraged bond return}_{t,T} = \text{YTM}_t - \text{Average}(R_t^f) \qquad (14.15)$$

Here, R_t^f is the overnight risk-free rate (e.g., the repo rate as discussed above), which is essentially set by the central bank. If we take the expectation of both sides of equation 14.15 and rewrite, we get the following relation, which is important in understanding the drivers of bond yields:

$$\text{YTM}_t = E_t(\text{Average}(R_t^f)) + \underbrace{E_t(\text{leveraged bond return}_{t,T})}_{\text{risk premium}} \qquad (14.16)$$

---

[2] Mathematically, this means looking at $f_t^{s,T}$ for a fixed future time s (say, $s = 1$ year) across a range of maturity dates T.

[3] Mathematically, this means looking at $f_t^{s,s+1\text{month}}$ across a range of future dates s.

Hence, a bond yield can be seen as the sum of two parts: (i) the expected average overnight interest rate over the bond's life, plus (ii) a risk premium. The first part is intuitive: An alternative to buying a one-year bond is to keep re-investing your money in the money market, earning the overnight interest rate every day. If the overnight interest rate is currently high and you expect it to stay high for at least a year, then you would require a higher yield on the one-year bond in order to buy it. Hence, when the central bank sets a higher interest rate, most bond yields tend to rise. This mechanism is very powerful for short-term bonds and less powerful for long-term bonds. Naturally, a one-month bond yield must be very close to the overnight interest rate, but a 30-year bond yield can deviate substantially.

The classic "expectations hypothesis" (EH) states that the risk premium is zero. The idea behind the EH is that fearless competition among arbitrageurs drives bond prices up to a level where their excess return is zero (i.e., their return is equal to the expected average short rate over their lives). The EH is clearly rejected in the data, however, as arbitrageurs are not fearless in the real world and they require compensation for taking risk. The EH fails in two ways: Bond risk premiums are not zero on average and they are not constant.

First, the average risk premium of a bond is positive (not zero). Hence, a leveraged bond position has historically made a profit on average, and this expected profit is called the "term premium." The term premium is compensation for "tying your money up" in a long-term bond (whose price can suddenly fall) rather than putting them in the risk-free money market. The term premium tends to increase with maturity, such that longer term bonds offer both greater risk and greater expected returns than shorter term bonds.[4]

The second issue with the EH is that it implies that bond yields *only* move based on changes in current and future overnight interest rate expectations. Bond yields do change over time due to changes in the short rate, but bond yields also move around for several other reasons. Hence, bonds' expected returns (i.e., risk premiums) vary across time and across bonds. For instance, as we discuss below, a bond's expected return changes over time as its carry changes. Furthermore, a bond's expected return may change if investors' risk appetite changes, if pension funds' interest-rate hedging demand varies, if there is significant demand for certain bonds (e.g., by the Chinese investing their currency reserves), or if the government issues new bonds. Such supply and demand effects underlie what is called the "preferred habitat theory" of the yield curve.

---

[4] The expected excess return per unit of risk, i.e., the Sharpe ratio, is highest for short-term bonds. This is because short-term bonds must be leveraged to earn a large excess return as investors cannot "eat" risk-adjusted returns. Furthermore, investors who want to earn the term premium prefer unleveraged long-term bonds to leveraged short-term bonds and, therefore, short-term bonds must offer a larger Sharpe ratio (Frazzini and Pedersen 2014).

14.3. TRADING ON THE LEVEL, SLOPE, AND CURVATURE OF THE TERM STRUCTURE

The collection of yields of all bonds across maturities is called the "term structure," as discussed earlier. The term structure moves around over time, changing its shape. In principle, there are an infinite number of shapes of the term structure, but much of the variation can be captured by its level, slope, and curvature. Fixed-income arbitrage traders can trade on each of these dimensions of the term structure.

Trading on the Level

Trading on the level of the term structure simply means betting on whether interest rates are going up or down. If you think interest rates are rising, then you short bonds—any kind of bonds or bond futures might do the job as you are simply betting on the level of all interest rates. Similarly, if you think interest rates are falling, then you buy bonds.

Directional "level" trades are driven by views on what the central bank is doing or views on the underlying macroeconomic fundamentals, most notably inflation and growth. Therefore, such directional macro bets are really the territory of the global macro traders, whereas fixed-income arbitrage traders typically focus more on relative-value trades.

Fixed-income arbitrage traders might bet on cross-country differences in the level of interest rate. For instance, they might invest in bonds in certain countries that are deemed likely to experience falling yields while shorting bonds in countries where interest rates are more likely to rise. Such a relative-value trade would be hedged against the global level of interest rate while betting on local differences.

Trading on the Slope

Fixed-income arbitrageurs can also trade on the slope of the term structure. For instance, a fixed-income arbitrage trader might buy a so-called "curve steepener" by buying 2-year bonds while shorting 10-year bonds. This is called a steepener because it profits if the yield of 2-year bonds falls relative to the yield of 10-year bonds, a steepening of the yield curve. The reverse trade is naturally called a "flattener."

Let us consider how such a trade might be sized. Suppose that the trader buys a single 2-year bond—how many 10-year bonds should be shorted against it? If we denote by x the number of 10-year bonds that are shorted, then we have the following P&L from an immediate change of yields:

$$\text{P\&L}^\$ \cong -\bar{D}^2 P^2 \Delta \text{YTM}^2 + x \cdot \bar{D}^{10} P^{10} \Delta \text{YTM}^{10} \qquad (14.17)$$

Here, we label all variables related to the 2-year bond with a superscript "2" (i.e., its modified duration is $\bar{D}^2$, its price is P^2, and its yield change is ΔYTM^2) and similarly for the 10-year bond. Different traders scale their slope trades slightly differently, but a natural choice is to make the portfolio duration neutral, i.e., immunized against changes in the level of the term structure (to keep the bets on the slope separate from bets on the level). To do that, we choose $x = \bar{D}^2 P^2 / (\bar{D}^{10} P^{10})$. This position size means that a change in the level of the yield curve with $\Delta \text{YTM}^2 = \Delta \text{YTM}^{10}$ will result in a P&L of approximately zero. Furthermore, the P&L will be positive when the yield curve steepens, $\Delta \text{YTM}^2 < \Delta \text{YTM}^{10}$, and vice versa for a flattening curve.

For example, if we consider two par bonds with $P^2 = P^{10} = 1,000$, 4% coupons, and modified durations of $\bar{D}^2 = 1.9$ and $\bar{D}^{10} = 8.1$, then $x = 0.23$. Hence, the slope trade uses a position sizing such that it shorts about a quarter 10-year bonds for every long 2-year bond. This position sizing is due to the fact that the long-term bond price is much more volatile and much more sensitive to changes in the level of the yield curve.

Rather than choosing the hedge ratio based on duration matching, some traders alternatively choose the hedge ratio to match the volatilities of the long and short positions. This would be the same as duration matching if the bonds have the same yield volatility (because return volatility is approximately duration times yield volatility), but the long-term bond yields tend to be less volatile than short-term bond yields.

Trading on the Curvature: Butterflies

Fixed-income traders often seek to identify points along the yield curve that appear relatively "rich" or "cheap." For instance, some fixed-income traders compare the curvature of the yield curve to its typical historical shape and bet on mean reversion of the curvature. They model the shape of the term structure and look at points where a bond's actual yield differs significantly from the model-implied yield. Academic economists call such a discrepancy a "pricing error," meaning that they assume that the market price is correct and that their term structure model erroneously misses the mark. Traders are less modest. They call such a discrepancy a "trading opportunity." If the actual bond yield is below the model-implied yield, then the fixed-income trader may sell short on this bond, hoping that its price will drop as its yield converges to the model-implied rate.

How do we know whether a discrepancy between a market yield and a model-implied yield is a pricing error or a trading opportunity? Well, said simply, if trading on the discrepancy loses money, then it is a pricing error, otherwise it is an opportunity. How do you know this in advance? You never know for sure, but there can be several indications. For instance, if the bond that appears to have a "too low" yield has just been bought in large numbers by price-insensitive insurance companies who need it for a specific reason, then such demand pressure gives a trader confidence that the anomalous price presents an opportunity. Furthermore, systematic traders backtest trading on such price discrepancies in general to see if the trading signal has worked in the past.

A butterfly trade is betting against such an anomalous bond while at the same time hedging by buying two "surrounding" bonds, as seen in figure 14.4. The "center" bond C has a strangely low yield, for instance, because several pension funds have been buying significant amounts of this bond as it is their preferred way to match their liabilities. A fixed-income arbitrageur observes this low yield and decides that it is driven by the pension funds' buying pressure rather than economic fundamentals. Hence, the arbitrageur decides to sell short this bond.

As a hedge, the arbitrageur buys the "left-side" bond L of lesser maturity and the "right-side" bond R of greater maturity, also shown in figure 14.4. The left-side bond is shorter term than C, and the right-side bond is longer term, so overall the hedge portfolio is similar to C, but it has a higher average yield. The hedge can therefore eliminate a lot of risk and seeks to exploit the relative valuations of the bonds. How exactly should the hedge portfolio weights be chosen? The beauty of the butterfly trade is that it can hedge both the risk of changes in the level and slope of the term structure.

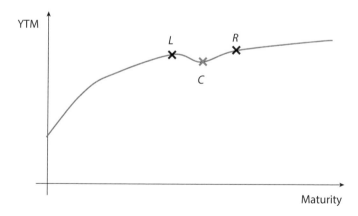

Figure 14.4. Butterfly trade.

A fixed-income arbitrageur determines that the yield on bond C is too low and short-sells this bond. As a hedge, the arbitrageur buys bonds L and R.

In practice, there are several ways to specify the hedge, and we consider a simple example. If the arbitrageur sells short bond C and buys x^L of the left-side bonds and x^R of the right-side bonds, then the profit or loss will be

$$\text{P\&L}^\$ \cong \bar{D}^C P^C \Delta\text{YTM}^C - x^L \bar{D}^L P^L \Delta\text{YTM}^L - x^R \bar{D}^R P^R \Delta\text{YTM}^R \quad (14.18)$$

This expression is getting a bit complex, so let us try to simplify it as follows. Rather than keeping track of the number of bonds, let us keep track of the dollar duration that it achieves. Specifically, we let $D^{\$,L} = x^L \bar{D}^L P^L$, $D^{\$,R} = x^R \bar{D}^R P^R$, and $D^{\$,C} = \bar{D}^C P^C$ so that we can write equation 14.18 as

$$\text{P\&L}^\$ \cong D^{\$,C} \Delta\text{YTM}^C - D^{\$,L} \Delta\text{YTM}^L - D^{\$,R} \Delta\text{YTM}^R \quad (14.19)$$

To hedge changes in the level of the term structure, the arbitrageur must be immune to shocks with $\Delta\text{YTM}^C = \Delta\text{YTM}^L = \Delta\text{YTM}^R$, as seen in figure 14.5. Hence, the position sizes must satisfy the following relation:

$$D^{\$,C} = D^{\$,L} + D^{\$,R} \quad (14.20)$$

The slope is hedged similarly, as seen in figure 14.6. Suppose that the typical slope change is given by $\Delta\text{YTM}^L = \beta\Delta\text{YTM}^C$ and $\Delta\text{YTM}^R = \gamma\Delta\text{YTM}^C$ (where the parameters β and γ could for instance be derived from a term structure model). Then the slope is hedged by choosing

$$D^{\$,C} = \beta D^{\$,L} + \gamma D^{\$,R} \quad (14.21)$$

Solving two equations with two unknowns gives

$$D^{\$,L} = \frac{\gamma - 1}{\gamma - \beta} D^{\$,C} \quad \text{and} \quad D^{\$,R} = \frac{1 - \beta}{\gamma - \beta} D^{\$,C} \quad (14.22)$$

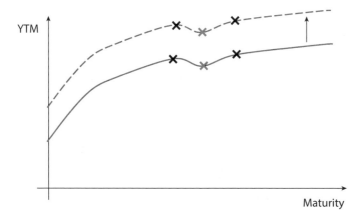

Figure 14.5. Butterfly trade: Change in the level of the term structure.

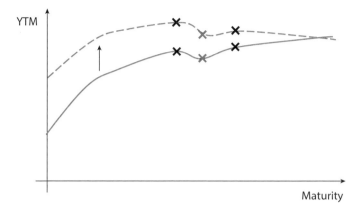

Figure 14.6. Butterfly trade: Change in the slope of the term structure.

For example, suppose that $\beta = 0.9$ and $\gamma = 1.1$, as might be the case in figure 14.6. Then we see that $D^{\$,L} = D^{\$,C} = 0.5\,D^{\$,C}$. This is an intuitive choice: The hedge has the same overall dollar duration as the bond being shorted with half the duration coming from a shorter term bond and the other half coming from a longer term bond. Given that this hedge is duration matched, level changes are hedged, and given that the hedge contains both short- and long-term bonds, slope changes are hedged.

Lastly, suppose that there is a change in the size of the "kink" in the yield curve around bond C. For simplicity, suppose that the yield of bond C changes by ΔYTM^C while the other bonds don't move, $\Delta YTM^L = \Delta YTM^R = 0$ as seen in figure 14.7. In this case, the profit or loss is

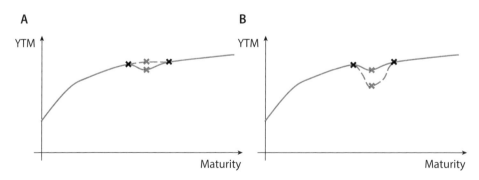

Figure 14.7. Butterfly trade: Change in the "kink" of the term structure.
Panel A: Convergence.
Panel B: Divergence.

$$P\&L^\$ \cong D^{\$,C}\Delta YTM^C \neq 0 \qquad (14.23)$$

We see that the hedge is powerless with respect to changes in the kink. Indeed, the arbitrageur is precisely betting on the kink, so he does not want this risk to be hedged. The arbitrageur is hoping that the kink disappears ($\Delta YTM^C > 0$), leading to a profit, as seen in Panel A of figure 14.7. Alternatively, Panel B of figure 14.7 shows a situation where the arbitrageur loses money as the kink widens, for instance, because the pension funds that have been buying bond C suddenly need to buy even more of these bonds.

14.4. BOND CARRY AND CARRY TRADES

Fixed-income traders search for high returns as expected returns vary over time and across bonds. One of the characteristics that predict high returns for a bond is a high carry.[5] Hence, bond carry can be used to trade on the level, slope, and curvature of the yield curve and also in the trades that we consider next, such as the off-the-run vs. on-the-run bond trade.

A bond's carry is its return if the market conditions stay the same. A simple measure of carry is its return if its own YTM stays the same. This carry measure is simply the bond's YTM as seen in equation 14.7. A more sophisticated measure of bond carry is the return if the *entire term structure of interest rates* stays the same:[6]

$$\text{bond carry}_{t,t+1} \cong YTM_t^{\text{maturity } T} - \bar{D}_{t+1}(YTM_t^{\text{maturity } T-1} - YTM_t^{\text{maturity } T}) \qquad (14.24)$$

Here, the first term is the bond's current yield, and the second term is called the bond's "roll-down return." The roll down is the expected price appreciation due to the bond nearing maturity (assuming that the term structure stays the same), as seen in figure 14.8.

For example, in the fall of 2013, the U.S. 10-year Treasury yield was about 2.6%, very low compared to history. However, the yield curve was relatively steep, implying a roll-down return of 1.6%, computed as the product of an 8-year duration and a 0.20 percentage point difference between 9- and 10-year

---

[5] Koijen, Moskowitz, Pedersen, and Vrugt (2012) show that bond carry predicts bond returns. Ilmanen (1995) and Cochrane and Piazzesi (2005) document other predictors of bond returns.

[6] Equation 14.24 is an approximation; the exact carry is the forward rate $f_t^{T-1,T}$. It may be surprising to rediscover the forward rate as the bond carry, but this is intuitive upon reflection. If the yield curve stays the same, then the bond will earn its carry between t and $t+1$ and the yield $YTM_t^{\text{maturity } T-1}$ for its remaining life $t+1$ to T, averaging its current yield $YTM_t^{\text{maturity } T}$. The forward rate is the yield such that the bond yield today equals the return of first earning the $YTM_t^{\text{maturity } T-1}$ from t to $T-1$ and then earning the forward rate from $T-1$ to T. Since it does not matter which yield is earned first, the carry equals the forward rate.

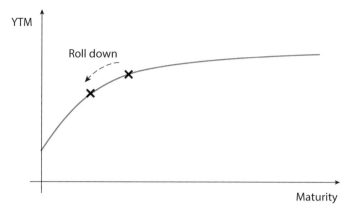

Figure 14.8. Carry of a bond: yield plus roll down.

Treasury yields. Hence, the total carry was 2.6% + 1.6% = 4.2%, which was not that low, especially compared to the short-term interest rate of less than 0.25%.

Of course, a bond's realized return typically differs from the carry. The bond's realized return is its carry plus the price appreciation due to the change in the term structure of interest rates, as seen in figure 14.9.

The expectations hypothesis (EH) discussed above proposes that a bond's expected return is constant. Hence, according to this hypothesis, a high bond carry does *not* predict a high return because a high carry is assumed to be offset by a low price appreciation (due to an unfavorable change in the yield curve). Empirically, the EH is a failure, which is good news to bond traders, because it means that the carry can be used as a trading signal.

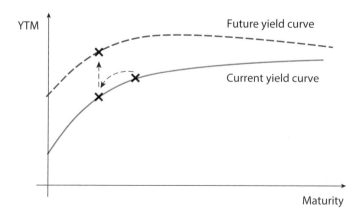

Figure 14.9. Carry vs. return of a bond.

14.5. ON-THE-RUN VS. OFF-THE-RUN

A classic government bond arbitrage is to trade on-the-run Treasuries against off-the-run Treasuries. This trade can be seen as a carry trade, a value trade, or a convergence trade. In particular, it typically involves buying cheap high-carry bonds against more expensive low-carry bonds, hoping that the bond prices will converge for a quick profit. Let's see how.

On-the-run Treasuries are newly issued government bonds. Since they are just issued, they have a lot of trading activity and are very liquid, i.e., they are easy to buy and sell at low transaction costs. Furthermore, on-the-run Treasuries are easy to finance for a leveraged trader as lenders like this safe and liquid collateral, implying that on-the-run bonds tend to have low repo rates. Off-the-run Treasuries are old bonds, and they tend to have worse market and funding liquidity. As a result, off-the-run Treasuries are cheaper and offer higher yields.

The yield spread between on- and off-the-run bonds varies substantially over time, as seen in Panel A of figure 14.10. The on-the-run/off-the-run spread reaches highs during liquidity crises such as the 1998 Long-Term Capital Management (LTCM) event and the global financial crisis of 2008–2009. The spread is low during times of abundant liquidity when traders reach for yield. For example, in early 2007 before the crisis, the spread had been getting lower and more stable over time as fixed-income arbitrage traders with ample liquidity eliminated most spreads.

Panel B of figure 14.10 shows the interesting shape of the yield curve during the global financial crisis in November and December 2008. The yields of old 10-year Treasuries that were originally issued as 30-year Treasuries deviated substantially from those of newly issued 10-year Treasuries. At times of greater liquidity, the yield curve has its more normal smooth shape.

The typical on-the-run/off-the-run trade is done by buying the "cheap" off-the-run Treasury and selling short on the "expensive" on-the-run trade. The profit or loss of a leveraged position over a single time period is

$$\text{P\&L}_{t,t+1} = \text{yield differential} - \text{financing spread} + \text{price appreciation differential}$$

$$\cong (\text{YTM}_t^{\text{off}} - \text{YTM}_t^{\text{on}}) - (\text{repo}_t^{\text{off}} - \text{repo}_t^{\text{on}}) - \bar{D}(\Delta\text{YTM}_{t+1}^{\text{off}} - \Delta\text{YTM}_{t+1}^{\text{on}})$$

$$(14.25)$$

Here, the first term, the yield differential, is positive since the cheap off-the-run bond offers a higher yield. The second term, the financing spread, detracts from the P&L as the off-the-run has a higher financing rate. The last term, the relative change in yields, is obviously not known in advance. The hope is that the on- and off-the-run yields will converge as the on-the-run becomes less new and less special, leading to a positive P&L.

Fixed-income arbitrage traders try to put on this trade when the on- vs off-the-run spread has blown out, but, of course, it can always blow out some

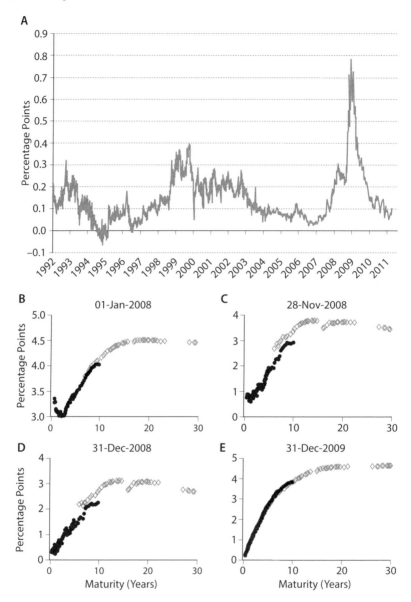

Figure 14.10. The on-the-run/off-the-run yield spread.

Panel A shows the yield spread between on- and off-the-run 10-year Treasury bonds over time. Panel B shows, at four selected dates, the entire yield curve where the (off-the-run) bonds originally issued as 30-year bonds are represented as diamonds and all other securities are plotted as solid circles. The disconnect between on- and off-the-run 10-year bonds during the global financial crisis is evident.

Sources: Panel A: Using data from AQR Capital Management. Panel B: Gürkaynak and Wright (2012).

more. A fixed-income trader will sometimes reverse the trade, buying on-the-run bonds while shorting off-the-run bonds. This reverse trade is a bet that their yield spread will widen in the near term, for instance, because the current spread is unusually low or because of an impending liquidity crisis.

14.6. SWAPS AND SWAP SPREADS

An interest-rate swap is a derivative that exchanges the cash flows of a fixed-rate loan to those of a floating-rate loan. The counterparty paying the fixed rate is called the "payer," and the counterparty receiving the fixed rate is called the "receiver." We will take the viewpoint of the receiver (who faces an interest-rate risk similar to that of an investor who is long on a bond).

The receiver earns a fixed rate called the swap rate, YTM^{swap}, and must pay a floating LIBOR rate, r_t^{LIBOR}. Hence, each time period, the net payment is $YTM^{swap} - r_t^{LIBOR}$ multiplied by a notional principal amount (say, $100,000) and the time between payments. There is no payment of face value at maturity since the notional principal amounts cancel out between the fixed-rate and floating-rate loans being exchanged. Traditional over-the-counter swaps set the swap rate such that the present value was zero at initiation, but entering into a swap is typically associated with a margin requirement. A swap has limited counterparty credit risk, since it has a market value close to zero and is marked to market.

The swap receiver has a similar position to being long on a leveraged government bond. The owner of a Treasury bond (at par) financed at the repo rate also receives a fixed coupon payment of $YTM^{Treasury}$, while paying interest on the repo financing, $repo_t$. Such a leveraged bond has little initial payment since the loan finances the purchase (subject to a margin requirement) and, if the position is held to maturity, the face value is used to repay the loan—in complete analogy to the swap. The yield of the leveraged bond net of financing is $YTM^{Treasury} - repo_t$.

The *swap spread* is the difference between the YTM on the Treasury and the fixed rate of the comparable maturity swap:

$$\text{swap spread} = YTM^{swap} - YTM^{Treasury}$$

The swap spread tends to be positive or, said differently, the swap rate tends to be above the Treasury rate. The swap spread is positive for several reasons. Most importantly, the swap's floating rate is LIBOR, which tends to be above repo rate. Hence, since the swap has a higher floating rate on one side, it must also have a higher fixed rate on the other side of the exchange. The LIBOR rate is higher than the repo rate since the LIBOR rate corresponds to an unsecured (i.e., risky) bank loan, whereas the repo rate corresponds to a loan secured by Treasury collateral.

While a positive swap spread is to be expected, the typical swap spread trade has nevertheless been to buy a swap spread "tightener" (as opposed to a "widener"), in which a trader goes long on a swap while shorting a leveraged Treasury. A swap spread tightener is a bet that the swap spread will narrow in the near to medium term, or that the swap spread is larger than the expected average financing spread, $r_t^{\text{LIBOR}} - \text{repo}_t$, over the life the securities. Historically, the swap spread has often been wider than the financing spread, implying a positive carry for the tightener.

14.7. CREDIT RISK AND CREDIT TRADING

Corporate bonds naturally offer higher yields than government bonds since corporations can go bankrupt and default on their bonds. (Governments can default too, but this is often seen as less likely in most countries and, to focus on corporate credit risk, we ignore government credit risk for now.) The credit spread is the promised yield of a corporate bond over and above the yield of a government bond of comparable maturity:

$$\text{YTM}^{\text{corporate bond}} = \text{YTM}^{\text{government bond}} + \text{credit spread}$$

The credit spread naturally depends on the credit risk, which can be broken into two parts: (i) the probability that a default happens, and (ii) the loss rate in case of default.[7] The product of the default probability and the loss rate is the expected loss from default. The credit spread is typically higher than the expected loss from default as investors require a risk premium as compensation:

$$\text{credit spread} = \underbrace{\text{default probability} \cdot \text{loss rate}}_{\text{expected loss from default}} + \text{credit risk premium}$$

Fixed-income arbitrageurs may trade corporate bonds employing credit analysis to evaluate a corporation's fundamental default risk. They then ask the question, "How wide is the credit spread relative to the bond's risk of default and expected recovery rate?" A high credit spread relative to the risk means a high expected return. Fixed-income traders buy such cheap high-expected-return bonds and hedge the interest-rate risk by shorting government bonds or swaps. The firm-specific default risk can then be largely diversified away, but changes in the overall marketwide default risk remain. Some fixed-income traders decide to bear the marketwide default risk, whereas others try to hedge it by shorting overvalued corporate bonds or by shorting credit indices such as the CDX. Similar trades can be implemented with credit default swaps (CDSs), sovereign bonds, and loans.

---

[7] The loss rate is the percentage loss in default, and it is closely linked to the so-called *recovery rate*. If a defaulted bond has a loss rate of 40%, then it corresponds to a recovery rate of 60%.

Fixed-income traders also consider relative value trades across asset classes. They trade corporate bonds against the corresponding CDSs, betting on the so-called CDS-bond basis. They trade the CDX credit index against the constituent CDSs or the tranches of the CDX against each other. Finally, they may perform "capital structure arbitrage," where they trade corporate bonds against equity on the same company, or junior debt against senior debt, or relative value among bonds denominated in different currencies, or CDS against equity and equity options. Capital structure arbitrage is based on the idea that different claims on the firm (stocks and corporate bonds) should be closely linked as they all depend on the value of the company. For instance, by looking at the stock price, the stock return volatility, and the level of debt, we can estimate (using the Merton (1974) model) how close the firm is to default because default happens when the firm value drops to the level of the debt and equity is wiped out. This gives an estimate of the fair value of the corporate bond, which can be compared to the market value of the bond. If there is a discrepancy, the corporate bond can be traded against the equity.

14.8. MORTGAGE TRADING

Fixed-income traders also often trade mortgage-backed securities (MBSs), that is, securities backed by mortgage payments, often guaranteed by an agency. The simplest securities are pass-through bonds, where the owner of a bond essentially receives her share of the overall mortgage payments.

The simplest mortgage-related trade is the so-called "mortgage basis trade." This trade invests long in MBS and hedges the interest-rate risk by shorting government bonds or swaps. The basic idea is to try to benefit from the MBS yield being higher than the government bond yield. The higher MBS yield is naturally compensation for the several risks that underlie this trade. First, the MBS could have some default risk, although this risk might be small due to the high quality of the collateral, the overcollateralization, and the government guarantees. Prepayment risk can be a serious risk, which is associated with negative convexity: Lower interest rates do not help the MBS as much as the government bonds (which are being shorted) because low interest rates lead to more prepayments, thereby reducing the maturity. On the flip side, higher interests rates hurt the MBS about as much as government bonds as prepayments drop. Lastly, the MBS basis trade is subject to liquidity risk as MBS's market liquidity can suddenly drop in a crisis and they can become harder to borrow against.

More complex trades include long–short relative-value trades on MBS "to-be-announced" (TBA) futures, tranches of mortgage pools (including interest-only and principal-only tranches), private-label mortgage pools, commercial mortgage backed securities (CMBS), and real estate investment trusts (REITs).

14.9. INTEREST-RATE VOLATILITY TRADING AND OTHER FIXED-INCOME ARBITRAGES

Some fixed-income traders also trade interest-rate related option instruments. For instance, they trade swaptions, caps, floors, and options on bond futures. This involves both directional volatility trades and relative value trades. A directional volatility trade means comparing a derivative's implied volatility with the arbitrageur's own prediction of actual volatility and buying the derivative if the implied volatility is low, while hedging the interest rate risk with bonds, bond futures, or swaps. Conversely, if the implied volatility is high, the arbitrageur will reverse the trade and short the derivative. Fixed-income arbitrage traders also perform relative-value volatility trades, in which they compare the pricing of different derivatives and go long–short based on the relative attractiveness.

Finally, fixed-income arbitrageurs pursue a variety of other trades such as municipal bond spreads, emerging market bonds, the bond futures basis relative to the cash market (based on cheapest-to-deliver considerations), structured credit, and break-even inflation trading.[8]

14.10. INTERVIEW WITH NOBEL LAUREATE MYRON SCHOLES

Myron Scholes was awarded the Nobel Prize in 1997 for his new method of determining the value of derivatives, notably the famous "Black–Scholes–Merton formula." He has held several professorships, currently the Frank E. Buck Professor of Finance, Emeritus, at the Stanford Graduate School of Business, and has served as the chairman of Platinum Grove Asset Management, a principal and limited partner at Long-Term Capital Management, and a managing director at Salomon Brothers. Scholes earned his Ph.D. and MBA at the University of Chicago and his BA at McMaster University.

> **LHP**: *I clearly remember the first time I met you—the day you won the Nobel Prize. You were at LTCM at the time, but suddenly showed up at Stanford University. I skipped class to attend the press conference.*
>
> **MS**: Obviously, it was a great excitement. It's hard to describe it. I was giving a talk at Pebble Beach—that's why I was in the area—and I was informed just before the talk. Afterwards, I went to Stanford where I was professor emeritus.

---

[8] See Huggins and Schaller (2013) for a "practitioner's guide" to a number of fixed-income arbitrage trades, Munk (2011) for an extensive analysis of fixed-income models, and Duarte, Longstaff, and Yu (2007) for an analysis of risk and return in certain fixed-income arbitrage trades.

LHP: *How did you decide to apply your academic ideas to real markets?*

MS: Well, I was an academic for many years and felt that to gain experience and new insights into how the intermediation process worked, it would be interesting for me to take a break from being an academic full time and become involved in the industry.

It's one thing to look at the water from afar; it's another thing to look at it right up close. From afar, it looks pretty calm; up close, it looks chaotic. I felt that the experience of the chaotic world, married to my theoretical abilities, would allow me to gain unique perspectives. For that reason, I gravitated to work for a while at Salomon Brothers.

LHP: *When most people think about the Black–Scholes formula, they think first about equity options, but you focused on fixed income arbitrage—why?*

MS: Right. The fascination with fixed-income arbitrage came about after many years of thinking about the idea that there are natural segmented clienteles. Insurance companies and pension funds tend to be at the longer end of the interest rate curve. Macro hedge funds try to express their macro views at the 10-year part of the curve, and other issuers—mortgage issuers and so forth—are also at the 10–15 year part of the curve. The shorter end of the curve tends to be the area where banks and corporations and others are borrowing or investing.

And so, as in the Modigliani view (as expressed in his presidential address to the American Finance Association), clienteles arise that lead to partially segmented markets. This creates opportunities for intermediaries to marry the disparate parts of the curve together, making the market more efficient. The idea of how clienteles arise in markets and how intermediaries make them appear seamless are a fascinating part of the fixed-income market, which is mostly an institutional market.

Also, fixed income has many embedded options and convexity issues—I was attracted to these complicated models. Many entities do not wish to hold instruments that have these embedded options, or a wish to reduce the convexity risk. They sell it off. As a result, there's an opportunity for investors who understand convexity and convexity hedging to intermediate in the market and assume and carry the risk forward in time.

LHP: *So, at the high level, fixed-income arbitrage traders intermediate between clienteles and accommodate convexity hedging. Can you talk more specifically about some of the fixed-income arbitrage trades?*

MS: Yes, fixed-income arbitrage is intermediating supply and demand imbalances that result from flows in the marketplace. To do that, one has to be able to understand and react to those flows. Most of the opportunities are mean-reverting trades. The major question is how long before mean reversion occurs and to what extent flows will continue in the opposite direction before investors step in or change holdings to mitigate the supply–demand imbalance in the market. The system is a combination of positive and negative feedback.

In a mean-reverting business, it is necessary to understand why prices are deviating from equilibrium or model values, to estimate the speed of mean reversion and how long it will take the price to return to equilibrium values, and to consider how much capital is necessary to support the position to determine the expected return on that capital.

The four major categories of trades in fixed-income arbitrage are curve trades, spread trades, convexity trades, and basis trades.

LHP: *Can you explain these four main trades? Basis trades I would define as trading two different securities that are almost identical but trade at different prices, or baskets of securities.*

MS: Yes. Basis trades are important. Spread trades are more directional and are on two different instruments that are similar. For example, you have a spread between government bonds and swaps. Or, even trade on spreads between Italian and German bonds. And, this might extend to spreads between swaps in Germany and the underlying bonds in Italy. Therefore, some of these trades are not only directional but have credit components.

LHP: *And then take views on how those spreads are going to change over time?*

MS: Yes, as I said, spread trades are more directional. If you understand what causes the imbalances, then you have an opportunity to intermediate even if you are taking some directional and credit risk. For example, there are times when investment banks issue a large volume of structured products, and the investment banks want to lay off their risks by using the swap market. These demands might involve hedging in the swap market, which causes spreads to go out or go in relative to other underlying bonds. Notice that the banks use market prices to determine the price at which they transact with their clients. They use relative prices to set prices in the market. Intermediaries use equilibrium models to determine prices at which to intermediate.

LHP: *Then there is curve trading.*

MS: Well, suppose that managed futures funds or macro traders such as George Soros believe that, say, bond prices in Japan are going to go up or yields are going to fall. They express their view by buying Japanese bond futures contracts because, for them, the futures contract is just the easiest way to express their views. They generally won't buy Japanese government bonds outright. They don't have the facility to do so. Their expertise is macro trading, deciding whether Japanese bonds will rise or fall in price.

The dealers will be on the other side of these futures contracts (demanded or supplied). The dealers must hedge their risks, for they make money on the bid–offer price differences of the futures contracts and not by predicting the direction of the markets. Therefore, for example, they directly hedge their risk by buying the cheapest-to-deliver bond, which most likely would be the

7-year bond, to hedge a futures contract that they sold to the macro traders. That creates imbalances between the adjacent maturities of bonds. The 7-year bond becomes expensive relative to some combination of the 10-year and 5-year bonds in the market. This creates a supply–demand imbalance in the market. The curve trader would then short the 7-year bond and buy the 10-year and the 5-year in the correct combination to hedge risks. There is a very short time period between the 7-year, 10-year, and 5-year part of the curve. The 7-year will become a 5-year bond in a few years. Longer term curve trades exist between the 10-year and 30-year part of the term structure. Notice here that because of clientele effects, bond prices are not always efficient. It is the role of intermediaries to make them efficient and earn a profit by doing such.

As another example, in Europe many pension funds—the Netherlands, for example—are required to hedge their pension liabilities by buying bonds at the long end of the curve if they take losses in the equity portions of their pension funds. In 2002, when the equity markets fell (as was the case in 2008), the pension funds were forced to liquidate equities and buy bonds at the long end of the curve. (Most pension promises are long-dated and become even more so as interest rates fall.) Under severe constraints, any government pension funds were forced to hedge their liabilities quickly. They received in swaps at the very long end of the curve (later to move out of swaps into bonds). As a result, they bid up the prices of swaps and the yields that they were receiving on their swaps were very low relative to bonds, because of the imbalances that they caused in the markets. As a result, the long end of the curve was very expensive relative to the intermediate parts of the interest rate curves. Therefore, it's possible to do curve trades where by selling the 30-year (in swaps) and buying the 10-year and then hedge the risks of changes in the slope of the curve and the level of the curve by selling at the 2-year part of the curve as well. Here, it is possible to do either curve trades (only in swaps) or combinations of curve and spread trades depending on demands and costs of putting on and maintaining the positions.

LHP: *You also mentioned convexity trading.*

MS: Yes. There are two types of convexity trading in mortgage markets. One type occurs when refinancing waves occur. During these waves, which generally occur when mortgage rates fall and refinancing demands expand dramatically, mortgage originators promise mortgagees a new mortgage, a forward delivery of a mortgage contract at some date in the future. When the refinancing demand accelerates, the mortgage originators need more time to complete the paperwork. As a result, in the short run, the supply of mortgages increases dramatically: For example, I have an old mortgage on my home, and with a refinance I'm going to take out a new mortgage a month or two months hence. Because of the friction of not being able to close the new mortgage at the moment originators lock the new mortgage rate, the originators want to hedge the risks associated with their forward delivery of mortgage contracts until they're placed and the old mortgages are paid off. So, as the supply of refinancing increases, there's a huge demand for convexity hedging by mortgage originators (they have granted an option and, without offsetting the risk, they will lose if interest rates rise), and that creates an opportunity to intermediate the imbalances generated by granting this lock-rate option.

The other kind of convexity trading has to do with mortgage servicers, who receive a fee each year for servicing the mortgage as long as the mortgage contract remains outstanding. If interest rates rise, the probability of refinancing is lower and the servicing fees are extended, which is great for them. On the other hand, if interest rates were to fall, they worry about refinancing and whether their mortgage servicing fees will be truncated. So they try to hedge the change in the length of their service fees by either buying at the long end of the curve or buying structured products originated by investment banks, such as constant maturity swaps or constant maturity mortgage obligations to protect their income flows. They are buying option protection. As a result, intermediaries are on the other side and intermediate these imbalances.

Fixed-income imbalances occur in these wholesale markets. What are the particular constraints and demands of clients and what are the dynamics of these demands? How do broker-dealers satisfy these demands, and, how in turn does this lead to clientele effects (pricing supply and demand imbalance transmission in particular regions or instruments) that can be intermediated across the curve (or regions). The clientele demands are satisfied and hedged within the clientele vertical. Fixed-income arbitrage is more horizontal across the curve.

LHP: *If you saw an apparent opportunity, but you couldn't actually identify the flow or you couldn't identify the demand pressure that was creating that opportunity, would you hesitate to put on the trade?*

MS: Oh, sure. If the flows are not understood, you hesitate. Most of the fixed-income business is a negative-feedback-type business unless you're directional, which is positive feedback or trend following. Trend following always competes with mean reversion, and the question is how you combine those two. You're always worried about the flows. If the return on capital is too low, you're not going to enter the trades initially, even though there is an opportunity to intermediate; you wait until you understand the flows. But, as described above, with interest rate movements, it is possible to predict flows even without actually observing them.

LHP: *If you don't know the source of the trading flows, then you don't know whether there's going to be a lot more behind it?*

MS: That's correct. That is the positive feedback or momentum effect. An intermediary will lose money by stemming the flow, and losses are taken on initial positions. If correct, however, the opportunity for mean reversion has increased. It is possible to add to positions.

LHP: *How do you know the source of trading flows and know how to time the trade?*

MS: Knowing the source of the imbalances helps to understand the market. This is where experience and knowledge of the business are important. With an equilibrium interest-rate model, it is possible to spot imbalances analytically. The broker-dealers help explain why the imbalance exists. One of the interesting aspects of fixed-income arbitrage is that it's akin to the reinsurance business in the sense that you're reinsuring the risks of the broker-dealer community. Broker-dealers are going to tell hedge funds, generally, what's happening; it's in their interest do so if they want to transfer their risks. They make a spread by satisfying their customers' demands and hedging. If they can reduce the costs of hedging, their customers will want more of their services. So, just as insurance companies reinsure with reinsurance companies, the same thing occurs in the financial markets when broker-dealers offload risks. They are willing to give up returns to hedge risks and explain to others why they wish to hedge.

LHP: *So, when you talk about positive- versus negative-feedback trading, you have in mind that negative feedback is when you're trading against the flow and being compensated for providing liquidity, while positive feedback is where you're trying to ride the trend?*

MS: That's correct. The idea is, by not intermediating immediately until your return on capital is higher, you're going with the flow, essentially. If something's a nickel cheap, you might not go in. If it's a dollar cheap, you go in. Intermediaries are always worried that the flows will continue against them. That part is invisible to them. The market demand might evolve as a wave builds up. The intermediary makes money when the wave subsides. Then the flows and equilibrium pricing are in the same direction.

LHP: *Or you might even short at a nickel cheap?*

MS: You might. Trend following is based on understanding macro developments and what governments are doing. Or they are based on statistical models of price movements. A positive up price tends to result in a positive up price. Here, however, it is not possible to determine whether the trend will continue.

LHP: *Why do spreads tend to widen during some periods of stress?*

MS: Well, capital becomes more scarce, both physical capital and human capital, in the sense that there isn't enough time for intermediaries to understand what is happening in chaotic times. Finance is in volatility time, not calendar time. When times are very quiet, intermediaries have a lot of time to figure things out, ask questions, put on trades, etc. When markets are very volatile, intermediaries don't have enough calendar time to make decisions. They don't have enough human capital to throw into the breach. That is why volatility time is so crucial to understand market pricing. As a result, intermediaries withdraw capital from the market. Capital goes to the sidelines until they can figure out whether and how to intermediate. Intermediaries lose on their invested capital because flows go against them as they are reducing risks; they become demanders of liquidity as they have to reduce risk. And, in chaotic markets, institutions and investors demand more intermediation services. Spreads widen, and market prices deviate from equilibrium values. At times of shock, market participants must sort out to what extent equilibrium prices have changed and to what extent supply–demand imbalances have increased. This takes time.

LHP: *In closing, what do you think is the main takeaway from your experiences at Salomon Brothers, LTCM, and Platinum?*

MS: Capital structure issues are very important in how to run a fixed-income arbitrage business. If done within a hedge fund, it generally means that leverage is part of the capital structure. This means that it is necessary to plan for shocks and losses across positions that are held at times of shock. It's one thing to have the skills and be able to understand imbalances and to intermediate imbalances, but it's very tough and very important to understand the efficacy of the capital structure—the debt and duration of the debt against positions, the equity underlying the positions, and the trust of investors supporting the business. It's tough because you're dealing with three things simultaneously: the assets you acquire; the business that you're in; and how you actually finance activities, whether it's debt, equity, or combinations of them and the demands of equity holders and of debt holders at a particular time. So, in times of shock, to provide reinsurance services (intermediation services) to the dealer community, and to borrow from them as well becomes very tough. If the intermediaries get into difficulties, then their horizons become very short term, and so they are more reticent to lend at the same time you're providing services to them. And, at times of shock, intermediaries must take losses on existing positions, reduce risk, find time to analyze opportunities, and maintain the trust of their investors taking these losses. A leveraged business is much more difficult to run than a long-only business. And, the correct form might be to intermediate within a long-only business and borrow securities within the long-only structure to enhance returns. This reduces the deadweight costs of the leverage component of the intermediation process.

CHAPTER 15

Convertible Bond Arbitrage

We predict and analyze the price relationships which exist between convertible securities . . . and their common stock. This allows us to forecast future price relationships and profits. We do not need to predict prices of individual securities in order to win.

—Thorp and Kassouf (1967)

15.1. WHAT IS A CONVERTIBLE BOND

A convertible bond is a corporate bond that can be converted into stock. Hence, a convertible bond is effectively a straight bond plus a warrant, that is, a call option to buy a newly issued share at a fixed price. A convertible bond has several important characteristics: Its *par value* is naturally the amount the owner will receive at maturity (if the bond has not been converted or called before then), and the *coupon* is the interest payments along the way. The *conversion ratio* is the number of stocks received upon conversion for each convertible bond. The *conversion price* is the nominal price per share (in terms of the bond's par value) at which conversion takes place. Hence, the following relation clearly holds:

conversion ratio = par value/conversion price

The so-called *parity conversion value* is the value of the convertible bond if it is converted immediately:

parity conversion value = conversion ratio × stock price

Many convertible bonds are *callable,* and some convertibles also have other option features. If a convertible bond is callable, then the issuer can redeem the bond before maturity (that is, pay the par value and stop paying coupons), subject to certain restrictions. A typical restriction is a *call protection*, meaning that the bond cannot be called for a certain time period.

Convertible bonds have been issued at least since the 1800s, among other things to finance railroads in the United States in the early days. Today, convertible bonds are often issued by smaller companies with a significant need for cash. Firms issue convertible bonds for a variety of reasons: Convertible bonds have lower financing cost (i.e., lower coupons) than straight debt because the buyers also receive the convertibility option. While convertible bonds dilute the equity, convertibles do so less than actual equity issues (e.g., the earnings per share is less diluted). Furthermore, it is possible to sell convertible bonds quickly as hedge funds and other arbitrageurs can hedge convertible bonds better than straight bonds. Convertible bonds are usually sold via an underwriting process, which can take as little as one day. The bonds are often sold as so-called 144a securities, meaning that they are yet to be registered with the Securities and Exchange Commission (SEC). In this case, the convertible bonds can only be traded among qualified institutional buyers (QIBs), so they are especially illiquid until they are registered. When the bonds get registered (often after 3 to 6 months), then they can be sold in the public market. Because of a liquidity risk premium and adverse selection, convertible bonds are reportedly sold at an initial average discount (similar to the average initial public offering (IPO) underpricing of equities). Hence, part of the profit from convertible bond arbitrage comes from participating in the primary market and being active enough to secure allocations of bonds in oversubscribed issues.

15.2. THE LIFE OF A CONVERTIBLE BOND ARBITRAGE TRADE

Convertible bond arbitrage has been known almost as long as convertible bonds. Weinstein gave a description of a simple convertible bond arbitrage trade in his 1931 book, *Arbitrage in Securities*. Thorp and Kassouf developed the trade significantly in their book from 1967, *Beat the Market*, foreshadowing the Black–Scholes–Merton formula for option pricing.

At a high level, the trade is simple: buy a cheap convertible bond and hedge it by shorting the stock. Form a whole portfolio of such positions, and possibly overlay hedges for interest rate and credit risk. The trick is knowing whether a convertible bond is cheap and determining the appropriate hedge—and here is where the option pricing techniques come in handy.

Interestingly, convertible arbitrage tends to be one-sided, that is, the trade is usually to buy the convertible bond and short the stock. However, if the convertible bond is overpriced, hedge funds sometimes reverse the trade and short the convertible bond while buying the stock. The reason that the trade tends to be long on the convertible bond is that convertibles have historically been cheap, perhaps as compensation for liquidity risk.

Indeed, the cheapness of convertible bonds is at an efficiently inefficient level that reflects the supply and demand for liquidity: Convertible bonds are issued by firms who have a need for quickly raising cash and they are mostly bought by leveraged convertible arbitrage hedge funds. When the supply of convertible bonds is large relative to hedge funds' capital and access to leverage, then the cheapness increases. For instance, when convertible bond hedge funds face large redemptions or when their bankers pull financing, then convertible bonds become very cheap and illiquid.

Figure 15.1 illustrates the life of a trade. The trader first acquires a long position in the convertible bond by buying it at a discount in the primary market or finding a cheap convertible in the secondary market. The trader then hedges his convertible bond by shorting the underlying common stock. The trader may refine the hedge by shorting a straight bond or by trading options, but such hedges are often very expensive, making it more economical to diversify away the idiosyncratic credit risk and hedge overall credit and interest-rate exposures at the portfolio level.

Over time, the convertible arbitrage trader will receive coupons on the convertible bond, compensate any dividends on the short stock position, and adjust the hedge as the stock price changes.

The trade can end in a number of different ways, as seen in figure 15.1: The convertible bond may be converted to stock. In this case, most of the shares are used to cover the short position in the hedge and the rest are sold. Conversion

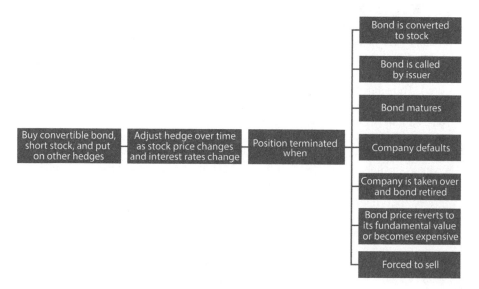

Figure 15.1. The life of a convertible arbitrage trade.

is typically the end of a successful trade (and I discuss below when conversion is optimal). The convertible bond may also simply mature or be called by the issuer. Other possible outcomes are that the company defaults or is taken over, and such events are usually negative for the convertible arbitrage trader. Finally, the trader might decide to sell his position in convertible bonds, either to take profit when the bond has richened sufficiently or because of forced selling due to margin calls.

15.3. VALUATION OF CONVERTIBLE BONDS

Convertible bonds can be valued using option pricing techniques. A simple method is to consider the value of a straight bond and then add the value of a call option computed using the Black–Scholes–Merton model. This method is not exact since it does not take into account that the conversion implies that the stock is bought for convertible bonds rather than cash, and the value of bonds varies over time. Furthermore, this method does not account for all the special features in the convertible bond's indenture, such as the possible callability. Hence, most convertible bond pricing models are based on extensions of the basic Black–Scholes–Merton framework solved numerically using binomial option pricing techniques or partial differential equations. Said simply, such models construct a tree of all the possible ways that the stock price can evolve, compute the convertible bond value at the end of each branch of the tree, and then work backward in the tree to compute the current value.

Rather than going through the details of this calculation (which is standard financial engineering by now), let us gain some intuition for how convertible bond values depend on stock prices, as seen in figure 15.2. The dotted line shows the value of a straight bond (i.e., a bond without the convertibility option). The value of a straight bond is independent of the stock price when we assume that there is no risk of default; hence, the dotted line is horizontal. The dashed line shows the parity conversion value, that is, the value of converting immediately. Naturally, the parity conversion value is linear in the stock price and the slope is the conversion ratio. When the convertible bond matures, its value is the upper envelope of these two lines: a hockey-stick shape with value 1,000 for stock prices between 0 and 50 and increasing value for higher stock prices. Indeed, for stock prices below 50, the owner of the convertible bond can choose not to convert and receive the value of the bond and, if the stock price is above 50, the owner can optimally convert.

Before maturity, the convertible bond value is given by the smooth curve (solid line), which is above the hockey stick due to option value. To understand why, suppose for instance that the stock price is 50. Clearly, the convertible bond is worth more than 1,000 since, if the stock price goes up, the convertible

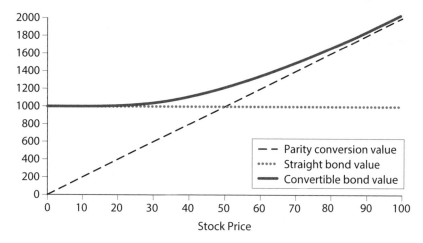

Figure 15.2. How the value of a convertible bond depends on the stock price: the case of no default.

bond will be worth more than 1,000 and, if the stock price goes down, the bond will be worth 1,000. An average of 1,000 and something above 1,000 is above 1,000! How much above? That depends on how much time is left and the volatility of the stock.

While figure 15.2 considered the example of a convertible bond issued by a firm with no risk of bankruptcy, figure 15.3 considers what happens if bankruptcy is a possibility. The top panel puts the value of the entire firm on the *x*-axis, rather than the stock price. The firm is assumed to have a total debt of 100 million, so bankruptcy occurs when the firm value drops below this level. Assuming that all bond holders have equal seniority (e.g., because the convertible bond is the only debt outstanding), we see that the value of an unconverted bond at maturity increases from 0 to the par value as the firm value increases from 0 to 100 million, and the straight bond value stays at this level for higher firm values. The risk of default is similar to being short a put option written on the value of the firm. The value of the convertible bond some time before maturity now has a more complex shape: concave for very low values of the firm (due to default risk) and convex for intermediate and high values (due to convertibility option value).

Panel B of figure 15.3 depicts the convertible bond value as a function of the stock price. The parity conversion value is the same as before, but now the value of straight debt is different: this figure plots the value of the straight debt reflecting default risk at some time before maturity (because the value at maturity is difficult to depict with the stock price on the *x*-axis). Again we see the convex/concave shape of the convertible bond value.

A

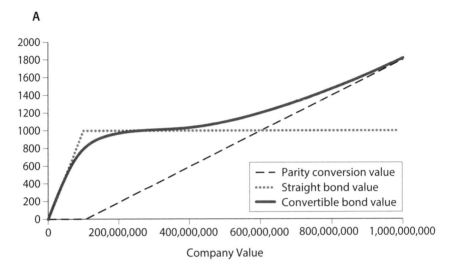

Company Value

B

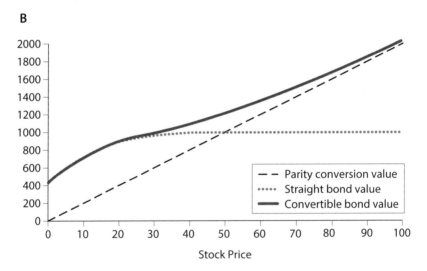

Stock Price

Figure 15.3. How the value of a convertible bond depends on the firm value and stock price.

　　Panel A. Convertible bond value vs. firm value.

　　Panel B. Convertible bond value vs. stock price.

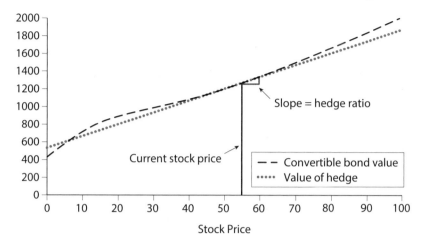

Figure 15.4. Hedging a convertible bond.

15.4. HEDGING CONVERTIBLE BONDS

Computing the value of a convertible bond and its hedge ratio are closely intertwined. Indeed, the optimal hedge ratio captures the *change* in the value of the convertible bond per unit of change in the underlying stock.

The hedge ratio is the number of stocks that a market-neutral arbitrageur should short for every convertible bond, usually denoted by delta, Δ. The arbitrage trader needs to choose the hedge ratio so that the stock-price sensitivity of the hedge equals the stock-price sensitivity of convertible bond, as seen in figure 15.4.

Figure 15.4 shows the optimal hedge if the current stock price is 55. The dotted line is the tangency of the convertible bond value, and its slope is the hedge. The hedge ratio clearly depends on the stock price, so as the stock price moves around, the convertible bond arbitrageur needs to readjust the hedge. For very high stock prices, conversion becomes ever more certain and the hedge ratio approaches the conversion ratio. The hedge ratio drops for lower stock prices, but it can pick up for stock prices so low that credit risk becomes a serious concern.

15.5. WHEN TO CONVERT A CONVERTIBLE

A Wall Street saying holds that one should "never convert a convertible." The reason is that it is usually better to keep the options open: Either convert later if the stock price keeps rising or receive the face value of the bond if the stock price falls. The reason that conversion should usually be postponed corresponds to the reasons for postponing the exercise of an American call option.[1]

There are, however, several important exceptions to this never-convert-before-maturity rule: First, if the stock is about to pay a dividend, then early conversion can be optimal. Indeed, converting the bond to stock before the dividend payment means that you receive the dividend. In contrast, failure to convert means that you will not receive the dividend and, furthermore, the stock price is expected to drop after the dividend date, reducing the value of the conversion option. Said differently, if money is about to leave the firm, you may protect your investment best by claiming part of this money and, to do so, you need to convert the bond to stock.

A second example where conversion may better protect the investment is an impending merger. If the merger makes the debt riskier and conversion is not possible in the merged company (e.g., because it is a private company), then early conversion is optimal.

Third, financial frictions can lead a convertible bond manager to convert the bond. For instance, if the stock has a high lending fee, it is expensive to short the stock. This leads to a constant drag on the hedged convertible bond position, similar to the drag of a stock that continually pays dividends. Therefore, it can be optimal to convert such convertible bonds.

Converting a deep-in-the-money convertible bond can also be optimal in light of funding costs. For such bonds, the cost of converting early is small (the bond will almost surely be converted eventually anyway since it is deep-in-the-money), and these small costs can be more than outweighed by reduced funding costs. Indeed, a convertible bond ties up capital that could otherwise be used for other trades, and it is associated with funding costs due to the financing spread, that is, the difference between the interest earned on the cash collateral supporting the short stock position and the interest rate paid on any leverage of the convertible bond. An alternative to converting a bond is selling it, but this may not be preferable, given the large transaction costs for convertible bonds and given that the potential buyers may face similar funding costs.

---

[1] The rule for optimal option exercise without frictions is due to Merton (1973), and the analogue for convertible bonds is due to Brennan and Schwartz (1977) and Ingersoll (1977). Jensen and Pedersen (2012) show that it can be optimal to convert early due to short sale costs, funding costs, and trading costs.

15.6. PROFITS AND LOSSES IN CONVERTIBLE ARBITRAGE

What Money Flows In and Out?

The convertible bond position generates income from the coupon paid by the bond. If the convertible bond is leveraged—which it is for most arbitrage traders—then interest payments must be made for the financing. Furthermore, the convertible bond trader must cover the cost of dividend payments on the short equity position as well as short-selling costs, especially for stocks that are "on special" (i.e., stocks with high demand for short-selling relative to the supply of lendable shares). In fact, companies with many outstanding convertible bonds are more likely to face high short-selling costs because of the demand to borrow the shares from owners of convertible bonds.

The primary driver of profit and loss, however, is changes in the prices of the stock and the convertible bonds. Stock price changes naturally feed into the convertible bond price, but, as discussed in detail below, these price moves are not perfectly offsetting. Convertible bond prices are also affected by changes in the volatility of the stock price and in the supply and demand for convertible bonds. The demand for convertible bonds is driven by flows to convertible bond hedge funds and mutual funds, risk appetite of these investors, and the financing environment, which affects convertible bond arbitrageurs' ability to take on leveraged positions.

Gamma: Making Money from Ups and Downs

One of the surprising characteristics of a hedged convertible bond position is that it can profit both from stock price increases *and* drops. Indeed, when the stock price moves up, the convertible bond moves up by *more* than the stock hedge, leading to a profit. The convertible bond moves by more because it benefits both from the higher value of the stock and from a higher chance of converting. When the stock price moves down, the convertible bond suffers *less* than the stock hedge, also leading to profit. The convertible bond moves by less because its downside is limited due to its bond characteristics.

Figure 15.5 and table 15.1 illustrate an example in which the stock price first jumps up from 55 to 85 and then jumps back down to 55. The property of benefiting both from up and down moves is called convexity, which refers to the shape of the value of the convertible bond in figure 15.5—it "curves upward" relative to the dotted line for the hedge (a formal definition is given in the chapter on fixed-income arbitrage). This property is also called positive gamma, where gamma is the second derivative of the value of the convertible bond with respect to the price of the stock.

A

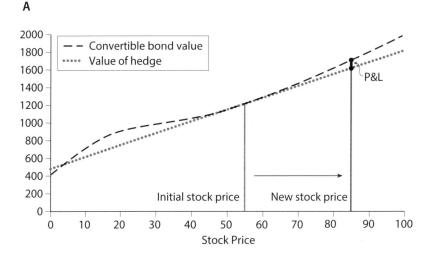

B

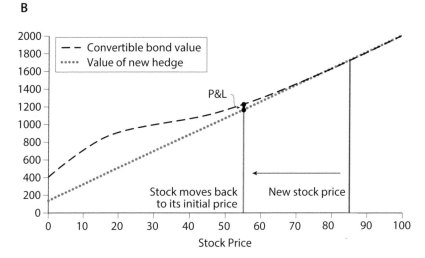

Figure 15.5. The profit and loss (P&L) of convertible bond arbitrage when the stock price increases and decreases.
Panel A: P&L of convertible bond arbitrage when the stock price increases.
Panel B: P&L of convertible bond arbitrage when the stock price decreases.

As seen in Panel A of figure 15.5, the convertible bond value increases by more than the stock hedge when the stock price goes from 55 to 85. Specifically, as seen in table 15.1, the convertible bond increases by $500.17, more than offsetting the increase in the hedge of 13.4 shares, $403.00. The difference, $97.17, is the profit on the hedged position.

TABLE 15.1. THE PROFIT AND LOSS (P&L) OF CONVERTIBLE BOND ARBITRAGE WHEN THE STOCK PRICE INCREASES AND DECREASES

P&L When Stock Price Moves from $55 to $85	
Long 1 convertible bond	$500.17
Short 13.4 shares	−$403.00
Total	$97.17
P&L When Stock Price Moves from $85 to $55	
Long 1 convertible bond	−$500.17
Short 18.6 shares	$558.16
Total	$57.99
P&L of Total Round Trip	$155.16

When the stock price drops back from 85 to 55, why isn't the initial profit simply reversed? The initial profit would be reversed if the hedge had not been adjusted in the meantime, of course. It is the change in the hedge that makes the difference: With the stock price at 85, the initial hedge of 13.4 shares short is no longer appropriate. This is because the convertible bond is now more in-the-money, that is, more certain to be converted; it has therefore become more equity sensitive. Hence, the correct hedge has increased to 18.6 shares.

Given this new hedge, a drop in the stock price leads to a larger drop in the value of the hedge than the value of the convertible bond. Hence, the drop in the stock price leads to a profit of $57.99, as seen in table 15.1. Note from table 15.1 that the net profit/loss of the convertible bond itself is exactly zero from the round trip: the initial profit of $500.17 is exactly erased when the stock price drops back, for obvious reasons. The profit from the round trip trade comes from the asymmetry of the hedge.

So convertible bond arbitrage can make money from both ups and downs in the stock market—does this mean that the strategy can never lose money? Surely not. As we will see, the strategy can lose money in several ways. First of all, the position is not convex everywhere. As seen in figure 15.5, the value of the convertible bond bends down for low stock prices, a negative gamma coming from the default risk having the effect of a short put option. Hence, certain extreme negative stock price moves are often bad for convertible bonds. For example, the default of the firm can lead to losses for the convertible bond arbitrageur.

Time Decay: Losing Money for Nothing

We have seen that convertible bond arbitrage can profit both from ups and downs in the stock market, but another surprising effect is that the strategy loses from the *lack* of stock price moves. If time passes without stock price moves, then this is a loss to the convertible bond arbitrage trader!

Figure 15.6 illustrates this effect, called time decay (or theta, the sensitivity with respect to time). Recall that the convertible bond value is strictly above the parity conversion value and the value of a straight bond because of option value. Hence, when you buy a convertible bond, you are paying a premium for the potential to make money from ups and downs. This price premium is key to understanding time decay. As time passes, the future opportunities to make money from ups and downs diminish. Hence, the option value diminishes and the convertible bond price therefore shrinks toward the values of straight debt and parity conversion, as seen in figure 15.6. This shrinking option value is a loss to the convertible bond trader—i.e., time decay.

Hence, stock price ups and downs lead to profit, but losses arise when the clock is ticking without stock price moves. The total profit over the life of the trade depends on how many stock moves you get vs. how many stock price moves you implicitly paid for when you bought the convertible.

Vega: Hoping for Lots of Ups and Downs

Since the hedged convertible bond position profits from price moves up and down, a higher stock price volatility means that the convertible bond is more

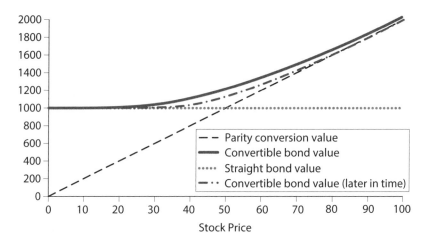

Figure 15.6. The loss for convertible bond arbitrage caused by time decay.

valuable. A higher perceived stock price volatility does not just imply higher future profits; rather, it raises the current price of the convertible bond given that the market is forward looking. Hence, increases in perceived stock price volatility tend to increase the price of convertibles, while drops in volatility have the opposite effect. The price sensitivity to volatility is called *vega*, so traders say that convertible bond arbitrage has positive vega since the convertible is long on an embedded call option.

Alpha and Cheapness

The alpha of convertible bond arbitrage comes from buying convertible bonds that are cheap relative to their fundamental value. Convertible bonds have historically been sold at an average discount to the value of their components (bond + option) for several reasons.

First, many buyers of corporate securities shy away from convertible bonds or require a large return premium since convertible bonds require expertise to trade, have large transaction costs, face market liquidity risk (meaning transaction costs sometimes increase dramatically and dealers even stop making markets), are difficult and expensive to finance, and face funding liquidity risk (meaning that margin requirements can increase or financing can be withdrawn).

Second, issuers of convertible bonds are willing to accept a liquidity discount if they are in need of cash and can sell convertible bonds more quickly and at lower investment-banking fees than other sources of financing.

Hence, convertible bond arbitrage earns a liquidity risk premium for holding an asset with market and funding liquidity risks, providing financing for companies that might otherwise have difficulty borrowing.

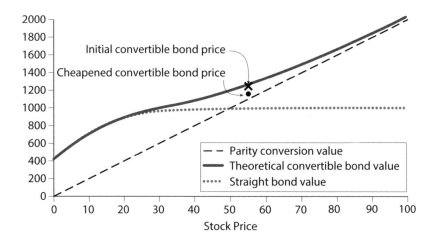

Figure 15.7. Cheapening of a convertible bond.

282 • Chapter 15

The liquidity discount of a convertible bond is illustrated in figure 15.7. The initial price of the convertible bond (indicated by the x in the graph) is below the theoretical value (the solid line). This discount in the price is the source of alpha in convertible bond arbitrage. In contrast, if the convertible bond were bought at its theoretical value, the alpha of the strategy would be zero, and paying a price above the theoretical value would be associated with negative alpha.

If convertible bond market conditions worsen (without a change in the stock price), then the convertible bond will cheapen further relative to the theoretical value, as seen in figure 15.7. This would lead to a loss for the arbitrageur but would set up higher expected profits in the future.

15.7. TYPES OF CONVERTIBLE BONDS

Convertible bonds are sometimes classified loosely into several categories, as illustrated in figure 15.8. Furthermore, some convertible bond managers specialize in a particular type of convertibles, whether it be distressed, busted, hybrid, or high-moneyness convertibles. Such specialization can increase a manager's expertise, but it can also be associated with additional transaction costs if bonds are bought and sold as they move between categories.

High-moneyness convertible bonds are in-the-money and therefore highly equity sensitive. Some convertible arbitrage managers believe that such high-money convertibles offer the highest risk-adjusted returns, but these bonds also require the most leverage to generate significant risk and total return.

Hybrid convertible bonds are closer to being at-the-money and are therefore especially sensitive to equity volatility. *Busted* convertibles are out-of-the-money

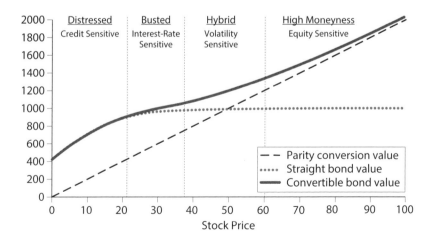

Figure 15.8. Types of convertible bonds.

and therefore have little optionality, but the stock price is nevertheless not so low that credit risk plays as significant a role as it does for *distressed* convertibles.

15.8. HEDGEABLE AND UNHEDGEABLE RISKS FOR A PORTFOLIO OF CONVERTIBLES

Market Risk, Interest-Rate Risk, and Credit Risk

The most obvious risk in owning a convertible bond portfolio is equity market risk, but the delta hedging discussed above largely takes care of this. Convertible bonds also face interest-rate risk since higher interest rates makes the bond's fixed coupons less valuable. Interest-rate risk can be hedged by shorting bond futures, straight corporate bonds, Treasuries, or interest-rate swaps.

Furthermore, convertible bonds face credit risk. While the equity hedge partially protects against the risk of default, this hedge often does not fully cover the loss on the convertible bond in case of default. Each bond's default risk can be hedged by buying credit default swap (CDS) protection (if CDSs are traded for that firm) or by selling straight corporate bonds. However, buying protection on all convertible bonds in a portfolio is expensive and associated with large transaction costs. Alternatively, a convertible arbitrage trader can make sure that her portfolio is well diversified, largely diversifying away idiosyncratic credit risk. Changes in marketwide credit risk can then be hedged with a credit default swap index such as CDX or iTraxx. Convertible bonds also face risks in connection with takeovers and other corporate events. Such event risk is difficult to hedge, but it can be diversified away to some extent.

Valuation and Liquidity Risk: Efficiently Inefficient Convertible Bond Prices

The major risks that cannot be hedged or diversified away are (1) a systematic cheapening of convertible bonds relative to their theoretical value, (2) funding liquidity risk, and (3) market liquidity risk. What is worse, these three risks are closely connected and often materialize at the same time. A cheapening of convertible bonds leads to losses for convertible bond traders, which creates funding problems. Such funding problems can lead to forced selling, and, as traders rush for the exit, market liquidity dries up, creating a downward spiral of prices and liquidity. Such liquidity events occurred in the convertible bond markets in 1998, 2005, and, most violently, in 2008.[2]

---

[2] Such liquidity spirals are analyzed theoretically by Brunnermeier and Pedersen (2009) and empirically in the convertible bond market and other markets by Mitchell, Pedersen, and Pulvino (2007) and Mitchell and Pulvino (2012).

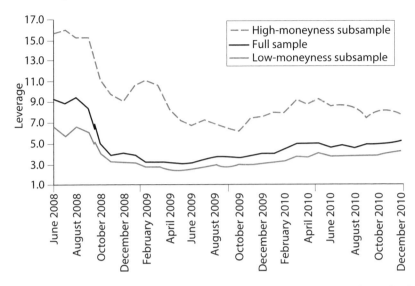

Figure 15.9. Available prime broker leverage for a large convertible bond arbitrage fund. Leverage is measured as the value of the long convertible bond positions relative to the net asset value.

Source: Mitchell and Pulvino (2012).

Figure 15.9 shows the available leverage for a large convertible arbitrage hedge fund from its prime brokers, June 2008 to December 2010. We see that convertible bonds with high moneyness can be leveraged more than low-moneyness bonds because their unhedgeable risk is smaller. More importantly, the available leverage fell significantly (that is, margin requirements went way up) during the global financial crisis when Lehman Brothers failed and most brokers were in trouble. In fact, this figure understates the magnitude of the funding crisis in the convertible bond markets as margin requirements went up even more for many smaller hedge funds and some simply had their financing pulled and were forced to liquidate.

The prices of convertible bonds fell dramatically as a result. An extreme example of the price drop of convertible bonds was that convertible bonds sometimes even traded cheaper than comparable bonds without the convertibility option! Figure 15.10 shows the average and median difference in yield between convertible bonds and straight bonds issued by the same company. Specifically, the sample consists of 596 busted convertible bonds trading below par, with at least one year of remaining life and with straight debt outstanding with a similar maturity date. Even though the convertible bonds have been chosen to have low option value (since they are trading below par), they still have significant optionality and therefore convertible bonds should naturally have a lower yield than straight bonds. Normally, this is indeed the case, and figure 15.10 also

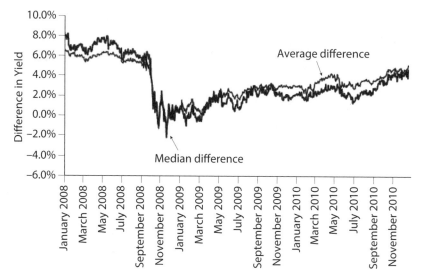

Figure 15.10. The yield difference between straight bonds and convertible bonds.
Source: Mitchell and Pulvino (2012).

shows a yield difference above 6% in the early time period. However, the liquidity crisis that hit the convertible bond market when Lehman Brothers failed was so severe that the yield difference collapsed to near zero and, in some instances, it even went negative! The market for convertible bonds was dominated by leveraged long–short hedge funds, which had severe liquidity problems due to the liquidity problems of their brokers, while the market for straight bonds was dominated by unleveraged long-only investors less affected by these events.

A similar liquidity event happened in the convertible bond market in 1998 in connection with the collapse of the hedge fund LTCM. As seen in figure 15.11, the price of convertible bonds dropped significantly relative to their theoretical value and, as a result, convertible arbitrage initially suffered losses and earned high returns as the cheapness diminished.

Mergers, Takeovers, and Other Sources of Risk

Mergers, takeovers, special dividends, and corporate restructurings present risk for convertible bond owners as other stakeholders may extract value from the firm, the convertible may be redeemed and lose its option value, or the convertible may be adversely affected by the fine print of the contract.

A takeover can be both good and bad. If the convertible is in-the-money and the takeover bid makes the stock price jump up, then this typically leads to profits for the hedged convertible due to its convexity.

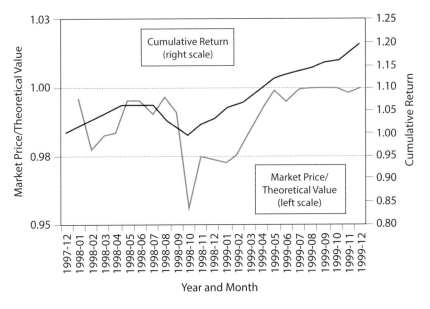

Figure 15.11. Price-to-theoretical value of convertible bonds, and return of convertible bond hedge funds.

Source: Mitchell, Pedersen, and Pulvino (2007).

However, consider the case of a takeover below the conversion price so that the convertible bond remains out-of-the-money. If the convertible bond is redeemed or loses its option value in the merged company (e.g., if it is a private company with a worse credit), then the convertible bond price will fall to the par value or below. At the same time, the stock price will increase on the takeover announcement, hurting the short stock hedge. Hence, in this situation, the convertible bond arbitrageur may lose both on the long convertible bond and on the short stock.

To limit this takeover risk, most convertible bonds are now issued with takeover protection clauses that allow the convertible bond owner to put the bond back to the issuer at par value in the event of a takeover and possibly to give the convertible bond owner the right to additional shares under certain conditions.

15.9. INTERVIEW WITH KEN GRIFFIN OF CITADEL

Kenneth C. Griffin is the founder and chief executive officer of Citadel, one of the world's largest alternative asset managers and securities dealers. Griffin received a bachelor's degree from Harvard University while starting and running two hedge funds at the same time. Shortly after he graduated, he founded

Citadel in 1990, and his youthful success quickly made him a legend. He started with a focus on convertible bond arbitrage, and Citadel now includes a number of hedge funds engaged in several alternative investment strategies.

LHP: *I would like to first ask you about the legend of your dorm room trading and the beginning of your trading career.*

KG: I began trading my freshman year at Harvard. There was an article in *Forbes* about why Home Shopping Network was extremely overvalued. After reading the article, I bought puts on the stock. Shortly thereafter, the stock plummeted and I made a few thousand dollars. But when I exited the position, the market maker paid me the intrinsic value less a quarter of a point for the options.

LHP: *So that got you thinking about market making, transaction costs, and arbitrage?*

KG: Yes, I realized that on a risk–reward basis, that market maker's transaction was far better than my investment. I had great appreciation for the fact that I was quite lucky, whereas the $50.00 the market maker earned was basically risk free. That piqued my interest to understand what investments sophisticated market participants engage in. I started to view the markets through the lens of relative value trading rather than just directional positioning.

LHP: *How did you figure out that you could make money trading convertible bonds, and how did you start trading?*

KG: In my time at college, I came across an S&P bond guide at Baker Library at Harvard Business School. In the back of the S&P bond guide, they list convertible bonds. For each bond they provide the coupon, the conversion ratio, the conversion value—all the salient terms of the instrument. Based on the market prices in that book, there appeared to be some bonds that were mispriced. I made it my mission to educate myself on these instruments and to understand the pricing and trading of convertibles.

LHP: *Was the insight just based on some back of the envelope calculations, or did you need to already appreciate something like the Black–Scholes Formula or the binomial option pricing model at that time?*

KG: Back of the envelope, some common sense, and a bit of naïveté as to the dynamics around why these mispricings might exist. Many mispricings were driven by the inability to borrow the underlying common stock and therefore the convertible bond traded close to conversion value because the arbitrage was difficult. Nonetheless, I didn't understand these dynamics at the moment. As I looked at the S&P guide at the Baker Library, it caught my interest.

LHP: *Then you started reaching out to more people and actually started trading on these things.*

KG: I dove into understanding the convertible market and came across a number of articles and books written over the years on convertible bond arbitrage. I put together a small partnership with a friend to manage money in the space. We raised about $250,000 from friends and family to deploy this strategy. It was actually $265,000—strange the numbers you remember. That was in September of 1987.

LHP: *That was a unique time—the following month was the crash.*

KG: Exactly. And not fully understanding how these bonds would behave in a downward market, my hedging strategy was generally to be short in extra margin of stock to compensate for the uncertainty in the bear market case.

LHP: *Good move.*

KG: Yes, that helped to preserve capital in the crash of '87. The crash of '87 created a number of dislocations in the marketplace that I was able to capitalize on with respect to my small fund and, on the back of that, I raised a second fund. I was managing just over a million dollars in college between these two funds.

LHP: *Help me visualize you in college running these funds—how did you actually do it?*

KG: I had a satellite dish on top of my dorm. I set up a phone and fax machine. I arranged to pull a cable down an unused elevator shaft, up to the roof of the building, and had a satellite dish on the roof to get real-time streaming stock prices. I had to pull some wires down the hall, but no one seemed to mind.

LHP: *How did you do the trades?*

KG: I traded between classes. I used a lot of pay phones on campus.

LHP: *Were those to adjust your hedge or to put on new convertible positions or to take convertible positions off?*

KG: All of the above. There would be a couple of trades a week to adjust the stock hedges and then other trades to buy and sell convertibles.

LHP: *How did you decide which bonds to buy and when to buy? Did you have a computer, and did you have a valuation model?*

KG: Back then all the decisions were made using paper and pencil and trying to approximate where I thought the bonds should trade based upon cash flow differentials, creditworthiness, and the inherent call protection of the bond. I started to piece together simplistic models based upon the principles of Black–Scholes. The real work in modeling convertibles hit its stride around 1991, two years after I graduated.

LHP: *In the early days, how did you even keep track of your portfolio of bonds? Was it you had it in your head, or you had it in a notebook, or you had it in a computer?*

KG: I organized it in my head. There weren't that many positions, and I assure you this was the greatest interest of my day! I could tell you conversion ratios to coupons on pretty much any of the positions at that time. I had spreadsheets and papers everywhere! When I was in a class, I'd have my HP 12C calculator, a scrap of paper, and think through the information in my head, and I'd make decisions.

LHP: *How did you find time for all this? You still had to do your classes.*

KG: I had a less than perfect attendance record.

LHP: *What were the challenges and advantages in running a small fund?*

KG: One of my advantages at that time was that I wasn't managing a lot of money. What you need to think about when you're in that position is not how much you have, but how to make the most of what you have. I realized that being small, I could borrow quantities of shares that were inconsequential to a large player—even though they were quite consequential to me! So those very convertibles that were mispriced because it was hard to borrow the stock represented the majority of my portfolio at the time.

LHP: *So how did you manage to borrow the stock for shorting?*

KG: I would do things like open accounts at Charles Schwab. They would have the stock in their retail accounts, and I could carry the longs and the shorts there. None of the large hedge funds were using Charles Schwab as a prime broker back in the late '80s or early '90s.

LHP: *So you developed an edge in convertibles for firms with hard-to-short stocks?*

KG: Yes. I would call two or three dealers, and the dealers would call me with incoming securities that they thought might be of interest to me. I built a reputation as the go-to person for names related to hard-to-borrow stocks.

LHP: *Being part of the flow is very useful in convertible bond arbitrage, but it seems amazing that dealers would be calling a college kid.*

KG: Yes, I suppose you're right. But you know, many trades in the convertible market back then were just a few hundred thousand dollars. There were a lot of small trades. So a hundred thousand dollar trade, I could do that, and so I'd be on the list for that phone call. Today we'll trade 15 or 20 million bonds on the wire, but back then the market was far smaller with fewer players. And there was a large retail component to the order flow that swept through the marketplace. A dealer might have an incoming retail order in a name like Chock Full o'Nuts, the coffee company. They knew that was a stock that I was routinely able to borrow and that I'd have an interest in trading with them.

LHP: *One of your first motivations was thinking about who earns the transaction costs, but you probably also had to pay large spreads on the convertible bonds, especially being a small hedge fund?*

KG: Given that I was trading from my dorm room, I was a bit of a novelty on Wall Street to say the least. Contrary to conventional wisdom on how Wall Street treats people, I was treated extraordinarily well by people in the industry who would do business with me on very fair terms because they were good people and wanted to help me out. A number of people who traded with me in college are still friends today.

LHP: *How did you evolve from there?*

KG: After college, I came to Chicago to manage money for a prominent fund of funds. The convertible market became less opportunity-rich, so I put our resources into trading convertibles and equity warrants in Japan, which became a focus of the firm back in the early '90s. One of my great mentors, Frank Meyer, stressed to me that many businesses are cyclical over time and that, being early in my career, I should consider designing a firm built on a robust platform, and a multitude of strategies, rather than just one strategy.

So, in the early '90s we stretched into convertibles on a global basis, into statistical arbitrage strategies in 1994, and into risk arbitrage in roughly 1994 and 1995. Over the course of time, we've probably added a dozen distinct investment strategies to our platform at Citadel.

LHP: *How much did you plan the whole evolution of the firm?*

KG: I can't say there was a master plan. But I knew early on that I loved this business. I wanted to build something unique with people who were as excited about the possibilities as I was, and continue to be. I work with incredibly talented and driven colleagues. They have taken Citadel into strategies, areas of the world and businesses that were never in the original game plan. I am grateful and humbled and incredibly excited about what we will do together for years to come.

LHP: *Among the trades that you did over your career, is there one that stands out?*

KG: I remember an investment in Glaxo, a U.K.-listed pharmaceutical company that issued a yen-denominated convertible bond in the Japanese market; a yen-denominated Tokyo Stock Exchange-listed convertible against a U.K.-listed company. It was exciting to be at the forefront of global finance, and that trade still stands out years later.

LHP: *So you're trading across three continents, and the security was not well understood?*

KG: Japanese local investors really didn't know what to do with this convertible issued by a U.K. pharmaceutical company. And foreigners, who were major owners of Glaxo, weren't thinking about looking to Japan to identify and source cheap convertible paper.

LHP: *Do you think that being the first to understand a security is a typical characteristic of a good trade?*

KG: Being the first trade makes for great stories, but it generally doesn't make for great businesses. Great businesses are defined by being exceptionally good at what you do, day in and day out. It's finding the sweet spot of where liquidity exists in the marketplace. That is, trading securities that are liquid enough that you can take meaningful positions but where you can still be better than others in understanding what defines and drives value through fundamental research or quantitative analytics.

CHAPTER 16

Event-Driven Investments

Risk arbitrage, generally, is investing in securities of corporations going
through a corporate event where the return is not based on the stock going up
and down, but the success and completion of the event.

—John A. Paulson

Event-driven investment is an opportunistic strategy of investing around
corporate-specific events and possibly marketwide events. Event-driven managers continually look for many types of "events" and try to find trading opportunities that arise in this connection.

The classic event-driven trade is merger arbitrage (also called "risk arbitrage"). Merger arbitrage tries to profit from the price moves that happen when
a merger is announced. Just as the merger of two companies can lead to opportunities from the temporary price moves, so can corporate events that do
the opposite, namely split a company into smaller pieces. Such events include
spin-offs, split-offs, and carve-outs.

Another class of trades is related to changes in the capital structure of a firm,
such as share buybacks, debt exchanges, security issuances, or other capital
structure adjustments. Some event-driven managers specialize in distressed
firms, trading in a range of securities when corporations face financial distress,
bankruptcy, or lawsuits. Such distressed investment often requires an active involvement in the firm, leading event managers to serve on creditor committees,
try to renegotiate debt, or find ways to turn the business around.

A third class of trades tries to profit from discrepancies between different
types of securities. Capital structure arbitrage trades different securities issued
by the same firm against each other, for instance, buying corporate bonds while
shorting the stock. Event-driven managers sometimes also trade on specialized
security structures such as closed-end funds, exchange traded funds (ETFs),
special purpose acquisition companies (SPACs), and private investment in public equity (PIPE).

A fourth class of events relates to changes in the market structure for the securities, e.g., if a stock is included in an index such as the S&P 500 stock market index, or is excluded from an index.

Beyond corporate events, event-driven managers may also look for events in other markets or asset classes. The most famous example is the trade by the event-driven hedge fund manager John A. Paulson, which has been called "the greatest trade ever." Paulson shorted derivatives related to subprime mortgages, which in 2007–2008 became one of the most profitable trades in the history of hedge funds, reportedly making more than $15 billion. This credit bet could also be considered a global macro trade.

While the events differ greatly across all these trades, they share a similar portfolio construction methodology. The portfolio is constructed based on two principles: (1) isolate the event-specific risk and hedge out market, interest-rate, and credit risks; and (2) diversify across many events to minimize idiosyncratic event risk. For example, the event manager constructs his portfolio such that he will profit if a merger is completed and lose if the merger fails. The risk associated with the failure of the merger is the risk he wants to be compensated for taking, and this risk cannot be eliminated—but it can be largely diversified away by holding many small positions related to many different mergers. Warren Buffett puts it this way:

> Of course, some investment strategies—for instance, our efforts in arbitrage over the years—require wide diversification. If significant risk exists in a single transaction, overall risk should be reduced by making that purchase one of many mutually-independent commitments. Thus, you may consciously purchase a risky investment—one that indeed has a significant possibility of causing loss or injury—if you believe that your gain, weighted for probabilities, considerably exceeds your loss, comparably weighted, and if you can commit to a number of similar, but unrelated opportunities. Most venture capitalists employ this strategy. Should you choose to pursue this course, you should adopt the outlook of the casino that owns a roulette wheel, which will want to see lots of action because it is favored by probabilities, but will refuse to accept a single, huge bet.
>
> —Warren Buffett, Annual Report, 1993

Let us discuss these strategies in more detail.

16.1. MERGER ARBITRAGE

Mergers and Acquisitions

Companies are being bought and sold all of the time. In many of these transactions, the buyer and/or seller is a private company, but merger arbitrage traders

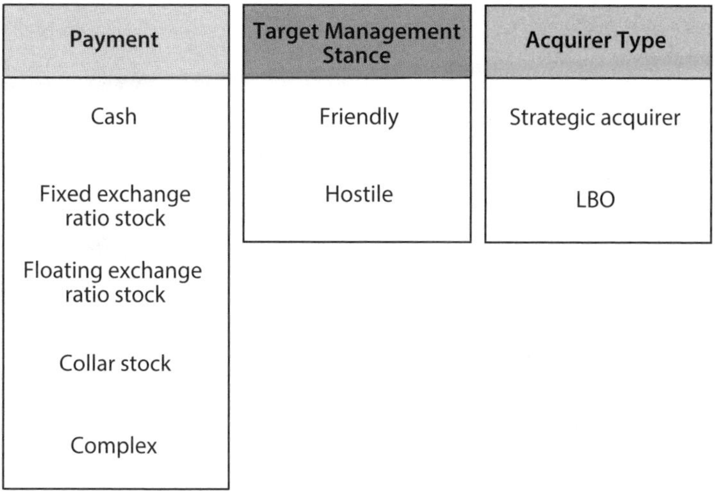

Payment	Target Management Stance	Acquirer Type
Cash	Friendly	Strategic acquirer
Fixed exchange ratio stock	Hostile	LBO
Floating exchange ratio stock		
Collar stock		
Complex		

Figure 16.1. Types of merger deals.

only get involved when the company that is being bought—the "target"—is a publicly traded company. As seen in figure 16.1, there are several types of mergers. The acquirer can be another company with potential synergies, that is, a strategic buyer, or the acquirer can be a (private equity) leveraged buyout (LBO) fund. The bid can be "friendly," meaning that it is backed by the target company's management and/or board, or it can be "hostile," meaning that the target company's management opposes the takeover. The type of acquirer and the stance of the management can significantly affect the chance that the deal goes through.

Deals also differ in the types of payments offered for the target company. Sometimes the acquirer offers to buy the company for cash. For instance, LBO deals are often done with cash as the acquirer does not have shares to offer. Alternatively, a strategic buyer may offer to pay for the target with its own shares. For instance, the acquirer may offer 2 shares of its own stock for every 1 share of the target company, called a 2-for-1 "fixed exchange ratio." A stock deal can also have a "floating exchange ratio," meaning that the number of shares depends on the acquirer's stock price at some point after the merger announcement. For example, the floating exchange ratio can be set so that the offer price is $100 worth of the acquirer's stock, where the number of shares is determined on February 1. Said differently, the offer is to give a number of shares equal to $100/P$, where P is the acquirer's stock price on February 1. Stock merger deals may also have optionality, e.g., to limit the value of the offer on the downside and upside. Such deals are sometimes referred to as collar deals. Merger offers can be rather complex and may involve other corporate securities, such as bonds issued by the acquirer.

Merger Arbitrage and Why It Works: Efficiently Inefficient Deal Spreads

When a merger is announced, the acquirer offers to buy the target firm at a premium to its current price to make the current owners willing to sell. For instance, if the stock price has been trading around $100 per share, an acquirer may offer $130 per share. After the announcement, the target stock price jumps up. It is important to recognize that this initial jump in the target stock price is typically *not* what merger arbitrage is about. It is very difficult for merger arbitrage traders to anticipate in advance which firms will be taken over (and those who really do know in advance often end up in jail for insider trading).

Merger arbitrage is about buying the target stock price *after* the announcement, i.e., after the target's stock price has already jumped up. So why should this trade be profitable if the target price already reflects the merger offer? The reason is that the target price typically does not jump up to the value of the offer; it only increases part of the way. For instance, if the acquirer offers $130, the target price might jump up to $120. Hence, the merger arbitrage manager will make $10 per share if the merger is completed. This potential profit should naturally be seen in light of the potential risk. If the merger fails, the target stock price will likely drop back to around $100, leading to a loss for the merger arbitrage manager of $20. The offer value may also be renegotiated, up or down, or a competing bidder may offer a higher price. Hence, the expected profit of this merger arbitrage trade depends on the probability of a successful merger, the expected losses in case of failure, and the profit in case of completion.

While the expected profit of a merger trade is complex to evaluate, it is straightforward to compute the profit of the merger trade if the current merger offer goes through, which is called the *deal spread*:

$$\text{deal spread} = \frac{\text{offer value} - \text{target stock price}}{\text{target stock price}}$$

In the example above, the deal spread is $10/$120 = 8.3%. Hence, if the merger offer goes through as stated, the merger arbitrage manager stands to earn an 8.3% profit. This measure of deal spread can potentially be refined to incorporate dividend payments before the expected time of the merger and possible implementation costs.

Does the existence of a positive deal spread mean that merger arbitrage makes money on average? Not necessarily. After all, the deal spread reflects actual deal risk. In other words, the deal spread should usually be positive just to offset the losses from failed deals to ensure *zero* average profits for arbitrageurs. However, historically the deal spread has been wider than the break-even deal spread, meaning that merger arbitrage has been a profitable trade.

There are several reasons why merger arbitrage has been profitable historically, but the main reason is that, when a merger is announced, many existing investors *sell* their shares in the merger target. This selling means that the target price does not increase as much as it might have otherwise, leaving open a deal spread large enough to make merger arbitrage profitable on average.

Many investors sell the merger target because they recognize that the target company's stock price can suddenly drop if the merger is called off. The typical owner of the stock, be it a mutual fund or an individual investor, bought the stock because she likes the company. When the acquirer offers to buy the whole company, such investors may feel vindicated in having bought the stock as the acquirer may like the company for the same reasons that the original owners did. However, even investors who had expertise in selecting the stock in the first place may feel that their expertise does not lie in evaluating the deal risk. Indeed, during the period of merger uncertainty, the key determinants of the target price are suddenly not its growth prospects and business efficacy; the key determinants become whether the target board and shareholders will accept the offer, whether the acquirer will revise or cancel the offer upon due diligence, the legal issues of whether the merger will be allowed by the regulator, and whether the acquirer will get the needed financing.

Since many stock owners are not comfortable with the deal risk, they will essentially demand "insurance" against the risk of deal failure. They get this "insurance" in the simplest possible way: they sell the stock. The price of this insurance is the deal spread.

Said differently, the natural owners of the stock suddenly become sellers for the stock. While new natural owners of the company will arrive after the merger is resolved (one way or the other), the market temporarily faces a significant demand for liquidity.

The merger arbitrage traders buy the target when other investors sell. Hence, they provide liquidity to all those who want to get out of the stock to avoid deal risk. Said differently, the merger arbitrage traders are providing insurance against the deal risk, and their average profit is the insurance return or the compensation for liquidity provision. How do merger arbitrage managers handle deal risk? They diversify across many deals, trying to make sure that no one deal failure will be detrimental for their overall portfolio.

The deal spread reaches an efficiently inefficient level where merger arbitrage managers are compensated for their liquidity provision. At times when the total number and risk of merger deals is large relative to the merger arbitrage capital, the expected return increases. The deal spread also tends to be efficiently inefficient when compared across different merger deals. Indeed, since merger arbitrage managers try to figure out which deals are more likely to fail and which are likely to go through, buying the target shares only in the deals they think will succeed, riskier deals tend to have wider deal spreads.

The Life of a Merger Arbitrage Trade

The life of a merger arbitrage trade starts when a merger is announced. This typically happens when the market is closed and, if the market is open, trading is temporarily halted. After the market opens, the merger arbitrage manager assesses the price and the target stock, weighing the deal spread and the possibility of an even higher bid against the risk of deal failure. If the manager likes the trade, he buys shares in the target stock and hedges by short-selling the acquirer in the amount described below (which can be zero). We will return to how to size the position and its hedge.

> First, one of our analysts screens the tape for any new deals that are announced. Once a deal is announced, we do a detailed financial analysis. We examine the performance of the company, its growth in sales, EBITDA [earnings before interest, taxes, depreciation, and amortization], net income and earnings per share; we compute the merger multiples to EBITDA, EBIT and net income; we look at the size of the acquirer vis-à-vis the target, and the premium being paid. We then make an overall assessment of the financial merits of the deal. Generally, we look for healthy companies being purchased at reasonable multiples without excessive premiums. The second stage of our research is to participate in the management conference calls; review the Wall Street research, SEC filings and the merger agreement. In our review of the merger agreement, we look for any unusual conditions to the merger such as due diligence, financing, business or regulatory conditions. We are basically looking for solid merger agreements with minimal conditions. We also examine regulatory issues that could affect the timing or the ultimate approval of the transactions. We have very good outside antitrust counsel and we have an in-house lawyer to look at any legal issue that may affect the outcome of a transaction. Generally, the focus of our research is to eliminate deals that are riskier and have a lower probability of being completed. We look at the remaining lower risk deals on a return basis and we try to focus on deals with lower risk and higher potential returns.
>
> —John A. Paulson, 2003 (as quoted by *Hedge Fund News*)

When the merger arbitrage position is on, the manager waits for the deal to close, following the events as they evolve. In the meantime, the long position in the target stock earns any dividends paid by the target company while having to compensate for dividends paid by the acquirer. Furthermore, the merger arbitrage manager incurs transaction costs when buying the target and shorting the acquirer, short-selling costs, and funding cost.

Figure 16.2. The life of a merger trade.

The typical closure of the trade is simply that the merger is completed and the merger arbitrage earns the deal spread. However, several other outcomes are possible, as seen in figure 16.2. An even better outcome is that another potential acquirer makes a competing bid to buy the target firm, raising the offer value. Sometimes several bidders drive up the price such that the merger arbitrage profit increases significantly above the initial deal spread. If the market assesses the possibility of competing bids as very likely, the deal spread can occationally be negative, meaning that the target price is above the current bid. Some merger arbitrage managers might liquidate their positions when the deal spread turns negative, while others might add to their positions, namely those who have strong views on the likelihood of competing bids.

A merger deal may also be renegotiated, which can lead to a higher or lower bid price, depending on the circumstances. The worst outcome is that the merger fails. This typically results in the target stock price falling back to the level it had before the merger announcement. The target stock price could drop even further, for instance, if the merger failed because of some bad news about the company, or because the preannouncement price already had a premium associated with the possibility of a merger, or simply because of general market movements. The target stock might also drop to a level above its premerger price, for instance, because the merger bid revealed a potential of the target company that may still be unlocked even without this particular merger.

Over the life of the merger trade, the deal spread opens and narrows depending on how the likelihoods of the different outcomes evolve. Figure 16.3 shows the median deal spread among deals that ultimately succeed and fail, respectively. We see that successful deals tend to have lower deal spreads, which typically start around 8% and narrow gradually over time as success is ever more certain and each potential obstacle is overcome. Deals that ultimately fail tend to have larger deal spreads, starting around 20%. Hence, while the market does not know in advance which deals will fail, the market recognizes that certain

Figure 16.3. Evolution of the merger arbitrage deal spread before resolution.
Source: Mitchell and Pulvino (2001).

deals are riskier and, naturally, the riskier deals are more often those that fail.
As the deal fails, the deal spread widens more than 15 percentage points, gapping out to around 30%.

The Case of Arcata Corp.

Warren Buffett gives an interesting example of a merger arbitrage trade in the
1988 annual report of Berkshire Hathaway:

> To evaluate arbitrage situations you must answer four questions: (1) How
> likely is it that the promised event will indeed occur? (2) How long will
> your money be tied up? (3) What chance is there that something still better
> will transpire—a competing takeover bid, for example? and (4) What will
> happen if the event does not take place because of anti-trust action, financing
> glitches, etc.?
>
> Arcata Corp., one of our more serendipitous arbitrage experiences, illustrates the twists and turns of the business. On September 28, 1981 the directors of Arcata agreed in principle to sell the company to Kohlberg, Kravis,
> Roberts & Co. (KKR), then and now a major leveraged-buyout firm. Arcata
> was in the printing and forest products businesses and had one other thing
> going for it: In 1978 the U.S. Government had taken title to 10,700 acres of
> Arcata timber, primarily old-growth redwood, to expand Redwood National
> Park. The government had paid $97.9 million, in several installments, for this

acreage, a sum Arcata was contesting as grossly inadequate. The parties also disputed the interest rate that should apply to the period between the taking of the property and final payment for it. The enabling legislation stipulated 6% simple interest; Arcata argued for a much higher and compounded rate.

Buying a company with a highly-speculative, large-sized claim in litigation creates a negotiating problem, whether the claim is on behalf of or against the company. To solve this problem, KKR offered $37.00 per Arcata share plus two-thirds of any additional amounts paid by the government for the redwood lands.

Appraising this arbitrage opportunity, we had to ask ourselves whether KKR would consummate the transaction since, among other things, its offer was contingent upon its obtaining "satisfactory financing." A clause of this kind is always dangerous for the seller: It offers an easy exit for a suitor whose ardor fades between proposal and marriage. However, we were not particularly worried about this possibility because KKR's past record for closing had been good.

We also had to ask ourselves what would happen if the KKR deal did fall through, and here we also felt reasonably comfortable: Arcata's management and directors had been shopping the company for some time and were clearly determined to sell. If KKR went away, Arcata would likely find another buyer, though of course, the price might be lower.

Finally, we had to ask ourselves what the redwood claim might be worth. Your Chairman, who can't tell an elm from an oak, had no trouble with that one: He coolly evaluated the claim at somewhere between zero and a whole lot.

We started buying Arcata stock, then around $33.50, on September 30 and in eight weeks purchased about 400,000 shares, or 5% of the company. The initial announcement said that the $37.00 would be paid in January, 1982. Therefore, if everything had gone perfectly, we would have achieved an annual rate of return of about 40%—not counting the redwood claim, which would have been frosting.

All did not go perfectly. In December it was announced that the closing would be delayed a bit. Nevertheless, a definitive agreement was signed on January 4. Encouraged, we raised our stake, buying at around $38.00 per share and increasing our holdings to 655,000 shares, or over 7% of the company. Our willingness to pay up—even though the closing had been postponed—reflected our leaning toward "a whole lot" rather than "zero" for the redwoods.

Then, on February 25 the lenders said they were taking a "second look" at financing terms "in view of the severely depressed housing industry and its impact on Arcata's outlook." The stockholders' meeting was postponed again, to April. An Arcata spokesman said he "did not think the fate of the acquisition itself was imperiled." When arbitrageurs hear such reassurances, their minds flash to the old saying: "He lied like a finance minister on the eve of devaluation."

On March 12 KKR said its earlier deal wouldn't work, first cutting its offer to $33.50, then two days later raising it to $35.00. On March 15, however, the directors turned this bid down and accepted another group's offer of $37.50 plus one-half of any redwood recovery. The shareholders okayed the deal, and the $37.50 was paid on June 4.

We received $24.6 million versus our cost of $22.9 million; our average holding period was close to six months. Considering the trouble this transaction encountered, our 15% annual rate of return excluding any value for the redwood claim—was more than satisfactory.

But the best was yet to come. The trial judge appointed two commissions, one to look at the timber's value, the other to consider the interest rate questions. In January 1987, the first commission said the redwoods were worth $275.7 million and the second commission recommended a compounded, blended rate of return working out to about 14%.

In August 1987 the judge upheld these conclusions, which meant a net amount of about $600 million would be due Arcata. The government then appealed. In 1988, though, before this appeal was heard, the claim was settled for $519 million. Consequently, we received an additional $29.48 per share, or about $19.3 million. We will get another $800,000 or so in 1989.

Implementing Merger Arbitrage: How to Determine the Hedge

Merger arbitrage is about earning the deal spread as a compensation for taking the risk that the deal fails. Hence, the risk that the deal fails cannot be hedged—this is precisely the risk that the merger arbitrage manager wants to take. In fact, event arbitrage is about isolating the event risk and hedging out other risks (and diversifying across a number of unrelated events, as discussed in more detail later). Let us see how to isolate the deal risk and hedge out unnecessary risks.

The right hedge depends on the type of payment in the merger deal. Recall that figure 16.1 gives an overview of the main types of merger payments. The simplest merger trades involve cash deals, that is, deals where the acquirer simply offers to buy the target for cash. Figure 16.4 shows an example in which the acquirer offers $60 per share for the target. Of course, the value of the offer is independent of the price of the acquirer in this case. Therefore, the merger trade is very simple: You buy the target and that's it. No deal-specific hedge. (The manager may still apply some overall portfolio hedges as discussed below.)

Figure 16.5 shows the value of a fixed-exchange ratio stock deal. In this example, the acquirer offers 1.2 shares for each of the target shares. Hence, when the arbitrageur buys the target, she is clearly exposed to the risk that the acquirer's stock price drops in value. To hedge this risk, she can simply short-sell 1.2 shares of the acquirer for every share of the target that she buys.

Figure 16.4. How the value of the offer depends on the acquirer's stock price: Cash deal.

Figure 16.6 illustrates how to think of a floating-exchange ratio stock deal. The acquirer offers $60 worth of the acquirer's stock based on average price over a *pricing period*. Initially, before the pricing period, this is just like a cash deal. Hence, no hedge is needed in this time period. After the pricing period, the deal becomes just like a fixed-exchange ratio deal. During the pricing period, the exchange ratio is gradually determined so that the merger arbitrageur gradually increases her hedge from zero to the full hedge.

Lastly, figure 16.7 shows the value of two different types of collar stock mergers, that is, mergers where the payment (the cash amount or the number of

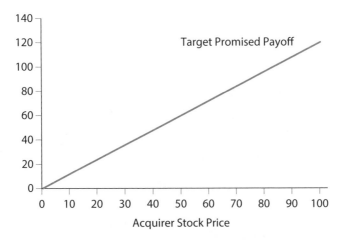

Figure 16.5. How the value of the offer depends on the acquirer's stock price: Fixed-exchange ratio stock deal.

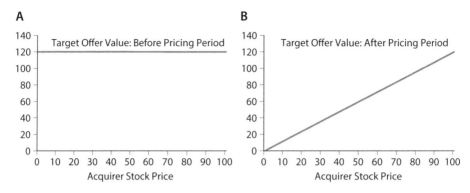

Figure 16.6. How the value of the offer depends on the acquirer's stock price: Floating-exchange ratio stock deal.
    Panel A: Before the pricing period.
    Panel B: After the pricing period.

the acquirer's shares) is adjusted depending on the circumstances. Hence, the promised payment has built-in option features like a collar option strategy. The payment structure in Panel A is sometimes called a "Travolta" deal, and the structure in Panel B an "Egyptian" deal (cf. the arm positions of John Travolta in Saturday Night Fever and a classic image of an Egyptian). The graphs show the values at the time of the merger completion, which are piecewise linear, like option payoffs. Hence, if options are available, such deals can be hedged using a portfolio of stocks and options that match the merger payoff. If options are not available or are expensive to trade, the merger arbitrageur can instead

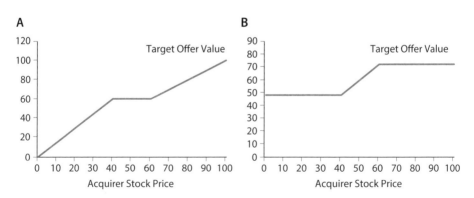

Figure 16.7. How the value of the offer depends on the acquirer's stock price: Collar deals.
    Panel A: "Travolta" collar deal.
    Panel B: "Egyptian" collar deal.

use the option technique called delta hedging. This means varying how much of the acquirer's stock is shorted over time.

Which Merger Acquirers Talk up Their Stock Price and When?

Acquirers in stock mergers have an incentive to boost their stock prices. Consistent with this, Ahern and Sosyura (2014) find that "fixed exchange ratio bidders dramatically increase the number of press releases disseminated to financial media during the private negotiation of a stock merger, compared to floating exchange ratio bidders, who do not have an incentive to manage their media during the merger negotiation. This effect is associated with short-lived increases in both media coverage and bidder valuation." Furthermore, they find that floating-exchange rate bidders disseminate more news around the pricing period, perhaps trying to talk up their stock price when it matters the most.

Merger Arbitrage Portfolio

Portfolio construction is an important part of merger arbitrage. The merger arbitrage manager must decide which merger targets to buy and how to size the positions. To do this, the merger arbitrage manager must first consider the available universe of mergers at any given time.

There are a lot of mergers and acquisitions going on almost all the time. Mitchell and Pulvino (2001) identify 9,026 U.S. merger transactions from 1963 to 1998, corresponding to 251 transactions per year on average. The number of transactions was lower in the early time period, peaked in the late 1980s, and has remained relatively solid since then. Each deal lasts about 3 months on average. Hence, having 251 transactions per year at a 3-month average duration implies that about 63 mergers were going on at any point of time in the United States during this period. The last decade, there have often been more than 100 U.S. mergers going on at each time, and more globally.

Given the available universe of merger deals, the merger arbitrage manager must decide on the number of deals to invest in, the maximum weight in any one deal, and which deals to buy. Some merger arbitrage managers are relatively concentrated, viewing their edge as taking significant bets on deals that have been very carefully analyzed. However, many merger arbitrage managers prefer to be well diversified, limiting the maximum weight in any one deal to be no more than 3–10% of the overall portfolio. To see why, consider what happens when a merger deal fails. For instance, suppose that the target of a cash merger increases 20% in value following the merger announcement and, when the merger is called off, the target price drops 20%. If the merger arbitrage manager buys the target with 5% of his capital, his loss will constitute

5% × 20% = 1% of his capital. To consider a more extreme case, consider an investment of 10% of the assets in a deal, leading to a 50% drop in the target price (relative to a potential hedge in a stock deal)—this implies a 5% loss of the overall capital. While such losses are painful, the merger arbitrage manager can nevertheless still hope to be up for the year. Some managers find the potential loss of 5% of capital on a single deal to be too large, whereas others may want to take a significant bet on deals where they have strong conviction of completion. If the maximum position size is set more conservatively to 3%, then the merger arbitrage manager needs to invest in a wide variety of merger deals, covering a large fraction of all deals that take place, and this is in fact a typical behavior among merger arbitrage managers.

As we will see in the historical return numbers below, the return to a diversified portfolio of merger arbitrage deals has been very good. That is, merger arbitrage managers have done well simply earning the deal-risk liquidity premium, even without special information regarding particular deals. Consistently, Warren Buffett (1988 annual report) says of merger arbitrage that "the trick, à la Peter Sellers in the movie, has simply been Being There."

Merger arbitrage managers also try to diversify across deal types and may size their positions differently across deal types. For instance, cash deals are more exposed to market risk (as explained below), so some merger arbitrage managers limit their overall exposure to cash deals. Furthermore, deal risk differs across deal types, as we discuss next.

Risk in Merger Arbitrage

The risk that any given merger deal fails is not negligible: about 10% of all deals fail. There exist some general patterns regarding which deals are more likely to fail (see Mitchell and Pulvino (2001), Table V). Naturally, hostile deals are more likely to fail than friendly deals as the acquirer must fight to gain control. LBOs are more likely to fail than strategic deals, likely because LBOs have a greater dependence on external financing and the deal may fall through if the acquirer cannot get financing. Also, smaller deals are more likely to fail, perhaps because large deals have been studied more carefully by the acquirer and the target has been subject to more general scrutiny by equity analysts. Furthermore, deals subject to more regulatory scrutiny are more likely to fail, e.g., deals that may be conceived as creating a monopoly. The simplest predictor of deal failure risk is the deal spread—deals with big spreads have big risk! Indeed, the market distinguishes good and bad deals ex ante, a sign of efficiently inefficient merger spreads.

Deal risk also changes over time, depending on the state of the takeover market. When the overall stock market is falling significantly, the risk of deal failure is higher. This is especially true for cash deals. To understand this, suppose that company A makes a bid to acquire company B for $100 million in cash, but before the deal is consummated, the overall stock market falls 30%. Then the bid may suddenly look too high—now the acquirer can consider buying another company for about 30% less than the time of the original offer. Therefore, the acquirer is likely to withdraw its offer or renegotiate it. If, on the other hand, the original merger offer had been to pay $100 worth of A's own stock, then the situation would have been different. In this case, the value of the offer would have likely fallen with the market as A's stock price would have adjusted. Therefore, the offer value might continue to look reasonable for A (and possibly B). Hence, deal failure risk depends on the overall market conditions, which shows up in the historical returns to merger arbitrage that we study next.

Historical Return of Merger Arbitrage

To evaluate the risk and return of a diversified merger arbitrage portfolio, Mitchell and Pulvino (2001) collect a large data set of mergers from 1963 to 1998 and construct a systematic strategy that they denote the "risk arbitrage index manager" (RAIM). The hypothetical RAIM invests in all cash and stock mergers available in each month (i.e., it excludes merger deals with more complex deal terms). The simulated strategy starts with $1 million in 1963 and invests in all deals, value weighting each deal subject to two constraints:

- Position limit 1: No deal can account for more than 10% of the simulated net asset value (NAV).
- Position limit 2: No deal must imply a trade so large that it would move the target or acquirer by more than 5% according to an estimated market impact function.

Based on these assumptions, the returns of merger arbitrage are simulated, accounting for transaction costs due to brokerage fees and market impact costs. The RAIM merger arbitrage index realizes an arithmetic average annual return of 11.1% (10.64% with geometric compounding) with an annual volatility of 7.74% over the time period from 1963 to 1998. Given the risk-free rate over this time period, this corresponds to an annual Sharpe ratio of 0.63 (0.57 with geometric compounding), which is higher than the Sharpe ratio of the overall equity market of 0.40 over the same time period.

Hence, merger arbitrage delivered significant positive excess returns after transaction costs. Let us see whether these returns were market neutral or exposed to market movements.

Figure 16.8 plots the excess returns of the RAIM merger arbitrage index vs. the excess return on the overall stock market. We see that merger arbitrage returns are largely uncorrelated with the market in mild bear markets and in bull markets. However, in significant bear markets—when the overall stock market drops more than 5% in a month—the correlation increases significantly.

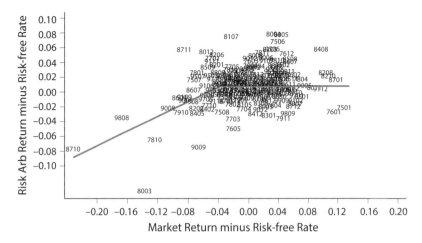

Figure 16.8. The excess return for merger arbitrage vs. the market excess return. Each data point is marked by the year and month it occurred, YYMM.

Source: Mitchell and Pulvino (2001).

The return of a diversified merger arbitrage portfolio does not depend directly on the stock market since the merger portfolio is hedged (i.e., it is a long–short portfolio). However, the merger arbitrage portfolio depends *indirectly* on the stock market since the overall rate of deal failure does. When the market return is close to zero or positive, marketwide events have little effect on whether a merger is completed so the merger arbitrage return depends largely on idiosyncratic events. Hence, in this range of market returns, merger arbitrage has a stock market beta close to zero (indicated by the flat line segment in the figure).

But, as seen to the left in figure 16.8, merger arbitrage has a positive beta when the stock market is significantly down as merger arbitrage shares the overall market pain in significant bear markets. This market exposure happens because a large drop in the market increases the general risk of deal failure (as discussed above). In particular, acquirers are more likely to walk away from their bid in down markets, especially if they made a cash bid that suddenly looks too expensive. Furthermore, obtaining financing becomes more difficult in down markets, especially if a credit crunch hits the financial sector.

The non-linear market exposure means that the standard capital asset pricing model (CAPM) model is not appropriate to evaluate the performance of merger arbitrage. The merger arbitrage payoff resembles a risk-free bond plus idiosyncratic noise and less a short put option on the market. Hence, when computing the alpha of merger arbitrage returns, we need to take into account that simply selling put options on the market earns a risk premium. To do this, one can regress the merger arbitrage excess return on both the excess return of the stock market index and the excess return of shorting put options:

$$R_t^{\text{RAIM}} = \alpha + \beta^{\text{MKT}} R_t^{\text{MKT}} + \beta^{\text{PUT}} R_t^{\text{SHORT-PUT}} + \varepsilon_t$$

This regression shows a statistically significant loading on put options and a significant positive alpha. This implies that merger arbitrage has delivered positive excess returns even accounting for the non-linear market exposure. Hence, merger arbitrage managers earn a premium for providing liquidity to market participants who sell merger deals, essentially providing "insurance" against deal risk.

Portfolio-Level Hedges for Merger Arbitrage

As we have seen, a merger arbitrage portfolio has a non-linear market exposure even when every deal in the portfolio is hedged. This portfolio exposure is the result of the increase in the general risk of deal failure that happens in bear markets, especially for cash deals. To hedge this non-linear risk, the merger arbitrage manager can overlay the strategy with portfolio hedges such as selling equity index futures or buying index put options, but most managers don't use such hedges as they tend to be expensive. If used, these hedges should be sized to remove the market-directional risk of the portfolio and therefore depend on the value of all the deals in the portfolio and the composition of deals across deal types.

16.2. SPIN-OFFS, SPLIT-OFFS, CARVE-OUTS

What Are Spin-Offs, Split-Offs, Carve-Outs?

The opposite of a merger happens when a company is divided into separate pieces and, interestingly, both mergers and divestments create opportunities to event managers. A company can sell a subsidiary in various ways, for instance by selling to another company in a private divestiture or by selling to the public. Selling to the public can be done with several methods, including a spin-off, a split-off, or a carve-out. In a spin-off, a subsidiary of the parent company is made into a separate firm and the shareholders of the parent company receive shares in the subsidiary on a pro rata basis (so no cash changes hands). A split-off is similar, except that the shareholders of the parent company must elect whether or not to tender parent shares in exchange for shares in the subsidiary.

Spin-offs and split-offs are illustrated in figure 16.9, which also shows how carve-outs work. In an equity carve-out, the parent sells some shares of the subsidiary while retaining a fraction of the shares on its own balance sheet. The carve-out creates a market for the subsidiary shares, and it is commonly followed by a later spin-off or split-off of the remaining parent shares. The carved out shares in the subsidiary company can be sold in a so-called partial initial public offering (IPO) or can be awarded to parent shareholders on a pro rata basis.

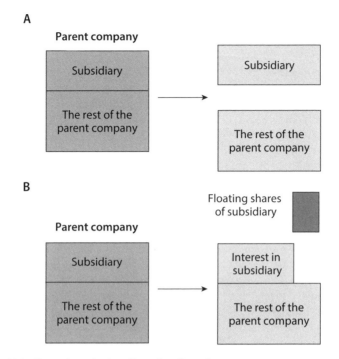

Figure 16.9. Illustration of spin-offs, split-offs, and carve-outs.
Panel A. Spin-offs and split-offs.
Panel B. Carve-outs.

Trading on Spin-Offs and Split-Offs

Spin-offs and split-offs give event managers an opportunity to bet on the separate prospects of the subsidiary and the rest of the parent company, their separate management teams, and business potentials. Furthermore, the corporate event can initially lead to supply and demand imbalances as investors are re-optimizing their portfolios. For instance, the subsidiary often faces initial selling pressure as many investors want to keep their shares in the parent stock, not the subsidiary. This is especially the case if the subsidiary is in a different industry than the parent or if the parent is in an equity index and the subsidiary is not. Subsidiaries in a spin-off are likely to face greater selling pressure than those being split off because *all* original shareholders in a spin-off receive shares in the subsidiary, while shareholders must elect to buy shares in a split-off. Furthermore, investors may initially feel that they have insufficient knowledge of the subsidiary and the subsidiary typically has low analyst coverage in the beginning.

Over time, the selling pressure ends, investors learn about the subsidiary and its management, and analyst coverage picks up. Furthermore, the subsidiary and the rest of the parent each can benefit from being a more focused company with more incentivized management, fewer agency problems, and so on, leading to potential strong performance over the medium term.

Trading on Carve-Outs

While investments in spin-offs and split-offs are often not arbitrage trades, carve-outs can present more true event-driven arbitrage opportunities. Since the parent firm owns a significant fraction of the subsidiary, event managers can sometimes profit from trading the parent against the subsidiary.

Table 16.1 illustrates the balance sheet of the parent firm and the "stub," that is, the parent firm excluding the interest in the subsidiary. Since assets always equal liabilities, we see from the balance sheet of the parent that the market values (MVs) of the various pieces must satisfy this equation:

$$\text{MV (other assets)} + \text{MV (stake)} = \text{MV (liabilities)} + \text{MV (parent equity)}$$

Similarly, from the stub's balance sheet we see that

$$\text{MV (stub equity)} = \text{MV (other assets)} - \text{MV (liabilities)}$$

Combining these relations gives the following natural relation:

$$\text{MV (stub equity)} = \text{MV (parent equity)} - \text{MV (stake)}$$

Event managers really pay attention when they find a *negative* stub value. This means that one can buy the parent equity for less than the value of its stake in the subsidiary, which seems like a great bargain.

TABLE 16.1. STYLIZED BALANCE SHEETS OF THE PARENT FIRM AND THE STUB

Panel A. Stylized Balance Sheet of the Parent Firm

Assets	Liabilities
Other assets	Liabilities
Stake in subsidiary	Parent company equity

Panel B. Stylized Balance Sheet of the Stub (the Parent, Excluding the Subsidiary)

Assets	Liabilities
Other assets	Liabilities
	Equity of stub

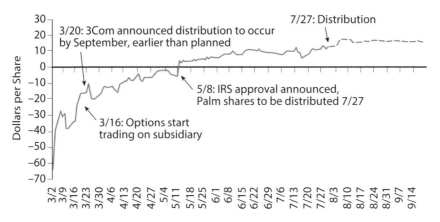

Figure 16.10. Stub value for 3Com during Palm carve-out in 2000.
Source: Lamont and Thaler (2003).

A negative stub value is a real arbitrage when it is known that the parent will distribute its shares of the subsidiary. For instance, if the parent has N shares of the subsidiary for every parent share outstanding, then an event manager can buy shares in the parent and short-sell N times as many shares of the subsidiary. The event manager is essentially paid to take on this position because of the negative stub value (although the position nevertheless ties up capital due to margin requirements). When the parent distributes the subsidiary shares, the event manager can use these shares to cover her short positions. This leaves the event manager owning the shares of the rest of the parent, which is worth no less than zero (due to limited liability).

Such negative stub values occurred several times during the tech bubble when an "old economy" firm ("brick and mortar business") carved out a tech subsidiary. The price of the tech subsidiary skyrocketed relative to the parent stock price, creating a negative stub value. Figure 16.10 shows an example of the stub value of 3Com/Palm during the end of the tech bubble. The stub value started highly negative and eventually turned positive.

Negative stub values are, however, not risk-free arbitrage opportunities. Several things can go wrong. First of all, the parent firm may not distribute the shares of the subsidiary even if the parent announces an intention to do so. For instance, the distribution can have negative tax consequences unless the IRS approves a tax-free distribution. What is worse, the parent company can go bankrupt or be delisted.

Furthermore, short-selling the subsidiary can be costly, difficult, and risky. Indeed, shares in a subsidiary with a negative stub value are often expensive to sell short, and sometimes it is even difficult to locate lendable shares for the short sale. (The capitalization of the high lending fee can even contribute to the high price of the subsidiary, as discussed in chapter 8.) Furthermore, if the event trader manages to put on the short position, she risks having her position closed down at the worst possible time if she can no longer borrow the share (a "buy-in"). Also, the stub value can fluctuate wildly, creating the risk of short-term losses and margin calls.

Studying 82 negative stub-value situations, Mitchell, Pulvino, and Stafford (2002) find that for "30 percent of the sample, the link between the parent and its subsidiary is severed before the relative value discrepancy is corrected. Furthermore, returns to a specialized arbitrageur would be 50 percent larger if the path to convergence was smooth rather than as observed."

What happens if the parent retains the shares in the subsidiary? Is a negative stub value still an arbitrage opportunity in this case? Possibly, possibly not. If the parent is a sound firm with little debt, the market should recognize the discrepancy and the stub value turn positive over time. On the other hand, if the parent has large liabilities that are worth more than the value of its assets outside the subsidiary, then there is nothing strange about having a negative stub value. Or if the management is entrenched and expected to waste significant assets, then this can also explain a low stub value. That being said, event managers also sometimes get excited about buying positive stub values if the stub value seems low relative to the value of the rest of the parent company. When evaluating such cases, the event manager must consider the value of the subsidiary, value the rest of the parent, and consider the various liabilities.

16.3. DISTRESSED INVESTMENT AND OTHER EVENT-DRIVEN INVESTMENTS

Distressed Investments

Some event-driven managers specialize in distressed investments, often the debt of firms in financial distress. Distressed firms include both firms that are already in default (e.g., in Chapter 11 in the United States) and struggling firms that are getting close to bankruptcy. Such struggling firms are sometimes defined as those with a credit spread over comparable-duration Treasuries of more than 1,000 basis points (bps). This credit spread means that the price of the firm's debt is so low that its yield to maturity is more than 10 percentage points higher than the yield on Treasuries. While this credit spread is large, so is the risk of not getting paid. In fact, a passive investment to distressed debt has historically not been well compensated according to some indices, surprisingly.

Hence, distressed managers must be active to add value. Indeed, companies in distress often present significant opportunities and risks as the underlying business is in flux and the various stakeholders may attempt to extract the remaining value. An event manager can approach a distressed investment in many different ways. In particular, an investor can take an ownership in debt or equity and attempt to help improve the business. For bankrupt companies, the event manager can try to help the company get a new start by securing debtor-in-possession (DIP) financing, which is more senior than all unsecured creditors (and therefore must be approved by the bankruptcy judge) or help the company emerge from bankruptcy with exit financing.

The event manager must also actively protect his investment, for instance, by serving on the creditor committee. Indeed, equity holders or other debt holders may try to extract value from the company, which can be detrimental to the remaining debt holders. Event managers can also try to renegotiate the debt or to buy securities directly from the firm, the firm's bank, or other stakeholders (e.g., bond holders). The event manager can even seek to get control of the company.

Event managers also sometimes try to profit from the price pressure that occurs when companies are downgraded to speculative grade, enter financial distress, or go bankrupt. Such situations can lead to selling pressure as many investors need to, or want to, offload distressed securities. The event managers can provide liquidity, but they need to carefully study risk, including the chance that the business can be turned around so that the company becomes profitable, the chance that the company can survive until then, the recovery in case of default, and each security's place in the capital structure.

Capital Structure Arbitrage

A classic arbitrage trade is to trade one security against another security issued by the same firm. For instance, to buy a corporate bond of a company while shorting the equity, to trade a company's stock against its preferred stock, or credit default swap (CDS) against stocks or bonds. This so-called capital structure arbitrage is not a bet on whether the company is good or bad as a whole but rather a bet that one part of the capital structure is cheap relative to another.

This trade is based on the idea that all claims to the firm (equity and liabilities) are really derivatives of the firm value and arbitrage opportunities arise if these securities are not priced consistently. For instance, the event manager can consider the equity price, firm leverage ratio, and equity volatility to determine the fair value of the corporate bonds and then buy low and sell high.

Changes in Capital Structure

Another event arbitrage play is to trade around changes in a firm's capital structure, for instance, share buybacks, share issuances, debt issuances, or debt exchanges. One set of event trades speculates that the capital structure change favors one part of the capital structure (at the expense of other parts). For instance, an equity issue may benefit bond holders and the market may not immediately fully price this in.

More broadly, when a firm buys back shares or retires debt, this often signals management confidence. On the other hand, issuance of securities, especially stocks, can signal that the securities are overvalued or that there are agency problems in the firm. However, participating in a security offering can be profitable if there is an average underpricing and if the event manager can avoid adverse selection in terms of allocation of shares—e.g., if the event manager is allocated shares even in the most oversubscribed offerings. Furthermore, the market for rights offerings sometimes involves arbitrage opportunities, as do when-issued markets.

Special Security Structures and Market Dislocations

Event managers also find opportunity in special security structures, such as ETFs and closed-end funds. Sometimes the value of the holdings of such securities differs significantly from the value of the shares, which gives rise to trading opportunities betting that the values will converge. Also, apparent mispricing can occur for special purpose acquisition companies (SPACs) and private investments in public equity (PIPEs), but these are highly illiquid investments subject to liquidity risk.

Event opportunities can also arise in connection with firm-specific or marketwide market dislocations. For instance, if a firm's equity is included in a stock index, this has historically led to a predictable average increase in price around the inclusion date as index investors buy, although this effect is not strong anymore. Similarly, a stock that is excluded from an index may drop in price around the deletion. In terms of dislocations for a broader market, John A. Paulson's subprime trade is the most famous and most profitable example.

16.4. INTERVIEW WITH JOHN A. PAULSON OF PAULSON & CO.

John A. Paulson is the president and portfolio manager of Paulson & Co. Inc., specializing in global merger, event arbitrage, and credit strategies. Founded in 1994, Paulson & Co. has received numerous awards and became widely known for the successful bet against the subprime market in a trade that has been called "The Greatest Trade Ever." Paulson graduated from New York University in 1978 and received his MBA from Harvard Business School in 1980. Before forming his investment management firm, he was a general partner of Gruss Partners and a managing director in mergers and acquisitions at Bear Stearns.

LHP: *How did you originally get interested in event-driven investment?*
JAP: I first learned about risk arbitrage when I was a student at NYU and I signed up for a seminar-type course taught by Gustave Levy. He was the

Chairman of Goldman Sachs and a graduate of NYU, and he had previously run the risk arb desk at Goldman Sachs. Unfortunately, right before the course started, Gustave Levy passed away. John Whitehead was made the Chairman, and John Whitehead stepped into Gustave's shoes and took over the class.

John knew how important the class was. He taught and he also brought in the head partners in charge of mergers and acquisitions, risk arbitrage, and corporate finance to teach one class each. That partner who was running risk arbitrage at the time was Bob Rubin, who ultimately became Chairman of Goldman Sachs and then Treasury Secretary. So that was my initial introduction to risk arbitrage.

Risk arbitrage has been an important investment strategy for Goldman Sachs and Bear Stearns for—looking back—for approximately the last 80 years. And it has been such a profitable part of the firm that the successive chairmen and heads of the firm have tended to come from the risk arb department. That's what happened with Gustave Levy, and that's what happened with Bob Rubin. And it's not hard to see why. If you're allocated $1 billion in capital and you're up 20%, then your group just produced $200 million of profits for the firm. It's very hard to produce individually those kinds of fees as a traditional investment banker giving advice on mergers or corporate finance. So the risk arb departments at both Bear Stearns and Goldman, when they were partnerships, generally became the most profitable parts of the firms.

When hedge funds started, the partners or junior people left the banks and formed their own hedge fund to do this same strategy. As time went on, the investment banks had so many conflicts of interest that it became difficult for them to compete against the hedge funds, which didn't have any conflicts of interest. And now these investment banks have gone public and they've become regulated by the government. And under the new rules, what's now called the Volcker Rule, they're not allowed to do proprietary trading any more. So the banks are sort of out of this business today. That has left hedge funds as the dominant players now in risk arbitrage.

LHP: *Can you describe your investment process?*

JAP: Risk arbitrage, generally, is investing in securities of corporations going through a corporate event where the return is not based on the stock going up and down but the success and completion of the event. The primary area of risk arbitrage tends to be merger activity. The second most important part for us is bankruptcy investing, when corporations go bankrupt and they reorganize in bankruptcy. This involves some very significant restructuring of the debt—either turning it into equity and reemerging as a private company, or other types of maneuvers. And then the third category would be more general, other types of corporate restructurings, which includes spin-offs and recapitalizations like the one at Apple, where companies borrow money and then pay their shareholders a big dividend.

LHP: *How do you approach merger arbitrage?*

JAP: In a merger situation, generally what happens is that the acquirer makes a bid for the target, either all cash bid, or a stock bid, or a combination of cash or stock, or any other form of consideration, where the target stock runs up close to the offer price but trades at somewhat of a discount to the offer price because of the risks of failure of deal completion.

LHP: *And you seek to earn that spread?*

JAP: Yes. That spread, adjusted for the time outstanding, becomes the annualized return from investing in a risk arbitrage situation. Take a simple example: Company A is trading for $30; it receives a $50 bid, and the stock goes to $49. And there's a $1 spread left. You buy it for $49 to make $1 when you sell it for $50.

But if the deal breaks down, the stock could fall back to $30. So in this case, you would have $1 on the upside, but $19 on the downside. Obviously, it's not a game for the faint of heart. Most people who owned the stock before, they don't want to hold onto it. They don't like that risk–return, so they sell it.

Now, why would I buy it? If I buy the stock for $49, I make $1; a dollar simply over $49 is about a 2% return. But let's say the deal closes in 60 days, 2 months. It's a tender offer. If you can make a 2% return in two months, that is equivalent to a 12% annualized rate of return. So it looks like a small amount of money, but on an annualized basis, could be a decent return. If you do that repeatedly, you could earn a return that on average is more than the return in the market.

The other advantage of this strategy is that it doesn't depend on the overall market. Let's say you buy the stock at $49, but after you buy it, the stock market falls 30%, the whole market crashes. Well, that shouldn't affect the outcome of this particular transaction. The companies involved are not paying attention to the market. So sure enough, 60 days later, this deal closes, I've still made a 12% annual return in an environment where the market went down. So not only are the returns on average higher than the market, they're also uncorrelated to the market. You don't need the market to go up in order to make this return.

LHP: *But there are risks, though?*

JAP: Yes, and what you need is an expertise in evaluating deal completion risk. With 19 points in the downside and one on the upside, what is the actual risk of this deal being completed? What is the regulatory risk? Will they get antitrust approval? Assessing that risk is very specialized to our profession. For example, the average investors who owned the stock before the bid may have no idea about antitrust law. They don't know what the issues are, how many deals have been approved, how many deals haven't been approved. They don't know the antitrust situation in the U.S. or Germany or China. Plus, there are many different regulatory approvals in addition to antitrust.

Average investors also don't read the merger agreement, which dictates the terms upon which the merger would be completed. Certain merger agreements could have an out; for instance, if the market falls 10%, the buyer has the right to walk. Well in that case, with the stock market falling 30%, the buyer would say, "Hey, I don't want to buy this anymore." He has a legal right to exit.

So before you start playing the arbitrage, you certainly need to read the merger agreement, but to fully understand the merger agreement, you have to be a very good merger lawyer. To play this game, you need a lot of expertise related to the issues that affect deal completion. You have to be able to understand merger agreements. You have to understand regulatory issues. And it's not just antitrust. There's all sorts of banking regulations, insurance regulations; there's federal regulations, and state regulations.

LHP: *And the deal could fail because of problems with the financing of the trade?*

JAP: Yes, it could be the financing. So you have to know does the acquirer have the money? Is there bank financing? Is it contingent on bank financing? Have you read the terms of the bank financing? Certain bank commitments are very tight, very difficult to get out of. Certain of them are very wide. So without doing all this work, you're at a disadvantage in evaluating this particular risk.

So that's where the experts come in. That's all we do. So we have an advantage in playing this game against basically 99% of the market that's getting engaged in the security after a bid is announced. And we can turn that knowledge into an investing advantage and use it to produce returns on an average better than the market that are also uncorrelated.

LHP: *But you're not just competing with the general public—there are other merger arb experts out there.*

JAP: Yes, there are other merger arbs out there, but they have various degrees of expertise. Our advantage is our expertise. Now, where did I get my expertise? Before I started working in risk arbitrage, I was a partner in mergers and acquisitions. All I did was live and breathe mergers, financing agreements, merger agreements, hostile bids, friendly bids, spin-offs, etc. So I had a high degree of expertise in all these issues when I started the firm. Now, I'm not a lawyer, I'm a banker, and while I've negotiated a lot of legal agreements, I know my limitations so we hired top M&A attorneys to be our legal advisors.

LHP: *So how do you apply this expertise in merger arbitrage? For instance, do you try to anticipate that bids will be topped by competing bidders?*

JAP: Well, when we talk about deal spreads, it's the initial way to look at merger arbitrage. But you also have to do the valuations. Say Company B is paying $50 a share for Company A, but what multiple of earnings is that? What multiple of EBITDA [earnings before interest, taxes, depreciation, and amortization]? How's Company A growing? What other acquisitions occurred in this sector? Could there be someone else that could pay a higher price?

The first thing we do is we compute all the acquisition multiples: multiple of earnings, book value, EBITDA, EBIT. I compare it to the growth rate. And then we go into our proprietary database of all public data on acquisitions that have occurred in different industries. So if this is in, let's say, the media industry or the telecom sector, I can immediately pick up a comp [comparison] sheet. I can see everyone that bought everyone in TV stations over the last 5 or 10 years and what multiple they paid. Let's say, the average multiple is 12. And then I look at this deal. This deal's being done at 10. This immediately raises a red flag—it seems to be somewhat underpriced.

Well, why is this underpriced? Was this an auction? When the company sold itself, did they hire a Goldman Sachs and shop it to all the media companies? If they did, then everyone already saw it and it's unlikely someone else is going to bid.

If, however, we find that this was just a negotiation between the buyer and seller, then other people did not know this was for sale. So they're going to hear about it the first time when this deal is announced. And they're going to do the multiples, and they're going to see this is trading for less than the others and may encourage some interest. Now all the other bankers, they're going to want to get a fee. So they'll likely go to their clients and say, "Do you see this company? It's trading for $10x$. You just bought someone at $12x$ in the same territory. Why don't we see if we can make a higher bid?"

Then you've got to read the merger agreement. Is there any particular shareholder that locked up their stock? Is there voting stock and non-voting stock? What's the agreement between the shareholders and the buyer? Is there a breakup fee in the merger agreement? If someone else comes in, do you have to pay a premium to the previous buyer, which may dissuade someone else coming in?

At the end of the day, if the deal looks cheap and you can identify other potential acquirers, then instead of taking an average position of 1% or 2%, you say: "You know what? I think it's a very high probability this deal gets closed, and very, very low chance it's not completed. And a reasonable probability someone else may come and bid." In that case, I'm not just going to take an average position, I'm going to take a 10% position in this portfolio. I'm going to buy as many shares as I can get, maybe even up to 10% of the company.

LHP: *So even when you really like a deal, you have a position limit, which is both 10% of your own assets and 10% of the company?*

JAP: Yes, we do have position limitations. Because after all, no matter how sure you are or how sure you think you are, or how you think it could work out, you play this enough times, it's not always going to work out as anticipated. So you always have to watch the downside. If you overconcentrate and you're wrong, you could get hurt. We generally limit our largest position size to 10%, so we'll always operate in a diversified sense. Now, obviously, if I put 100% of my money in a deal that gets a topping bid, I make a fortune. But if something goes wrong, something breaks the bid, you can lose a fortune. We're not into losing a fortune.

The key thing in making money is not losing money. You have to think first about the downside and size your position to not how much money you could make, but how much money you could lose. You've got to set your limits based on your tolerance for loss within the overall portfolio.

LHP: *So you overweight deals that could receive a topping bid while staying relatively diversified?*

JAP: Yes. If I like the company, I'll buy up to 10% of the company. When the deal is announced and the stock goes from $30 to $49, a lot of the institutions don't want to hold it for the last dollar, so as they sell, I can quickly get 9.9% of the company. Now let's say we're right and someone else comes along, and instead of offering $50 they offer $60. So instead of making $1, I'll make $11. If $1 was a 12% rate of return, $11 would be 120%. So this can turn into a very high-return strategy. Weighting your portfolio to that deal means that, if that happens, it's going to have a disproportionate effect in your portfolio.

LHP: *Can you give a specific example of such a trade?*

JAP: We did it with Sprint last year. SoftBank made a bid to buy 70% of Sprint for $5.75 a share. So we did the multiples like I just described, and it was a low multiple relative to other wireless companies that traded. We thought there's a chance someone else could come in. So we bought 220 million shares of Sprint. Obviously, we made a big investment. So let's say $5.75 times 220 million, we put about $1.3 billion into this one stock. And then we waited. Well, lo and behold, Dish showed up and offered $7 a share. And that forced SoftBank to come back at $7.75 a share. We wound up making $2 a share very quickly on 220 million shares or, in real-life terms, $440 million in this one merger transaction.

LHP: *What are the other elements of merger arbitrage?*

JAP: Obviously, you can see when a deal's announced, it could be at a 30%, 50%, or even higher premium to where the stock traded the day before or a week before the announcement. So this is a big payday if you could anticipate which company could be taken over next and then own that stock prior to the announcement of the bid.

Obviously, that's where it creates a possibility for fraud; that's where insider trading comes in, where people try to gain an advantage by trading on inside information. That's something we're not interested in. We have very strict policies here about having access to inside information. If, by any chance, we inadvertently get inside information, then we obviously won't trade the stock. But that doesn't mean you can't try to figure out which company will be taken over next. There's nothing illegal about doing that as long as you're doing it based on an industry analysis and not on any special information.

We've set up our firm to have experts in each industry, so when there's a merger announced in, say, telecom, we have people that only do telecom mergers. So we have both the industry expertise and the merger expertise. In the case of the telecom industry, by having people that focus just on that and meeting with all the executives and doing this for years and understanding who bought who, why they bought that company, and who may want to buy someone else.

LHP: *So you try to anticipate mergers before they happen in an industry going through a consolidation?*

JAP: Exactly. When you start to see consolidation in the industry, it starts to become kind of apparent who's next. In the telecom sector, you have Verizon, which is biggest. Then you have AT&T. But then you have the smaller players. You have Sprint. You have T-Mobile. Before this, we had MetroPCS, and then Leap Wireless, then Clear Wireless, so you had seven national players. As the industry's growth started to slow and the need for capex [capital expenditure] started to grow, it was apparent that these smaller guys could not survive as independents any more. So it was possible for us to anticipate, who is likely going to get acquired and acquire those stocks in anticipation of them being acquired. And then, the way it worked out, they were all acquired: Sprint by SoftBank, MetroPCS by T-Mobile, Clear Wireless by Sprint, and Leap by AT&T. In the case of Leap, we had a 9.9% stake and AT&T paid a 110% premium.

LHP: *Let's turn to distressed investment and bankruptcies. How do you trade these?*

JAP: Bankruptcy investing is also a very attractive area where there's a limited amount of expertise. When a company goes bankrupt, bondholders often don't know what to do with the bonds. You get a lot of the traditional holders selling the securities. Then people who specialize in bankruptcies buy these securities and go through the process of restructuring the company, either reorganizing the company so it emerges as a well-capitalized, hopefully, healthy company or, on the other side if the business prospects are poor, investors may go through a liquidation. It's very complex. You need a similar but different set of skills than a merger arbitrage. You need different legal expertise, although the financial analysis can be similar.

LHP: *Can you give an example of a bankruptcy trade?*

JAP: We have many examples, as we were very active in the bankruptcy investing in the last recession. I'll give you one. It was a hotel chain called Extended Stay Hotels. They have about 670 owned and operated hotels across the U.S., and they were purchased in a leveraged buyout in 2007 for $8 billion, $7 billion of debt and $1 billion of equity. At the time, they were making about $550 million of EBITDA, so they were bought at a relatively high multiple of 15 times EBITDA, thinking that the earnings would continue to grow.

Lo and behold, the economy went into a recession after Lehman Brothers failed. As economic activity collapsed and business activity fell, people started traveling less. The occupancy at Extended Stay Hotels fell, and their EBITDA went from $575 million to $250 million. At $250 million, they couldn't support $7 billion of debt, so they defaulted on their debt and went into bankruptcy.

We knew this company. We knew the capital structure. We also know that hotels are cyclical: They go down in recessions and they go up when the economy recovers. So there was nothing the matter with the chain. The problem was that they had too much debt and the cycle turned against them.

So we thought this would be an attractive company to control, and we bought a big chunk of debt in bankruptcy. There was another hedge fund that we knew that also bought a big chunk of debt in bankruptcy. As the economy started to recover, we decided we wanted to lead a reorganization of Extended Stay. But the other hedge fund also decided the same thing. Rather than compete, we decided to pool our respective debt positions together. By doing that, we controlled over one-third of the debt. In bankruptcy, you need two-thirds of the creditors to approve a bankruptcy plan. Controlling one-third of the debt essentially gave us veto power over any reorganization.

Since no one could reorganize this company without our approval, we were in the pole position to lead the restructuring. At the end of the day, we did that. We brought in Blackstone as a partner and wound up buying the company out of bankruptcy by paying off all the creditors for $3.9 billion in cash, down more than 50% from what their company traded for two years before. As part of this structure, we put up $500 million, Centerbridge put up $500 million, and Blackstone put in $500 million. Together we put in $1.5 billion of equity and then raised $2.4 billion of first mortgage debt.

So we had the $3.9 billion, and we bought Extended Stay, a 50% discount to the price paid three years before. We did some management changes, some restructuring, but basically, as the economy recovered, the earnings went up. Now Extended Stay is back to the level of profitability it was before, making roughly $600 million in profits. Then we took it public and with the proceeds we paid down the debt. Now the company again has a value of $8 billion. We paid off about $400 million of debt, so there's only about $2 billion of debt. So that means the equity value is $6 billion. So we put in $1.5 billion in 2010, and now that $1.5 billion is worth $6 billion. That's a good example of a bankruptcy reorganization.

LHP: *Your most famous credit play is your subprime trade. When I interviewed Soros, he actually said that you sized that trade based on his ideas about how to go for the jugular when the payoff is very asymmetric—is that right?*

JAP: Yes, it's true. And it is important to read books like the one you're writing. When I was starting in the business, I read a book on Soros, called *Soros on Soros*. It was his investing philosophy. I remember when he decided to short the pound, one of his analysts came in, they were discussing it, and George thought it was a great idea. The analyst suggested a certain size. George said well, that's too small. Good investment ideas don't come around that often. When you find a great one, you can't be passive. You have to go for the jugular, he said.

LHP: *So how did you apply this for the subprime market?*

JAP: We had been involved in bankruptcy reorganizations, like the one I described before, coming out of the recession of 2002, but by 2006 the credit market had become so frothy and yields had become so tight that we sold our long positions. We felt that the best opportunities were on the short side. We did a pretty thorough analysis of all the credit markets and felt that the most overvalued securities were subprime mortgage securities. At the time, the BBB-rated tranches of subprime securities were trading only for 1 percentage point more than Treasuries, so if you shorted a subprime bond and went long a Treasury bond of the same maturity, you earned, let's say, a 5% yield from the Treasury bond and paid a 6% yield on the subprime. Your net cost was 1% to be short the subprime.

We felt ultimately that these BBBs in a housing downturn could go to zero; we had found a tremendously mispriced security with a very asymmetrical return profile—if the worst happens, you pay 1%, and if what you expect to happen actually happens, you make 100%. It was 100-to-1 risk–return trade-off. And the more work we did on these subprime securities in the housing market, the more convinced we became that the probability of these going to zero was very, very high. The economics just didn't make any sense at all. And we were right in the middle of a tremendous credit bubble.

So we initially shorted $100 million of these bonds, and $100 million is a lot of money. But, we said it's only costing us $1 million. At the time we're managing $6 billion. So we said, "Well, don't look at the $100 million, just look at the cost of the trade: when you go long and short against Treasuries, we couldn't lose more than $1 million a year." So we said, "Let's size it up." We took it up to $500 million; still can only go down $5 million a year. So we took it up to $1 billion, $2 billion, $3 billion. As the work went on, we became more and more convinced this was going to happen. So how big should we get with this?

That's when I remembered George Soros's comment. When you really find the great investment, "you have to go for the jugular." So I said, "You know what? Forget about the numbers. This is the greatest risk–return trade-off I've ever seen. I'm not going to sit here with this—we're going to go for the jugular." Ultimately, we took the position up to $25 billion short securities. George's comment was a big part of us sizing up that position.

LHP: *What analysis made you convinced that the subprime BBB securities would collapse?*

JAP: It is worthwhile to understand what the structure of subprime securities were. These structures were amazing credit contraptions. Let's say they took $1 billion of subprime mortgages and they put them into a pool, then they sold securities against that pool that were tranched into about 15 different layers. So that means if a loss happened, that started at the bottom; whereas the most senior tranches got paid off first. The top layer was AAA securities and then they had AAA1, 2, 3, 4, 5, and 6, which represented about 70% of the structure. After these seven layers of triple-A, they had AA-plus, AA-flat, AA-minus. And then they went to A-plus, A-flat, and A-minus. Then came the BBBs (BBB-plus, BBB-flat, BBB-minus), and, below these, the non-investment-grade BB securities and the equity tranche.

The BBBs had so much demand because they were the last investment-grade layer and therefore had the highest yield amongst all the investment grades. A lot of institutions globally wanted investment-grade securities but wanted the most yield they could get. So there was an enormous demand for the BBB securities.

But all you needed was a loss of 6% in the subprime pool and the BBB was wiped out. Losses first hit the equity layer. A 3% total loss and the equity layer would be wiped out. Then you had the BB tranches. Then BBB-minus, then BBB, then BBB-plus. Then you go to the A on up. But the cutoff point for the BBB securities was only about 5%, and it was only 1% thick, so a 6% loss would wipe it out.

When the market started to implode, the default rate in subprime securities went from 10% to 15% to 20% to 30% to 40%. Once a loan defaults and then you sell the house, the recovery on these loans was less than 50%. So if you take a 40% default rate and a 50% recovery, you're talking about losses that are going to extend up to 20% of the capital structure. So that's what was happening. The BBBs wiped at 5%.

LHP: *How did you manage to stay in the trade to the end? As the crisis gradually unfolded, many investors might have been tempted to close the position halfway when you were already up tremendously.*

JAP: That's a very good question. When the BBB started to fall, they fell from par to 90, 80, 70, 60, 50—people were saying, "Why don't you get out? You made all this money. Where are you going to take it?" They didn't understand that the loss rates in these pools were now obvious. The default rates were so high. The foreclosures were happening, and our prediction was these pools were going to lose north of 20%. And that was just almost in the bag, if you just let the thing run out, the defaults run into foreclosures. That's what you're going to get. And all I needed was 5% to make 100 cents on the dollar. So I'm saying, "Why am I going to close that at 50? All I've got to do is be patient and as the default rate continues to rise, as house prices continue to fall, as losses build up, these securities are going to be wiped out."

So I wasn't looking at these and thinking "Those fell from 100 to 50. Oh, I'm scared, they may go back to 100." If you knew the underlying collateral and had all the data, you knew they were toast. There was no hope of any recovery. And if we just waited, the market would eventually catch up and they'd go to zero. And that's what we did. We waited and they went to zero.

References

Abreu, Dilip, and Markus Brunnermeier (2003), "Bubbles and Crashes," *Econometrica* 71, 173–204.

Acharya, V., and L. H. Pedersen (2005), "Asset Pricing with Liquidity Risk," *Journal of Financial Economics* 77, 375–410.

Agarwal, Vikas, Naveen D. Daniel, and Narayan Y. Naik (2009), "Role of Managerial Incentives and Discretion in Hedge Fund Performance," *Journal of Finance* 5, 2221–2256.

Ahern, Kenneth, and Denis Sosyura (2014), "Who Writes the News? Corporate Press Releases during Merger Negotiations," *Journal of Finance* 69, 241–291.

Amihud, Y., and H. Mendelson (1986), "Asset Pricing and the Bid–Ask Spread," *Journal of Financial Economics* 17, 223–249.

Aragon, George O., and Vikram Nanda (2012), "On Tournament Behavior in Hedge Funds: High-Water Marks, Fund Liquidation, and Managerial Stake," *Review of Financial Studies* 25, 937–974.

Ashcraft, Adam, Nicolae Gârleanu, and Lasse Heje Pedersen (2010), "Two Monetary Tools: Interest Rates and Haircuts," *NBER Macroeconomics Annual* 25, 143–180.

Asness, C. (1994), "Variables That Explain Stock Returns," Ph.D. Dissertation, University of Chicago.

Asness, C. (2003), "Fight the Fed Model," *Journal of Portfolio Management* Fall, 11–24.

Asness, C. (2004), "An Alternative Future," *The Journal of Portfolio Management* 31, 8–23.

Asness, C. (2007), "How I Became a Quant," *How I Became a Quant: Insights from 25 of Wall Street's Elite*, Richard R. Lindsey and Barry Schachter (Eds.), John Wiley and Sons, Hoboken, NJ.

Asness, C., A. Frazzini, and L. H. Pedersen (2012), "Leverage Aversion and Risk Parity," *Financial Analysts Journal* 68(1), 47–59.

Asness, C., A. Frazzini, and L. H. Pedersen (2013), "Quality Minus Junk," Working paper, AQR Capital Management and New York University.

Asness, C., A. Frazzini, and L. H. Pedersen (2014), "Low-Risk Investing without Industry Bets," *Financial Analysts Journal* 70, July/August, 24–41.

Asness, Cliff, Tobias Moskowitz, and Lasse Heje Pedersen (2013), "Value and Momentum Everywhere," *The Journal of Finance* 68(3), 929–985.

Asness, C., R. Krail, and J. Liew (2001), "Do Hedge Funds Hedge?" *Journal of Portfolio Management* 28(1), 6–19.

Baker, Malcolm, and Jeffrey Wurgler (2012), "Behavioral Corporate Finance: An Updated Survey," *Handbook of the Economics of Finance*, 2, 351–417.

Baltas, A.-N., and R. Kosowski (2013), "Momentum Strategies in Futures Markets and Trend-Following Funds," working paper, Imperial College, London.

Barberis, N., A. Shleifer, and R. Vishny (1998), "A Model of Investor Sentiment," *Journal of Financial Economics* 49, 307–343.

Berk, Jonathan B., and Richard C. Green (2004), "Mutual Fund Flows and Performance in Rational Markets," *Journal of Political Economy* 112, 1269–1295.

Berk, Jonathan B., and Jules H. van Binsbergen (2013), "Measuring Skill in the Mutual Fund Industry," working paper, Stanford University.

Bikhchandani, S., D. Hirshleifer, and I. Welch (1992), "A Theory of Fads, Fashion, Custom, and Cultural Change as Informational Cascades," *Journal of Political Economy* 100, 992–1026.

Black, F. (1972), "Capital Market Equilibrium with Restricted Borrowing," *Journal of Business* 45, 444–455.

Black, F. (1992), "Beta and Return," *The Journal of Portfolio Management* 20, 8–18.

Black, F., and R. Litterman (1992), "Global Portfolio Optimization," *Financial Analysts Journal* September/October, 28–43.

Black, F., M. C. Jensen, and M. Scholes (1972), "The Capital Asset Pricing Model: Some Empirical Tests." *Studies in the Theory of Capital Markets*, M. C. Jensen (Ed.), Praeger, New York, 79–121.

Black, F., and M. S. Scholes (1973), "The Pricing of Options and Corporate Liabilities," *The Journal of Political Economy* 81, 637–654.

Bollen, N. P., and R. E. Whaley (2004), "Does Net Buying Pressure Affect the Shape of Implied Volatility Functions?" *Journal of Finance* 59, 711–753.

Brennan, M. J., and E. S. Schwartz (1977), "Convertible Bonds: Valuation and Optimal Strategies for Call and Conversion," *The Journal of Finance* 32, 1699–1715.

Brinson, Gary P., L. Randolph Hood, and Gilbert L. Beebower (1986), "Determinants of Portfolio Performance," *Financial Analysts Journal* 42(4), 39–44.

Brunnermeier, Markus, and Stefan Nagel (2004), "Hedge Funds and the Technology Bubble," *Journal of Finance* 59, 2013–2040.

Brunnermeier, Markus, Stefan Nagel, and Lasse Heje Pedersen (2008), "Carry Trades and Currency Crashes," *NBER Macroeconomics Annual* 23, 313–348.

Brunnermeier, M., and L. H. Pedersen (2005), "Predatory Trading," *Journal of Finance* 60, 1825–1863.

Brunnermeier, M., and L. H. Pedersen (2009), "Market Liquidity and Funding Liquidity," *The Review of Financial Studies* 22, 2201–2238.

Budish, Eric, Peter Cramton, and John Shim (2013), "The High-Frequency Trading Arms Race: Frequent Batch Auctions as a Market Design Response," working paper, University of Chicago.

Buraschi, Andrea, Robert Kosowski, and Worrawat Sritrakul (2014), "Incentives and Endogenous Risk Taking: A Structural View on Hedge Fund Alphas," *Journal of Finance*, forthcoming.

Calvet, L. E., J. Y. Campbell, and P. Sodini (2007), "Down or Out: Assessing the Welfare Costs of Household Investment Mistakes," *Journal of Political Economy* 115, 707–747.

Clarke, R., H. de Silva, and S. Thorley (2013), "Minimum Variance, Maximum Diversification and Risk Parity: An Analytic Perspective," *Journal of Portfolio Management* 39, 39–53.

Cochrane, John, and Monika Piazzesi (2005), "Bond Risk Premia," *American Economic Review* 94, 138–160.

Cohen, Lauren, Karl B. Diether, and Christopher J. Malloy (2007), "Supply and Demand Shifts in the Shorting Market," *The Journal of Finance* 62, 2061–2096.

Constantinides, G. M. (1986), "Capital Market Equilibrium with Transaction Costs," *Journal of Political Economy* 94, 842–862.

Cramer, J. (2002), *Confessions of a Street Addict,* Simon & Schuster, New York.

Cutler, D. M., J. M. Poterba, and L. H. Summers (1991), "Speculative Dynamics," *Review of Economic Studies* 58, 529–546.

Damodaran, A. (2012), *Investment Valuation: Tools and Techniques for Determining the Value of Any Asset,* John Wiley & Sons, New York.

D'avolio, Gene (2002), "The Market for Borrowing Stock," *Journal of Financial Economics* 66, 271–306.

Daniel, K., D. Hirshleifer, A. Subrahmanyam (1998), "A Theory of Overconfidence, Self-Attribution, and Security Market Under- and Over-Reactions," *Journal of Finance* 53, 1839–1885.

De Bondt, W. F. M., and R. Thaler (1985), "Does the Stock Market Overreact?" The *Journal of Finance* 40(3), 793–805.

De Long, J. B., A. Shleifer, L. H. Summers, and R. J. Waldmann (1990), "Positive Feedback Investment Strategies and Destabilizing Rational Speculation," *The Journal of Finance* 45, 379–395.

De Long, J. B., Andrei Shleifer, Lawrence H. Summers, and Robert J. Waldmann (1993), "Noise Trader Risk in Financial Markets," *Journal of Political Economy* 98, 703–738.

de Roon, F., T. E. Nijman, and C. Veld (2000), "Hedging Pressure Effects in Futures Markets," *Journal of Finance* 55, 1437–1456.

Dechow, Patricia M., Richard G. Sloan, and Amy P. Sweeney (1996), "Causes and Consequences of Earnings Manipulation: An Analysis of Firms Subject to Enforcement Actions by the SEC," *Contemporary Accounting Research* 13, 1–36.

Derman, Emanual (2004), *My Life as a Quant,* John Wiley & Sons, Hoboken, NJ.

Desai, Hemang, K. Ramesh, S. Ramu Thiagarajan, and Bala Balachandran (2002), "An Investigation of the Informational Role of Short Interest in the NASDAQ Market," *The Journal of Finance* 57, 2263–2287.

Dimson, E. (1979), "Risk Measurement When Shares are Subject to Infrequent Trading," *Journal of Financial Economics* 7, 197–226.

Duarte, Jefferson, Francis A. Longstaff, and Fan Yu (2007), "Risk and Return in Fixed-Income Arbitrage: Nickels in Front of a Steamroller?" *Review of Financial Studies* 20, 769–811.

Duffie, D. (2010), "Asset Price Dynamics with Slow-Moving Capital," *Journal of Finance* 65, 1238–1268.

Duffie, Darrell, Nicolae Gârleanu, and Lasse Heje Pedersen (2002), "Securities Lending, Shorting, and Pricing," *Journal of Financial Economics* 66, 307–339.

Duffie, D., N. Gârleanu, and L. H. Pedersen (2005), "Over-the-Counter Markets," *Econometrica* 73, 1815–1847.

Duffie, D., N. Gârleanu, and L. H. Pedersen (2007), "Valuation in Over-the-Counter Markets," *The Review of Financial Studies* 20, 1865–1900.

Edwards, W. (1968), "Conservatism in Human Information Processing," *Formal Representation of Human Judgment*, Kleinmutz, B. (Ed.), John Wiley and Sons, New York, 17–52.

Engle, Robert, Robert Ferstenberg, and Jeffrey Russell (2012), "Measuring and Modeling Execution Cost and Risk," *The Journal of Portfolio Management* 38(2), 14–28.

Fama, E., and K. French (1993), "Common Risk Factors in the Returns on Stocks and Bonds," *Journal of Financial Economics* 33, 3–56.

Fama, E., and K. French (2010), "Luck versus Skill in the Cross-Section of Mutual Fund Returns," *The Journal of Finance* 65, 1915–1947.

Fama, E. F., and MacBeth, J. D. (1973), "Risk, Return, and Equilibrium: Empirical Tests," *Journal of Political Economy* 81(3), 607–636.

Frazzini, A. (2006), "The Disposition Effect and Underreaction to News," *Journal of Finance* 61, 2017–2046.

Frazzini, A., and L. H. Pedersen (2013), "Embedded Leverage," working paper, AQR Capital Management and New York University.

Frazzini, A., and L. H. Pedersen (2014), "Betting Against Beta," *Journal of Financial Economics* 111(1), 1–25.

Frazzini, Andrea, Ronen Israel, and Tobias Moskowitz (2012), "Trading Costs of Asset Pricing Anomalies," working paper, AQR Capital Management and University of Chicago.

Frazzini, Andrea, David Kabiller, and Lasse Heje Pedersen (2013), "Buffett's Alpha," working paper, AQR Capital Management.

Fung, W., and D. A. Hsieh (1999), "A Primer on Hedge Fund," *Journal of Empirical Finance* 6, 309–331.

Fung, W., and D. A. Hsieh (2001), "The Risk in Hedge Fund Strategies: Theory and Evidence from Trend Followers," *Review of Financial Studies* 14, 313–341.

Gabaix, X., A. Krishnamurthy, and O. Vigneron (2007), "Limits of Arbitrage: Theory and Evidence from the Mortgage-Backed Securities Market," *Journal of Finance* 62, 557–595.

Gârleanu, N., and L. H. Pedersen (2007), "Liquidity and Risk Management," *American Economic Review* 97, 193–197.

Gârleanu, N., and L. H. Pedersen (2011), "Margin-Based Asset Pricing and Deviations from the Law of One Price," *The Review of Financial Studies* 24, 1980–2022.

Gârleanu, N., and L. H. Pedersen (2013), "Dynamic Trading with Predictable Returns and Transaction Costs," *Journal of Finance* 68, 2309–2340.

Gârleanu, N., and L. H. Pedersen (2014), "Dynamic Portfolio Choice with Frictions," working paper, University of California, Berkeley.

Gârleanu, N., L. H. Pedersen, and A. Poteshman (2009), "Demand-Based Option Pricing," *The Review of Financial Studies* 22, 4259–4299.

Gatev, Evan, William N. Goetzmann, and K. Geert Rouwenhorst (2006), "Pairs Trading: Performance of a Relative-Value Arbitrage Rule," *The Review of Financial Studies* 19(3), 797–827.

Geanakoplos, John (2010), "The Leverage Cycle," *NBER Macroeconomics Annual* 24, 1–65.

Geczy, Christopher C., David K. Musto, and Adam V. Reed (2002), "Stocks Are Special Too: An Analysis of the Equity Lending Market," *Journal of Financial Economics* 66, 241–269.

Goetzmann, William N., Jr., Jonathan E. Ingersoll, and Stephen A. Ross (2003), "High-Water Marks and Hedge Fund Management Contracts," *Journal of Finance* 58, 1685–1717.

Graham, J. R. (1999), "Herding among Investment Newsletters: Theory and Evidence," *Journal of Finance* 54(1), 237–268.

Graham, B. (1973), *The Intelligent Investor,* HarperCollins, New York.

Graham, B., and D. Dodd (1934), *Security Analysis,* McGraw-Hill, New York.

Grant, J. (1838), *The Great Metropolis,* vol. II, E. L. Carey & A. Hart, Philadelphia.

Greenwood, Robin, and Dimitri Vayanos (2014), "Bond Supply and Excess Bond Returns," *Review of Financial Studies* 27, 663–713.

Griffin, John M., and Jin Xu (2009), "How Smart Are the Smart Guys? A Unique View from Hedge Fund Stock Holdings," *Review of Financial Studies* 22, 2531–2570.

Griffin, Paul A. (2003), "A League of Their Own? Financial Analysts' Responses to Restatements and Corrective Disclosures," *Journal of Accounting, Auditing & Finance* 18, 479–517.

Grossman, S. J., and J. E. Stiglitz (1980), "On the Impossibility of Informationally Efficient Markets," *American Economic Review* 70(3), 393–408.

Grossman, S. J., and Z. Zhou (1993), "Optimal Investment Strategies for Controlling Drawdowns," *Mathematical Finance* 3, 241–276.

Gürkaynak, Refet S., and Jonathan H. Wright (2012), "Macroeconomics and the Term Structure," *Journal of Economic Literature* 50(2), 331–367.

Harrison, J. Michael, and David M. Kreps (1978), "Speculative Investor Behavior in a Stock Market with Heterogeneous Expectations," *The Quarterly Journal of Economics* 92, 323–336.

Harvey, Campbell R., and Yan Liu (2013), "Backtesting," working paper, Duke University, Durham, NC.

Harvey, Campbell R., Yan Liu, and Heqing Zhu (2013), ". . . and the Cross-Section of Expected Returns," working paper, Duke University, Durham, NC.

Hong, H., and J. Stein (1999), "A Unified Theory of Underreaction, Momentum Trading and Overreaction in Asset Markets," *Journal of Finance* 54(6), 2143–2184.

Hou, Kewei, Mathijs A. van Dijk, and Yinglei Zhang (2012), "The Implied Cost of Capital: A New Approach," *Journal of Accounting and Economics* 53, 504–526.

Huggins, D., and C. Schaller (2013), *Fixed Income Relative Value Analysis: A Practitioners Guide to the Theory, Tools, and Trades,* John Wiley & Sons, West Sussex, U.K.

Hurst, Brian, Yao Hua Ooi, and Lasse Heje Pedersen (2013), "Demystifying Managed Futures," *Journal of Investment Management* 11(3), 42–58.

Hurst, Brian, Yao Hua Ooi, and Lasse Heje Pedersen (2014), "A Century of Evidence on Trend-Following Investing," working paper, AQR Capital Management, Greenwich, CT.

Ilmanen, Antti (1995), "Time-Varying Expected Returns in International Bond Markets," *Journal of Finance* 50, 481–506.

Ilmanen, Antti (2011), *Expected Returns: An Investor's Guide to Harvesting Market Rewards,* John Wiley & Sons, Chichester, U.K.

Ingersoll, J. E. (1977), "A Contingent-Claims Valuation of Convertible Securities," *Journal of Financial Economics* 4, 289–321.

Jagannathan, Ravi, Alexey Malakhov, and Dmitry Novikov (2010), "Do Hot Hands Exist among Hedge Fund Managers? An Empirical Evaluation," *The Journal of Finance* 65, 217–255.

Jegadeesh, Narasimhan, and Sheridan Titman (1993), "Returns to Buying Winners and Selling Losers: Implications for Stock Market Efficiency," *The Journal of Finance* 48(1), 65–91.

Jensen, Mads Vestergaard, and Lasse Heje Pedersen (2012), "Early Option Exercise: Never Say Never," working paper, Copenhagen Business School, Copenhagen.

Jones, Charles M. (2013), "What Do We Know about High-Frequency Trading?" working paper, Columbia Business School, New York.

Jones, Charles M., and Owen A. Lamont (2002), "Short-Sale Constraints and Stock Returns," *Journal of Financial Economics* 66, 207–239.

Ketchum, Richard G., and John H. Sturc (1989), Prepared Statement from Division of Enforcement, Securities and Exchange Commission, before the House Committee on Government Affairs, Subcommittee on Commerce, Consumer, and Monetary Affairs, Washington, DC, Dec. 6.

Keynes, J. M. (1923), "Some Aspects of Commodity Markets," *Manchester Guardian Commercial,* European Reconstruction Series, Sec. 13, 784–786.

Keynes, John Maynard (1936), *The General Theory of Employment, Interest and Money,* Harcourt, Brace, and World, New York.

Khandani, Amir E., and Andrew W. Lo (2011), "What Happened to the Quants in August 2007? Evidence from Factors and Transactions Data," *Journal of Financial Markets* 14, 1–46.

Kiyotaki, N., and J. Moore (1997), "Credit Cycles," *Journal of Political Economy* 105, 211–248.

Koijen, Ralph, Tobias Moskowitz, Lasse Heje Pedersen, and Evert Vrugt (2012), "Carry," working paper, London Business School, London and AQR Capital Management, Greenwich, CT.

Kosowski, R., A. Timmermann, R. Wermers, and H. White (2006), "Can Mutual Fund 'Stars' Really Pick Stocks? New Evidence from a Bootstrap Analysis," *Journal of Finance* 61, 2551–2595.

Kosowski, Robert, Narayan Y. Naik, and Melvyn Teo (2007), "Do Hedge Funds Deliver Alpha? A Bayesian and Bootstrap Analysis," *Journal of Financial Economics* 84, 229–264.

Krishnamurthy, Arvind, and Annette Vissing-Jorgensen (2012), "The Aggregate Demand for Treasury Debt," *Journal of Political Economy* 120, 233–267.

Lakonishok, Josef, Andrei Shleifer, and Robert W. Vishny (1994), "Contrarian Investment, Extrapolation, and Risk," *The Journal of Finance* 49(5), 1541–1578.

Lamont, Owen (2012), "Go Down Fighting: Short Sellers vs. Firms," *Review of Asset Pricing Studies* 2, 1–30.

Lamont, Owen, and Richard H. Thaler (2003), "Can the Stock Market Add and Subtract? Mispricing in Tech Stock Carve-Outs," *Journal of Political Economy* 111(2), 227–268.

Lefèvre, E. (1923), *Reminiscences of a Stock Operator,* John Wiley & Sons, New York.

Lin, Hai, Junbo Wang, and Chunchi Wu (2011), "Liquidity Risk and Expected Corporate Bond Returns," *Journal of Financial Economics* 99, 628–650.

Liu, H. (2004), "Optimal Consumption and Investment with Transaction Costs and Multiple Assets," *Journal of Finance* 59, 289–338.

McLean, R. David, and Jeffrey Pontiff (2013), "Does Academic Research Destroy Stock Return Predictability?" working paper, University of Alberta, Edmonton.

Malkiel, B. G. and A. Saha (2005), "Hedge Funds: Risk and Return," *Financial Analysts Journal* 61, 80–88.

Mallaby, S. (2010), *More Money than God,* Penguin Press, New York.

Merton, R. C. (1973), "Theory of Rational Option Pricing," *The Bell Journal of Economics and Management Science* 4, 141–183.

Merton, R. C. (1974), "On the Pricing of Corporate Debt: The Risk Structure of Interest Rates," *Journal of Finance* 29, 449–470.

Miller, Edward M. (1977), "Risk, Uncertainty, and Divergence of Opinion," *The Journal of Finance* 32(4), 1151–1168.

Mitchell, M., L. H. Pedersen, and T. Pulvino (2007), "Slow Moving Capital," *American Economic Review* 97, 215–220.

Mitchell, Mark, and Todd Pulvino (2001), "Characteristics of Risk and Return in Risk Arbitrage," *The Journal of Finance* 56(6), 2135–2175.

Mitchell, Mark, and Todd Pulvino (2012), "Arbitrage Crashes and the Speed of Capital," *Journal of Financial Economics* 104(3), 469–490.

Mitchell, Mark, Todd Pulvino, and Erik Stafford (2002), "Limited Arbitrage in Equity Markets," *Journal of Finance* 57(2), 551–584.

Moskowitz, T., Y. H. Ooi, and L. H. Pedersen (2012), "Time Series Momentum," *Journal of Financial Economics* 104(2), 228–250.

Munk, C. (2011), *Fixed Income Modelling,* Oxford University Press, Oxford, U.K.

Nagel, Stefan (2012), "Evaporating Liquidity," *Review of Financial Studies* 25, 2005–2039.

Novy-Marx, R. (2013), "The Other Side of Value: The Gross Profitability Premium," *Journal of Financial Economics* 108(1), 1–28.

Pastor, Lubos, and Robert F. Stambaugh (2003), "Liquidity Risk and Expected Stock Returns," *Journal of Political Economy* 111, 642–685.

Pastor, Lubos, and Robert F. Stambaugh (2012), "On the Size of the Active Management Industry," *Journal of Political Economy* 120, 740–781.

Pastor, Lubos, Robert F. Stambaugh, and Lucian A. Taylor (2014), "Scale and Skill in Active Management," working paper, University of Chicago.

Pedersen, L. H. (2009), "When Everyone Runs for the Exit," *International Journal of Central Banking* 5, 177–199.

Perold, A. (1988), "The Implementation Shortfall: Paper Versus Reality," *Journal of Portfolio Management* 14, Spring, 4–9.

Preinreich, Gabriel A. D. (1938), "Annual Survey of Economic Theory: The Theory of Depreciation," *Econometrica* 6, 219–241.

Sadka, Ronnie (2010), "Liquidity Risk and the Cross-Section of Hedge-Fund Returns," *Journal of Financial Economics* 98, 54–71.

Scholes, M., and J. Williams (1977), "Estimating Betas from Nonsynchronous Data," *Journal of Financial Economics* 5, 309–327.

Schwager, Jack D. (2008), *The New Market Wizards: Conversations with America's Top Traders*, John Wiley & Sons, Hoboken, NJ.

Shefrin, H., and M. Statman (1985), "The Disposition to Sell Winners Too Early and Ride Losers Too Long: Theory and Evidence," *Journal of Finance* 40, 777–790.

Shiller, R. J. (1981), "Do Stock Prices Move Too Much to Be Justified by Subsequent Changes in Dividends?" *American Economic Review* 71, 421–436.

Shleifer, A. (1986), "Do Demand Curves for Stocks Slope Down?" *Journal of Finance* 41, 579–590.

Shleifer, Andrei (2000), *Inefficient Markets: An Introduction to Behavioral Finance*, Oxford University Press, Oxford.

Shleifer, A., and R. Vishny (1997), "The Limits of Arbitrage," *Journal of Finance* 52(1), 35–55.

Silber, W. L. (1994), "Technical Trading: When It Works and When It Doesn't," *Journal of Derivatives* 1(3), 39–44.

Soros, George (2010), *The Soros Lectures at the Central European University,* PublicAffairs, New York.

Staley, K. F. (1997), "The Art of Short Selling," John Wiley & Sons, New York.

Stambaugh, R. (1999), "Predictive Regressions," *Journal of Financial Economics* 54, 375–421.

Stattman, Dennis (1980), "Book Values and Stock Returns," *Chicago MBA: A Journal of Selected Papers*, 5, 25–45.

Swensen, D. (2000), *Pioneering Portfolio Management: An Unconventional Approach to Institutional Investment,* Free Press, New York.

Taylor, J. B. (1993), "Discretion versus Policy Rules in Practice," *Carnegie-Rochester Conference Series on Public Policy* 39, 195–214.

Thorp, Edward O., and Sheen T. Kassouf (1967), *Beat the Market,* Random House, New York.

Tversky, A., and D. Kahneman (1974), "Judgment under Uncertainty: Heuristics and Biases," *Science* 185, 1124–1131.

U.S. Commodities and Futures Trading Commission and Securities and Exchange Commission. (2010). "Findings Regarding the Market Events of May 6, 2010," Report of the Staffs of the CFTC and SEC to the Joint Advisory Committee on Emerging Regulatory Issues, Washington, DC.

U.S. Securities and Exchange Commission (1963), "The Market Break of May 1962," Chapter XIII in "Report of the Special Study of Securities Markets," Washington, DC.

Vayanos, Dimitri, and Paul Woolley (2013), "An Institutional Theory of Momentum and Reversal," *Review of Financial Studies* 26, 1087–1145.

Wason, P. C. (1960), "On the Failure to Eliminate Hypotheses in a Conceptual Task," *The Quarterly Journal of Experimental Psychology*, 12, 129–140.

Weinstein, Meyer H. (1931), *Arbitrage in Securities,* Harper & Brothers, New York.

Welch, I. (2000), "Herding among Security Analysts," *Journal of Financial Economics* 58, 369–396.

Welch, I., and A. Goyal (2008), "A Comprehensive Look at the Empirical Performance of Equity Premium Prediction," *Review of Financial Studies* 21(4), 1455–1508.

Wurgler, J., and E. V. Zhuravskaya (2002), "Does Arbitrage Flatten Demand Curves for Stocks?" *Journal of Business* 75, 583–608.

Index

A page number followed by f refers to a figure and a page number followed by t indicates a table.